Divine Art,
Infernal Machine

Divine Art,
Infernal Machine

The Reception of Printing in the West
from First Impressions
to the Sense of an Ending

ELIZABETH L. EISENSTEIN

PENN

UNIVERSITY OF PENNSYLVANIA PRESS

PHILADELPHIA · OXFORD

Copyright © 2011 University of Pennsylvania Press

Published by
University of Pennsylvania Press
Philadelphia, Pennsylvania 19104-4112

Printed in the United States of America on acid-free paper
10 9 8 7 6 5 4 3 2 1

Library of Congress Cataloging-in-Publication Data

Eisenstein, Elizabeth L.
Divine art, infernal machine : the reception of printing
in the West from first impressions to the sense of an
ending / Elizabeth L. Eisenstein.
    p.   cm.
Includes bibliographical references and index.
ISBN 978-0-8122-4280-5 (acid-free paper)
    1. Printing—Europe—History.   2. Printing—Social
aspects—Europe—History.   3. Books—Europe—
History.   4. Europe—Intellectual life.   I. Title.
Z124.E368   2011
686.2094—dc22   2010018016

Contents

Illustrations

Preface

This book deals with attitudes toward printing and printers expressed by observers in the Western world during the past five centuries. As far as I know, no one has yet explored this topic. The field is much too large to be covered in a single book. Its chronological range extends too far, some might say, to be covered even in a multivolume collaborative work. Surveying developments over the course of many centuries, however, does make it possible to observe continuities and ruptures that are hidden from view by special studies of a more limited scope. A case in point is offered by Michael Warner, who has called for a "history of the way we think about and perceive print."[1] In keeping with this project, Warner provides a fascinating close-up view of the role played by print in shaping an Anglo-American republican ethos. But his sharply focused treatment of an eighteenth-century political ideology is accompanied by a blurred and distorted presentation of previous developments. The views of early printers are wrongly characterized (see below). Puritan attitudes are lumped together as reflections of a vaguely defined "traditional culture of print." The *un*traditional aspects of early print culture are ignored, along with significant links between seventeenth-century Puritans and eighteenth-century republicans.

By extending coverage to encompass many centuries, I hope to bring out neglected continuities as well as to indicate significant ruptures. What follows is intended merely as a suggestive sketch. It is highly selective, drawing material from only a few regions and social sectors, and is loosely organized along chronological lines.

Anyone who attempts to trace views of printing over the course of centuries has to confront one problem at the outset, namely, the transformation of printing processes themselves. A sixteenth-century commentator who referred to the art of artificial writing had in mind a wooden handpress and the inking of carefully aligned pieces of metal. By the nineteenth century, printing meant steam-driven rotary presses and linotype machines. Thereafter, the press was replaced by photographic processes, and "hot type" was superseded by "cold." A literal-minded historian of technology might argue that, although sixteenth-century commentators and twentieth-century ones both refer to printing, they are in fact referring to entirely different things. A similar point pertains to the role of the printer. There's a world of difference between the multifarious activities undertaken in a single printing house under the guidance of a single master printer during the first century after Gutenberg and the diverse tasks performed by different specialists in the many different branches of a later book trade.

Fortunately, this argument need not detain us for long. The views to be discussed here seem to have been relatively unaffected by the several mutations printing and printers have undergone. Indeed, the persistence of similar reactions to similar problems is striking. Some hark back to the earlier age of scribes, and some were carried over into later considerations of new communications technologies. In 1946, Harold Nicolson, who had been speaking on the BBC to an audience estimated at some twenty million, wrote in his diary that he had "no sense of audience." "To whom am I talking?" he asked. An audience of readers had been replaced by one of listeners, yet the sense of estrangement from an invisible public remained.[2] A book entitled *Amusing Ourselves to Death*[3] raised alarms about the effects of television. Concern about the public's preference for entertainment over instruction long preceded television. The same point applies to reports of violent crime. Torture, rape, and murder were prominently featured in sixteenth-century street literature and in Jacobean plays.[4] Disdainful remarks about sound bites are now often coupled with respectful comments about print journalism. When print journalism monopolized the scene, however, it was accused of mindlessness and warmongering (see Chapter 6). As these examples may suggest, looking at the way previous generations viewed printing may help us place current debates about new media in some sort of historical perspective.

Current reactions to new media may also lead to a more sympathetic understanding of previous reactions to older ones. I must confess, however, that I have more difficulty sympathizing with negative than with positive views of Gutenberg's invention. I imagine that a similar bias is shared by many of my readers: that they regard printing in a positive light—if not as a divine art or mighty engine, then at least as a useful invention.

Our American heritage (and, despite current debates about multiculturalism, we do all still live under a single Constitution, and in that sense do share a common heritage) owes too much to the Enlightenment to be neutral on this particular topic. Opponents of printing have almost always been placed in the enemy camp. Take the much-cited comment of 1671 (made in a letter to the Committee on the Colonies) by William Berkeley, colonial governor of Virginia. "I thank God there are no free schools nor printing and I hope we shall never have these [for] a hundred years; learning has brought disobedience and heresy and sects into the world and print has divulged them . . . God keep us from both." Eleven years later, in 1682, after an abortive attempt to set up a press in Jamestown, a new governor enforced the royal order that "no person be permitted to use any press for printing upon any occasion whatsoever."[5] It seems unlikely that there are many Americans today who would approve of the position taken by either colonial official.

To be sure, I feel less secure now about making any statement concerning contemporary views on our topic than I would have during my own college days. At that time it was assumed that printing, along with the compass and gunpowder, had been advantageously deployed in the West as nowhere else in the world, thus ensuring Western superiority over other cultures in accordance with a providential design. There was always some ambivalence about guns. In the sixteenth century, Rabelais had described artillery as the devil's work. In the same passage, however, he attributed the invention of printing to divine inspiration.

Today, there is not only an increasing revulsion against weapons of mass destruction, but also considerable ambivalence about Western technologies of all kinds. Triumphalism is out of fashion, along with ideas of progress and other "Whiggish" views of historical development. As with all generalizations, this one needs qualification. An exception must be made for those advocates of digitalization who regard "dead-tree editions" as hopelessly out of date. Current enthusiasm for the World-Wide Web does seem to have a triumphal air. Enthusiastic reports about the marvels of electronic media, however, are in marked contrast to the sober assessments of historians who deal with print. The approach that is currently favored by the latter is exemplified by James Raven's magnificent study of the English book trade. Raven's readers are warned repeatedly against "being prone to triumphalism" and against associating print culture with "progressive forces."[6]

The compass as a symbol of voyages of discovery is in growing disrepute for having made possible the despoiling of peaceful civilizations and the rape of virgin lands. Columbus, once hailed by American literati as an unquestioned culture hero, now appears to have become, if not a deep-dyed cultural villain, then, at the very least, a highly problematic figure.[7] And this leads me to wonder: what fate is now in store for Gutenberg?

Is he yet another of those numerous historic figures whose significance has been overblown by a Eurocentric bias? In the context of world history he was hardly a pioneer. The Chinese had been printing on paper long before he was born. Even though it now commands a high price on world markets, the Gutenberg Bible is not cherished in the same way throughout the world. Other icons are more significant to followers of other faiths. The Muslims objected to the printing of their sacred text; reliance on hand-copying scarcely inhibited the spread of the Koran. Several recent studies have underscored the point that the cultural configuration described by Marshall McLuhan in his *Gutenberg Galaxy* reflected peculiar conditions and applied only to a small portion of the globe.[8] The introduction of printing in neighboring regions such as Russia, not to mention exotic areas such as Japan, had very different consequences from those it had in Western Europe.[9] Regional variation marked the reception of printing in British India, with distinctively different results for Hindi, Urdu and Tamil cultures. Goa, under Portuguese rule, experienced, among other developments, an early Catholic monopoly and a seventy-year ban (1754–1821).[10] Let me take this occasion to issue a plea for more such studies. The different forms taken by print culture throughout the world seem to be especially suitable for comparative, collaborative work.

But, of course, a concern to avoid parochialism and to engage in comparative study does not really take us out of our own orbit. Such concern is deeply embedded in Western Christendom and helps to distinguish our culture from others. The point that the Chinese had developed printing before it was known in the West, for example, was asserted by sixteenth-century commentators—not only by Montaigne, who is often cited in this connection,[11] but also by Louis LeRoy, who credited the Asians in order to counter German claims (see Chapter 3). It was reiterated in later histories of printing before becoming a commonplace in our own day. This is only one instance where what appears to be a recent phenomenon (the vogue for multicultural perspectives) turns out to be embedded in a distant past. All this is by way of asking you to make a mental note to underline the words "in the West" in my subtitle. Institutions and traditions which were peculiar to Western Europeans shaped reactions to Gutenberg's invention and entered into the myths that were woven around it.

Before turning to look at some of the early reactions that are discussed in Chapter 1, let me end this preface with a citation with which I agree. It describes the opinion of Thomas Holcroft, as reported by William Hazlitt, and was selected by the late Roy Porter to epitomize the ideals of the British Enlightenment. It suggests why I find the injunction not to align printing with "progressive forces" difficult to obey.

> He believed that truth had a natural superiority over error, if it could only be heard; that if once discovered, it must, being left to itself, soon spread and triumph: and that the art of printing would not only accelerate this effect, but would prevent those accidents that had rendered the moral and intellectual progress of mankind hitherto so slow, irregular, and uncertain.[12]

Chapter 1

First Impressions

The Presse, the most-honorable Presse, the most-villainous Presse
—Gabriel Harvey (1593)

Prologue: Some Foundation Myths

Let me start with some of the foundation myths that reveal long-lasting attitudes toward printing on the part of Western Europeans. They concern Gutenberg's one time partner, Johann Fust (sometimes spelled Faustus). He helped to subsidize the operations of the Mainz press, and his daughter married Peter Schoeffer, who fathered the first Mainz printing dynasty. Thus, there is good reason to consider him as a founding father of the new industry.

The mythic dimension is supplied by the long-lived confusion between Johann Fust, who died in 1466, and the necromancer "Doctor" Johann Georg Faustus, whose life provided the prototype for the *Faustbuch* and who was born around 1480.[1]

According to the anticlerical author of an eighteenth-century dictionary, Fust was wrongly confused with "one Johann Faust, a fraudulent magician" owing to "lies circulated by monks who hated anyone associated with the invention of printing."[2] A nineteenth-century biographical dictionary provides a different, more detailed version:

FUST, or FAUSTUS (JOHN) a citizen of Mainz and one of the earliest printers. He had the policy to conceal his art; and to this policy we are indebted for the tradition of "The Devil and Dr. Faustus," handed down to the present times. About 1460, he associ-

ated with John of Guttemburgh . . . and . . . having printed off a
. . . number of copies of the Bible, to imitate those which were
commonly sold in MS, Fust undertook the sale of them in Paris,
where the art of printing was then unknown. As he sold his printed
copies for 60 crowns while the scribes demanded 500, this created
universal astonishment: but when he produced copies as fast as they
were wanted and lowered the price to 30 crowns, all Paris was agi-
tated. The uniformity of the copies increased the wonder; informa-
tions were given in to the police against him as a magician; . . . a
great number of copies being found [in his lodgings], they were
seized; the red ink with which they were embellished was said to be
his blood; it was seriously adjudged that he was in league with the
devil; and if he had not fled, most probably he would have shared
the fate of those whom ignorant and superstitious judges condemned . . . for witchcraft.[3]

Whereas the first version took for granted the hostility of monks (a common misconception even now), this one depicts a mystified urban populace.
It takes note of the sudden rise in output, drop in price, and uniformity of
copies which led contemporaries to suspect magic. In view of recent asser-
tions that the handpress was incapable of standardizing texts and that uniformity came only in the nineteenth century, it's worth citing the early
eighteenth-century version of a similar tale by Daniel Defoe:

the famous doctors of the faculty at Paris, when John Faustus
brought the first printed Books that had been seen in the World or
at least had been seen there, in to the City and sold them for Manuscripts: They were surprized . . . and questioned Faustus about it;
but he kept affirming that they were manuscripts and that he kept a
great many Clarks employ'd to write them thus satisfying his ques-
tioners for a while. But then *they observed the exact agreement of every*
Book one with another, that every line stood in the same place, every
page [had] a like Number of lines, every line, a like number of words;
if a word was misspelled in one, it was misspelled also in all; nay, that
if there was a Blot in one, it was alike in all; they began again to
muse, how this should be . . . not being able to comprehend the
Thing . . . [they] concluded it must be the Devil, that it was done
by Magic and Witchcraft . . . [and that] . . . poor Faustus (who was

indeed nothing but a meer Printer) dealt with the Devil . . . [This is
the] true original of the famous Dr. Faustus . . . of whom we have
believed such strange things . . . whereas poor Faustus was no Doctor and knew no more of the Devil than any other body.[4]

Defoe, who certainly knew his way around printing shops, thus held the
handpress capable of the sort of standardization that recent critics have
deemed impossible.[5] He also reflected the superior attitude of an eighteenth-
century writer who treated belief in magic and witchcraft as evidence of
ignorance about the actual workings of a machinery behind the scenes. In
his account, however, ignorance was deliberately cultivated by the secretive
bookseller who pretended his products had been hand-copied.

In the tales of Fust-cum-Faustus, the duplicative powers of print are
mistaken for magic by the uninitiated.[6] Different attributes, entailing expro-
priation and exploitation, also became associated with Gutenberg's onetime
partner. Long after printing had ceased to be viewed as a magical art, it
continued to be stigmatized as a mercenary métier. Johann Fust was less and
less likely to be accused of sorcery, but more and more likely to be viewed as
an exploitative capitalist who robbed an unworldly, impractical inventor of
the fruits of his labor.[7] In this instance, the wordplay is not on the variant
spelling of Fust as Faust but on the meaning of "Fust" as "fist"—as something that is, by its nature, "grasping."[8] To cite a standard nineteenth-century
reference work: "greedy, crafty, and heartless speculator, who took a mean
advantage of Gutenberg's necessity, and robbed him of his invention."[9] This
mythic Fust has recently been described by a Marxisant literary critic as embodying Western printing's primal crime. In her view, the document attesting
to the lawsuit that Fust won against Gutenberg (the most valuable piece of
evidence concerning the Mainz invention) points to the "legitimation" of the
capitalistic control of the book trade: "capital, comes to control the book
trade and the skilled labor of printers and writers alike."[10] In another version,
industrial sabotage is at work. The poor inventor who was robbed turns out
to be, not the "German" Gutenberg of Mainz, but the "Dutchman" Lawrence Hans (Laurens Coster) of Haarlem, who was robbed "on a Christmas
daye att night, of all his instrumentes by John Faustus who fled to Mentz in
Germany."[11]

The split identity of the inventive craftsman/thieving financier is a remarkably persistent feature of Western literature on printing. It reappears in
the eighteenth-century good author/bad bookseller fiction (with the gifted

author replacing the inventive artisan as a victim of the exploitative book-seller). It is elaborated in more recent studies of the "social history of ideas."[12] Despite the well-documented existence of commercial copying centers before Gutenberg's day, the sinister figure of the exploitative capitalist appears to have no equivalent in stories about scribes and copyists.[13] It makes its debut only after the advent of printing, when would-be authors became reliant on "the commercial judgment of publishers to establish their place in the world of letters."[14] It looms ever larger as the centuries progress until it merges with antisemitic propaganda during the Dreyfus years, when Fust (who came of Christian burgher stock) gets recast as a usurious Jew.[15]

We need not wait for centuries to pass to encounter complaints about the sharp dealings of the greedy printer or profiteering merchant/publisher. But such complaints should not be mistaken, as they frequently are, for a repudiation of the craft itself. More often than not, they were directed only at the shortcomings of certain practitioners. When medieval anticlerical writers condemned the lechery or gluttony of monks who fell short of embodying an ascetic ideal, they took a different position from that of eighteenth-century philosophers who rejected "penance, mortification, self-denial, humility, si-lence, solitude, and the whole train of monkish virtues."[16] Similarly there is a difference between objecting to error-filled editions and repudiating the art of printing. When Conrad Leontorius attacked ignorant and careless printers, he was not rejecting the "divine art," as he called it, but rather deploring the way it was being mistreated. He went on to compliment his friend Johann Amerbach on his superior products.[17]

Initial Reactions: Pros and Cons

This brings me to the question that the rest of this chapter will explore: how did Gutenberg's contemporaries and immediate successors react to the advent of printing? The question has received different and often contradictory an-swers. According to Paul Needham,

> The invention of printing made a striking impression on the literate
> minds of the time . . . historians are often tempted to produce an
> artificially "balanced" view . . . by arguing that to contemporary
> eyes, the new invention held both advantages and disadvantages; or
> that printed books infused themselves so gradually into the Euro-

Mais la mort de ses associés et de nouveaux embarras d'argent empêchèrent Gutemberg de conduire à bien ses travaux : vers 1445, pauvre et découragé, il dut quitter Strasbourg emportant avec lui le peu qu'il possédait, pour retourner à Mayence, sa patrie.

A Mayence il demanda l'appui financier d'un riche banquier juif, Jean Faust, qui, frappé du mérite de son invention, consentit à lui prêter de l'argent. Mais il le fit de façon à tenir dans sa griffe d'usurier le malheureux grand homme qui ne se défiait pas de lui.

Toutefois, grâce à l'appui de son associé Faust, Gutemberg put enfin terminer son œuvre et faire paraître sa fameuse Bible que ses caractères gothiques faisaient ressembler à un manuscrit, ce qui fut le but primitif de l'inventeur. L'imprimerie dès lors était créée (**1450**).

Quand Faust se fut mis au courant de l'invention de Gutemberg, il lui chercha querelle pour le remboursement de ses prêts d'argent, le chassa de chez lui et le dépouilla de tout son matériel. Le pauvre grand homme, victime de son infâme associé, se vit de nouveau réduit à la misère (1461).

Figure 1.1. Details from Image d'Epinal #382 (1890). Gutenberg travels from Strasbourg to Mainz to get financing for his invention from Johann Faust. The Jewish banker supports printing the Mainz Bible, then bankrupts the inventor and confiscates his equipment. Courtesy of the Musée National de l'Éducation.

pean world that no dramatic date of cultural change can be identified . . . it is abundantly clear that from the earliest days of their
appearance, printed books were considered and accepted as a great
success in their own right, that is, as more than an ersatz for manuscripts.[18]

The two separate issues that are intertwined in this citation need sorting
out. Whether printing "made a striking impression" from the first is a different matter from whether the invention was invariably accepted as a "great
success." On this last point Needham's verdict seems to be too sweeping,
even though citations from the writings of contemporaries seem to bear him
out.

Thus, a letter of 1455 written to a Spanish cardinal by a future pope
about seeing unbound quires of a printed Bible (probably the forty-two-line
Gutenberg Bible) conveys both an immediate and highly favorable impression. The text was exceedingly clean, wrote Aeneas Sylvius Piccolomini. It
was without error and could be read without glasses. Several people reported
that over one hundred copies were finished.[19] This letter has the additional
significance of showing that the printing of a sacred text was welcomed without any reservations by highly placed churchmen. A different social position
was occupied by the Venetian physician Nicolaus Gupalatinus. He also took
a favorable view. He persuaded the first native-born Italian printer to print a
medical treatise and described the press as a "miracle worth celebrating, one
unknown to all previous ages."[20]

I agree with Needham that the "artificially balanced" view presented by
many authorities does not do justice to the initial enthusiasm that was exhibited by such individuals. Division of opinion over the invention often gets
concocted, seemingly out of thin air, with "triumphalist" accounts set against
imaginary "catastrophist" ones.[21] Of course, opinions were likely to vary,
depending on the position of those who expressed them. Churchmen, scholars, and book hunters were unlikely to share the same outlook as manuscript
dealers or professional scribes and illuminators. The latter groups are often
thought to be opponents of the new art on the mistaken assumption that
printing deprived them of their livelihood. But, on the contrary, they were
kept busier than ever. The demand for deluxe hand-copied books persisted,
and the earliest printed books were hybrid products that called for scribes
and illuminators to provide the necessary finishing touches.[22]

"There was an immense range of individual opinions," writes Martin

Lowry, "all can be placed somewhere between committed acclamation and absolute rejection."[23] Even this seemingly cautious assessment still tends to obscure Needham's point that there was an actual imbalance—that acclamation outweighed rejection.

Indeed, there is little evidence of absolute rejection. The foundation myths that depict hostile monks and urban crowds making accusations of witchcraft, profiteers engaged in industrial sabotage, or scribes deprived of their livelihood seem to be baseless. It's true that François I temporarily banned printing after the affair of the placards, and two colonial governors in seventeenth-century Virginia banned printing from that colony.[24] But neither episode had much effect, and neither occurred in the fifteenth century.

There is little or no evidence of absolute rejection in the fifteenth century, while there is much evidence of "committed acclamation." Nevertheless, fifteenth-century commentators were not always single-minded about the new presses. Initial enthusiasm can be documented, but so can subsequent disillusion and disappointment. The fifteenth-century scholar who wrote that he sometimes "wondered whether printing was a blessing or a curse"[25] was not a figment of a later imagination. Nuances get lost when one cites, as Needham does, only favorable comments without pausing over negative ones. As later discussion suggests, negative views are not hard to find. Indeed, a "protracted debate . . . on whether the new art was a force for good or for evil" has been discerned by Brian Richardson.[26] The existence of negative views is not in doubt. What needs more attention is that such views were most often directed not at the new art itself but rather at its unworthy practitioners. This was especially the case with authors who often regarded printers, much as earlier writers had regarded copyists, with considerable ambivalence.

On the other question, of gradual infusion as opposed to dramatic change, Needham's view seems to be sustained by unambiguous evidence. The future pope and the Venetian physician cited above were by no means alone. An admiring comment about a wonderfully efficient new technique for reproducing books was made in 1466 by Leon Battista Alberti.[27] Martin Lowry describes Venetian literati as being disoriented and "thrown into complete disarray" by the advent of printing.[28] His account has persuaded others that the sudden increase in output stunned contemporaries, "almost literally overwhelming them."[29] Thus it does seem "abundantly clear" that the invention made an immediate and striking impression, at least upon literati.

Nevertheless, there are book historians who argue that the impression first made by the new technology was so faint as to be almost imperceptible. According to a favorable review of Silvia Rizzo's study, for example, the author "shows convincingly . . . that in the mind of the humanists there was no distinct line of demarcation between the manuscript book and that printed by movable type."[30] As is often the case when dealing with the shift from script to print, one is presented with two seemingly incompatible models of change. For Rizzo, the change was so gradual that it almost went unnoted. For Needham, it was so marked that it aroused immediate comment. Different kinds of evidence are presented to substantiate these different views.

The arguments favoring gradualism tend to pass over fifteenth-century reports of excited comment while stressing the similar uses that were initially made of hand-copied and printed books. Whereas manuscripts and printed products are now assigned to separate categories by curators and dealers, fifteenth-century readers found both kinds of books for sale in the same locales, often in the same shops. Purchasers placed them together in the same cabinets or on the same shelves and sometimes had them covered by the same bindings. The contrast with twentieth-century practices is striking and helps to explain why authorities insist that "the fifteenth century . . . made little distinction between hand-written and press-printed books."[31] Moreover, during the fifteenth century a carryover of format and layout reinforced the impression of similarity. When discussing a particular text, readers did not always make clear whether it was hand-copied or not. One is reminded of present-day encounters with computer printouts that are often mistakenly described as typescripts (not to mention typescripts that also get called manuscripts).[32]

Indeed, at first no distinctive neo-Latin terminology was employed to distinguish printed from hand-copied products. It is because "liber, volumen, codex were used indiscriminately" for both kinds of books that Rizzo concludes the humanists drew no clear line of demarcation between the products of the pen and the products of the press.[33] In support of her view, she cites Armando Petrucci's comment that "printing did not . . . provoke any fundamental modifications in the typology of book production. The first printers, indeed, restricted themselves to transferring into new books the sizes, dispositions of text, characters, and ornament found in manuscript."[34] Several authorities also note how lines of demarcation were smudged by the way scribes copied printed books even while printers were reproducing hand-copied ones.[35] Continuity is also stressed in David Shaw's study of neo-Latin synonyms for printing, which considers implements as well as books. Like Rizzo, Shaw finds that special terminology for the new technology was slow to develop. Printing, he notes, was at first described as "writing with a hand of brass" or with a "brazen pen."[36]

But philology is not always an adequate guide in such matters. Calling a computer printout a "typescript" rather than "hardcopy" does not indicate failure to distinguish word processor from typewriter. Similarly, using the same terminology was not incompatible with recognizing the stunning novelty of presswork. Distinctions between manuscript and printed text were clearly drawn by the humanists. They not only created dialogues about the merits and defects of the new medium,[37] but were also sufficiently impressed by its advantages that they sought out printers when it came time to duplicate their own work. (It was in this way that the first Paris press was set up within the precinct of the Sorbonne.)

Uncertainty over terminology, however, does need attention when considering the fate of scribes. The tendency to exaggerate the number of scribes who turned to printing and the difficulty of arriving at an accurate estimate has been demonstrated by Sheila Edmunds. She points to the "unsettled" character of the occupational nomenclature used in fifteenth-century tax rolls. (Even today there's a certain ambiguity in the way we use the term printing. The phrase: "I was taught to print" may mean merely that I was not taught to use cursive style when forming my letters.) During the fifteenth century the meaning of such labels as "scriptor" or "schreiber" (scribe) and "impressor" or "drucker" (printer) was much more ambiguous than is acknowledged by many authorities.[38]

Edmunds does agree, however, that there is at least one well-substantiated case of a scribe turned printer—that of Peter Schoeffer, who was born near Mainz, studied at Erfurt, and worked as a calligrapher at the Sorbonne. After being hired by Gutenberg's financier and partner, Johann Fust, he married Fust's daughter and became the founder of Europe's first printing dynasty.[39] As a scribe, Schoeffer produced a colophon praising the city of Paris, "completed by me, Peter of Gernsheim . . . in the year one thousand four hundred forty-nine, in Paris, most glorious of all cities."[40] As a printer he produced several colophons that paid tribute to the city of Mainz.[41] But there the similarity ends.

Aside from containing a civic tribute, the contents of Schoeffer's printed colophons departed from precedents set by scribes. So did the colophons of most early printers. In this regard, Michael Warner's claim that "early printers . . . in no way distinguished their work from hand-produced documents"[42] is plainly wrong. The claim is contradicted by the numerous self-congratulatory statements made by the practitioners of the new craft: "And who dare glorify the pen-made book, / When so much fairer brass-stamped letters look?"[43]

The colophon, like the codex form, was inherited from the hand-copied book. It represents what Petrucci describes as an unchanged typology. But it also contained striking evidence of discontinuity. From the beginning, new wine was poured into the old bottle. Copyists were more likely to complain about frozen fingers and cramped hands than to praise the implements they used. To cite the colophon of a scribe in 954: copying "extinguishes the light from the eyes . . . bends the back . . . crushes . . . the ribs . . . brings forth pain to the kidneys and weariness to the whole body . . . the [last] line is as sweet to a writer as the port is to a sailor. Three fingers hold the pen but the whole body toils."[44] This chatty, often-cited tenth-century example is not characteristic of the more laconic colophons of the later Middle Ages. Still, even at a later date, it was not unusual to find expressions "of gratitude or relief at the termination of [the scribes'] irksome labors."[45] In contrast to scribes, early printers were much more likely to praise their tools than to dwell upon the hardship of their craft.[46] "This noble book . . . without help of reed, stilus, or pen, but by the wondrous agreement, proportion, and harmony of punches and types, has been printed and finished."[47] So goes part of a colophon of 1460, often attributed to Gutenberg himself.

The art of artificial writing was one of the first (perhaps the very first?) of the new technologies developed in the post-classical world where contemporary reactions are documented. For printing had the unique property of being an invention that could advertise itself, and printers had a strong incentive to take advantage of that fact. Given the need to pay for expensive reams of paper before embarking on a project, much was at stake in persuading patrons and prospective purchasers of the merits of a particular printed product. Alfred Pollard's useful collection of early colophons offers numerous instances of denigrating the work of scribes while hailing the new and improved products that came off the handpress. To cite only two examples—the first comes from a 1478 edition of a medieval commentary on Justinian's corpus: "The Volumes of the Sacred Law had died, / So much were they by error damnified; / Which had so deeply steeped each mouth and pen, / To free them seemed too hard for mortal men; / . . . Buy, then, these flawless books with a light heart; / And, buying, praise the printer for his art."[48] The second is taken from a colophon to Pliny's *Natural History* (Venice, 1469): "I, erst so rare few bookmen could afford me, / And erst so blurred that buyers' eyes would fail—/ To Venice now 't was John of Speier restored me, / And made recording brass unfold my tale."[49] Of course such claims, more often than not, were wide of the mark. "The printing industry, though boasting superior correction, offered little or no inherent gain in textual accuracy."[50] Pliny's text, far from being "restored" by John of Speyer's edition, was full of gross errors with blank spaces left for Greek terms.[51]

Nevertheless the idea that "recording brass" could best withstand the ravages of time, that the texts of ancient authors were not only being recovered but also being preserved, became a commonplace observation. The great value placed on preservation was inherited from scribal culture.[52] From the days of St. Jerome to those of Jean Gerson, the preservative powers of writing had loomed large in tributes paid to scribes. "It is the scribes who . . . give lasting value to passing things . . . Without them the Church would see faith weakened . . . justice lost, the law confused and the Gospel fallen into oblivion."[53] When it came to giving lasting value to passing things, however, the press was believed to be superior to the pen. Printing came to be known as a divine art partly because it was regarded as the art which preserved all other arts.[54]

The advantages of typography over hand-copying were repeatedly enumerated not only by printers, but also by the editors, authors, translators, and glossators who composed the dedications, letters, prefaces, and other front matter that got added to numerous early editions.[55] This paratextual material seems to undercut the claim that no distinct line of demarcation was drawn "in the minds of the humanists" between manuscript and printed book. After all, much of the "front matter" was written by "humanists." Thus a Milanese humanist, Bonus Accursius, in a prefatory letter to a 1475 edition of Ovid's *Metamorphoses*, described why printed books were superior to manuscripts: "when the impression . . . is correct . . . it runs through all the copies always in the same order, with scarcely the possibility of error—a thing which in a manuscript is apt to result very differently."[56] Modern-day scholars who stress the incapacity of the handpress to produce truly standard editions may regard this opinion as naive and misleading.[57] The fact remains that the Milanese humanist held this opinion. In so doing, he clearly distinguished between manuscript copies and printed editions.

When assessing what went on in "the minds of the humanists," the carryover of nomenclature and typology seems to me to count for less than do

the paratexts of printed books that repeatedly alerted readers to the benefits of
the new technology. In addition, there were actions that spoke, perhaps,
more loudly than did words. In 1470, Guillaume Fichet, the rector of the
Sorbonne, together with Johann Heynlin, the college librarian, invited three
German printers to come to Paris to set up, within the college precincts, the
first French press. One may assume that the two scholars thought the services
of printers were different from (and, indeed, preferable to) those of scribes.[58]
Fichet's often cited tribute leaves no room for doubt on the matter:

> Bacchus and Ceres were made divinities for having taught humanity
> the use of wine and bread. Gutenberg's invention is of a higher and
> more divine order. It enables all that has been thought and said, to
> be preserved and transmitted to posterity.[59]

As we have seen, Fichet and Heynlin were by no means the only "humanists"
who expressed enthusiasm for the new craft.[60]

Numerous learned tributes in praise of printing echoed not only earlier
works in praise of scribes but also other panegyrics composed in imitation of
ancient Latin models. A passage taken from a humanist's tribute to his celebrated teacher, Guarinus of Verona, illustrates the sort of tribute that would
be transposed into a eulogy of Gutenberg's art. The passage deals with Guarinus's birth. A favorable conjunction of planets shows the heavens preparing
for the momentous occasion when a child, long promised to the land, will be
born. He is destined to inaugurate a new Augustan age. Mercury is depicted
prophetically describing to the Muses the future glory that Guarinus will
bring to his birthplace, Verona, a glory even greater than that of two other
famous native sons: Catullus and Pliny. "Through you [Guarinus] the
mouths of men long mute will speak, you will bring their dead names to
life."[61]

To place the early praise of printing in an appropriate context, this rhetorical tradition should be kept in mind. The extravagant claims made for
humanist culture heroes would be transferred with little change to claims
made on behalf of Gutenberg and other early printers. These claims were
transferred also to the infant art itself, which was born in Mainz under the
aegis of Minerva—an art that inaugurated a new order of the ages while also
enabling dead authors to speak.

Celebrating the resurrection of dead authors and the recovery of lost
wisdom was, once again, a legacy from the age of the scribe. But the praise

of printing also looked forward to the dawning of a new age. It included comment on the superiority of the moderns who had been favored by Providence with a tool unknown to the ancients. One of Peter Schoeffer's many colophons boastfully asserted that Providence had not considered antiquity worthy of the art which had been granted to his own times.[62] The same point, connecting the invention with the superiority of the moderns, was made in a preface of 1522 by the Italian printer, Alessandro Paganini.[63]

This was a relatively new way of thinking about a post-classical invention. A list of such inventions had already been compiled by a Vatican librarian before Gutenberg. But it had not been aimed at documenting superiority over the ancients. Rather, Tortelli's *De Orthographia* was concerned with the coining of new Latin terms for objects unknown to antiquity, such as the stirrup, the grist mill, the mechanical clock, eyeglasses, and the like. After being issued in print in 1471, the work was expanded to include more recent innovations and went through some thirteen editions before 1500. Verses in praise of printing (alluding to Mercury and Minerva) were added to the editions. Successive editions of *De Orthographia* register a significant shift: from concern with classical terminology to a celebration of progress in technology.[64]

Tributes to printing as a divine art then subsumed several humanist themes. Printing was credited with restoring ancient wisdom and preserving it for posterity, with spreading letters and learning, and with demonstrating the superiority of the moderns over the ancients. But there were also specifically Christian aspects to the chorus of praise. Aeneas Sylvius Piccolomini (who became Pope Pius II) was by no means the only influential churchman who looked favorably on the new craft. Another tribute comes from the bishop of Brescia, secretary to Pope Sixtus IV: "Merciful God instructed our contemporaries in a new art . . . thanks to typography . . . three men working in three months have printed 300 copies [of a 366-page folio of a commentary by Gregory the Great], a feat they could not have accomplished in their entire lives had they written with a pen or stylus."[65]

A preface composed in the 1460s to Augustine's commentary on the art of preaching (*De Arte Praedicandi*) noted that copies were hard to find "even in the great and well stocked libraries" and especially difficult to obtain for the purpose of copying—and, when found, were full of errors in transcription. So the preface writer set about comparing extant copies and produced an exemplar "by as much care and labour as I am capable of" in order that the

little book may be multiplied in this [corrected] state, and in such a
way that it may become rapidly and easily known in a short time,
for the use of many and to the common advantage of the Church
. . . this could not be done more expeditiously by any other method
or means . . . I have persuaded . . . Johann Mentelin, . . . master of
the art of typography, to [duplicate] this little book by means of
printing, having my copy before his eyes.[66]

Printing was valued not only for efficiently replicating the writings of
church fathers, but also for enabling the Roman Church to raise money
quickly, for serving as an aid to conversion and for demonstrating Western
Christendom's superiority over the infidel. As early as 1452, a papal legate
(possibly Nicholas of Cusa) had authorized the printing of thousands of in-
dulgences by a Mainz shop to raise money for the crusade against the Turks.[67]
"Printing was dedicated by the special grace of God to the redemption of the
faithful," wrote the author of a student manual illustrated with the first
printed regional map of Palestine.[68]

Above all, it was the capacity of print to standardize liturgy that evoked
enthusiasm from churchmen who had long been troubled by local variations
in prayer books and service books. "One of the principal ideas of the monastic reform . . . [was] that identical texts should be present in all monasteries."[69] The same concern preoccupied members of the secular clergy.
Nicholas of Cusa as Bishop of Brixen "had a concern bordering on mania
that the liturgies of his diocese should be centrally corrected."[70]

It is worth noting that the description of printing as a heavenly gift or
divine art did not command universal assent. Indeed, it is unlikely that such
a description would find favor from any faithful adherent of Islam. That
Western Christian leaders favored the printing of missals, psalters, and other
sacred texts was in striking contrast to the measures taken by the Ottoman
Turks, who prohibited the printing of any Arabic writings and whose prohibitions remained in effect for some three centuries.[71] In contrast to the
Koran, which continued to be copied out by hand, the Bible was, of course,
one of the very first major works to come off a European press. Nor did the
Roman church object to the setting up of presses within the walls of monasteries, abbeys, and convents. Indeed, the first press to be set up in Italy was
housed in a monastery.[72]

Equally remarkable were the numerous manuscripts previously preserved
in monastic libraries that were taken out of safekeeping and turned over to

lay craftsmen for the purpose of getting them printed.[73] "It was fortunate . . . for the growth of the early book trade . . . that these ecclesiastical curators . . . accepted and promoted the new art of printing immediately and enthusiastically."[74] The enthusiasm of the generous librarians may, however, have been misplaced. P. S. Allen notes that many manuscripts were sent to be printed with no arrangement being made for their return. It was assumed that the original codex no longer had any value once it had been duplicated in print. "That any degeneration might come in by the way, that the printed text might contain blunders, was not perceived."[75]

To be sure, there is at least one example where an abbot insisted that hand-copied texts were superior to printed ones. Often discussed, because it is so exceptional, this was the contrarian position taken by Johannes Trithemius (1462–1516), sometime abbot of Sponheim, whose praise of scribes has already been cited. Trithemius asserted that "monks should not stop copying because of the invention of printing."[76] Hand-copied works on parchment, he argued, would outlast printed works on paper. But this was really a non sequitur—an argument in favor, not of handcopying as against printing, but of durable skin as against perishable paper.[77] Durable skin, however, was no guarantee of durable texts—as is shown by the practice of scraping and revising parchments. In any case there was no necessary connection between a preference for hand-copying and a preference for skin. Many texts were copied by hand on paper and many deluxe editions were printed on skin. The abbot's plea for the continuation of hand-copying seems to have been designed largely for domestic consumption—perhaps partly to keep his monks busy and out of mischief and probably also because copying sacred texts was spiritually edifying. But he did not practice what he preached. He had his advice to monks printed and resorted to a nearby press for his other writings. His chronicles are now valued for recording conversations concerning Gutenberg, Fust, and Schoeffer and for containing passages that blessed the art of printing.[78]

The most often cited description of printing as a "divine," "holy," or "sacred" art (*"haec sancta ars"*) was produced under church auspices. It appeared in an editor's Latin introduction to the first printed edition of the letters of St. Jerome, turned out in Rome in 1468 by the two German printers, Sweynheim and Pannartz.[79] The editor, Gianandrea de Bussi, bishop of Aleria, had been in the service of Cardinal Nicholas of Cusa. His former master, de Bussi wrote, was pleased to see that this divine art which had been born in Germany had recently been introduced into Italy. This was neither the first nor the last time that it was said that Italians owed printing to the Germans—a point to be discussed later.

Here let me underline the defensive tone of de Bussi's praise of printing. It offers a valuable (albeit implicit) corrective to Needham's view that printing was hailed on all sides as a "great success," for it shows that the invention was not welcomed by everyone. Thus jealous collectors are chided for selfishly worrying that their own rare manuscripts would be devalued by the increased output of texts. This same theme would be sounded later in Elizabethan England by the first publisher of a vernacular poetry anthology. Robert Tottel argued, against "the vngentle horders vp of such treasure," that publication was beneficial to "the studious of Englishe eloquence."[80] With de Bussi as with Tottel, printing is associated with generosity—with "the act of sharing what was hoarded."[81]

De Bussi also addressed concern about the capacity of printing to multiply error.[82] He argued that the new abundance would facilitate comparison of different versions and lead to textual purification. In addition, he found merit in the lowered cost of books[83] because it put them within the reach of poor readers. (Poor readers, of course, did not refer to members of a "working class" but rather to needy clerics, such as de Bussi himself, and to other poor Latin-reading preachers, teachers, and students.)

Clearly this editor had a vested interest in promoting his own work and that of the two printers he used. But he was also writing as a churchman who cited the praises of a cardinal while introducing the letters of a church father. Although his defensive tone pointed to some hostility on the part of manuscript book collectors, he gave no sign of sensing any incompatibility between serving the church and promoting the printer's craft.[84]

Indeed, printing was frequently blessed by teachers and preachers for being so well designed to fulfill an apostolic mission of spreading glad tidings far and wide. Cloistered monks and nuns who followed rules of silence also welcomed typography. They had long been advised (by Cassiodorus and his successors) to take up their pens so they could preach without opening their mouths and make the Lord's teachings resound in the ears of all the nations. That the press was even more powerful than the pen for such a purpose was often repeated. For example, the 1476 editor of the collected sermons of a local preacher (printed by the Brothers of the Common Life in Rostock) explained, "this admirable book, which was lurking in the hands of a few in their cells, should be published abroad by the printing art, chief of all arts for the advantage of the holy church."[85] Perhaps the most celebrated quattrocento preacher to take advantage of being printed was Savonarola. He rapidly became the best-selling Florentine author; between 1495 and 1498, editions of his sermons came out at the rate of one every fortnight.[86]

Even after the fear of spreading heresies led to edicts requiring preliminary censorship, printing itself continued to be viewed by the church authorities as God-given. The major censorship decree issued by Pope Leo X at the Fifth Lateran Council of 1515 stated that printing had been "invented for God's glory, for the exaltation of the faith and the diffusion of art and learning." The decree listed various abuses that had to be curbed and warned against turning a blessing into a curse. But it also celebrated the benefits to mankind conferred by an invention which "had come down from the heavens as a gift from God."[87] This description of printing as a heavenly gift was later reasserted by anticlerical philosophes during the age of Enlightenment. By then, few writers, Protestant or Catholic, were likely to recall that a pope had once hailed Gutenberg's invention as God-given.[88] By then also the Sorbonne would be seen not as an institution that had housed the first French press but as one that persecuted printers and censored their output.[89]

As one might expect, in view of the enthusiastic support given by fifteenth-century scholars and churchmen, negative views of printing were quite muted at first. Opponents of the new art were especially disadvantaged because the most powerful organs of publicity were lodged in enemy hands. Probably the most celebrated opponent of printing was not a churchman but the Florentine manuscript book dealer, Vespasiano da Bisticci. When printing came to Florence, Vespasiano closed shop and then wrote his memoirs. There he described the beautiful manuscript books he had supplied to the Duke of Urbino and famously asserted that a printed book would have been ashamed in such elegant company:

> Where there was so much care to show honour to the contents of a book by the beauty of its outward form, it is intelligible that the sudden appearance of printed books was greeted at first with anything but favour. The envoys of Cardinal Bessarion, when they saw for the first time a printed book in the house of Constantine Lascaris, laughed at the discovery "made among the barbarians of some German city" and Federigo of Urbino "would have been ashamed to own a printed book."[90]

According to Curt Bühler, the manuscript books supplied by Vespasiano were beautiful to look at but extremely corrupt as texts, since the copyists had avoided making any corrections which might have spoiled the symmetry of each page.[91] The ducal library at Urbino soon contained printed volumes alongside hand-copied ones.

Vespasiano's comments on the "sudden appearance" of printed books support the view that printing made an abrupt, not a gradual, impression on contemporaries. But his account of elite rejection was too self-interested to be trusted. It has "been inflated into meaning noble patrons rejected print. . . . But [they] did nothing of the kind."[92] His views received little attention until the nineteenth century, when his *Lives* first appeared in print and attracted the attention of Jacob Burckhardt. Thereafter they received considerable exposure—resulting in the incorrect but prevalent opinion that printed books were disdained by Italian patricians as vulgar machine-made objects.[93]

Later objections to commodities produced by iron presses harnessed to steam need to be distinguished from earlier reactions to the output of the wooden handpress. In colonial America, it is true, the artisans who operated handpresses were sometimes called "meer mechanics" and were often disdained.[94] Similarly, the "vile meccanico" did not command admiration in Renaissance Italy. There, also, a satirical dialogue contrasted the "manual, plebeian" work of the printer with the "noble and honorable" work of the scribe.[95] But the nuns who ran the Ripoli press were not likely to be regarded as "rude mechanics." That nuns and monks did run early presses may serve to remind us that manual labor was by no means incompatible with monastic discipline. "The monastic association of prayer and work (*ora* and *labora*) exposed many sent to monasteries in their youth to the practice of manual arts and crafts."[96] Other associations, less pertinent to monks, are suggested by the hybrid terms "astronomer-printer, anatomist-printer, scholar-printer."[97] The printers who set up the first Paris press not only were skilled craftsmen but also had university degrees.[98]

In the larger establishments, journeymen typographers need to be differentiated from the entrepreneurs who hired them and the proof readers (correctors) who worked beside them. The literate compositor also needs to be distinguished from the often illiterate pressman. Nevertheless, all claimed to work under the aegis of Minerva, goddess of Wisdom.[99] Some master printers achieved respectability as civic leaders and wealthy burghers. Others, such as Amerbach and Aldus, won the friendship and admiration of numerous scholars. This was not true of Josse Bade (Badius), however. His efforts to gain admission to the republic of letters were repeatedly rebuffed. He was compared unfavorably to the great Budé, accused of writing barely passable Latin prose, and scorned less as a mechanic than as a tradesman.[100]

Many other printers who were similarly scorned as tradesmen appear in Martin Lowry's account of the Venetian scene before the arrival of Aldus Manutius. But Lowry's description of the "boorish grasping and provincial" printers who were "slipshod" in their work[101] seems somewhat overdone— designed, perhaps, to highlight by contrast the exceptional achievements of Aldus. Even before Aldus, some printers in Venice were deemed worthy of respect. Erhard Ratdolt, for example, was praised by a bishop of Augsburg for "his . . . diligence and the wonderful art of printing in which he excelled."[102] Ratdolt had turned out the *editio princeps* of Euclid, among other well regarded works, during his stay in Venice 1476–86.[103]

However much disdain was exhibited against printers as mechanics or tradesmen, there is little or no evidence that snobbery extended to the objects they produced.[104] It is true that when Leonardo da Vinci compared painting to printing, he praised the art that produced a unique object while denigrating the one that gave birth to an infinite number of children.[105] For the most part, however, the duplicative powers of print were welcomed by members of the learned community. They were pleased to gain increased access to the texts they required.

According to all available statistics of production and purchase, the flood of reading matter which poured from the presses after 1470 was aimed at the upper levels of society. It was the established sections of the reading public—priests, teachers in school and university, lawyers, doctors, students, secretaries and clerks—who first felt its first impact.[106]

Within this learned community, tributes to printing were sometimes counterbalanced by complaints about the mishandling of texts by ignorant editors, proofreaders, and printers. In his preface to an edition of Catullus of 1481, Joannes Calphurnius rejoiced at the good fortune that enabled him and his contemporaries to be supplied with a "huge abundance of books which former ages, and the one preceding ours, lacked." But, he wrote, "as the famous poet says, 'The rose is often closest to the thorn,'" and he went on to express irritation at the lack of "diligent and accurate" correction. (According to a recent authority, however, his own editing left much to be desired.)[107]

In 1470, a Florentine scholar, Niccolò Perotti, wrote to a Roman prelate (who was then a cardinal and later became Pope Paul II) that he had at first welcomed the "new art of writing lately brought to us from Germany" and anticipated that it would be a great boon. But his hopes were now dashed. Printers were turning out much too much trash. When good books did get printed they were so badly edited that the world would be better off not having any books at all than to have a thousand copies of such corrupt texts in circulation. One recalls Rabelais's later (apocryphal?) comment as an editor of medical works that one error could now kill thousands of readers.[108] If such ignorant editing was allowed to continue, Perotti went on, the Latin language itself would perish. He was so disturbed by the errors found in one newly printed classical work (edited by de Bussi) that he urged the recipient of his letter to persuade the pope to create a board of learned correctors and to insist that every text undergo scrutiny by a member of the board before it could be printed.[109]

Although this letter has been described as a "call for censorship," it would be more accurate (as Martin Davies notes) to describe it as a call for "institutionalized press correction."[110] Here again it is worth noting that Perotti was not rejecting the use of printing but was rather advocating placing the craft "under the control of enlightened patrons and officials."[111] Ironically enough, when Perotti published his own version of the same work, he was accused by another scholar of making some 275 dreadful errors himself.[112]

It seems likely that any board of learned correctors would soon be at loggerheads, if, indeed, an agreement could be obtained over who was fit to serve. As is often the case with academic infighting, scholarly squabbles had unanticipated benefits. Efforts at textual restoration,

> amid constant claims to have uncovered flaws in the work of their
> predecessors, led inevitably to bitter personal rivalries, as Pliny schol-
> ars competed for reputation, patronage and academic appointments.
> But these disputes over how to correct an obviously corrupt and
> very difficult classical text also led to explicit and fruitful discussion
> of the proper canons of editorial practice.[113]

The persistence of learned quarrels over each edition had the additional benefit of stimulating continuous investigatory activity.

In another instance, an Italian scholar expressed a kind of helpless ambivalence. "Texts would perish if it were not for printing; all writers have to give way before it," wrote Hieronimo Squarciafico in a work published in 1481.

He went on to describe the dream he'd had about his friend, the humanist Francesco Filelfo, who had died recently. The dream was set in the Elysian fields. There, philosophers, poets, and orators debated the question of "whether the newly invented art of printing was more to be praised or condemned." Some argued in favor of the new art that a large number of almost lost books could now be resurrected, thus ensuring lasting fame for authors. But others complained (as had Perotti) that texts were being so corrupted by ignorant handling that authors would not be able to recognize their own writings. The dream ends with Filelfo begging his friend to see that his name would not perish but also to take extra pains to ensure that his writings were published free of errors.[114]

As the foregoing suggests, attitudes toward early printing often reflected a traditional dilemma faced by all writers whose aspirations toward fame and immortality conflicted with their concern about losing control when a text was entrusted to others to be duplicated. This dilemma was by no means novel in the fifteenth century.[115] It was an inevitable concomitant of publishing texts by any means other than reading them out loud—as is suggested by the chorus of complaints about the carelessness of scribes.[116] After printing, however, both the hope of achieving lasting fame and the sense of losing control were intensified. In addition, the number of intermediaries who handled the text increased.[117]

In many instances, to be sure, close collaboration between author and printer made it possible to circumvent many difficulties. "The list of . . . close relationships between printers and savants could easily be extended to fill many pages."[118] In a few exceptional instances, from Regiomontanus to Benjamin Franklin, printer and author were the same. But there seems to be no limit to the number of authors who felt they had lost control once a manuscript had been handed over for printing. Adrian Johns cites a relevant complaint from Robert Burton: "If a printed book did not correspond to the writer's words . . . 'whom do you blame?' The corrector, the printer or 'everyone?' "[119]

With regard to the seventeenth-century scene, H. S. Bennett writes, "Authors have always considered themselves a downtrodden race and they certainly often had reason to think themselves so at this time." Once they had "delivered a manuscript into the printer's hands it practically passed out of their control."[120] Nor was it always possible to ensure that one's manuscript would not be kidnapped, so to speak, by pirate printers who felt no compunction at all about ignoring the author's wishes.

Recent studies of attitudes toward printing on the part of Renaissance writers have raised doubts about the once popular "stigma of print" thesis.[121] When writers informed readers of their reluctance to get printed, they were more likely to take refuge in formulaic statements (invoking the classical modesty trope) than to reveal their actual motives.[122] A "language of justification and disavowal"[123] masked a vast variety of diverse attitudes. Reactions were so diverse that they defy generalization. Some authors, such as Juan Luis Vives, exhibited little or no ambivalence. He wanted "to see his work published almost before the ink . . . [was] dry."[124] Often there was a conflict between an awareness of the benefits of print and the feeling that it was somehow indecorous to demonstrate this awareness too openly. When authors such as Bembo and Castiglione took the initiative to procure the services of printers, they tended to deny that they had done so by shifting responsibility to the insistence of friends—a tactic employed long before in ancient Rome.[125] Claiming foul play by unauthorized printers was a common ploy.[126] Samuel Daniel shifted responsibility not to a friend but to a "greedie printer" who had turned out his work uncorrected and thus Daniel "was forced to publish that which I never ment."[127] Thomas Browne used both ploys in his "To the Reader" address of 1643. He claimed that the insistence of friends *and* a previously corrupted pirated copy made it necessary for him to issue a corrected version of *Religio Medici*. After noting that he'd lived "to behold the highest perversion of that excellent invention," Browne cited the duty he owed his friends and the allegiance he "must ever acknowledge unto the truth" as an explanation for getting a corrected copy printed. Oddly enough he used the same printer who had presumably "pirated" the first corrupted version.[128]

In Elizabethan England (unlike France or Italy in the same period)[129] the propriety of printing had much to do with genre. It is often assumed that English aristocrats shied away from dealing with printers to avoid being tainted with "involvement in commercial affairs."[130] Yet they did not hesitate to arrange for the printing of their prose treatises.[131] Poetry was a different matter. It might circulate in hand-copied form for a friendly coterie, but it was unacceptable to have it printed and be seen by "the publique eie of the world."[132] "'Tis ridiculous for a lord to print Verses," wrote John Selden, "'tis well enough to make them to please himself, but to make them public, is foolish."[133] Not all poets agreed: Michael Drayton repeatedly complained against the fashionable avoidance of print. "Verses are wholly declined into chambers, and nothing [is] esteemed in this lunatic age, but what is kept in cabinets and must pass only by transcription."[134]

Despite Drayton's complaints, poets continued to be more hesitant than were preachers about having their work appear in print.[135] This may have been partly because of the disapproval of preachers who frowned on amorous verse. There was also the coupling of verse with street literature—ballads and songs. Verse was stigmatized for being ephemeral and frivolous as well as ungodly.[136] When gentle-born poets did have their verses printed, they often took refuge in anonymity.

But the "stigma of verse" (as May more accurately puts it) should not be generalized to encompass aristocratic distaste for commerce with printers. There was nothing ridiculous about a lord's having his name singled out in a printed dedication or other prefatory matter expressing gratitude for his support. Indeed most patrons, however high their rank, welcomed having the public told about their generous, Maecenas-like role. Praising a patron also had benefits for printers. An illustrious name acted as a kind of "celebrity endorsement."[137] It helped promote sales while paving the way for obscure writers to enhance their reputation. It was by means of a dedication that Erasmus first managed to get his name into print.

"The prospect of coming to the press was fraught with considerable anxiety . . . [as] the early modern author existed in a liminal state between patronage and copyright . . . Ben Jonson and Spenser express similar anxieties about allowing their words to circulate beyond their control."[138] No doubt the early modern author (especially the playwright or poet) was placed in "a complex and indeterminate position."[139] As noted elsewhere, in connection with Racine, the lofty position of the inspired "immortal" and arbiter of taste was not easily reconciled with that of supplying commodities sold on the open market.[140] Ben Jonson's "deeply ambivalent attitude" is well described by Ian Donaldson. Jonson was "attracted to an usual degree by the lure of the printing house" and had no wish to be a "côterie" poet like John Donne. But even while thinking of printed works as "vehicles of fame, couriers to posterity, monuments to art," he realized that they were also liable to be treated as "mere commodities . . . used to wrap spices, line pie dishes and clothe tobacco."[141]

That printing introduced a "commodification" of literature is currently a favorite theme.[142] But here, as elsewhere, it would be a mistake to underestimate antecedents in the age of scribes. Ancient authors had also wavered between thinking of themselves as immortals and as the producers of perishable goods. Horace hoped his works were "more durable than bronze" and "higher than Pharaoh's Pyramids" but also feared they might end up being used "to wrap pepper and frankincense" (or even worse—as Martial put it—to wrap "fried tuna").[143]

In any case, as Squarciafico's dream suggested, early modern writers were by no means of one mind about the advantages and disadvantages of printing. In their dealings with early printers, as in their later dealings with publishers and booksellers, authors often began by expressing gratitude only to end by expressing disgust. Few were likely to hold the same view throughout their lives.

Perhaps the most celebrated example of inconstancy was provided by Erasmus. When soliciting favors from a potential patron, he made much of the long-lasting celebrity conferred by print: "You will point out how much more credit I will do her by my learning than other divines whom she maintains. They preach obscure sermons: I write what will live forever; they . . . are heard in one or two churches; my books will be read in every country in the world."[144] His tribute to Aldus Manutius as a prince among printer-publishers encompassed a paean to the divine art itself for creating a library without "walls" or "other limits than the world itself." All scholars were indebted to the printer for having recovered the treasures of antiquity. Aldine editions served not merely a single generation or a single province but all the peoples of the entire world and all the generations to come.[145]

But there is also his later scathing portrayal of Aldus's father-in-law, Andrea Torresani of Asola, as a malevolent miser who starved visiting authors, watered their wine, and fed wet roots to the fire while amassing a fortune. In the same late *Colloquy*, Aldus himself is cast in the unheroic role of a deferential son-in-law who aids and abets his villainous relative.[146] In this instance Erasmus was reacting angrily to being accused (by Julius Caesar Scaliger) of exhibiting boorish behavior while taking advantage of the printer's hospitality. It has been said that "the ease with which Erasmus's long-declared veneration for Aldo could be transformed into contempt for an undignified commercial enterprise illustrates the equivocal status of even the most illustrious Venetian printer."[147] But Erasmus's angry riposte had more to do with the wounded vanity of an author than with the equivocal status of a printer. Aldus and his editions continued to be held in high esteem by almost all other literati. The colloquy did illustrate the fickle attitude of an ambitious author who had not hesitated to break an agreement with one printer (Badius) after deciding he'd be better served by another (Froben).

In his later years, especially after the Lutheran revolt cost him former friends and admirers, Erasmus adopted a sour tone when he wrote about the press. He made nasty remarks about the shortcomings of Froben's competitors, who "contaminated, mutilated and lacerated texts" and who were so eager to save every penny that they failed to employ any proofreaders.[148] In a late version of the same *Adage* that was initially dedicated to Aldus, the benefits of printing were almost eclipsed by complaints about increased output: swarms of new books were glutting the market and once venerated authors were being neglected. "To what corner of the world do they not fly, these swarms of new books? . . . . the very multitude of them is hurtful to scholarship, because it creates a glut, and even in good things satiety is most harmful." The minds of men "flighty and curious of anything new" are lured "away from the study of old authors."[149]

In addition to the grievances of temperamental authors, adverse comments came from printers themselves in the course of denigrating their competitors. In the early days of the craft competition was especially fierce. A free-for-all environment offered no protection to printers who produced costly first editions that provided competitors with copies that could be duplicated and sold at lower cost.[150] From the 1470s on, potential purchasers were repeatedly warned against the inferior editions of other printers. If the dozen previous editions of Cicero's letters were adequately edited, noted a printer in 1472, there would be no need for yet another. But the result has been "a tangled and contorted mass of corruptions produced by the greed of the avaricious."[151] "Purchase these, book-buyer, with a light heart, for you will find such excellence in this volume that you will be right in easily reckoning other editions as worth no more than a straw," advertised a Basel printer in 1494.[152] For colorful abuse of a fellow printer it would be hard to outdo a preface of 1570 by the celebrated Elizabethan, John Day. While warning his readers against the previous edition of 1565 by a "contemptible printer," Day likened the latter to a rapist who "entised into his house a faire maide and done her villanie, and after all to-bescratched her face, torne her apparel, berayed and disfigured her, and then thrust her out of doors dishonested."[153] On the negative side also were the frequent attacks made on journeymen, who served their masters as convenient scapegoats. The colophon of a 1494 history of Bologna told readers that whatever faults were to be found in the book were due not to the master printer, who was a man of exceptional ability and literary gifts, but rather to the carelessness of his workers.[154] In his *Ship of Fools* of 1494, Sebastian Brant underscored the reckless, roistering ways of printing workers.[155] As recent historians continue to remind us, real printing shops were noisy, dirty, and smelly[156]—attributes that have never been associated with Christian ideas of the divine.

The unavoidable presence of often boisterous, sometimes disorderly, and, occasionally, drunken workers opened the way for invidious comparisons with the quiet dedicated labors of the scribe. Little attention was paid to the fact that, after the twelfth century, most manuscripts had actually been duplicated not by dedicated monks but piecemeal by paid copyists and careless (often boisterous, disorderly, and sometimes drunken) students. We often forget that the beautiful illustrated manuscripts in our modern rare book collections were rare even in their own day. Doubtless some fifteenth-century manuscripts were "exquisitely handwritten," and "ornately bound," and "associated with . . . ostentatious expenditure."[157] But these costly objects were exceptional, not typical, products of late medieval book production. As noted above, complaints directed at printing workers largely echoed complaints previously directed at copyists. Scribal errors had been the bane of anxious authors from the days of Cicero to those of Petrarch.[158] But memories of the shortcomings of real scribes (they were called "the excrement of the universe" by Poggio Bracciolini)[159] soon faded. The best of the past would be set against the worst of the present. An idealized image of the pious copyist working for the glory of God set the stage for an invidious comparison with the actuality of disreputable printing workers striking for higher wages.[160]

This contrast became especially popular in a later age—an age marked by Luddite revolts, Gothic revivals, and the industrialization of printing and paper-making. Yet the difference between the peaceful scriptorium and the infernal din of the printing shop was already drawn in the fifteenth century by one disgruntled friar whose manuscripts have been unearthed in the twentieth century. (As was the case with Vespasiano da Bisticci, the friar's writings did not appear in print for hundreds of years. After being repeatedly recycled, Vespasiano's views are falling into disrepute even as the writings of the friar are now coming into vogue.)[161] He was a Dominican scribe and preacher named Filippo di Strata who resided in the monastery of San Cipriano in Murano. He observed the operations of the Venetian press in the last three decades of the fifteenth century when Venice was emerging as the central city of the European printed book trade.[162]

He objected first of all to increased output and the vulgarization of learning. The city was overflowing with books, he wrote contemptuously, so that men who could barely read were now forming libraries. The friar was by no means the last commentator to express concern about the flooding of markets with new books. But he was among the first. In this connection it is worth pausing over the often cited (and often misconstrued) passage from Ecclesiastes: "Of making many books there is no end." Richard de Bury, who cites the passage in *Philobiblon*,[163] makes it clear that the phrase does not express concern about flooded book markets but rather concern about the fragility and scarcity of hand-copied books. "It is meritorious to write new Books," de Bury asserts, "and to renew the old. [It is] needful to replace the volumes that are worn out with age by fresh successors. Hence it is that the Preacher says (Ecclesiastes 12) "of making many books, there is no end; *faciendi plures libros nullus est finis.*"

A remarkable epidemic of scribbling attracted the attention of ancient Roman satirists. In the age of the handpress, complaints came from one generation after another. Erasmus's concern about the "swarms of new books" has already been cited. Robert Burton found that the "vast chaos and confusion of books" contributed to bewilderment and melancholy.[164] In the seventeenth century Thomas Browne would put it in his marvelous prose: "'tis . . . the desires of better heads . . . to condemne to the fire those swarms and millions of Rhapsodies, begotten only to distract and abuse the weaker judgements of Scholars, and to maintaine the Trade and Mystery of typographers."[165]

But perennial complaints about there being too many books in the world were usually aimed at the need to separate the wheat from the chaff. The friar's elitist view that learning itself should be restricted was vigorously contested by teachers and translators who welcomed the popularizing potential of printing.[166] "Learning cannot be too common and the commoner the better. . . . Why but the vulgar should not know all," wrote John Florio,[167] whose English translations made Italian and French works known to writers in Shakespeare's time. Of course the cause of translation and popularization benefited from the evangelical tradition. In this regard, di Strata was an atypical member of a teaching and preaching order.[168] "Some members of the clergy, in particular the Franciscans and Dominicans, felt that the low price and the abundance of printed books were heaven-sent means of spreading enlightenment."[169] Printing seemed to them to be providentially designed to implement Erasmus's vision of plowboys, weavers, and housewives reciting the Psalms while at work.

But printing was also well designed to serve other less holy and edifying purposes. That printers profited from diversifying and that most readers preferred entertainment to instruction would be a source of disillusionment to each generation in turn. As Myron Gilmore put it, "even a John Stuart Mill did not envisage that when the plowboy had learned to read he was more likely to read the Hearst papers than the Psalms."[170] It was already apparent to our friar in late fifteenth-century Venice that printers would be more likely to profit from the popular appetite for sexually titillating stuff than from serving the needs of austere scholars and ascetic monks. "They basely flood the market with anything suggestive of sexuality," he complained, thereby corrupting the minds of "tender boys and gentle girls." The respectable art of writing should be "held to be noble . . . unless she has suffered degradation in the brothel of the printing presses. She is a maiden [virgin] with a pen; a harlot [whore] in print [*est virgo haec penna: meretrix est stampificata*]." (Little did he imagine that five hundred years later he would become celebrated for thus "gendering" pen and press.)[171]

In addition to the corrupting effect of cheap books catering to erotic fantasies and recycling pagan myths, di Strata was prophetically worried that evangelism itself was getting out of hand. Vernacular Bibles were spreading dangerous heresies, he complained. He concluded his denunciation by asserting that printing should be banished by law from Venice.

But the Venetian authorities had no desire to banish such a flourishing industry from the Republic.[172] Often at odds with the Roman pope, the authorities gave printers considerable latitude in turning out popular, often anticlerical works always provided they exhibited due respect for Venetian rulers. "Blistering criticism of the papal court went uncensored. Insult, slander, even obscenity against friars and priests were so common that anti-clericalism became a literary convention . . . authors only avoided criticism of things Venetian."[173] As elsewhere in numerous petty principalities and city states, the printing industry was welcomed for filling town coffers and enhancing civic pride.

Although Venetians could boast of having the most flourishing printing industry in late fifteenth-century Europe, they also had to acknowledge that foreign merchants and craftsmen were largely responsible for this fact. Among other adverse effects produced by printing, according to our friar, it opened the way for German intruders to debase Venetian intellectual life. From the very beginning, attitudes toward printing were shaped by its originating as a German invention and its having been introduced over the Alps and Pyrenees by itinerant German craftsmen. The English tradition is somewhat anomalous in this respect. Instead of Germans coming to England, an

English merchant went to Germany: Caxton learned the craft in Cologne and practiced it in Bruges before setting up shop in London and earning immortality among his countrymen.[174]

On the Continent, however, Gutenberg's compatriots were acknowledged to be the first to set up printing shops in Italy, France, and Spain.[175] The last part of the 1460 colophon usually attributed to Gutenberg has already been cited: "This noble book . . . [was made] without help of reed, stilus, or pen, but by the wondrous agreement, proportion, and harmony of punches and types." Other parts of the colophon are also worth noting. They assert that the new art was born in "the bounteous city of Mainz of the renowned German nation, which the clemency of God has deigned with so lofty a light of genius and free gift to prefer and render illustrious above all other nations of the earth."

Gutenberg was reticent, and it is uncertain if he wrote those words. His immediate successor, Fust's son-in-law, Peter Schoeffer, in striking contrast, was something of a publicity hound. As already noted, he made his name known as the author of numerous colophons which appeared during the 1460s and '70s. They praised Gutenberg and his invention and also paid tribute to the noble city of Mainz and to the special genius of the German nation. These colophons set the pattern for later developments. In Strasbourg, Lyon, Basel, and numerous other cities, printers publicized the local history and special virtues of the towns in which they worked. It was not just for their contributions to local prosperity but also for the way they enhanced civic pride and put provincial place names on the map—so to speak—that printers were invited by so many local rulers to set up the numerous presses which dotted the Italian peninsula.[176]

In the light of subsequent developments, it is worth pausing over the broader claims that linked the invention with the special genius of the German nation. To forestall anachronistic interpretations, we need to underscore the point that fifteenth-century references to "Germans" did not look forward to the modern nation state. In their colophon to an edition of Sallust in the 1470s, for example, the German printers who set up the first Paris press noted that the king of France was getting ready for war. By publishing a volume describing the brave and heroic deeds of the ancient Romans, the printers claimed, "[we] German printers" were adding to the French king's supply of fighters and were helping France stir up more recruits.[177] To find Germans boasting of recruiting soldiers for a French king puts us at some distance from later national rivalries.

Of course the term "nation" was used differently in Schoeffer's day than in our own. Among its diverse meanings, probably the most common was with reference to languages spoken by the different groups encountered at church council meetings or within the precincts of a university or in quarters set aside for foreign merchants. "Of the foreign 'nations' at the universities of Italy none was more numerous than the German, a title which embraced . . . not merely . . . the Swiss and Flemish and Dutch, but all who could by any stretch of imagination be represented as descendants of the Goths; Swedes and Danes, Hungarians and Bohemians, Lithuanians and Bulgars and Poles."[178]

German-speaking folk who came from Swiss towns, such as Zürich or Basel, would also be regarded as members of the German nation on other grounds, because their home towns were included within the political boundaries of the old Reich. A fifteenth-century reference to the German nation might carry with it the traditional opposition of German emperors to Italian popes; the formal grievances drawn up by imperial diets were presented to the papal curia in the name of the German Nation. The Holy Roman Empire provided Germans with their claim to be linked with antiquity, yet they had to grant to the Italians "proprietorship of Roman remains that were everywhere on the ground."[179]

In addition to imperial politics, there was a longstanding cultural rivalry with Italians which was of special importance to early printers and literati. "The fifteenth century saw a profusion of Italian complaints in elegant Ciceronian Latin about the Germans' loutish behavior and propensity to drink, not to mention their curious liberties, oral and written, with the Latin language." To most Italian humanists, "barbarus" and "Germanus" were synonymous terms.[180] The Germans were held responsible not only for barbarous Latin but also for allowing precious manuscripts to molder in the monasteries of northern Europe. In 1417, for example, after congratulating Poggio Bracciolini for "restoring to us the Orators, Poets, Historians, Astronomers" of antiquity, Franciscus Barbarus lashed out at "those Germans" who "ought to be branded with shame for leaving celebrated men buried alive for so long."[181] The Germans might retaliate against being charged with boorishness and drunkenness by accusing the Italians of sodomy and pederasty, but they still had to acknowledge the "Italian . . . preeminence in the world of learning."[182]

Until the mid-fifteenth century, Italian claims to superiority for having recovered the lost treasures of antiquity and for having revived true Latin eloquence had gone virtually unchallenged. By depicting printing as a peculiarly German contribution, Peter Schoeffer and other early printers used the new technology as a counterweight to the self-congratulatory literature that had come from beyond the Alps. A 1469 colophon to a second edition of Cicero's *Letters* published in Venice by a German printer offers one example: "From Italy once each German brought a book. / A German now will give more than they took."[183] The theme was sounded by scholars as well as by printers. Thus, Conrad Leontorius praised Johann Amerbach for defending "Germany from charges of barbarism by the accurate publications . . . of your publishing house."[184] Sebastian Brant cited newly printed editions of Cicero and Virgil to show how the muses had found a new home in Germany: "Through the genius and skill of the German people, there is now a great abundance of books. . . . Thanks be first to God and like thanks to printers. . . . Not only do the Germans excel in strength of character and arms, they hold the sceptre of the world as well."[185] The Germans also boasted of being the true heirs to ancient Roman technical ingenuity. They

> had invented gunpowder, and above all the arts of printing, the new medium of textual knowledge and the basis for Albrecht Dürer's European fame as an artist. In . . . verses from the *Amores*, Celtis placed the Germans at the end of a long medial chain: The Greeks call me *Sophia* and the Romans *Sapientia* / the Egyptians and Chaldeans discovered me, the Greeks wrote me / the Romans translated me and the Germans amplified me / . . . . Conrad Peutinger rebutted his own teacher Pomponio Leto's curious claim that the Italians had invented printing . . . [pointing out that Leto's example had involved no more than the stamping of coins].[186]

One much-published chronicle, first issued in 1483, assigned Gutenberg's invention to the year 1440. While thus fixing the year for all subsequent celebrations, the chronicler added: "How much students of letters owe to the Germans is beyond the power of words to express."[187] The date 1440 was taken up by others, including Hartmann Schedel in the *Nuremberg Chronicle*, where the Germans are again singled out for a tribute: "Who can say with what measure of praise, honor and renown are to be esteemed those Germans who, through their brilliant and clever skill, thought out and discovered the art of printing, by which the long closed fountain of untold wisdom in sacred and profane art was caused again to flow forth to all mankind."[188]

Let us now return to the question posed at the outset concerning early reactions to the advent of printing. As we have seen, different answers will emerge from special studies of limited scope: studying the vocabulary used to describe fifteenth-century books thus yields a result that is different from studying the contents of colophons, prefaces, and other paratextual material. But if we expand the scope of our inquiry to encompass comparative perspectives and compare Western Christian attitudes with those that prevailed throughout Islam, the answer seems clear enough. When contrasted with prohibitions that remained in effect for three centuries, the enthusiastic welcome printing received in the West stands out in bold relief. In Europe, indeed, positive responses far outweighed negative ones. The objections that were posed were aimed, not at the use of the handpress per se, but rather at its misuse or abuse by ostensibly unworthy practitioners. Insofar as actions should be considered along with words, much more was done to encourage than to discourage the establishment and use of presses throughout the Western world.

In this light, there does seem to be something rather artificial about the way recent authorities urge us to give equal time to those special cases where hand-copying was favored over recourse to print. Scribal publication was a "normal" procedure throughout the Islamic world; in Western Europe, it was increasingly exceptional. When pointing to the "normalcy of manuscript publication" in seventeenth-century England, it is worth keeping this significant contrast in mind.[189]

"There has been a tendency to exaggerate the unifying power of Gutenberg's invention," Roger Chartier remarked to an interviewer, "we cannot ignore the fact that there was not only a discourse of praise for Gutenberg's invention but also a discourse of resistance . . . aristocrats, scholars, the erudite . . . [who] believed that print culture was commercial . . . that the printing process was corruptive."[190] Granted that anxiety and ambivalence were often present, the phrase "discourse of resistance" seems oddly incompatible with the way most Europeans reacted to print during the age of the handpress.

There was a real "discourse of resistance" that was elaborated by opponents of diverse regimes. To evade official repression, dissidents often resorted to a clandestine trade in manuscripts (a practice that persisted into the twentieth century with the anti-Stalinist *samizdat*). But far from objecting to printing, dissidents took advantage of the handpress whenever they could—installing it in secret places and moving it around.

As for aristocrats, scholars, and other elites, the Venetian doges, the Sorbonne professors, and the cardinals and bishops who welcomed the industry were more characteristic of official reactions throughout Europe than was the contrarian friar whose demand for banishing printers has only recently been unearthed.[191] Moreover, calls for stricter censorship and other forms of regulation should not be confused with rejection. In Tudor England the demand for stringent regulation of the printed book trade, far from conveying any resistance to printing, was initiated by printers themselves. As noted above, the papal censorship edict of 1515 celebrated the new craft's benefits to mankind, even while warning against turning a blessing into a curse. But, however one may read this edict, it is not aptly characterized as representing a discourse of resistance.

When an early editor of St. Jerome's letters celebrated the virtues of printing in extravagant terms, we are told that "few of his readers agreed."[192] Perhaps so. Yet the fact remains that an extravagant praise of printing was reiterated in numerous colophons, prefaces, and chronicles. Had the new art not commanded the admiration of Latin reading scholars, it seems unlikely that German humanists would have made such a point of the German origins of the invention and also unlikely that they would have hit on it as means of countering Italian claims to cultural supremacy.[193]

The idea that printing was a providential gift had first been sounded by the Roman church in its crusade against the Turks. The same idea was then taken over by German humanists intent on countering Italian claims of cultural supremacy. After Luther, the invention that was hailed for emancipating Germans from cultural bondage to Italian humanists would be celebrated among Protestants generally for freeing them from spiritual bondage to Italian popes. The Roman church that had regarded printing as a weapon to be wielded against infidels found this same weapon being turned against itself.

Religious divisions would affect attitudes toward the invention during the ensuing centuries. But printing also was at issue in other more secular contexts. The capacity of "paper bullets" to undermine established institutions was welcomed by political dissidents even while alarming royal officials. Within a cosmopolitan commonwealth of learning, printing played a strategic role in bookish battles between ancients and moderns. The advancement of learning was credited to the increased availability of texts. At the same time, there was concern about information overload. These developments will be considered in the following chapters.

Chapter 2

After Luther: Civil War in Christendom

God graciously bestowed this Art of Printing on Mankind, for the Unveiling and Unmasking of this Mystery of Iniquity to the world. . . . Printing is like a Wing on which knowledge flies throughout the habitable world and is at this day a famous instrument of God's holy spirit to publish his sacred and infallible truth.

—Christopher Ness (1679)

It has been made a Question long agoe, whether more mischief then advantage were not occasion'd to the Christian world by the Invention of Typography.

—Roger L'Estrange (1660)

Printing as a Protestant Weapon

The same themes that had first been sounded by the Roman church were echoed by Protestants after 1517. Thus printing was celebrated by Luther and his successors, as it had been by earlier preachers and teachers, for the tremendous impetus it gave to the evangelical cause. But the Lutherans also assigned a new world historical role to printing by depicting it as the weapon that undermined papal rule. Even while attacking greedy printers, Luther hailed the press as a God-given instrument that made the difference between his success in defying the pope and the failure of precursors, such as Jan Hus, to achieve the same goal.

Long-standing German-Italian rivalries also inflected Lutheran discourse. The Germans congratulated themselves on being the first to be granted knowledge of a divine art that enabled them to break free of bondage to Rome and to bring the light of true religion to other God-fearing peoples. Printing thus figured prominently in triumphalist claims centering on the world historical mission of the Germans. A case in point was an *Address to the Estates of the German Empire* by the influential Lutheran historian, Johann Sleidan:

> As if to offer proof that God has chosen us to accomplish a special mission, there was invented in our land a marvelous, new, and subtle art, the art of printing. Each man became eager for knowledge, not without feeling a sense of amazement at his former blindness.[1]

It is tempting to read this passage as if Sleidan had in mind the advancement of learning and the dawning of the age of Enlightenment. But sixteenth-century Lutherans were more likely to envisage a future that was closed off by the coming of Judgment Day.[2] This was not true of all Protestants. Calvin, in particular, doubted the validity of the apocalyptic tradition, and Luther himself only adhered to it in later life.[3] Nevertheless, when considering attitudes toward printing (a medium that is often associated with cumulative cognitive advance), we need to be reminded that "the Reformation was not seen as the beginning of a 'modern' period of history but as a prelude to the End of all history."[4] The "magisterial reformers believed that they lived in the last age . . . the Second Coming ushering in Eternity was imminent."[5] In 1530 Luther rushed his translation of the Book of Daniel to the printers for fear that he would not get the work finished before the Second Coming.[6] In a telling metaphor, he likened his success in spreading the Gospel to the fate of a guttering candle:

> Just before it burns out [it] makes a last great spurt, as if it would continue to burn for a long time, and then goes out. So it now appears as if the gospel is going to spread far and wide, but I'm afraid that it will be extinguished . . . and the day of judgment will follow.[7]

Thus Gutenberg's invention was celebrated, not for initiating an indefinitely expanding knowledge industry, but rather as a signal that the anti-Christ (whether Turk or pope) was destined to be defeated and that the last days were close at hand.

Sleidan's view that the acquisition of printing was a sign of being chosen by God for a special antipapal mission was shared by other Protestants. It was forcefully expressed by the Marian exiles who found work in Continental printing shops during the 1550s in Strasbourg, Basel, and Geneva. Their travels followed a precedent set by William Tyndale, who, with his assistants and associates, had crossed the Channel in the 1520s in search of a printer for his English translation of the Bible. He found what he sought in Peter Schoeffer (a descendant of the son-in-law of Gutenberg's partner), who published Tyndale's New Testament in Worms in 1526.[8]

The special connection between Protestantism and printing that was eventually taken for granted among English-speaking people was not unrelated to the actual experiences, first of Tyndale and Miles Coverdale, then of John Bale,[9] and finally of the Marian exiles. All of them, when they traveled on the Continent, were never far from printing shops. One group of the exiles (including John Knox and William Whittingham, a disciple of Calvin and his kinsman by marriage) took up residence in Geneva. There they published the celebrated Geneva Bible, along with a stream of subversive tracts that justified political disobedience.[10]

The other group, which included John Bale and John Foxe, moved at first in Lutheran circles in Frankfurt and Strasbourg before settling in Basel.[11] At some point, Foxe may have met Sleidan, whose comment about Germany's "special mission" is cited above.[12] His later familiarity with a Latin treatise on printing[13] by Matthäus Judex, a German Lutheran, is well documented.[14] Judex (Matthäus Richter), like many others who wrote about printing, was puzzled why the invention was unknown for so long. He concluded that the art was only revealed to mankind at the very time that God had chosen for unmasking the anti-Christ.[15] Foxe's views on printing doubtless owed much to this sort of Lutheran influence, although he was more likely to side with Zwingli and Bucer than with Luther on doctrinal issues[16] and never ceased admiring Erasmus.[17] But his views of printing were probably also influenced by his working in milieux, especially in Basel, that were conducive to celebrating the divine art.

The first Latin versions of what later was known as the *Book of Martyrs* were written when their author was collaborating with Continental master printers, first in Strasbourg and then, most notably, in Basel, where Foxe worked for four years as a proofreader in the shop of Vesalius's printer, Oporinus.[18] During that interval Oporinus was preparing, among other notable projects, the publication of a gigantic fourteen-volume martyrology directed by Matthias Flacius Illyricus.[19] The first and several subsequent English versions of Foxe's expanding martyrology were written after the author's return to England, when he was a constant visitor to the Aldersgate printing house of John Day.[20]

"Hereby tongues are knowne, knowledge groweth, judgement increaseth, books are dispersed, the scripture is scene [sic], the Doctors be read, stories be opened, times compared, truth descerned, falsehod detected, and with fingers poynted, and all (as I sayd) through the benefit of printing."[21] In this passage, Foxe showed how much tributes to printing owed to the traditional praise of scribes.[22] His comments on the amplifying effects of the new medium also echoed earlier preachers. "By this printing as by the gift of tongues, and as by the organe of the Holy Ghost, the doctrine of the Gospell soundeth to all nations and what God hath revealed to one man, is dispersed to many and what is known to one nation is opened to all."[23]

But Foxe departed from scribal precedents when dealing with antipapal themes. As was true of Luther, he attributed the inability of Jan Hus, Jerome of Prague, and other heresiarchs to win their battle against the papacy to their being deprived of the invention that God had granted to a later age. The Dark Ages had been marked by withholding knowledge of the Gospel from the "simple and unlearned." "The Word was forgotten. . . . the people were taught to worship no other thing but that which they did see." Then came the great turning point. After the Council of Constance had condemned

> poor John Huss and Hierone of Prague to death for heresy . . . and after they had subdued the Bohemians and the whole world was under the supreme authority of the Romish See, in this very time so dangerous and desperate where man's power could do no more, the blessed wisdom and omnipotent power of the Lord began to work for his church not with sword and target to subdue his exalted adversary but with printing, writing and reading: to convince darkness by light, error by truth, ignorance by learning . . . either the Pope must abolish printing or he must seek a new world to reign over: for else as this world standeth, printing will doubtless abolish him.[24]

The first signs that the tide of battle was turning came from Erasmus and his Basel printer. "When Erasmus wrote, and Frobenius printed, what a blow thereby was given to all the friars and monks in the world? And who seeth not that the pen of Luther, following after Erasmus, and set forward by writing, hath set the triple crown so awry on the pope's head that it is never likely to be set straight again?"[25] Even while assigning credit to Erasmus and Luther for effective use of the new weapon, Foxe did not neglect the English antecedents of the antipapal campaign. In addition to such continental precursors as the Waldensians and the Hussites, he drew attention to native-born figures, such as the Lollards and William Wycliffe, who had persistently battled against "alien intruders for ever seeking to subvert the English State and corrupt the English Church."[26] Together with John Bale he helped to transport the world historical mission that had been assigned by Sleidan to the German people[27] and rooted it in the English past.[28]

Recently, questions have been raised about the extent to which Foxe stressed the English roots of the Reformation and thus fostered the idea of English exceptionalism.[29] According to Mozley, Foxe lost no opportunity to mention English precursors in order to counter German insistence that Protestantism originated with Luther.[30] Similarly, William Haller argues that Foxe shaped the English conception of an "elect nation." Against these views, it is said that Foxe always regarded the church as a cosmopolitan body comprised of Christians belonging to different countries and different epochs. He "saw nothing special about the fact that Wyclif was English."[31] Although the triumphalist aspects of some editions of the Book of Martyrs are acknowledged, its "religiously inflected exceptionalism" and "missionary imperialism," are attributed to later versions of the work, especially to Bright's post-Armada edition of 1589.[32]

Yet in his very first Latin version (Strasbourg, 1554) Foxe had "devoted the opening section to . . . Wycliffe and the Lollards" and paid tribute to "our countryman Wicliff" before he "plunged into the . . . narrative which was to be his life's work. Wycliffe's place in [this narrative] remained a leading one."[33] A passage which passed from the Latin edition to the English one of 1563 seems to confirm this verdict. When "all the world was in most desperate and vile estate, and . . . the lamentable ignorance and darkness of God's truth had overshadowed the whole earth, this man [Wycliffe] stepped forth like a valiant champion . . . 'Even as the morning star . . . so doth he shine and glister in the . . . church of God.'"[34] Indeed it was largely owing to the *Actes and Monuments* that "Wycliffe gained a notoriety he has never since lost," and "the Lollards were given new fame as the spiritual ancestors of sixteenth-century reformers."[35]

Even while reshaping the reputation of the Lollards as "forelders," and transforming William Wycliffe into the "morning star" of the Reformation,

Foxe did not neglect the Bible translator who was closer to his own time. His portrayal of William Tyndale as "the Apostle of England in our Later Age" owed much to his close collaboration, after his return from exile, with John Day, who had printed Tyndale's *New Testament* in 1548.[36] Day's Aldersgate printing house kept many presses in constant use. His output had been arrested (along with Day himself) during Mary Tudor's reign but flourished under Elizabeth, in large part due to William Cecil's patronage, which procured Day a monopoly on the printing of ABC books and the Psalms.[37] His edition of Euclid in English, with an introduction by John Dee, would become celebrated later on.[38] However, his epitaph showed that his contemporaries esteemed him for one work above all: He "set a Fox to wright how Martyrs runne from death to lyfe."[39]

Another of Day's publications, *The Whole Works of William Tyndale, John Frith and Doctor Barnes . . . Collected . . . in One Tome together Being Before Scattered . . .* (1573), contained a preface that provided yet one more opportunity for Foxe to hail the "science of printing" and those who practice it "as divinely ordained instruments for the furtherance of true religion and the repairing of Christs Church":

> We have great cause to geeve thanks to the high providence of almighty God, for the excellent arte of Printing, most happely of late found out, and now commonly practiced everywhere, to the singular benefite of Christes Church. [Printing had restored] the lost lyght of knowledge to these blynde tymes, by renuing of holsome and auncient writers: whose doinges and teachinges otherwise had lyen in oblivion had not the benefit of Printing brought them agayne to light, or us rather to light by them.[40]

The traditional scriptural dichotomies of darkness/light, blindness/seeing, ignorance/knowledge that were employed by early Protestants would continue to be associated with the advent of printing long after the invention had lost its religious overtones.[41] On a more prosaic level, Foxe presented what amounted to a blurb for John Day. He congratulated the printer for having collected together, and presented in a lasting form, writings that had been scattered in manuscript form and were thus vulnerable to being destroyed by the papists. "And woulde God the like diligence had been used of our auncient forelders, in the tyme of Wickliffe, Purvey, Brute, Thorpe, Husse, Hierome and such other, in searching and collecting their workes and writings.

No doubt but many thinges had remained in lyght, which now be left in oblivion. *But by reason the Arte of Printing was not yet invented, their worthy bookes were the sooner abolyshed.*"[42]

Foxe and Day often praised each other and seem to have collaborated amicably, despite arguing over the constant inclusion of new material that led to swollen volumes and increased costs.[43] One letter, cited in Oastler, however, casts a different light on their relationship. When William Turner, dean of Wells, wrote to Foxe complaining about the bloated size and expense of the successive editions of the *Actes and Monuments*, he implied that Day was a harsh taskmaster. "Printers generally prefer their books to be big for the sake of the big profit that they can make from them, rather than small and easily available to the small and wretched flock of Christ. I wish that your means were ample enough to save you from having to work for miserable, greedy, vainglorious and ignorant booksellers; for I hear that you are harshly treated, to use no stronger word, by your employer."[44]

As noted previously when discussing Faust/Fust, this is not the only instance where the printer is given a split persona—simultaneously praised for serving God and denounced for serving Mammon. Foxe's tributes to Day and his "excellente art" are not easily reconciled with the "miserable, greedy, ignorant" practitioner depicted by Turner. Nor does the comment about printers' preferring "books to be big" make much sense, since large books usually entailed losses and small ones, profits. Day's preface to *Gorboduc*, denigrating an earlier edition, showed that the printer could be vicious and abusive at times.[45] Nevertheless, Day's admiring biographer seems to have a sound basis for rejecting Turner's characterization as an "unwarranted slur."[46]

The four large and lavishly illustrated versions of Foxe (1563, 1570, 1578, 1583) that were issued by Day before his death in 1584 did indeed make a profit for the printer.[47] But they also cost him dearly. Day had to borrow hundreds of pounds and risked bankruptcy to pay the costs entailed. This book was the first work in England that rivaled the best continental work in size and quality.[48] Large sums of capital were risked on the monumental enterprise, one that had never previously been attempted by Day's colleagues. The 1570 edition with its 2,300 large folio pages and its 2.5 million words represented the largest project ever undertaken by an English printer in the age of the handpress. Moreover, even in its monumental form, the work reached too large an audience—too large a reading (and hearing) public—to be described as being unavailable to "a small flock."[49] In London, it was ordered to be read in city orphanages and the halls of city companies; it was to be provided by deans throughout England in their cathedrals and in their homes; and, it was to be found in many parish churches and in the colleges of Oxford and Cambridge.[50] Excerpts were incorporated in Holinshed's *Chronicles*; Francis Drake took a copy with him on his voyages.[51] A cheaper, abridged quarto edition was issued shortly after Day died. More abridgements followed along with further reduction in size. As David Kastan suggests, the work went from "monument to miniature."[52] Numerous later publications: "abridgements, annals, chronicles, histories, sermons etc" continued to convey Foxe's views on printing to later generations.[53]

Here as elsewhere, censorship contributed to extra publicity. When a new edition in 1637 was refused a license by Archbishop William Laud, Milton made sure that his readers learned of it.[54] Nor should we stop short with printed materials bearing Foxe's name. Jacobean drama "popularized and reappropriated the Book of Martyrs" by presenting scenes drawn from Foxe's work on the stage.[55] On national holidays, parades and pageants, bonfires and bells repeatedly reminded the populace of England's providential escapes from papal power.[56]

The title page of the 1570 edition of *Actes and Monuments of these Latter and Perilous Days* neatly illustrated the book's dichotomized scheme. On one side are the Protestants, who listen to their preacher while holding their books or turn to acknowledge the radiant aura of the Word (that is, the word for God in Hebrew letters—the so-called Tetragrammaton.) On the other side are the Catholics, who are holding beads instead of books. They follow their priests instead of the Word.[57] (As one French historian, who was friendly to the Reformation, put it: in post-Reformation Catholic Europe, "the priest reads for all.")[58] The woodblock also assigned a prominent role to the Day of Judgment. It employed the same iconographic scheme, dividing the saved from the damned, as was used by medieval sculptors on the portals of cathedrals. The fate of Protestants who are burned on earth but triumph in heaven is contrasted with the fate of Catholics who celebrate their sacrament of the Mass on earth but then get burned by an everlasting fire in the next world.

Just where Foxe placed the final act of these "latter and perilous days" is uncertain.[59] In the first English edition of 1563, the death of Mary Tudor and enthronement of Elizabeth found him in an optimistic mood that inclined him to postponing the Day of Judgment. In 1570, with the setbacks to the Puritan cause and the threat posed by Mary, Queen of Scots, a more pessimistic view prevailed.[60] In a still later edition, Judgment Day again receded.[61]

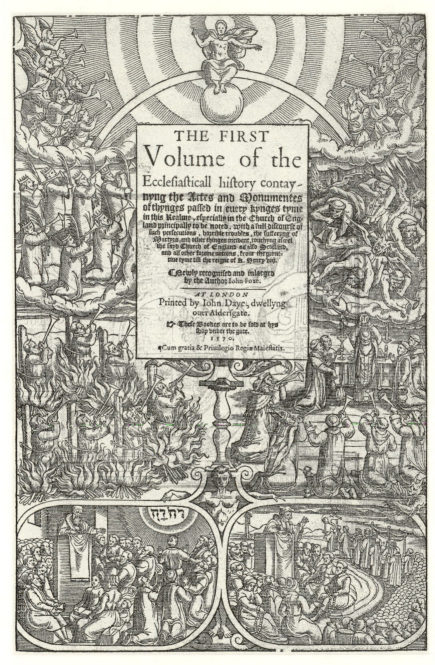

Figure 2.1. John Foxe, *Actes and Monuments* (1570), title page. Courtesy of the Folger Shakespeare Library.

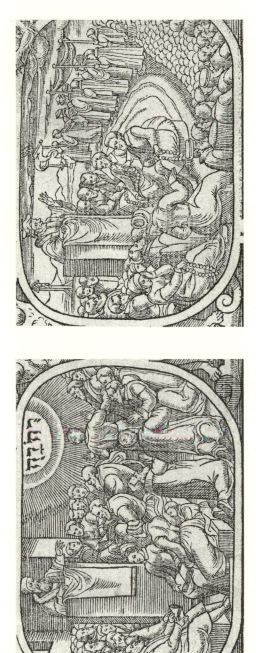

Figure 2.2. Detail from Foxe title page. Courtesy of the Folger Shakespeare Library.

In any event, the Book of Martyrs was destined to have a much longer life than its author may have granted to humankind.

Successive editions incorporated newsworthy events, such as the Massacres of St. Bartholomew's Eve (1572), the defeat of the Armada (1588), and the Gunpowder Plot (1605).[62] In the course of the seventeenth century, as noted below, Foxe's readers would celebrate printing not only as an antipapal weapon but also as a means of subverting bishops and even kings. His book served as a source of inspiration to religious dissidents from William Prynne to George Fox.[63] It was carried overseas by Puritans and pilgrims along with their translations of the Bible.

Foxe's celebration of printing has been singled out because of its extraordinary long-wave resonance among English-speaking peoples and its bearing on the connection between printing and Protestantism. This connection has been questioned in recent years by revisionists, who seek to remedy neglect of the "astonishingly rich culture of print" engendered by English Catholicism.[64] They object to the "lingering opinion that popery and printing press should be placed in stark opposition."[65] They point to Lutheran qualms about popular literacy and unguided scriptural reading. They conclude that, despite initial hesitancy, "in the long run the Counter Reformation proved no less willing to take advantage of print than its Lutheran and Calvinist counterparts."[66] Even while granting that their work has helped to rectify unbalanced treatments and has greatly enriched our understanding of post-Reformation English Catholicism, some of the revisionists' claims seem to me to be too strong.[67]

"Though Protestants liked to think that they had a special relationship with the printing-press," Alison Shell argues, we ought not to take their word for it. The large printed literature produced by the English counter-Reformation has been unfairly marginalized, Shell says. This large literature "prove[s] unanswerably that English Protestant printing initiatives stimulated a formidable degree of Catholic retaliation."[68] Since much of this literature was not only published overseas but also written in languages other than English, its neglect in histories (and bibliographies) of English literature seems unsurprising. But such questions are really beside the point. The point is that Protestants *did* think they had "a special relationship with the printing press." In a study devoted to early modern attitudes, there is no good reason not to take them at their word.

The disparate churches and sects that are grouped under the label Protestant disagreed on innumerable issues.[69] But like Foxe, all followed Luther in celebrating an invention that had purportedly freed parts of Western Christendom from the dominance of Rome, thereby ending a long dark interval of papal misrule. As studies of both Lutheran and Calvinist propaganda suggest, Protestant triumphalism placed the defenders of the Roman church in an awkward position. The very means they employed to rebut their opponents—vernacular pamphlets attacking Protestant views—undercut their position that it was wrong to air disputes over religion before a lay public. Pamphlet warfare in which texts responded to texts by means of excerpting and commenting had a dialogic character.[70] Readers who were caught up in the intertextual exchange had the sense of participating in an ongoing public debate—quite a different sense from that obtained from listening to a sermon, going to confession, or reciting a catechism.[71] In the course of refuting Protestant views, Catholic apologists had to describe the positions they opposed, thereby propagating the very ideas they wanted to expunge.[72]

The Roman church that had initially welcomed the divine art became much more ambivalent about the invention after the Protestant revolt. It tended to take a reactive rather than a proactive approach to the uses of print. Lay obedience was emphasized over lay learning. Latin liturgies were retained so that priestly mysteries remained veiled from the faithful. Debates at the Council of Trent ended with a victory for the *zelanti* who rejected the "inky divinitie" of the Bible reader. Both Protestant and Catholic clergymen distrusted the capacity of ordinary laymen to interpret scripture. But Catholics also were more prone to question the authenticity of scripture. They set the oral transmission of the living word of God by new orders of preachers and teachers against the "dumb judge," the "leaden rule" and the "dead letter" of the printed text.[73] Highlighting the role that oral modes had played in the dissemination of early Christianity, they "repeatedly pointed out that for 2,600 years from Adam to Moses there were no holy books, that it was at least twenty years before the Gospels were penned by the apostles, and that Christ himself had left nothing in writing."[74]

Decisions taken at the Council of Trent thus had the unanticipated effect of dividing the spoken word from the printed page. "Whereas many medieval theologians had thought in terms of the mutual coinherence of the written text and unwritten tradition, the polemical battles provoked by the Reformation . . . intensified a tendency to see them as separate receptacles of truth."[75]

Religious polarization thus split apart two modes of communication, oral and written, that had been, for the most part, previously joined. To be sure, speech had been contrasted with writing to the detriment of the latter in ancient Greece (notably in Plato's dialogue, *Phaedrus*, about the impairment of memory).[76] But during the medieval millennium speaking and writing had formed a continuum. Reading aloud was the common practice. The habit of dictating texts to scribes linked the spoken to the written word. Both were also linked when cloistered monks, who were under a rule of silence, were urged to "preach with their hands." In keeping with medieval views, printing was initially welcomed for extending the reach of *both* voice and pen. Preachers who were famous for their pulpit eloquence, such as Geiler von Keysersberg or Savonarola, were far from hesitant about transposing their sermons into print. To Christian scholars such as Erasmus, the eloquent orator appealing to the ear and the eloquent author appealing to the eye belonged within the same continuum.[77] "I feel that I have not been entirely deprived of a sermon," wrote Erasmus, "if I have heard Chrysostom or Jerome speak to me in writing."[78] Similarly, for Luther and his early followers, the high value assigned to the pulpit did not detract from the high value assigned to the press. To set one against the other went against the spirit of the Protestant Reformation.[79]

But reactions to decisions taken at the Council of Trent did set one against the other. Catholic emphasis on the contrast between "living voice" and "killing letter"[80] was countered by Protestant emphasis on the unreliability of oral traditions and insistence on the trustworthiness of the written word of God as embodied in Scripture. It is true that preaching was always regarded by Protestants as "the supreme engine of theological conversion."[81] Moreover, all parties were opposed to unsupervised lay reading.[82] Nevertheless, Reformation debates were increasingly marked by "a binary opposition between 'oral' and 'written.'" "From the beginning and for centuries thereafter, Protestant apologists would identify an essential difference between their Church and that of Rome around this issue."[83]

The binary opposition between oral tradition and written text had a counterpart in the opposition between ceremonial object and written word. According to Eamon Duffy,

> Behind the repudiation of the ceremonial by reformers lay a "radically different conceptual world, a world in which text was everything, sign nothing. The sacramental universe of late medieval Catholicism was, from such a perspective, totally opaque, a bewildering and meaningless world of dumb objects and vapid gestures, hindering communication."[84]

The two "conceptual" worlds thus hinged on two different means of communication, both designed to supplement the spoken word: by means of the written word on the one hand, and by means of image and gesture on the other.

Even while Protestants celebrated the capacity of print to replace "dumb show," Catholics were dismayed by the way Christian teachings were being "devocalized" and "desocialized" by typography.[85] "The words on a page are like a dead body stretched out on the ground" wrote the seventeenth-century French Oratorian priest, Bernard Lamy; "In the mouth of the one who advances them they are effective, on paper they are lifeless."[86] John Sergeaunt in late Stuart England pointed to the dangers of trusting matters of salvation to the care of "copiers and printers and translators and grammarians." Sacred writings tended to be reduced to "ink variously figured in a book, unsensed characters, waxen natured words . . . fit to be played upon . . . by quirks of wit."[87] Distrust of all written documents pertaining to Scripture was expressed by the Jesuit priest Jean Hardouin.[88] He saw forgers at work everywhere, and he was convinced that the records of early Church council decisions were also untrustworthy. For Hardouin, "there was no *history* of the church, but only *tradition*, only the oral tradition, kept alive from age to age, without the use of written records, by the perpetual presence of the Holy Spirit."[89]

The divorce of living word from dead letter by the leading councilors at Trent was reinforced by their opposition to Bible translation. Scriptural passages transposed into contemporary vernaculars were bound to seem livelier and less "leaden" than texts presented in the Latin of St. Jerome's day. The Sorbonne, which had presided over the installation of the first Paris press, took the lead in 1526 of enacting a total ban against the printing of vernacular Bibles in France.[90] To be sure, some vernacular translations were eventually printed under Catholic auspices, but only for the purpose of countering Protestant versions. Alexandra Walsham describes the "profound ambivalence" about biblical translation which characterized English Catholic attitudes both prior to and after 1582 when the Rheims-Douai Bible was published as an exceptional emergency measure.[91] She notes the sense of unease that accompanied its publication.

A cautious approach to exploiting the uses of print did not, of course, mean that that the Counter-Reformation church relied only on the spoken word to reach the laity. Ceremonies that offered the smell of incense, the sound of choral music, and surroundings embellished by newly commissioned Baroque artists were more likely to appeal to all the senses than was the resort to silent, colorless, odorless printed texts. Foxe's woodcuts were exceptional for a Protestant martyrology.[92] Moreover, by the second half of the sixteenth century, the post-Tridentine Church successfully mobilized printers for an aggressive counteroffensive.[93] The printing office that was set up in Rome in 1623 for the propagation of the faith was well armed with fonts in a vast variety of exotic languages.

The term "propaganda" is often traced to the creation of this new printing office that was set up to combat heresy and win new converts.[94] Yet, the Office of the Propaganda was a late reaction to earlier Protestant "propagations" that had first emanated from Wittenberg and other Lutheran towns as well as from Geneva and other Calvinist strongholds.[95]

The subversive implications of these "propagations" aroused alarm among statesmen as well as churchmen. In Tudor England, when Henry VIII was still a "defender of the faith," he warned against the "blasphemous and pestiferous English books printed in other regions and sent into this realm to pervert the people . . . to stir and incense them to sedition and disobedience . . . to the final subversion and desolation of this noble realm."[96] Harold Weber cites a number of such proclamations in order to indicate "just how frightening the state found print technology that stubbornly evaded its repeated efforts at control. The printed word becomes . . . a power unhealthy, infectious, subtly and mysteriously contagious. . . . A plague has invaded the body of the kingdom fragmenting a unity . . . that prohibitions and licensing procedures . . . attempt to recapture . . . these proclamations disclose . . . a dark and secret realm of books that mysteriously propagate themselves."[97]

Fear of contamination was especially strong when a Catholic queen ascended the throne. At the accession of Mary Tudor in 1553 a proclamation was issued against "lewd treatises in the English tongue . . . touching the high points of Christian religion" and against books that printers and stationers "set out to sale" because of "an evil zeal for lucre and covetousness of vile gain."[98] Recent studies have questioned the "Whiggish" description of Marian policy as sterile and reactionary. They point to measures that were taken to revivify Catholic spirituality during the short reign of the Catholic Queen.[99] Nevertheless, in England under Mary Tudor (as in Transylvania under the Catholic Polish king Istvan Bathori) royal policy toward printing became more negative.[100] At Mary Tudor's funeral, alarms were raised again about the contagion being spread from abroad. "The wolves be coming out of Geneva and other places of Germany . . . and have sent their books before, full of pestilent doctrines, blasphemy and heresy to infect the people."[101]

Of course, there was nothing peculiarly Catholic about fear of subversion or intolerance of dissent or concern about unregulated printing. Protestant authorities objected to heterodox publications and supported strong censorship measures, just as Catholic authorities did. When he cast volumes of canon law onto the flames in 1520, Martin Luther showed no hesitation about burning books that he deemed evil. The works of Rabelais and other libertines were banned in Calvinist Geneva. It was there, moreover, that Servetus was burned alive.

In all realms, heresy was regarded as "disease" or as a poison that posed dangers for the body politic.[102] Insofar as printing multiplied such dangers, all agreed there was need for new controls or antidotes. But where Catholic policies tended to stop short with these negative considerations, among Protestants printing was also assigned the positive functions of spreading the gospel and breaking free of papal rule. Polemicists consistently accused the Roman Catholic church of fighting tooth and nail to preserve a clerical monopoly on the Word. "Closely guarded in cloisters and ecclesiastical libraries, the Bible had been corrupted by the monastic scribes who were its 'ordinary jaylers.' But God had preserved his Holy Word . . . and eventually brought His people out of 'Aegypticall darkness' by means of the providential invention . . . of printing."[103] Realms that were liberated from Rome, moreover, were no longer subject to controls from a single center. The diversity of plural jurisdictions, together with rivalry between the rulers of small states, favored the expansion of the printing trades. A single list of prohibited books, periodically issued from Rome, limited the output of reading matter in Catholic lands even while opening markets for Protestant printers, who could take full advantage of the publicity that the Roman *Index of Prohibited Books* inadvertently gave to forbidden fruit.[104]

Although divisions between Catholic and Protestant over issues posed by printing were deep and abiding, they were by no means the only divisions that characterized the complex religious geography of early modern Europe. Ecclesiastical institutions within diverse dynastic states were subject to contradictory pressures. Lutheran authorities were less likely to promote lay Bible reading than were the Calvinists.[105] Catholic rulers were often at odds with Rome, and not all influential Catholic subjects were of one mind. Antipapal diatribes, often inspired by Paolo Sarpi's "histories" of the Inquisition and of the Council of Trent, were produced by adherents of the Gallican cause in

Catholic France as well as by Anglicans and Puritans in Tudor-Stuart England.[106] A Catholic League, not a Protestant one, sponsored printed campaigns justifying tyrannicide and popular sovereignty in Paris during the Wars of Religion.[107] Later on, also in France, Jansenist-Jesuit rivalries saw the Jansenists adopting positions that resembled Protestant ones, especially with regard to the printing of vernacular Bibles. In England, after the Elizabethan settlement, when Catholics became a persecuted and dissident minority, the recusants behaved much as did other nonconforming groups. During Elizabeth's reign, English Jesuits (like later French Jansenists) set up an underground press.[108]

But the use of the press by Catholic minorities (and Catholic rulers) needs to be distinguished from the celebration of printing as a providential event. This was a peculiarly Protestant phenomenon and was, with a few exceptions,[109] especially marked among the so-called radical Protestant sects. After the Elizabethan Settlement, pamphleteering campaigns mounted by "low-Church" Puritans placed the Anglican establishment in much the same defensive and reactive position as that assumed elsewhere by Catholic authorities. The pamphlet warfare unleashed by the Martin Marprelate tracts (1588–89)[110] offers a case in point:

> Martin Marprelate had seized a rhetorical terrain that could not be wrested from him, since descriptions of his tactics inevitably reproduced them. . . . The authorities who had orchestrated the anti-Martinist attack looked with horror on the turmoil they had created. Rather than quelling public desire for Marprelate writings [they] had spurred the popularity of the offending . . . tracts and had produced an appetite for all things Martin; rather than eliminating him from the cultural landscape, they had made [him] ubiquitous . . . making . . . issues of "Divinytie and State" a point of discussion.[111]

Such emphasis on the Marprelate pamphleteering, a recent critic has argued, overlooks previous English Catholic propaganda. Topical print controversy had been introduced before Marprelate by earlier Catholic tracts printed in Antwerp and elsewhere on the Continent expressing outrage over the execution of the Jesuit, Edmund Campion.[112] But the resonance of Marprelate among his countrymen was much more powerful and long-lasting.[113] According to Jason Scott-Warren, Marprelate's influence on Thomas Nashe was profound: "Nashe cut his teeth on the Martin Marprelate exchange." It taught him "about the power of print simultaneously to reveal and to conceal" the presence of an author. Nashe himself became a "present-yet-absent writer, familiar to a vast audience from which he is divorced by the intervening marketplace of print."[114]

Anglicans were especially perturbed by the way the Marprelate controversy had "made Divinity and State topics of public discussion." This development provoked anxiety among the authorities in Stuart England to the point of nostalgia for the days before printing. In a sermon of 1624, Joseph Hall, later bishop of Exeter, paid a tribute to Gutenberg: mankind was "highly beholden to that witty citizen of Mainz for his invention of this nimble Art of Impression." But he then complained that "nothing hath so much powere [as printing] to poison the world." In a serious vein he anticipated Andrew Marvell's satire by evoking the "times of our forefathers when every page and line was to pass . . . the pains of a single pen" when "books were scarce and if offensive could not light onto many hands to work a speedy mischief."[115] Seventeen years later, he would express outrage at the "furious and malignant spirits" everywhere that "burst forth into slanderous libels."[116]

The more Anglican bishops balked at airing issues associated with church policy, the more the reformers appealed for debate and sought to be answered in print.[117] "This is a Martinish and Counter-Martinish age," wrote Gabriel Harvey, "where the Spirit of Contradiction reigneth." In "title page after title page" of books by Puritan divines one finds the same citation from Luke 19:40: "I tell you that if these should holde their peace, the stones would crye."[118] Under Charles I, the opponents of Archbishop Laud were once again able to seize the initiative. When John Milton turned from poetry to polemic, he made much of Laud's purported refusal, in 1637, to license Foxe's *Book of Martyrs* for republication. The *Actes and Monuments* had become "so hateful to the Prelates," wrote Milton in his *Animadversions* (1641) that it had "almost come to be a prohibited book . . . two or three editions hath crept into the world by stealth not without the open regret and vexation of the Bishops."[119]

It seems doubtful that editions of Foxe ever "crept into the world by stealth" and likely that later historians have exaggerated the importance of Laud's refusal. Milton was not unaware of the publicity value of censorship. In *Areopagitica* (1644), he cited Francis Bacon's opinion: "The punishing of wits enchaunces their autority . . . and a forbidd'n writing is thought to be a certain spark of truth that flies up in the faces of them who seeke to tread it out."[120]

Nevertheless, it is clear that Laud was not enthusiastic about turning to print. For some time, he refused to open the presses even to his own adherents:

> Archbishop Laud had tried to prevent the use of the press in contro-
> versy even by his own adherents. Now he gave way and consented
> to try whether a pamphlet could succeed where surplice and prayer
> book, Star Chamber and High Commission had failed. . . . [He]
> put upon the Bishop of Norwich the task of preparing . . . a general
> defense of prelacy. It was submitted to him page by page for correc-
> tion and approval and issued from the press early in 1640 with the
> title "Episcopacy by Divine Right Asserted." It elicited a salvo of
> replies from the Puritan side and achieved a kind of immortality by
> deflecting Milton from his poem.[121]

Foxe's bellicose view of printing as a weapon aimed against papal despotism had gone together with celebrating the English monarchy as the head of
a church that was liberated from Rome. In the seventeenth century the same
bellicose approach was reworked into an attack not only on English bishops
but also on English kings. When John Bastwick, a Leveller, declared from
the pillory: "were the press opened to us, we would scatter [the Antichrist's]
kingdom," he was referring not to the kingdom of the pope but to that of
Charles I.[122]

Pamphlet Warfare: "The Media Explosion" of the 1640s

The fear that printing had given rise not only to the spread of heresy but also
to political sedition was intensified by the sectarian enthusiasm that exploded
during the seventeenth-century Civil War. "Martin Marprelate was a bonny
lad / His brave adventures made the Prelates mad / Though he be dead yet
he hath left behind / A generation of the Martin kind."[123] Thus the future
Leveller, printer, and publicist, Richard Overton, evoked the pamphlet wars
of the Elizabethan era.[124] He appropriated the voice and persona of Martin
(and his mischievous feminine alter ego Margery) in a "self-conscious act of
reclaiming and remaking the Puritan past."[125] During the seventeenth-cen-

tury Interregnum, the ghostly presence of the sixteenth-century pamphleteer was so ubiquitous that, as Joad Raymond observes, although fairies were frightened by printing, it "gave a new vitality to ghosts."[126] John Lilburne sought to reenact the role of one of Foxe's martyrs even while exhibiting a rare talent for exploiting printed publicity. After having been whipped and while standing with his head in the stocks, the irrepressible publicist managed to pull three pamphlets from his pocket and throw them at the crowd.[127] When exiled in Amsterdam in 1651, Lilburne followed the pattern established by the Marian exiles and issued a stream of subversive publications. Oliver Cromwell could banish Lilburne but could not keep his pamphlets out.[128]

The explosion of printed materials that resulted from the breakdown of press controls during the English Civil War (and that led to the large pamphlet collection of the bookseller George Thomason) has often been noted.[129] The Thomason collection was a "testament to posterity of a world dramatically invaded by and reordered in print."[130] "There had been polemical pamphlets before . . . but there had been nothing to match the development of 1641–42 when writers and publishers seized the opportunities created by the collapse of censorship and by the public excitement surrounding the breakdown of the monarchy."[131]

This outbreak of "unrestrained discursivity" (in Kristen Poole's phrase) gave rise to an alarmist literature reminiscent of the reigns of Henry VIII and Mary Tudor.[132] Thomas Browne wrote: "I have lived to behold the highest perversion of that excellent invention; the name of his Majesty defamed, the honour of Parliament depraved."[133] Once again the press was demonized; it was "Amsterdamnified," in the words of a royalist who complained "religion is now . . . common discourse . . . in every tavern and alehouse, where a man shall hardly find five together in one mind, and yet everyone presumes he is in the right."[134]

Not only servants of the crown but also Parliamentarians and Presbyterians and even, on occasion, Independents expressed concern about the seemingly uncontrolled output of printed materials. Binary metaphors of light/darkness and knowledge/ignorance were replaced by others less complimentary to Gutenberg's invention: filth/cleansing; contagion/quarantine; poison/antidote. "Amongst those innumerable *Locusts* that . . . were spewd from the Bottomless Pit, there crawl'd and swarm'd over the Kingdome, a Crew of Rascalls called *Martinists*; whose laxative Purity did . . . besquitter all *England* over . . . those *Martins* like Caterpillars encreased most pestiferously."[135] However mixed the metaphors, whether a plague of locusts or the onset of diarrhea, a sense of disgust was palpable. The pamphlets "spawned" by a "teeming" press were "unhealthy, infectious, unclean." "The Citie and Countrey is pestered, and the ayre thereof infected and poysoned with the sulphurous breathings of . . . vanitie, prophaneness and lyes."[136]

Fifteenth-century churchmen had welcomed printing for the promise it held of providing uniform liturgies.[137] In Tudor England, the reciting of the same prayers by all English-speaking people testified to the unifying powers of print.[138] "Heretofore there hath been a great diversitie in saying and singing in the Churches . . . henceforth all the whole realme shalle have but one use."[139] But the sects that proliferated during the Interregnum did not adhere to the liturgy contained in the Book of Common Prayer.[140] The "incksquittering treacherous pamphlets" issued by the sectarians showed that printing was also compatible with splintering and cacophony.

Outrage at the lies that were poisoning the air was expressed by radicals as well as conservatives. The former found it "insufferable and unjust" that a monopoly of printing during the Long Parliament was granted to the Stationers' Company, who were enabled to print "whatsoever . . . Pamphlets and Libells they please, though they be full of *Lyes* and tend to the poysoning of the Kingdom with. . . . Tyrannical principles."[141]

Attacks on the Catholic Church had employed the metaphor of a swarming beehive to indicate contempt for all those drones who mindlessly served the papal queen bee. The mid-seventeenth century saw something even worse: a swarm that escaped from containment—a ubiquitous swarm, teeming not just with bees but also with frogs, locusts, and all manner of loathsome creatures.[142] Not only did the pamphlets swarm, they also "spawned" with the irrepressible fecundity of snakes or maggots. The title of Thomas Edwards's *Gangraena*, a massive, seemingly unreadable yet widely read three-part work, spoke for itself. This 800-page, three-part *Catalogue and Discovery of many of the Errours, Heresies, Blasphemies and Pernicious Practices of the Sectaries of this time* (1646)[143] listed no less than 176 different "heretical" views that had been articulated in print.[144] It provoked numerous angry replies, leading the author (somewhat incongruously) to assume the mantle of a successor to John Foxe: "as the Jesuits and Papists did by Mr Foxe's Book of Martyrs, give out it was a Book of lyes. . . . Just so do the Sectaries now by my Book."[145]

Pamphlet warfare during the Interregnum led to exaggerated estimates of the power of the press. This is especially clear in Richard Atkyns's *Original and Growth of Printing*, which was published after the Stuart Restoration. It had started out as a broadsheet and was expanded into a thirty-two-page pamphlet by 1664. Printing, wrote Atkyns, "is of so Divine a Nature, that it makes a Thousand years but as yesterday, by Presenting to our View things done so long before; and so Spirituall withall, that it flyes into all parts of the World without Weariness . . . [it is] so great a Friend to the Schollar, that he may make himself Master of any Art or Science that hath been treated of for 2000 years before, in lesse than two years time." This extravagant tribute was accompanied by an anti-Catholic reference to the "sort of People . . . that account Ignorance the Mother of Devotion and . . . would not have even the Scriptures printed in the Mother Tongue."[146]

But Atkyns did not stop short with the usefulness of printing to scholars or with papal resistance to vernacular Bibles. The pamphleteer's main concern was to restore royal control over a medium that had been allowed to infect the populace, with dangerous consequences for all.[147] For this he blamed not the sectaries but the profit-seeking Stationers who had been allowed to take too many liberties. They had "filled the Kingdom with so many Books, and the Brains of the People with so many contrary Opinions, that these Paper-pellets became as dangerous as Bullets."[148] Until the Civil War, Atkyns wrote, fining, imprisoning, seizing books, and breaking presses had kept things under control. But when Parliament took control and liberty of the press was proclaimed, every malcontent was able to vent his passion, and the common people, who "believed even a Ballad, because it was in Print,[149] greedily suckt in these Scandals, especially being Authorized by a God of their own making."[150] Atkyns concluded that "Printing is like a good Dish of Meat, which moderately eaten of, turns to the Nourishment and health of the Body; but immoderately, to Surfeits and Sicknesses: As the Use is very necessary, the Abuse is very dangerous."[151]

Measures passed by Parliament after the coronation of Charles II showed how the authorities agreed with Atkyns in holding the media responsible for the horrors of the Civil War: "The growth and increase of the late troubles and disorders did in great measure proceed from a multitude of seditions, sermons, pamphlets and speeches, daily preached, printed and published."[152] Pamphlets, in the words of the poet George Wither (1588–1667), had "added fuel to the direful flame / Of civil discord and domestic blows / By the incentives of malicious prose." To control the "incentives of malicious prose" new regulations, including a new Licensing Act, were passed.[153]

When justifying the suppression of all news-sheets except for a government organ, Roger L'Estrange, "licenser of the Press," famously declared: "a public Mercury should never have my vote because I think it makes the multitude too familiar with the actions and counsels of their superiors, too pragmatical and censorious and gives them not only an itch, but a kind of colourable right and license, to be meddling with the Government."[154] It is in this context, after the restoration of Charles II, when memories of the pamphlet explosion were still fresh, that we ought to place the much cited comment made in 1671 by William Berkeley, who thanked God that there was no printing in Virginia.[155]

Similar alarms about the contagious character of printed materials were expressed by French authorities, who were also confronted by explosions of pamphleteering during the seventeenth century. Some five thousand "Mazarinades" were turned out between 1648 and 1652—within the same decade as the explosion in England. Although French pamphleteers were quick to distance themselves from English regicides and Puritan propaganda, the reception of their output was much the same.[156] Jeffrey Sawyer's study of French alarmist literature entitled *Printed Poison* and Luc Racaut's *Hatred in Print* contain much that resembles Harold Weber's *Paper Bullets*. George Wither's poetic reference to the "incentives of malicious prose" had a counterpart in the warning given by one of Marie de Medici's councillors against the "sweet and agreeable poison that slips easily into our minds."[157]

Their historic antipapist posture, however, made it more awkward for Protestants than for Catholics to advocate stringent press control. "Restraint of the Press," wrote Matthew Tindal after the Revolution of 1688, "is consistent enough with Popery, but for Protestants to attempt it, is to strike at the Foundation of their Religion."[158] "Without a doubt," ran an argument set forth in the House of Commons against renewing the Licensing Act, if the late King James had continued on the throne . . . books against Popery would have . . . been deemed offensive."[159]

Earlier, under Charles II, Charles Blount expressed similar views in his treatise aimed at Restoration licensing laws: they undercut "the great argument we make use of against the Mohametans and the Popish religion . . . that ignorance is the Mother of their Devotions." "How can we condemn the Papists," Blount asked, "for not daring to permit their common people to read the Bible when we inhibit the freedom of the press." Licensing was an "Old relique of Popery," an "Inquisition upon the Press which prohibits any Book from coming forth without an Imprimatur."[160] Here, as in many other places, Blount was echoing Milton's *Areopagitica*.

Although Milton's most celebrated treatise is often mentioned in connection with pleas for a free press, *Areopagitica* argued more vigorously against book banning in general than against new measures to control printing in particular. As often noted, it attacked not post-publication censorship but only pre-publication licensing.[161] It was aimed against a parliamentary ordinance that had been prompted by the Remonstrance of the Stationers' Company in April 1643.

This Remonstrance marked a departure from the antipapist position that had been adopted by Foxe and his successors. It made clear the vested interest of the Stationers in protecting their monopoly: "we must . . . give Papists their due; for . . . where the Inquisition predominates, . . . regulation is more strict by far, then it is amongst Protestants . . . for that cause not onely their Church is the more fortified, but the Art of Printing thrives, and the Artists grow rich also beyond any examples among us."[162] The claim that printing flourished better under Catholic rulers than Protestant ones seems to run counter to the conventional wisdom that prevailed during the Interregnum, when few English writers were inclined to give the papists and the Inquisition their due.

After the Stationers had opposed his pamphlet on divorce, Milton had expressed his contempt for their position. In his *Animadversions* (1641) he had denounced "your Monkish prohibitions and expurgatorious indexes, your gags and snaffles, your proud *Imprimaturs*."[163] In *Areopagitica*, however, he took a more circuitous route. Although he made a fuss over Laud's purported banning of Foxe's *Book of Martyrs*, Milton was much more ambivalent about print than Foxe had been. Unlike Foxe, for whom the advent of printing signified an epochal event, Milton resisted paying tribute to the press, even while celebrating books and the scribal arts.[164]

As a treatise that owed much to the classical republican tradition, *Areopagitica* celebrated the constitution of ancient Athens. Its very title drew attention to the rhetoric of Isocrates and the institutions of the Greek polis.[165] But ancient Greek institutions were ill-suited to dealing with new issues posed by print. The repeated insistence on the absence of licensing laws among the ancients (with the exception of imperial Rome) and the reference to Plato's laws for his ideal republic were of doubtful relevance to regulating the printed book trade.

Where it did touch on historical change, *Areopagitica* focused on England's role in the prelude to the Reformation. In keeping with themes sounded earlier, Milton singled out "Wicklef" for initiating the Reformation. "Why else was this Nation chosen before any other that out of her . . .

should be proclaime'd and sounded forth the first tidings and trumpet of Reformation of all Europ?"[166] Had it not been for Wycliffe's repression by "pervers prelates," Milton wrote, "the glory of reforming all our neighbors had bin compleatly ours."[167] But, unlike Foxe, Milton sidestepped the invention that purportedly enabled Luther and Calvin to prevail where Wycliffe and the others had failed. Following Paolo Sarpi, "the great unmasker of the Trentine Councel,"[168] he equated licensing with a repressive policy that had commenced, long before Gutenberg, with medieval popes and that culminated in the Counter-Reformation. "The project of licensing crept out of the Inquisition, was catcht up by our Prelates, and hath caught some of our Presbyters."[169] This

> project did not come from any ancient State, or politie, or Church, nor by any Statute left us by our Ancestors elder or later; nor from the moderne custom of any reformed Citty, or Church abroad; but from the most Antichristian Councel, and the most tyrannous Inquisition that ever inquir'd. Till then Books were ever as freely admitted into the World as any other birth; the issue of the brain was no more stifl'd then [sic] the issue of the womb . . . that a Book . . . should be to stand before a Jury ere it be borne to the World . . . was never heard before, till that mysterious Iniquity provokt and troubl'd at the first entrance of Reformation, sought out new limbos and new hells wherein they might include our Books also within the number of their damned.[170]

Elsewhere, it is true, there are topical references to printers and to the fears of contagion that printed products inspired.[171] There is also an intriguing reference to the prohibition of printing throughout the Ottoman Empire.[172] Milton's presentation of his pamphlet as a speech act—as if it was a parliamentary interjection—had political implications that pointed to the future: "Areopagitica thus imagined that pamphlets created a virtual parliament, broadening the franchise of representation to include non-MPs. . . . the arena of print is figured as a massive parliament-without-doors."[173] (This interpretation seems to foreshadow eighteenth-century views of a political arena that included members of a disenfranchised reading public and nineteenth-century conceptions of the newspaper press as a "grand national agora.")[174]

Nevertheless, the failure to distinguish between problems posed for the authorities before and after the advent of printing gave rise to some remarkable non sequiturs: "If we think to regulate Printing," *Areopagitica*'s readers are told, then we must follow Plato's laws for his ideal Republic and ban all recreations and pastimes together with poetry and music (other than in a Doric mode).[175]

Blount borrowed several arguments from *Areopagitica*[176] and similarly cited classical precedents that were of doubtful relevance. But, unlike Milton, he referred explicitly to the fifteenth-century invention. "Having thus demonstrated how much the world owes to learning and books, let me not be altogether unmindful of Faust and Gutenberg, . . . who by their ingenuity discovered and made known to the World that Profound Art of Printing which made Learning not only easy but cheap." Alluding to Milton's mention in *Areopagitica* of "Galileo grown old as a prisoner for thinking in Astronomy otherwise than his Dominican licensers thought," Blount sounded a remarkably modern note by describing licensing as "an embargo on science." He also anticipated Enlightenment propaganda by stressing the way printing had ended a priestly monopoly on knowledge. "Popish villanies proceed not more from sacerdotal malice than from their Laicks ignorance and servitude, without which the Clergy are wolves without teeth." To divest priests of their powers of doing ill, nothing more was needed "than to propagate Wisdom and Knowledge amongst the Populace."[177]

It was left to Milton's friend and fellow poet Andrew Marvell to provide the most memorable satire on negative views of printing.[178] This satire was an all-out attack on Samuel Parker, an Anglican divine, who had led a pamphlet campaign against easing restrictions on the nonconformists.[179] Parker later replied to Marvell's satire by accusing his opponent of reviving the tactics of the notorious Martin Marprelate, leading Dryden (who was also a target of Marvell), in a reverse formulation, to call Martin "the Marvell of those times." In his attack on Parker, Marvell pretended to read his opponent's thoughts:

> The Press (that *villanous* Engine) invented much about the same
> time with the Reformation, . . . hath done more mischief to the
> Discipline of our Church than all the Doctrine can make amends
> for. Twas an happy time when all Learning was in Manuscript, and
> some little Officer, like our Author, did keep the Keys of the Library.
> When the Clergy needed no more knowledg then [sic] to read the
> Liturgy, and the Laity no more Clerkship than to save them from

Hanging. But now, since Printing came into the world, such is the mischief, that a Man cannot write a Book but presently he is answered. . . . There have been wayes found out to banish Ministers, to fine not only the People, but even the Grounds and Fields where they assembled in Conventicles: But no Art yet could prevent these seditious meetings of Letters. Two or three brawny fellows in a Corner, with meer Ink and Elbow-grease, do more harm than *an hundred Systematical Divines* with their *sweaty Preaching*. And, which is a strange thing, the very Spunges, which one would think should rather deface and blot out the whole Book, and were anciently used to that purpose, are become now the Instruments to make things legible. Their ugly Printing-Letters, that look but like so many rotten-Teeth, How oft have they been pull'd out by B. and L. the Publick Tooth-drawers! and yet these rascally Operators of the Press have got a trick to fasten them again in a few minutes, that they grow as firm a Set, and as biting and talkative as ever. *O Printing!* how hast thou disturbed the Peace of Mankind! that Lead, when moulded into Bullets, is not so mortal as when founded into Letters![180]

Marvell thus celebrated printing for putting an end to a priestly monopoly—sarcastically described as that "happy time when all learning was in manuscript," when "the keys of the Library" were kept by church officials,[181] and so few laymen could read that those who could were able to claim benefit of clergy. Writing in reply to Parker's polemic, he not only made use of the "dialogic" effects of print but offered the self-reflexive comment: "a man cannot write a book but presently he is answered." He taunted church officials for being unable to prevent "seditious meetings of letters" while taking care to substitute provocative pseudonyms on his title page.[182] The fear that evangelism had gotten out of hand after pen was replaced by press was burlesqued by suggesting that "two or three brawny fellows in a corner" now could do "more harm" than hundreds of preachers. By likening official censors to barber-dentists who pull out rotten black teeth only to find them back in place as "biting and talkative" as ever, Marvell mocked alarms about infection together with zealous censors such as Roger L'Estrange (indicated by the initial "L"). The metaphor of letterforms as "teeth" led Marvell to allude to Ovid's Cadmus legend, an allusion that also appeared in *Areopagitica*. Whereas Milton, as elsewhere, sidestepped printing processes and took *books* to be as "lively, and . . . productive" as the legendary teeth that "spring up [as] armed men," Marvell, more suitably, takes the serpent's teeth to be "nothing else but the *letters* which he [Cadmus] invented."[183] The idea that inked pads were no longer employed to blot out and obliterate writing but were instead rubbed over pieces of metal to produce legible texts offered a powerful metaphor for the revolution wrought by print.

Finally, when Marvell coupled the two inventions that made use of lead—to mold bullets and pieces of type[184]—he unwittingly produced a phrase that struck a sympathetic nerve more than three centuries later among writers who had lost sight of his satirical intent ("O printing! how has thou disturbed the peace"). His meaning would be repeatedly misconstrued: "The invention of the printing press was no less traumatic and morally ambiguous than the invention of gunpowder; the pen was mightier than the sword, but the press outdid both."[185] Given its actual context, it would seem that Marvell did not associate either ambiguity or trauma with the invention. Rather, he was taking his opponent to task for equating a divine art conducive to the peaceful advancement of learning with a diabolical invention, a "villainous engine" that had increased the destructive capacity of war.

Chapter 3

After Erasmus: Propelling
the Knowledge Industry

And it cannot be but that each generation succeeding to the knowledge acquired by all those who preceded it, adding to it their own acquisitions and discoveries, and handing the mass down for successive and constant accumulation, must advance the knowledge and well-being of mankind: not infinitely, as some have said, but indefinitely, and to a term which no one can fix and foresee.

—Thomas Jefferson (1818)

Celebrating Technology/Advancement of Learning

The previous chapter has said little about the advancement of learning and much about disturbing the peace. What follows will attempt to redress the balance. For polarization is only part of our story. Erasmus had condemned Lutheran polemicists and had died within the Catholic Church. Many of his followers considered themselves to be members of a peace-loving cosmopolitan "Commonwealth of Learning." In their view, God was displeased by the monkish quarrels that had led to the Wars of Religion. This same view found favor among those who adopted a so-called "Erastian" approach. Princes, statesmen, and other officials who feared civil discord and valued domestic tranquility tended to agree with the position attributed to Henri IV, former Huguenot and founder of the Bourbon royal dynasty, who purportedly thought Paris worth a mass.

But the interests of dynastic rulers did not always coincide with those of scholars and literati. Whereas the former tended to favor censorship in order to preserve tranquility, the latter objected to having officials decide what they could read and/or blot out what they had written. Thus Clement Marot repudiated the intervention of censors who felt no qualms about "tampering and wrecking in the cabinet of the sacred Muses." He claimed the right to decide his reading matter for himself: "who denies that I may read everything. . . . The great Giver has given me the sense to select from books . . . and discard" from the same.[1]

Erasmus had resided in many regions and curried favor from numerous patrons, thereby avoiding dependence on any single one. Several of his followers, similarly, were without strong loyalty to the rulers of any one church or state. Whether nominally Catholic or Protestant (or, as in some cases, adhering to one confession and then another),[2] whether labeled Nicodemite, Libertine, Socinian, Latitudinarian, or neo-Stoic, these representatives of a "third force" were consistent in condemning zealots and extremists on both sides. "The tyranny of the ministers of Geneva leaves hardly any more liberty to the world than the Spanish Inquisition, though in the contrary fashion."[3] The "minimal creed" to which these savants adhered went together with "a fearless engagement with the wide world of knowledge."[4]

A similar ecumenical outlook was adopted by many of the master printers and publishers who served a learned Latin readership from numerous principalities and cities throughout Europe. Often acting under the protection of local rulers, they housed foreign editors and correctors and sought far-flung markets for their wares.[5] They sponsored commemorative histories of printing and echoed themes that had been sounded previously in early colophons, prefaces, and chronicles. Henri II Estienne's praise of printing in his commemorative brochure celebrating the Frankfurt Book Fair[6] was typical in this regard. Annals and chronicles continued to lavish praise on Gutenberg's invention.

Thus printing continued to be celebrated, as it had been before the Reformation, not for furthering the antipapist cause but for its contributions to letters and learning.

> The intelligence of men increases every day if only through the abundance of books being published . . . the study of letters amazingly flourishes in all parts of the world. In only one day one person prints and publishes what many could hardly write in one year . . . a large number of books of all sorts and disciplines have been spread throughout the world . . . many authors both Greek and Latin who

had been almost completely forgotten have been saved. It would not
be right to cheat the inventor of such an achievement of deserved
praise. Johann Gutenberg from Germany invented this art . . . in
the City of Mainz . . . and discovered with equal talent a new type
of ink. . . . There is no part of the world where Printing does not
flourish today.[7]

The citation comes from Polydore Vergil's *De Inventoribus Rerum*—a "foun-
dational work of reference" which ran through some hundred editions. After
its initial publication in 1499, it was repeatedly issued in Latin (Erasmus
urged Froben to publish one of the Latin editions). Vergil drew much of his
material from Pliny's *Natural History*, while departing from Pliny's antipro-
gressive verdict that "whatever is older is better." Vergil's work was translated
from the Latin into seven or more vernacular tongues, and was placed on the
Index.[8] The frontispiece that decorated several editions reflected a different
kind of polarization from that conveyed by antipapist reformers. Printing was
not presented as a metaphoric weapon in a war against the anti-Christ. On
the contrary, it was represented as a peaceful art and as such was contrasted
with real weapons that were newly designed to make use of gunpowder.[9]
According to Vergil, the invention of gunpowder was an "eternal disgrace."[10]
    Many other sixteenth-century writers represented printing as the antithe-
sis of gunpowder. In the 1530s, Rabelais set printing, as a divinely inspired
invention, against the diabolical invention of artillery.[11] The French poets
who comprised the Pléiade held similar views. Ronsard was especially emphatic in his condemnation of the new weaponry. He regarded gunpowder
as a "transgressive" invention that signified death and destruction and as the
"satanic double of . . . printing."[12]
    On the other hand there were those who, even while expressing repug-
nance at the unleashing of new destructive powers, also welcomed any new
devices that might prove helpful in the ongoing war against the Turks.[13]
Classical topoi that coupled "learning" with "arms," pen with sword,[14]
helped to legitimize the linkage of printing with gunpowder. Thomas Dekker
played with this topos, comparing "Pen" and "Inck" with "murdering engines of mankind, Guns and Powder. . . . The Pen is the Piece that shootes,
Inck is the powder that carries, and Wordes are the Bullets that kill. The one
doth onely destroy men in times of warre, the other consumes men, both in
warre and peace."[15] Both inventions were coupled as representing improve-

ments in the arts of war and of peace and were cited to counteract exaggerated reverence for the wisdom of the ancients.

Yet gunpowder and cannonry never served quite as well as did printing to symbolize human progress.[16] The opposite was true of the mariner's compass. As was the case with the new weaponry, the magnetic compass was an anonymous and complex innovation. It was also often coupled with printing and used as a shorthand way of referring to the well-publicized, definitely dated, and eponymous voyages of discovery. In this guise it was especially suitable for representing an irreversible movement from the old to new.

All three inventions were repeatedly mentioned as evidence that the moderns were superior to the ancients, at least in some respects. They were also cited to show that Christian Europeans were superior to the other peoples of the world. Many sixteenth-century commentators placed Gutenberg's invention in this particular context.[17] The following excerpts from the works of a few influential French savants are characteristic.

Guillaume Postel was an erudite visionary who had mastered Arabic as well as trilingual studies. Rather like Tommaso Campanella later on, Postel remained within the Catholic Church while expressing heterodox views as an enthusiastic millenarian. In his best-known work, *Concordia Mundi*, Postel presented printing as a means of fulfilling millennial prophecies entailing the spread of the Gospel and the conversion of all the peoples of the world. When coupled with the voyages of discovery, he believed, printing would ensure the worldwide triumph of Christianity. Postel was impressed by the intellectual progress made by European Christians in contrast to Muslims within the Ottoman Empire. In the West, he wrote, the study of Greek, Latin, Hebrew, and other languages had "made more progress in fifty years than in the previous thousand, while at the same time the Ishmaelites today no longer possess either letters or learning."[18] As did the Protestants, Postel regarded printing in a bellicose context. However, he aimed the new "weapon" not against the papacy, but against the infidel Turk. When writing to Christopher Plantin in connection with his Arabic translation of the Gospels, he described printing as "the lance and sword of Christ's victory."[19]

Jean Bodin in his *Method for the Easy Comprehension of History* (1565) criticized blind veneration of the ancients. "They who say that all things were understood by the ancients err not less than do those who deny them the early conquest of many arts." He pointed to the invention of the compass and the new "engines of war" and then asserted the "printing alone can easily vie with all the discoveries of all the ancients."[20] His praise of printing was

coupled with a denunciation of its misuse by radical pamphleteers. As was
true of later English authorities who reacted unfavorably to partisan pamphleteering during the Interregnum, Bodin was alarmed by the extreme views
expressed during the French religious wars. Anticipating Hobbes's reaction
to civil disorder, he wrote that the pamphleteers "open the door to a licentious anarchy . . . worse than the greatest tyranny in the world."[21] As was true
of most Catholics, Bodin rejected the Lutheran interpretation of scriptural
prophecies concerning the coming of the Last Judgment. Loyalty to the
French crown also led him to repudiate works that favored German exceptionalism and glorified the German empire.[22]

Bodin's praise of printing was largely confined to discounting the superiority of the ancients. It did not encompass a vision of an extended cognitive
advance. When modeling the course of human history, he turned not to
scripture but to classical theorists. "The path of change seems to go in a
circle."[23]

Louis LeRoy similarly adhered to a cyclical model even while singling
out Gutenberg's invention among the many novelties that had come into
view in recent years.[24]

> Besides the restoration of ancient learning . . . the invention of many
> fine new things . . . has been reserved to this age. Among these,
> printing deserves to be put first, because of its excellence, utility, and
> the subtlety of craftsmanship . . . more work is accomplished in one
> day than many diligent scribes could do in a year. . . . The invention
> has greatly aided the advancement of all disciplines . . . it seems
> miraculously to have been discovered in order to bring back to life
> . . . literature which seemed dead.[25]

LeRoy went on to note that the invention was attributed to the Germans.
After beginning in Mainz, it spread to the rest of Latin Christendom. But,
like his compatriot Bodin, he was wary of assigning too much credit to the
Germans. Recent reports from Portuguese travelers who had returned from
Asia with printed books, he wrote, suggested that "printing had long been in
use in those parts." It was carried through Tartary and Muscovy before its
arrival in Germany and its subsequent diffusion throughout Western Christendom.

While acknowledging, as would Montaigne in 1588,[26] that the Chinese
probably had printing before the West, LeRoy stressed the contrast between

Christendom, where God had shed his grace ("to whom the providence of God has especially entrusted the consummation of divine and human wisdom"), and Islam, which remained in darkness. "Deprived of this grace, the Mohammedans have entirely rejected printing, not using it at all among themselves, nor permitting the importation of books on their own affairs printed elsewhere in Arabic."

He went on to give second place to the invention of the compass and third place to "bombard" (cannonry and/or gunpowder), all of which were "by some destiny reserved to our age." Whereas this was seen by the millenarians to portend a triumphant interval before the coming of Judgment Day, LeRoy (like Bodin) had a less hopeful vision. If the memory and knowledge of the past serve as instruction to the present, he wrote, the "perfection of today" will give way to dislocation and chaos. Europe will be overrun by new barbarians and then subject to famine, pestilence, floods, fires, and earthquakes, "reducing [all things] to their former state of chaos." Nevertheless, he underlined the fallacy of thinking there was a golden age in the past or that the ancients knew more than the moderns.

Perhaps the most widely circulated early modern work that coupled printing with compass and cannon was pictorial rather than textual. It consists of a series of some two dozen prints, entitled *Nova Reperta*.[27] The engraved images illustrate the new powers acquired by Western Europeans. The series elaborates on themes introduced by early printers who boasted about their superior writing tools and advertised the globes, maps, and other instruments that were for sale in many printing shops. The inventions and discoveries that are depicted are imbued with religious (specifically Christian) significance, indicating that the celebration of technological progress had not yet been secularized. The title page offers a concise summary of the whole.

On the top left: a native of the New World points to a map of the new continent while holding a snake swallowing its tail (the ouroborus), which indicates the cyclical movement of time. The map is circled with the names of Columbus and Americus Vespucci. (In the sixteenth century, the naming of the new continent was closely linked to the act of discovery.) On the top right is the image of a windrose card symbolizing the invention of the magnetic compass, here wrongly credited to Flavius of Amalfi, a chronicler who merely reported what he had learned from sailors in his port town. Balancing the Native American on the top left, the top right has a bareheaded bearded old man, also holding an ouroborus. He appears to represent the end of a historic cycle and the disappearance of the old world known to antiquity.

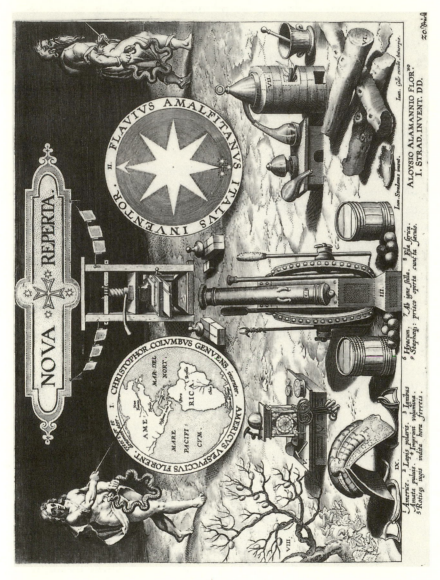

Figure 3.1. Jan van der Straet, *Nova Reperta* (ca. 1600), title page. Courtesy of the Smithsonian Institution Libraries.

In the center a cannon, flanked by barrels and cannon balls, illustrates the invention of gunpowder. It points upward to a printing press which is cleverly integrated into the title while occupying a central position. The ink pads and balls surmount the barrels of cannon balls; freshly printed pages link the press with the ornamental board carrying the title. The constellation Southern Cross is placed between the words "Nova" and "Reperta." (The discovery of the Southern Cross by maritime explorers was imbued with special Christian significance at the time.) Cannon, press, and Cross lead from bottom to top—from infernal regions to heavenly ones.

Scale and position distinguish the triad of printing, gunpowder, and compass from the other objects which are scattered on the ground in no special order. As noted earlier, almost every object shown had initially appeared on a list compiled by a Vatican librarian who was concerned about the legitimacy of using new Latin names to designate objects unknown in antiquity. Later writers such as Polydore Vergil added the printing press to the list of objects for which the ancients had no words. By the mid-sixteenth century, the objects which had once figured in a treatise on philology were being deployed to celebrate technology, with printing, gunpowder, and compass assigned central roles.

Beginning with the top tier, going from left to right, there are depictions of the silkworm, the mechanical clock, and the art of distilling. On the bottom tier, there is a saddle containing the modern invention of the stirrup and a portrayal of guiacum, the bark of wood from the New World (which was promoted as a cure for syphilis by the Fugger mining and merchant dynasty, who had a monopoly on this wood.) The full series of twenty-four plates contains a separate engraving for each object shown and includes several objects not shown, such as a water mill and armor-making.

One engraving, devoted to an object not displayed on the title page, dealt with the invention of eyeglasses. Because of its special relevance to book history, especially to the currently fashionable topic of the history of reading, it seems worth including here. One detail showed that the artist was well informed about chronology. He portrayed a stationer's shop, not a printing shop, indicating an awareness that spectacles were invented before printing. Unlike printing, which advertised itself, no inventor's name could be attached to eyeglasses. What little we know about this late thirteenth-century invention comes from the transcription of a fourteenth-century sermon given in Pisa.[28] In the distance is a blind man led by a dog. The caption reads: "Also invented were eyeglasses which remove dark veils from the eyes." The improvement of vision and the removal of dark veils resonated with neo-Platonic, Christian significance.

And so, too, did the discovery of the New World. As Guillaume Postel's writings showed, the voyages of discovery in the age of Columbus fueled millenarian expectations. To locate all the peoples of the world and convert them to Christianity was to pave the way for the Second Coming. The print entitled "Astrolabe" is only one of several engravings devoted to the voyages. The title refers to the mariner's instrument developed by Martin Behaim in 1480 and used by Columbus to help calculate latitude. But the instrument held by Americus in the print is actually an armillary sphere. (Was there a breakdown in communication between the caption writer in Antwerp and the artist in Florence?) The artist seems less concerned with describing a specific tool than with the symbolism of the cross making itself visible in the skies of the southern hemisphere. The caption reads: "Americus Vespucci found the cross with the four stars in the silent night." While the sailors sleep, Vespucci is awake and recalls Dante's description of emerging from the Inferno. (The artist had previously illustrated an edition of the *Commedia*.) There is a portrait of Dante on the left with excerpts from the first canto of *Purgatorio*: "I turned to the right and looked at the other pole and saw four stars never seen since Adam and Eve. The heavens rejoiced." The contrast between the wakeful discoverer and the sleeping sailors evokes Renaissance renderings of the risen Christ and sleeping soldiers. Is the open tomb represented by the open chest? There is a crucifix near the lantern.

In contrast to the depiction of a cross in the heavens is the portrayal of a cannon foundry. In the background, war is being waged against a fortified city. The caption reads: "Thunder and Lightening made by Hand. It seems to be a gift from the jealous underworld." Attributing the development of new weaponry to the infernal regions was in keeping with the views held by the caption writer and print publisher, who held to the irenic views that were discussed above.

The printing shop is displayed in another print. The caption reads: "Just as one voice can be heard by a multitude of ears, so a single writing covers a thousand sheets." The artist seems to have depicted one worker operating an instrument that required two operators. But he did at least convey a sense of numerous activities undertaken in a printing office: the operating of the screw press, the daubing of ink, the proofreader wearing spectacles, the compositors setting type.

The artist was literally most at home in his tribute to the brothers Van

Eyck for inventing oil painting. He depicted the interior of an artist's workshop containing several apprentices, models, and canvases. It is likely that Stradanus was portraying his own studio in Florence, where he stayed after studying under Vasari. Obviously he drew on Vasari's account of the lives of famous artists, where the invention of oil painting is credited to the Van Eycks. Perhaps he was also expressing pride in the accomplishment of fellow Flemings.

In addition to printing and painting, one more craft was required to produce the series. Figure 3.7 is a highly self-referential print—a depiction of the art in the act of deploying it—that is, an engraving of the process of engraving. The caption reads: "By a new art the engraver carves figures on beaten sheets and reproduces them on a press." The engraver is at right with his burin in hand, cutting lines on metal. In the center, plates are warmed and polished. On the left, the press rolls paper over the plates. In back the pulled papers are hung to dry.

As these three last plates show, diverse operations had to be coordinated to produce a series of this kind. The usual practice of attributing the series to the single figure of the artist conceals the complex cosmopolitan collaboration that was actually entailed.[29] At least three contributors are worth special notice. First the artist: Jan van der Straet (1523–1605), later known by his Latin name Stradanus, was a Fleming born in Bruges who studied in Florence under Vasari. He then turned out paintings, frescoes, and tapestry designs for Italian patrons including Grand Duke Cosimo de Medici and two popes. Attracted by the international market for prints, he formed a partnership with a Flemish firm of print publishers. The designs for *Nova Reperta* were sent by courier to Antwerp (at that time the major European printing center). There, the designs were rendered on metal by a distinguished engraver (Jan or Adriaen Collaert) working under the direction of the print publisher Philippe Galle (or Galleus, 1537–1612).[30] Galle, who belonged to an illustrious Antwerp dynasty, compiled and published numerous books of portraits and medallions as well as several other print series. One of his publications included a portrait of his friend, the greatest master printer of mid-sixteenth-century Europe, Christopher Plantin.

Plantin's *officina* in Antwerp served representatives of diverse confessions and dynastic states without being affiliated with any single one. He was associated with a secretive heterodox sect, the Family of Love, which allowed its practitioners to conform to local church customs while inwardly dissenting from orthodox creeds. He managed to win patronage both from the Spanish

15. Ioan. Stradanus invent. Ioan. Collaert sculp. CONSPICILLA. Ioan. galle excud.

Inuenta conspicilla sunt, quæ luminum Obscuriores detegunt caligines.

Figure 3.2. *Nova Reperta:* Spectacles. Courtesy of the Smithsonian Institution Libraries.

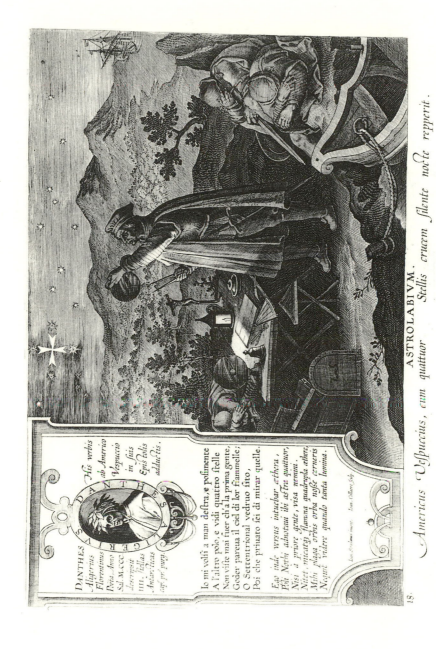

Americus Vespucius, cum quattuor Stellis crucem silente nocte repperit.

Figure 3.3 *Nova Reperta*: Astrolabe. Courtesy of the Smithsonian Institution Libraries.

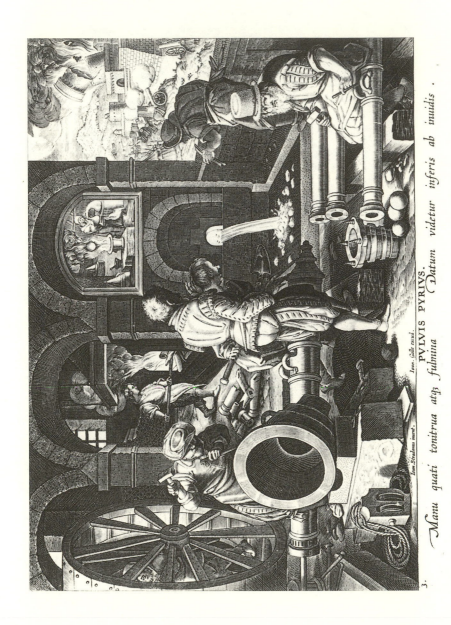

3.

PVLVIS PYRIVS.

Manu quati tonitrua atq̃ fulmina   Datum videtur inferis ab inuidis .

Ioan. Stradanus inuent.   Ioan. Galle excud.

Figure 3.4. *Nova Reperta*: Cannon Foundry. Courtesy of the Smithsonian Institution Libraries.

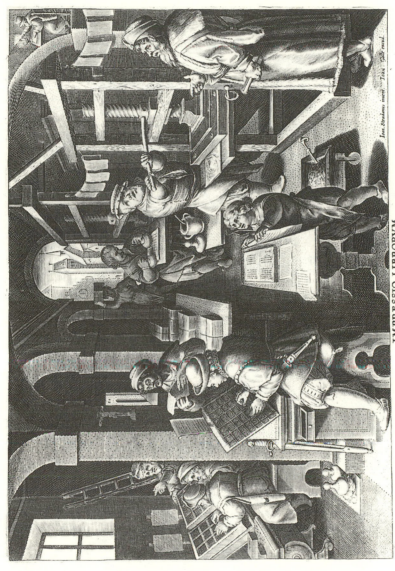

IMPRESSIO LIBRORVM.

Poteſt vt vna vox capi aure plurima :   Limant ita vna ſcripta mille paginas.

Figure 3.5. *Nova Reperta:* Printing Shop. Courtesy of the Smithsonian Institution Libraries.

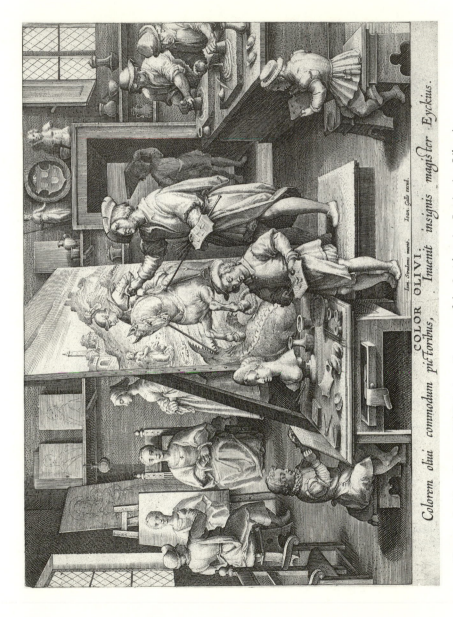

COLOR OLIVI.

Colorem oliui commodum picToribus, Inuenit insignis magiSter Eyckius.

Ioan. Stradanus inuent.   Ioan. Galle excud.

Figure 3.6. *Nova Reperta:* Oil Painting. Courtesy of the Smithsonian Institution Libraries.

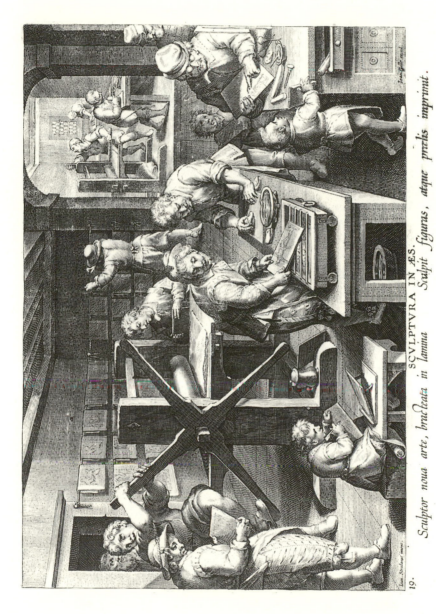

Sculptor noua arte, bractea in lamina SCVLPTVRA IN ÆS. Sculpit figuras, atque prælis imprimit.

Figure 3.7. *Nova Reperta*: Engraving. Courtesy of the Smithsonian Institution Libraries.

Catholic king Philip II and from the Protestant Dutch ruler William of Orange. He secured financing from Jews as well as Christians. He married off one daughter to a Catholic printer, who carried on the family business in Antwerp, while another wed a Calvinist scholar-printer who worked at the Dutch university of Leiden. The little book on the craft of printing that he authored contained a tribute to the invention.[31] He figures here not just because he helped to shape the cosmopolitan commonwealth of learning, nor because he was a friend of the print publisher, but also because his printing shop employed the third participant in the *Nova Reperta* series, the often neglected figure of the caption writer. Cornelius Kilian (Kilianus) served as Plantin's proofreader and editorial adviser. As a lexicographer, he produced the first Dutch-Latin dictionary. He was also Philippe Galle's cousin and was recruited by Galle to provide Latin captions for the series.

Nova Reperta shows how printers and engravers continued to elaborate on the self-congratulatory themes introduced by early printers who boasted about the superior new tools at their disposal. The sixteenth century saw Gutenberg's invention assigned a prominent position in celebratory discourse about new stars, new worlds, and new powers acquired by Western Europeans. But a full-blown description of these tools and of those who worked them did not appear until later in the seventeenth century, when Joseph Moxon disclosed all the tricks of his trade for public inspection in his *Mechanick Exercises* (1683).

This delay between the first use of the press and the detailed description of how it worked provoked speculation later on. The prolonged delay in disclosing technical details was noted by Isaac d'Israeli: "How has it happened that such a plain story as that of the art of printing should have sunk into a romance?" he asked, and then answered his own question. The "monopolisers" feared disclosing their trade secrets. They hid their work, even tried to blind their workmen, and pretended that their volumes were "the work of some supernatural agency." As with most trade secrets this one had to be jealously guarded "solely because the monopolisers dreaded discovery." As a result, rumors were floated about a "supernatural agency," and the foundation myths described in Chapter 1 took hold.[32]

Moxon introduced his detailed "how-to" treatise with a preface that drew on Renaissance efforts to dignify the craft by associating it with Vitruvian principles and Euclidean geometry. As was true of earlier printers, his commemoration of the invention was linked with advertisements for the instruments he made and sold. He acknowledged that the Chinese had had printing for many hundred years but noted that the Asian practice of "Cutting . . . Letters upon Blocks in whole Pages" differed from the much more recent European practice of "Printing with single Letters Cast in Mettal." The controversy over whether the European invention originated with Gutenberg in Mainz or Coster in Haarlem he deemed "undecidable." More important was obtaining acknowledgement that typography "in all its Branches" could be deemed "a Science"; perhaps even a "Science of Sciences" as "some Authors" said. John Dee in his preface to Euclid had claimed that architecture was a mathematical science (citing Vitruvius and Alberti in his support). Moxon cited Dee when making the same claim for typography.

> By a Typographer, I do not mean a Printer . . . any more than Dr. Dee means a carpenter or Mason to be an Architect: But by a Typographer, I mean such a one, who by his own Judgement . . . can either perform, or direct others to perform from the beginning to the end, all the Handy-works and Physical Operations relating to Typographie . . . .The Master Printer . . . is . . . as the Soul of Printing; and all the Work-men as members of the Body governed by that Soul.[33]

As was also true of the writings of earlier master printers, little or nothing is said of the business side of Moxon's enterprise. The muses loom large while mammon is kept out of sight. Yet Moxon was far from shy about advertising his products or competing in the marketplace of print. He took a special interest in navigation and astronomy. He made and sold globes at his shop "At the Sign of the Atlas," published Edward Wright's treatise on navigation, and he, himself, authored a "silent instructor": *A Tutor to Astronomie and Geography* (1659).[34] He was by no means the only master printer who devised, advertised, and sold navigational and astronomical instruments along with other printed materials. His Dutch contemporary, W. J. Blaeu, not only made and sold globes and navigational aids but also devised and advertised a presumably improved wooden handpress.[35] Thus press and compass were quite naturally coupled in the shops of printers-cum-instrument makers, even while the invention of printing and the discovery of a new continent were being assigned world historical significance in learned treatises.

As already noted with reference to sixteenth-century enthusiasts such as Postel, the seeming convergence of invention and discovery excited contemporary commentators. The Dominican visionary, Tommaso Campanella, was persuaded (as Postel had been) that the coincidence of America's discovery with the invention of printing opened the way for a worldwide triumph of Christianity. The entire world would become a single sheepfold under the guidance of a single shepherd, in accord with a Johannine prophecy in John 10:16.[36] For Campanella, "the new devices of printing, compass and arquebus possess an almost sacral quality."[37]

Unlike Postel, however, Campanella lived in an era when controversies were swirling around the new heliocentric world system. The idea of a sun-centered universe proved especially stimulating to his imagination and to that of his contemporaries. Johannes Kepler could scarcely contain his enthusiasm:

> What shall I say about today's mechanical arts. . . . Do we not . . .
> by the art of printing bring to light all the ancient writers, as many
> as are extant? . . . Every year, especially since 1563 . . . in all subjects
> the number of authors whose writings are printed is greater than the
> number of all the authors over the past one thousand years. Through
> them a new theology has been created . . . and a new jurisprudence;
> the followers of Paracelsus have created a new medicine, and the
> followers of Copernicus a new astronomy. For my part, I believe
> that now at last the world is alive, and indeed is in a state of intense
> excitement.[38]

Early humanists had celebrated printing largely because it enabled them to recover and preserve the almost lost tongues and texts of antiquity. By the time Kepler was writing, the twinned themes of recovery and discovery had begun to move apart. Ancient maps, charts, and texts, once arranged and dated, turned out to be dated in more sense than one. As fresh findings accumulated, modern navigators and stargazers turned out to know more about the heavens and earth than did ancient sages.[39] The recovery of old texts when taken together with an accumulation of new data, led Francis Bacon and others to reverse an old formula, making the so-called ancients youthful.[40] "Antiquitas saeculi juventus mundi" (Ancient time was the youth of the world). "From our age: if it but knew its own strength . . . much more might fairly be expected than from the ancient times, inasmuch as it is a more advanced age of the world, and stored and stocked with infinite experiments and observations."[41] If the moderns were less youthful and more adult, however, they were vulnerable to future enfeeblement and senile old age.

(This consideration would lead Fontenelle, later on, to abandon the metaphor of a single life span and to argue that humankind, unlike a single human being, would forever be able to profit from past experience.)[42] Bacon's confidence in future progress was qualified by his concern with political stability. The ancients could be successfully challenged, provided a program of research and development received adequate support from the state.[43] Nevertheless, his vision of the future was optimistic. Just as contemporaries surpassed the ancients, so too would future generations be able to profit from new experiments and observations, and thus venture even further into the unknown. As Richard Foster Jones observes, the voyages of discovery supplied the most often used metaphor for asserting the superiority of the moderns over the ancients:

> Note how frequently the Pillars of Hercules with their supposed inscription "ne plus ultra" are used to indicate the closed circle of ancient knowledge . . . the vast increase in geographical knowledge over that of the ancients operated consciously or unconsciously in undermining the superiority of the classical writers, a fact later conspicuously revealed in various geographical figures of speech used to express modern progress in knowledge.[44]

Not a figure of speech but a figure engraved on a seventeenth-century title page encapsulated this metaphor in its most memorable form. The title page[45] of Bacon's *Instauratio Magna* shows a ship sailing outside old limits (the pillars of Hercules, which enclosed the inhabited world of antiquity) into the vast unknown, on a voyage without end. Against the motto "Ne plus Ultra" ("Do not go too Far"), Bacon adopted the motto "Plus Ultra" ("Too far is not enough"):[46]

> that little vessels, like the celestial bodies, should sail round the whole globe, is the happiness of our age. These times . . . may justly use . . . plus ultra, where the ancients used non plus ultra. . . . This improvement of navigation may give us great hopes of extending and improving the sciences, especially as it seems agreeable to the Divine will that they should be coeval. Thus the prophet Daniel foretells that "Many shall go to and fro on the earth, and knowledge shall be increased," as if the openness and through passage of the world and the increase of knowledge were allotted to the same age,

Figure 3.8. Francis Bacon, *Instauratio Magna* (1620), engraved title page. Courtesy of the Folger Shakespeare Library.

which indeed we find already true in part: for the learning of these times scarce yields to the former periods . . . and in many particulars far exceeds them.[47]

As had the earlier Protestants, Bacon assigned special significance to the timing of the advent of printing. (It was, he wrote, "ordained by God.") But whereas Foxe saw the hand of Providence in rescuing Luther from the fate of Hus, Bacon had in mind the coincidence of overseas exploration with the increased output of books: "as if the . . . thorough passage of the world and the increase of knowledge were allotted to the same age."[48]

The metaphor of sailing beyond ancient limits neatly coupled the exploration of space and cumulative cognitive advance. It also tended to detach the "increase of knowledge" from increases in the destructive power of weaponry. Yet overseas conquests hinged rather more on guns than on printing. To be sure, some European mariners also deployed new printed products, such as the tables of declination, that might have helped them set their course. One story, taken from Samuel Eliot Morison's biography of Columbus, suggests that the use of printed materials was not always innocuous.[49] When Jamaican natives balked at supplying Columbus and his retinue with food, Columbus got out his astronomical tables that had been printed some years before in Nuremberg. The natives were told that the gods would eliminate moonlight if adequate supplies were not forthcoming. On the next night indeed an eclipse occurred; there was no more trouble about provisions.[50] Whether apocryphal or not, the story indicates how printing enters into Bacon's most famous aphorism: "knowledge is power."

That the same age was granted the use of two new instruments, compass and printing, had been regarded as providential by visionaries such as Guillaume Postel and Tommaso Campanella. Postel's vision of the eventual conversion of all the peoples of the world entailed expansion over space. Bacon also envisaged a temporal process: the advancement of learning and the increase of knowledge would unfold over the course of time. Accordingly, the classical aphorism "Veritas Filia Temporis" (Truth is the Daughter of Time) acquired new meaning. Previously associated with courtroom verdicts that saw false rumor defeated by veracious testimony, the motto was reinterpreted by Bacon and his followers to designate an indefinitely extended series of investigations.[51] "Rightly is truth called the daughter of time, not of authority."[52] "It would be a disgrace to mankind if wide areas of the physical globe, of land, sea and stars, have been opened up and explored in our time while the boundaries of the intellectual globe were confined to the discoveries and narrow limits of the ancients."[53] Later in the century Joseph Glanvill explicitly used *Plus Ultra* to designate "the progress and advancement of knowledge."[54] As a new mode of communication, the printing press pointed to a sequence of discoveries that extended into an indefinite future; an endless series of voyages on "strange seas of thought." Natural philosophy was recast as a progressive construction based on cooperation that was never finished but was always perfectible.[55]

As did many followers of Erasmus, Bacon disdained theological disputation: "controversies of religion must hinder the advancement of sciences."[56] Nevertheless, his celebration of printing was still strongly inflected by scriptural prophecy. The invention had been regarded by the Lutherans as a sign that the last days were very close at hand. It was regarded by Bacon and his followers as signifying the coming of a more extended interval during which man's dominion over nature, which had been lost at the Fall, would be restored. Thus printing loomed large in George Hakewill's refutation of a traditional pessimistic work entitled *The Fall of Man* (1616).[57]

In *Novum Organum,* as in the citation above from the *Advancement of Learning,* Bacon referred to the prophecy contained in Daniel (12:4): "Many shall runne to and fro and knowledge shall be increased," "thus plainly hinting and suggesting that fate (which is Providence) would cause the complete circuit of the globe (now accomplished, or at least going forward . . .), and the increase of learning to happen at the same epoch."[58]

That this particular prophecy was favored by seventeenth-century Baconians is fully documented in Charles Webster's magisterial study, *The Great Instauration.*[59] The prophecy was frequently cited in that influential group of central Europeans who spent time in England during the Thirty Years War: Jan Comenius, Samuel Hartlib, and John Drury. They regarded printing, much as had Postel and Campanella, as a providential gift that pointed toward the achievement of universal concord (a Concordia Mundi) based on the conversion of all the peoples of the world. As Protestants they favored the propagation of the Gospel by means of translation.[60] But they also placed special emphasis on the opportunities extended by printing for the "open communication of useful knowledge."[61] Comenius drew plans for a college to be founded in London whose members would divide responsibilities and correspond with learned men throughout the world.[62] Hartlib organized an "Office of Address for Communications," which mutated into an "Agencie for Universal Learning."[63] Later, Hartlib's onetime associate Henry Oldenberg, as secretary to the Royal Society, would not only elicit contributions from foreign virtuosi but also enable them to publish their findings when they were hindered from printing in their native lands.[64]

The dialogic potential of printing proved alarming to orthodox church-men and government officials. It was seen in a more positive light when applied to interchanges concerning natural phenomena and the promotion of useful knowledge. This was no less true on the Continent than among the English Baconians singled out by Webster.[65] Indeed, when Hartlib sought to organize a new system for exchanging useful information and laid plans for an "Office of Address for Communications," he looked to Paris for his model. There, Théophraste Renaudot (a French physician turned publicist, protégé of Richelieu and founder of the official *Gazette*) had pioneered with a "Bureau d'Adressse" that acted as both a labor exchange and a central clearinghouse for medical information.[66] Also in Paris, the abbé Mersenne dreamed of setting up an organization that would bring together all the learned men of Europe.[67] Even while remaining in a Paris convent, Mersenne took part in a movement that valued cooperative ventures more highly than "solitary spiritual wisdom."[68] It is worth noting that Mersenne and many of his correspondents were not animated by the scriptural prophecies that had been repeatedly cited by the Puritans and millenarians described by Webster. Yet they shared the same faith as the English circle around Hartlib in the value of collaborative ventures and communicable knowledge.

Insistence on the value of collaboration was of course the hallmark of the greatest of all eighteenth-century ventures in encyclopedism. In his article on "art," Diderot noted that he was echoing Bacon, "whom I never tire of praising because I never tire of reading him." He mentioned the three inventions that were unknown to the ancients and that have "transformed the face of the earth. . . . What a revolution these discoveries have brought about . . . typographic characters have created enlightened communication between learned men of all countries and all future time."[69]

The foregoing has stressed the enthusiastic reception of Gutenberg's invention and the part played by printing in shaping early ideas of progress. The loss and erosion that occurred when texts had to be transmitted by hand-copying had been arrested; an incremental "increase in learning" was set in motion by the duplicative powers of print. The buoyant and optimistic outlook that resulted had been expressed in the sixteenth century by Rabelais, among others, ("all the world is full of learned men, of most skilled preceptors, of vast libraries")[70] and by Ramus ("in our century we have seen greater progress in . . . works of learning than our ancestors had seen in the whole course of the previous fourteen centuries").[71] Seventeenth-century enthusiasm was exemplified by the citation from Kepler given above.

But attitudes toward printing were rarely unmixed. The "vast libraries" mentioned by Rabelais grew larger in the next century, a development that was encouraged by members of the cosmopolitan commonwealth of learning, but also one that proved worrisome to librarians.[72] Justus Lipsius evoked Alexandria while expounding on the role libraries might play in his own strife-ridden time by providing a space for study that was open to all and free of partisanship. "What Lipsisus saw in Alexandria was not only the union of high purpose and deep learning but a community of scholars open to all points of view."[73]

A similar vision animated Gabriel Naudé, whose advice on how to construct a library (*Avis pour dresser une bibliothèque*, 1627) was translated from the original French into Latin and many vernaculars.[74] Naudé served diverse patrons, guiding the collections of French *parlementaires* and of cardinals Barbarini in Rome, and Richelieu and Mazarin in Paris. His ideal library embraced all types of books and all forms of learning, and was open to all points of view. It should not leave out "any of the works of the leading heretics or partisans of religions different from our own."[75] It should also be capacious enough to make room for new findings: "nothing makes a man more of a senseless pedant than to despise modern authors and remain attached only to certain of the ancients." Naudé's acceptance of all points of view did not prevent him from taking sides in the battle between ancients and moderns, where he proved to be an unabashed modern: "it is much easier at present, to procure thousands of Books, then it was for the Antients to get hundreds . . . it would be an eternal shame . . . to come beneath them in this particular, which we may surmount with so much advantage."[76]

Overload: Lost in the Crowd

The advantages that accrued to the moderns, however, represented a mixed blessing. For the goal of collecting all learned works from all eras was better suited to the age of the scribe, when texts were in relatively short supply, than to the age of the printer, when the unending output threatened to become unmanageable.[77] "By the second half of the seventeenth century the sense of a crisis due to information overload had reached such proportions that printing, long praised as a 'divine' invention, had to be defended against the charge of bringing on a new era of barbarity."[78]

Leibniz, when addressing Louis XIV in 1680, paid tribute to the way printing duplicated books and thus made it possible "to preserve the greater part of our knowledge."[79] But he also expressed alarm about the "horrible mass of books" that kept on growing. Unless contained and restrained, he advised, the increase in output would result in intolerable disorder, and it would become "a disgrace rather than an honor to be an author."[80] A "swarm" of sectarian pamphlets had alarmed authorities in France and England during the religious wars. The proliferation of learned tomes and treatises did not arouse the same fears of heretical contamination, but did engender concern nevertheless:

> the multiplication of books was felt as an oppression and bewilderment. When Barrildo, a peasant in Lope de Vega's play *Fonte Ovejuna*, remarks that "since so many books have been printed learning spreads," Leonelo, a student, replies: "You ought rather to say unlearning spreads; for a too great swarm of objects confuses the mind, and should one not dread the task of reading only the titles of all the books?"[81]

Compiling "only the titles of books" soon taxed the capacity of even the most energetic and erudite bibliographers. In the preface to his massive bibliography, the *Biblioteca Universalis* (1545), Conrad Gesner had complained of the "confusing and harmful abundance of books."[82] A century later, a Jesuit scholar, Father Philip Labbé, had compiled a "Bibliothèque des Bibliothèques" consisting solely of the names of those who had compiled bibliographies.[83] Listing "only the titles of books" became subject to infinite regress. In the early nineteenth century, Isaac d'Israeli noted that almost 400 years had passed "since the art of multiplying books has been discovered" and the "superfluity of knowledge in billions and trillions, overwhelms the imagination!" He commented on the "enormous swarm of bibliographical errors" yet to be uncovered and listed the names of some fifty bibliographers whose massive tomes still needed correcting.[84] The twentieth century saw the compilation of bibliographies of bibliographies of bibliographies. A fourth term will probably be needed before all is converted to an electronic database.

To be sure, complaints about an overabundance of reading materials predated Gutenberg by hundreds of years—as was noticed earlier. Ann Blair

offers an apt medieval citation from Vincent of Beauvais about "the multitude of books, the shortness of time and the slipperiness of memory."[85] After
printing introduced a sharp rise in output, many complaints were aimed
merely at the way good books were outnumbered by bad ones, the latter
being turned out, as Sir Thomas Browne complained, solely for the benefit
"of the trade of typographers."[86] Increased output also provoked elitist objections about casting pearls before swine; even the best books were liable to be
misread when made available to unworthy, ignorant readers.

The concern expressed by some seventeenth-century savants, however,
was of a different order. The preservative powers of print had eased the task
of transmitting what remained of ancient texts. Indeed, more and more remnants of the classical past were being recovered and secured. At the same time,
fresh data pertaining to new worlds and new stars were also accumulating.
"Collecting and codifying constantly progressing and changing materials"[87]
posed new challenges. The glut of information seemed too much to be
crammed into a single volume or to be absorbed by any single reader. "How
is it possible to understand the whole universe?" asked François de Grenaille,
"these big volumes that our century has published to instruct us frighten
most minds not only because it is impossible to carry them but because their
length makes us dread reading them."[88]

The ambivalence that marked so many reactions to printing was especially pronounced on this issue. Ambivalence went so far as to lead some
savants to treat the destruction of the Alexandrian Library as a "fortunate
misfortune."[89] As early as the 1560s, Louis LeRoy felt so overwhelmed by all
the new books that he welcomed the demolition of ancient ones: "If all that
had been written by the auncient Philosophers . . . had come into our hands,
all had bin full of books and we should have no other mouvables in our
house but bookes: we should be constrained to go, sit and lie upon bookes."[90]
Sir Thomas Browne's complaint about there being too many books was accompanied by the suggestion that a new bonfire was needed, similar to "the
combustion of the Library of Alexandria."[91] Later on, vicarious pleasure at
the idea of future book-burnings would be manifested in the utopian visions
of Louis Sébastien Mercier and Étienne Cabet. In his *Year 2440*, Mercier
characteristically assigned an approximate numerical value to the books that
were to be destroyed: "five or six hundred thousand commentators, a billion
romances, eight hundred thousand volumes of law, etc."[92]

Contemporaries were caught between long-lived fears of loss (stemming
from repeated catastrophes in the age of scribes) and an increasing anxiety

aroused by the astonishing multiplicity of books. Perhaps the wisest comment came from the extremely prolific polymath Daniel Georg Morhof,[93] whose *Polyhistor* reached some 2,000 pages in its final form: "One should not think that this remarkable art should be condemned; for nothing is good with which some evil from the vice of men is not admixed."[94] Most writers were less judicious. Leibniz was by no means the only librarian who believed the new abundance, if unrestrained, would lead not to an advancement of learning but to a descent into chaos. "The situation seemed absolutely dire" to Adrien Baillet, the biographer of Descartes who served as librarian to Guillaume-Henri de Lamoignon, chancellor of France: "We have reason to fear that the multitude of books which grows every day in a prodigious fashion will make the following centuries fall into a state as barbarous as that of the centuries that followed the fall of the Roman empire."[95]

The idea that the knowledge industry was headed toward dislocation and chaos ("'tis all in pieces, all coherence gone") was in sharp contrast to the hopeful Baconian vision of indefinitely extended cognitive advance. Yet it would be a mistake to take all such alarms too literally. Almost all of them were sounded by authors who were justifying the presentation of their own work to a presumably overburdened reader. When Vincent of Beauvais referred to the multitude of books and the shortness of time, it was in the preface to his own four-volume medieval compendium, *Speculum Maius*. Similarly, Baillet's description of the "dire" situation was set forth to justify the publication of his multivolume bibliographical survey, *Jugements des savans sur les principaux ouvrages des auteurs*.[96] Even Leibniz proposed to cope with the "horrible mass" by producing yet more volumes. Rather like the earlier humanist who asked the pope to appoint a committee, he urged Louis XIV to empower the royal academies to "stop the publication of bad and superfluous books" and also to empower them to sponsor a multivolume encyclopedia that would present extracts and addenda compiled by specialists in diverse fields.[97] Ironically then, the "perception of an overabundance of books fueled the production of many more books, often especially large ones, aimed at remedying the problem."[98]

To the problem of an overabundance of books was added that of overabundant volumes, resulting in a reaction against previously respected forms of book learning. Erudite Latin-writing compilers, such as Morhof, "who had loaded seventeenth-century bookshelves to breaking point" tended to fall out of favor.[99] Their works, which bristled with paratextual material, gave rise to numerous parodies. The output of "Martinus Scriblerus" is most celebrated among English readers.[100] But the work of one "Dr. Mathanasius," which was published in 1714 and composed by Thémiseul de Saint-Hyacinthe, was no less noteworthy. What purports to be a long-lost, recently recovered, anonymous poetic masterpiece (*Le chef d'oeuvre d'un inconnu*) is so smothered by learned commentary that one page has barely enough room for more than a single exclamation: "Ah!"[101] Swift and Pope would plan to counter the English version of the *Journal des savants* (*History of the Works of the Learned*) with a satire entitled "Account of the Works of the Unlearned."[102]

The weighty tomes of verbose Latin writing scholars also came under attack from natural philosophers, who found more value in the terse reports of mariners, craftsmen, and mechanics.[103] The distinction between Latin works that had been much copied and corrupted over the course of centuries and newly composed works (often in the vernacular) that contained fresh data was not always made clear. "Away with books!" became a popular slogan: "The difference between my philosophising and that of Pico is this: I learn more from the anatomy of an ant or a blade of grass . . . than from all the books that have been written since the beginning of time . . . human books . . . have been copied badly . . . without attention to the things that are written in the original book of the universe."[104]

Insistence on doing away with books, however, was almost always expressed in a bookish form. When Descartes described how he abandoned bookish studies and set out to see the world, he did so in a printed work.[105] "Away with books!" was itself a topos inherited from the ancients. It became little more than a ritualistic rhetorical flourish. Still, the "primitivist" trend did serve to propel vernacular science writing in new directions.

> [There] has been a constant resolution to reject all the amplifications, digressions, and swellings of style; to return back to . . . primitive purity, and shortness . . . a close, naked, natural way of speaking . . . bringing all things as near the mathematical plainness as they can; and preferring the language of artizans, countrymen and merchants before that of wits or scholars.[106]

The attack on verbosity went together with objections to secrecy and obfuscation. Anticipating recent calls for "transparency," Bishop Sprat referred dismissively to the "smoky" style employed by alchemists. The demand for "mathematical plainness" was intended to dispel some of the semantic confusion that contributed to a sense of disorder and chaos.

But the new vogue for science writing scarcely eased concerns about overload. "By a paradoxical twist, this shift toward empirical study and data collection produced a new problem, that of comprehending and managing the swelling sea of scientific information." In the mid-eighteenth century, Diderot complained: "it will be almost as convenient to search for some bit of truth concealed in nature as it will be to find it hidden away in an immense multitude of bound volumes."[107] Diderot also complained about other aspects of the reaction against Latin learning. Compilers of reference works could no longer afford to confine themselves to reading Latin but had to master a growing number of different vernaculars. Diderot was especially alert to this problem, having had to master English in order to translate several reference works into French.[108]

D'Alembert wrote in a similar vein about "the practice of writing everything in the vulgar tongue." He approved of the substitution of French for Latin, in the belief that it had contributed to the spread of the Enlightenment. But problems ensued when the practice was imitated by other countries. After the English had imitated the French, d'Alembert complained, Latin had taken refuge in Germany, only to lose ground there. "I have no doubt that Germany will soon be followed by the Swedes, the Danes, and the Russians. Thus before the end of the eighteenth century, a philosopher will be required to burden his memory with seven or eight different languages. . . . having consumed . . . precious time . . . in learning them, he will die before beginning to educate himself."[109]

The vernacular translation movement that inspired these warnings had begun to affect encyclopedias in the late seventeenth century. A series of vernacular encyclopedias appeared, beginning with Furetière's three-volume French *Dictionnaire universel* (The Hague, 1690) and continuing with John Harris's English *Lexicon Technicum* (1704–10). Harris took note of the provisional character of his work, given the inevitable advances that lay in the future. "It is easie to see that new Matter will continually occurr . . . and, consequently, that there can be no such thing as a Perfect Book of this Kind, so I thought it better to send out an imperfect one than none, and to afford some Help to Mens Improvement."[110] The modest tone was absent from the next in the series, Ephraim Chambers's large and influential *Cyclopedia* of 1728. The *Cyclopedia* played a significant role in shaping Samuel Johnson's plans for a *Dictionary*[111] and Diderot's plans for the *Encyclopédie*. (Diderot had been commissioned to translate Chambers's *Cyclopedia* into French.) In his work, Chambers devoted a special section to "The Multitude of Books." There he observed: "Multitude of BOOKS has long been complained of: . . . They are grown too numerous, not only to procure and read, but to see, learn the names of, or even to number." He presented his own work as a solution to the problem. It " 'would answer all the Purposes of a Library" and would be more useful "than any, I had almost said all, the Books extant.'" In a prospectus for his second edition, he "boldly described the *Cyclopedia* as the 'best book in Universe' [sic],"[112] adding that it would provide England with the same resources as were supplied on the Continent by "Royal, Imperial, . . . [and] Ducal Academies."[113] As Daniel Rosenberg points out, "the rhetoric of overload" helped to drive the market in encyclopedias.[114]

The market for reference works was also driven by new learned review journals, often initiated by booksellers and publishers seeking to advertise their own products.[115] They offered digests of recent publications and coordinated findings sent in from all parts of Europe.[116] Booksellers also devised new systems for arranging titles in the catalogues they issued.[117] So, too, did librarians and auctioneers. The new system that was advocated by Gabriel Naudé,[118] of shelving by subject matter rather than by chronology (thus combining ancient with modern works), won the favor of Richard Bentley but provoked Jonathan Swift and helped to inspire Swift's celebrated attack on Bentley in his *Battle of the Books*.[119]

Efforts at reorganization were not only aimed at relieving the increasing burden felt by erudite polymaths. There were also attempts to make books more readable and accessible to an expanding public. In the 1680s, Fontenelle started out to translate an "unreadable Latin treatise by a Dutchman,"[120] and found that it contained numerous digressions and allusions, resulting in a "learned disorder." Although savants were accustomed to such a work, the less learned, more worldly readers for whom Fontenelle's translation was designed—"the ladies and, quite frankly, most of the men of this country"—were ill served by it. So, instead of a faithful translation, Fontenelle ruthlessly eliminated all that was extraneous, and changed the whole arrangement of the book.[121] Such methods were the stock in trade of popularizers, whose output won favor from publishers and booksellers seeking to enlarge markets for their wares. Fontenelle was vigorously attacked by Swift but was later hailed by d'Alembert for "throwing off the yoke of pedantry."[122] (Of course, objections to pedantry long preceded printing, as is indicated by the many classical allusions offered by Montaigne.)[123]

The so-called "superfluity" of books was regarded as a problematic by-product of printing by scholars who were trying to produce definitive compilations. As noted below, it also seemed oppressive to ambitious writers who sought to follow Erasmus and achieve lasting fame. But increased output was welcome to those who agreed with Comenius that learning ought to be widely shared.[124]

The spread of learning as well as its "increase" had been an integral part of the program developed by Hartlib and his circle.[125] It was greeted with enthusiasm by those who espoused the cause of the "moderns" against the "ancients." William Wotton, who had been engaged by the Royal Society to defend that institution against its opponents, was especially explicit about the contributions made by Gutenberg's invention.[126]

Unlike the ancients, Wotton argued, the moderns did not need to fear conquests by barbarians. In a passage that anticipated Enlightenment views, expressed most famously by Gibbon, Wotton argued that in order to conquer, barbarians would have to have mastered all the new arts of war and peace that were known to his age—in which case they would be barbarians no longer.[127] The advantages conferred by printing were so obvious that it seemed like a waste of time to dwell on them. But, Wotton wrote, Sir William Temple's ill-advised defense of the ancients called for a response.

Among other advantages, Wotton pointed out, printing lowered the cost of books and thus made them more accessible.[128] Printed texts were also more legible than were most handcopied ones. Books could be supplied with indexes and other "divisions" that were "cumbersome" in manuscripts. Notices of "new" and "excellent" books were more easily disseminated. Texts were better preserved entire and not so liable to be corrupted by "the ignorance or malice of transcribers." This was of special significance ("of great moment") to mathematics, "where the alteration of a letter, or a cypher" might make a "demonstration unintelligible." The same point applied to "anatomy, mechanicks, geography, and natural science," where unreliable hand-copying had been replaced by "engraving upon wood or copper."[129]

Wotton's reference to the usefulness of printing for mathematics and the life sciences is worth underscoring. Galileo's sarcastic comment about the stupid scholar who persisted in studying nature by looking only at books is sometimes cited without noting that the comment was coupled with insistence that decoding nature's secrets required expertise in mathematics.[130] Consulting logarithm tables was a different activity from nature study.

The reaction against verbosity went together with increased use of print-

made tools, tables, charts, and exactly repeatable pictorial statements—
materials that hand-copying had been unable to duplicate accurately and in
quantity.[131] Although not as spectacular as the discovery of new worlds and
new stars, and less appealing to poetic imagination, the rapid development
and publicizing of mathematical tools in particular: decimals, logarithms,
Cartesian coordinates, calculus (or the method of "fluxions") were the most
striking achievements of the so-called century of genius. Advances in mathematics gave proponents of progress a telling argument.[132] Whereas the meaning of the polyglot Scripture gave rise to dispute, the proof of a theorem
seemed to call forth universal consent. Nevertheless, the virtuosi were not
reluctant to cite proof texts from Scripture. In addition to the citation about
"running to and fro and increasing knowledge," they made frequent references to "ordering all things in measure and number and weight."[133] This
scriptural passage was a favorite of Sir William Petty (1623–87),[134] who was
among the founders of the Royal Society, and who pioneered statistical analysis of mortality rates. Petty's posthumously published *Political Arithmetic*
(1691) set the stage for future applications of mathematics to human affairs,
with results that have been controversial, to say the least. As noted below,
Condorcet was especially enthusiastic about this approach.[135]

The vogue for mathematical reasoning provided satirists with new targets. In addition to attacking pedantry and verbosity, they could make fun
of the reductionist implications of subjecting all phenomena to "measure,
number, and weight."

> In spite of Addison's response to many other new concepts of the
> day . . . he lost no chance for laughter at . . . absent-minded mathe-
> maticians who in their preoccupation with one subject forgot the
> world about them . . . Swift's Laputans excel in theoretical learning
> . . . .They can solve equations—but they cannot build houses.[136]

Of course, Jonathan Swift did not stop short with satirizing the new
vogue for mathematical reasoning. In his *Battle of the Books* and *A Tale of a
Tub* he took aim at all the arguments set forth by William Wotton and
sent poisoned darts at Wotton himself.[137] He exhibited his contempt for the
disciples of Francis Bacon and the very idea that there could be any "universal
improvement of Mankind."[138]

> The whole course of things being . . . entirely changed between us
> and the ancients . . . we of this age have discovered a shorter and

more prudent way to become scholars and wits, without the fatigue of reading or thinking. The most accomplished way of using books at present is twofold: either first to . . . learn their titles exactly and then brag of their acquaintance; or secondly . . . to get a thorough insight into the index by which the whole book is governed . . . the arts are all in a flying march and therefore more easily subdued by attacking them in the rear. . . . Thus men catch knowledge by throwing their wit upon the posteriors of a book.[139]

He questioned the modernity of the "discoveries" of Copernicus and William Harvey, hinting that they were probably "derived" from ancient sources.[140] He was also contemptuous of the busy spirits of the Royal Society and the toys they were given to play with in order to divert them from disturbing civil order by meddling in politics and public affairs.[141] Even worse than those "busy spirits" were the political pamphleteers, "infinite swarms of . . . Rogues and Raggamuffins," "mercenary scriblers, who write as they are commanded by the leaders . . . of sedition, faction, corruption and every evil work."[142] This characterization might seem to fit Swift's own services in 1710–14 as the chief propagandist for the Tory ministry under the earl of Oxford. But although he was a scribbler, Swift was not (like Daniel Defoe) a mercenary one. He had refused to take money for his services, even while he "hoped for a bishopric as his reward."[143] But Swift was also scornful about the activities of less partisan journalists who "wrote to the moment" and catered to a public avid for the "latest news."[144]

He was no more respectful of the weighty works of scholars and antiquarians who were engaged in restoring monuments of the past. He observed how preface writers tended to complain about the inordinate numbers of authors even while acting as authors themselves. Such complaints, he noted, came from the very same writers who produced the most "voluminous" products, thereby evoking the story of a very fat fellow who repeatedly complained of being stifled and squeezed in a large crowd until someone cried out that his carcass was taking up more room than anyone else.[145] It was true that the output of news writers was quickly erased, whereas heavy tomes were more likely to be preserved. But preservation meant only becoming dusty and worm-eaten in the large libraries that served as a final resting place.[146] Huge scholarly compendia provoked Swift; but so too did efforts at abridgement and popularization. In his *Battle of the Books* he described how Homer hurled Perrault at Fontenelle and dashed out both their brains.[147] He disdained reliance on commonplace books, indexes, and epitomes that seemed designed to save one the trouble of "reading and thinking."[148] Indeed, there seems to have been no genre, no sort of printed product that met with Swift's approval.

The same sense of being victimized by overproduction that had alarmed Leibniz and other librarians who faced a "horrible mass of books" had its counterpart in Swift's writings.[149] But the difficulty of organizing a vast and constantly growing collection was not Swift's main concern. Swift became melancholy when he entered a library, less because its contents were hard to arrange than because the best authors got lost in the crowd: "the best Author is as much squeezed, and as obscure, as a Porter at a Coronation."[150] Even worse, in his view, was the rapid rate of publication, which entailed a constant turnover of products. "The concern I have most at Heart," he wrote in his prefatory letter "To Prince Posterity," was the fate of "poets . . . whose immortal productions" were no longer likely to reach future readers. "Altho' their Numbers be vast and their Productions numerous . . . yet are they hurryed so hastily off the Scene, that they escape our Memory." As Anne Kelly notes, in each of the three works published together in 1704, Swift revisits a scene that is obviously traumatic: "It entails the rapid disappearance of pages posted on street corners to advertise new works. The author prepares a copious List of titles . . . the originals to be posted fresh upon all the Gates and Corners of Streets but returning in a very few Hours . . . he finds they were all torn down and fresh ones in their Places."[151] He penned some verses "on the death of Doctor Swift" (1731), where a country squire goes to the shop of a London publisher and searches in vain for a work by an author whose "way of writing" had become obsolete.[152]

Perhaps it was partly to ensure that his *Tale of a Tub* could not be so hastily hurried off the scene that Swift weighed down his fable with such an elaborate apparatus of title pages, prefaces, dedications, introductions, and the like.[153] The Scriblerians were contemptuous of polymaths and pedantic editors who smothered lines of poetry with learned marginal allusions. When they took on the role of pedantic commentator themselves, it was ostensibly for the purposes of parody and perhaps partly to guide the reactions of readers along desirable lines. But their elaborate and often facetious framing devices may have been devised, also, to give proper heft to a short poem or fable. As noted in the opening lines of Swift's *Tale*: "Whoever hath an Ambition to be heard in a Crowd, must press, and squeeze, and thruste, and climb."[154] It made sense to thicken one's own work if one was aiming at squeezing out the rest.

Swift, of course, managed to overcome the threat of obsolescence and achieve lasting fame by shrewdly calculating the market for printed materials and by cultivating his own personal celebrity. "The death of Dr. Swift" proved to be a literary event with a very long life indeed.

Chapter 4

Eighteenth-Century Attitudes

Hail Mystick Art! which Men, like Angels, taught,
To speak to Eyes and paint unbody'd thought!
Though Deaf, and Dumb; blest Skill, reliev'd by Thee,
We make one Sense perform the Task of Three.
We see, we hear, we touch the Head and Heart,
And take, or give, what each but yields in part.
With the hard Laws of Distance we dispense
And without Sound, apart, commune in Sense;
View, though confin'd; Nay; rule this Earthly Ball,
And travel o'er the wide expanded ALL.
Dead Letters, thus with Living Notions fraught
Prove to the Soul the Telescopes of Thought;
To Mortal Life a deathless Witness give;
And bid all Deeds and Titles last, and live
In scanty Life, ETERNITY we taste;
View the First Ages, and inform the Last.
Arts, Hist'ry, Laws, we purchase with a Look,
And keep, like Fate, all Nature in a BOOK.
—Constantia Grierson, "The Art
of Printing. A Poem" (1764)

Prelude and Preview

Many of the same attitudes that had been manifested in previous centuries were carried over into the long eighteenth century. Tributes to the "divine art" were richly orchestrated and illustrated by printers, engravers, and publishers. Literati continued to complain about vulgarization, with special emphasis on commodification and the profiteering of bookseller-publishers. The latter were invidiously compared with the early master printers of a lost "golden age." At the same time, an emotional investment in the fate of fictitious characters generated fan letters from readers and turned authors into celebrities. A prevailing culture of improvement went together with celebrating the advancement of learning and the invention that made it possible. Concern about overload was taken as indicating the need for new reference works, especially updated encyclopedias.

Whereas the replaying of earlier themes with variations characterized the literary scene, departures from precedent marked political discourse within the Atlantic world. Whether printing was welcomed or deplored, there was general agreement that it had fundamentally altered the conduct of affairs of state. In Georgian England, the Wilkes affair demonstrated how disenfranchised subjects could be mobilized to take political action. In Bourbon France, the emergence of "public opinion" as a new force was much discussed. The replacement of political oratory by printed discourse was welcomed by French Academicians, who associated demagoguery and religious "enthusiasm" with speech, and thoughtful appraisal with reading. This view was common among French Revolutionary leaders, such as Condorcet, who believed that the use of print would lead to the ultimate triumph of reason over revelation and science over superstition. This was neither the first time nor the last one that the capacity of the printed word to excite emotional responses was underestimated.

Literary Responses: Mystic Art/Mercenary Trade

The poem with which this chapter starts provides a useful reminder that reader response has a "mystical" component. It was composed by a learned lady who was acquainted with Jonathan Swift. It conveys a positive, celebratory attitude that is in marked contrast to the views of the satirist. Whereas Swift reflected the anxieties of an ambitious author, Grierson adopts the posture of an enthralled reader who endows print with remarkable life-enhancing powers. In this regard, her treatment also contrasts with that of the post-Tridentine Church. Among Catholic controversialists after Trent, the dead letters of printed texts were invidiously contrasted with the spoken word and the living presence of the priest. For Grierson, however, through the magic of print, one sense is able to perform the task of three.[1] Distance, time, and even mortality are overcome. The armchair traveler is enabled to survey the whole wide expanded universe, relive the entire course of human history, and commune with fellow readers who are dispersed.

The poem is concerned solely with the experience of the reader. The mystical component is activated by reading books, not by producing or marketing them. One might assume, wrongly, that the poem reflected a learned lady's distance from the prosaic actualities of printing and book-selling. Grierson certainly was a learned lady. But she was also the wife, assistant, and sometime proofreader of the king's printer in Dublin. Her poem, far from indicating a distance from the printing shop, reflected a venerable printing house tradition, one that went back to the earliest days of the wooden handpress, when humanist editors and correctors drew on classical mythology to compose their encomiums. To be sure, the references to telescopes and the "wide expanded ALL" postdate the age of Erasmus.[2] But the reference to angelic powers is in keeping with Renaissance tributes. One recalls how the rector of the Sorbonne in 1470 depicted printing as a gift of the gods and compared Gutenberg to Bacchus and Ceres.[3] Grierson's concern with the enthralled reader also looks forward to very recent publishing strategies where "the pleasures of imaginative absorption" play a significant part in decisions to select or promote a given work of fiction.[4]

Grierson's was by no means the only eighteenth-century poem in English in praise of printing to come from someone associated with the trade. One pamphlet of 1752 that combined excerpts from printing histories with brief bits of rhymed verse and one long poem seems worth singling out. One jingle evokes the *Book of Martyrs* tradition: "The noble art of printing found / No sooner but it Rome did wound / and ever since, with nimble Ray / Spreads knowledge to a perfect Day." The long poem is titled *A Contemplation on the Mystery of Man's Regeneration in Allusion to the Mystery of Printing*. It starts: "Great blest Master-Printer, / Come into thy Composing-Room: / Wipe away our foul Offences; / Make, O make our Souls and Senses, / The Upper and the Lower-Cases."[5] It suggests that the "metaphoric excess" of Benjamin Franklin's famous epitaph (in which Franklin imagines his resurrection as appearing in "a new and more perfect Edition, Corrected & amended") was by no means peculiar to the prototypical American man of letters.[6]

The colony of Virginia, which had been inhospitable to printing under two governors in the 1680s and '90s, proved more welcoming to Robert Parks in 1730. His printing office in Williamsburg issued the first poem printed in Virginia: "TYPOGRAPHIA: AN ODE, ON PRINTING," by John Markland, a former London pamphleteer turned Virginian lawyer. "Happy the Art, by which we learn / The Gloss of errors to detect / The Vice of Habits to correct / And sacred Truths from falsehood to discern."[7] Some remarkable verses were also offered by the English author of "An Essay on Writing and the Art and Mystery of Printing" (1696). They describe "an art from heaven" that "could transcribe whole books without a hand": "The letters all turn'd mutes, in iron bound, / Never prove vocal, till in ink they're drown'd."[8]

Commemorative volumes in prose also came from printing shops. One notable example was produced by Benjamin Franklin's first English master, Samuel Palmer. Palmer had the unusual distinction of teaching the ten-year-old duke of Cumberland to print "under the eye of his father George II."[9] Palmer died before his history of printing was complete. After his death, it was stitched together by a collaborator, resulting in numerous inconsistencies.[10] It claims to be the first history in English of the fifteenth-century invention. Yet one chapter draws on a previous English account by Richard Atkyns. After complaining that printing, "the nurse and preserver of arts and sciences," had "not left the least sketch of its own history," it goes on to mention early printed records described by previous authorities. Nevertheless it contains some astute observations. For example, it questions the custom of taking the year 1500 as a cutoff point to mark the end of the era of incunabula, in view of the continuing operations of such master printers as Manutius, Badius, Amerbach, and Froben.[11]

One of the eighteenth century's most memorable tributes to printing was presented not in textual but in graphic form. It appeared as an engraved frontispiece in one of the many books that commemorated the 300th anniversary of the invention. As was the case with Constantia Grierson, its author was thoroughly familiar with printing house practices. Prosper Marchand (1678–1754) had himself been a privileged printer in Paris on the rue St. Jacques before he converted to Protestantism in 1709. Thereafter, he took up residence in the Dutch Netherlands, where he spent the ensuing four decades working in diverse capacities in the book business.[12]

Marchand's intimate acquaintance with all aspects of the eighteenth-century book trade included the experience of observing his own book being processed for publication. As was often the case with authors, he found himself at odds with his publisher. He was especially angry because his book failed to appear in time for either the Leipzig or Frankfurt Bookfairs of 1739.

The usual authorial impatience at delay was intensified by anxiety over beating out competitors who were rushing to press with commemorative volumes.[13] Marchand's book finally appeared in the spring of 1740, having missed the important deadline. The author blamed not only his publisher but also printing workers for holding up the project and wrote angrily about their laziness and dissipation.

There is a striking contrast between the actual operations that vexed the impatient author and the idealized ones depicted at the top of his first page. Minerva has taken charge of foundry and printing shop. The motto "Ars Artium Conservatrix" is held by putti, who are portrayed playfully doing the tasks that were normally undertaken by sweaty, grimy workingmen. We are at a considerable distance from the actual operations of which Marchand complained. Yet we are not entirely out of the orbit of early modern artisans. Minerva had served as a kind of patron saint for journeymen typographers. Sixteenth-century Lyonnaise printing workers had carried an image of the goddess through the streets on festival days.[14] The connection goes back to Gutenberg's era. There is a reference by Fust's son-in-law, Peter Schoeffer, to the birth of printing in Mainz under the aegis of Minerva.[15] Her presence in the engraving thus represents the perpetuation of a long-lived craft tradition which was coextensive with the age of the wooden handpress.

Of course Minerva's presence signified more than the survival of a particular craft tradition. This particular goddess was loaded, indeed overloaded, with esoteric meanings among eighteenth-century cognoscenti. In the guise of Athena she presided over the numerous learned societies called "Atheneums"—not to mention John Dunton's influential (albeit largely virtual) Athenian Society.[16] Her repeated appearance in earlier engravings by Marchand's best friend and closest collaborator, illustrator Bernard Picart, has given rise to speculation concerning a special Minerval brand of Freemasonry.[17] A characteristic engraving by Picart, showing Minerva and putti, decorates the frontispiece of the 1717 issue of a cosmopolitan review journal published in The Hague.[18] This journal was run by an editorial board to which Marchand belonged along with other French émigrés and some Dutch savants. Members of this board figure prominently in Margaret Jacob's account of the "radical enlightenment."[19]

In 1736 a medal bearing Minerva's image was struck in Berlin to commemorate the founding of a francophone, quasi-Masonic society that sought to propagate Johann Christian Wolff's philosophy. Soon thereafter, Wolff's forbidding Latin works would become more accessible in a multivolume French translation entitled *La Belle Wolffienne* produced by Henri-Samuel

Figure 4.1. Prosper Marchand, *Histoire de l'Origine et des Premiers Progrès de l'Imprimerie* (1740), First Page. Courtesy of the Folger Shakespeare Library.

Formey, a Huguenot émigré who became secretary to the Berlin Academy of Sciences and kept his readers abreast of the Francophone literary scene.[20] On the medal, the image of the goddess was coupled with the celebrated motto of the Enlightenment: "Sapere Aude!" [Dare to Know!].[21]

Minerva appears in a loftier position on the frontispiece to Marchand's work. Together with Mercury, she escorts the spirit of printing as it descends from the heavens holding a wooden handpress. The instrument is received by five European powers, each shown holding medallions with engraved portraits of celebrated master printers. As noted elsewhere,[22] Marchand was responsible for the iconography. The grouping of European nations and the selection of printers for the medallions convey his particular approach to printing history. His text, as well as its illustrations, reflect his anticlerical views and suggest that he accepted the Lutheran view of printing as heaven-sent to aid the antipapist cause.[23]

Not all eighteenth-century writers invoked angelic powers and the Goddess of Wisdom when they considered the operations of the wooden hand-press. (Indeed, the goddess herself eventually became tainted by association with tawdry bestsellers. William Lane's Minerva Press, which started in 1770, "was a byword for sensational and violently sentimental novels.")[24]

As the previous chapter suggested, men of letters often took a more jaundiced view of printing than did printers and publishers. Jonathan Swift's circle of friends was especially successful in conveying a darker vision. This vision was graphically embodied in a print that appeared in two successive issues of the *Grub Street Journal* published in October 1732. It was reproduced in the 1920s in Ralph Straus's study of the much hated and much abused publisher-bookseller Edmund Curll. It has surfaced again in recent studies in a way that suggests it appeals also to the postmodern imagination.[25] The print is usually taken as a caricature of Curll, who is shown wearing a monstrous mask and performing multiple roles as pamphleteer, journalist, printer, publisher, pornographer, and literary agent.

No doubt Curll is the butt of several of the visual jokes in this particular satiric print. But the significance of the caricature is not confined to scoring points against the bookseller-publisher who became notorious as Pope's bête noire (and who appears in the print costumed as a bête noire). The texts beneath the picture indicate a wider range of concerns. The disreputable aspects of popular journalism loom large, but other topics are also discussed. Of particular interest are those passages which satirize commemorative histories of printing and thus provide an intriguing counterpoint to Marchand's

Figure 4.2. Marchand, *Histoire de l'Origine et des Premiers Progrès de l'Imprimerie* (1740), Frontispiece. Courtesy of the Folger Shakespeare Library.

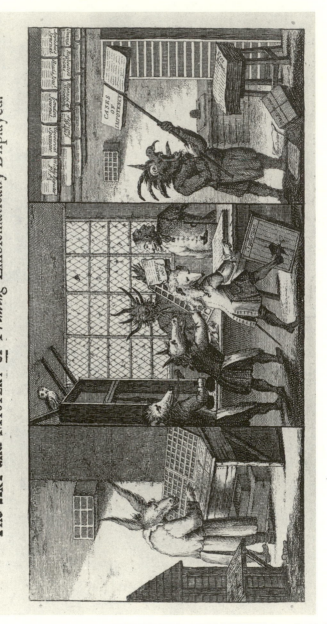

Figure 4.3. *Grub Street Journal* 147, October 26, 1732, first page. Courtesy of the Folger Shakespeare Library.

celebratory text. Incidentally, both images—of printing as a heavenly gift and as a bestial enterprise—were produced in the same decade of the 1730s.[26]

In contrast to Marchand's depiction of master printers such as Gutenberg and Caxton on commemorative medallions in heroic guise, the *Grub Street Journal* describes an encounter with black and dirty newsboys who were *so* black and dirty that they were known as "printers' devils." They are overheard discussing the origin of their name, which is derived from a Monsieur De Vile or DeVille who purportedly came to England with William the Conqueror. Among his descendants, one son worked for the famous Caxton in the 1470s—first as an errand boy, then as an apprentice. After he became a master, he was known as the printer Deville.

In another version, "upon a very reputable account," John Faustus (German, Johann Fust of Mainz) was the first inventor of printing, "which art so amazed the world that they thought him a conjurer and called him Dr. Faustus and his art the black art. As he kept a constant succession of boys to run on errands who were always very black, these they called devils." The mock historical inquiry on the origins of the printer's devil concludes with the comment that "printers use devils as booksellers use authors . . . all the world agrees their God is MAMMON."[27]

Another section deals with the Janus-like figure who is supervising the shop. There is an evocation of Renaissance tributes to printing. The two-faced figure is said to represent the art of typography itself, which looks both to the past and to the future—which retrieves the transactions of past ages and transmits them to posterity. But Janus is described as being two-faced in another sense. In the guise of the bookseller, he responds to the customer who asks how a book is selling by replying, "extremely well." But to the author who asks the same question he replies: "very indifferently." In the guise of a printer, Janus issues books which are godly and books which are lewd. As a mercenary author, the same figure defends both virtue and immorality and places his pen at the disposal of Whigs and Tories alike.

The text encompasses divisions of labor within the printing office. The conventional history of the trades is satirized in the course of settling scores with personal enemies. Dog, horse, and swine are assigned multiple roles as Grubian authors and printing workers. The passages that deal with animals bristle with allusions to the literary and journalistic politics of the day. To pursue them here would take us far afield. But there is one creature which seems worth further notice. Minerva's owl is shown accompanying the wooden handpress in its descent from the heavens in Marchand's version. It

Figure 4.4. Alexander Pope, *The Dunciad*, title pages from the 1728 ed. left; 1729 Variorum ed. right. Courtesy of the Folger Shakespeare Library.

is transmogrified into an anti-Minerval owl, shown sitting atop a bookcase in a printing office. This Grub Street owl is associated not with wisdom but with stupidity—not with clear sight but (as is true of real owls) with weak vision. This is the same owl, familiar to all Pope scholars, that figures in *The Dunciad* title pages: in one edition, alone, in the other sitting on top not of a bookcase but of a pile of worthless books carried by an ass.[28] This owl belongs not to the goddess of Wisdom, daughter of Jove, but to "Dulness, daughter of Chaos and Eternal Night."[29]

Pallas for Wisdom priz'd her favorite Owl,
Pope for its Dulness chose the self-same Fowl:
Which shall we choose, or which shall we despise,
If Pope is witty, Pallas is not wise.[30]

The contrasting images, heavenly and bestial, may be taken to represent two of the literary fictions which prevailed in the eighteenth century, according to Dustin Griffin.[31] *The Grub Street Journal* caricature thus embodies the Scriblerian fiction of the author's fall from grace into the diabolic zone inhabited by money-grubbing printers and booksellers. The image of printing as a gift of the Gods evokes the category Griffin calls the fiction of the Republic of Letters—a fiction that, he says, originated in France. When contextualizing the two fictions, Griffin seems to be on target when he points to the London milieu associated with Curll and his colleagues. But when dealing with developments across the Channel, he stresses the political absolutism of Bourbon rulers and thus, in my view, points in the wrong direction. It is true that English writers, such as John Dryden and some of his successors, tended to contrast the generous patronage of French kings with the negligent attitude of English rulers. They envied royal sponsorship of a French Académie that presumably guarded French literature from contamination.[32] Certainly the German-speaking Hanoverians were unlikely to be compared (as was Louis XIV) with Maecenas or Augustus.

Nevertheless, the Bourbon realm is not an entirely appropriate context within which to situate a Republic of Letters. The idea of a Respublica Litterarum originated not in France but in Renaissance Italy.[33] It was initially propagated by wandering scholars, such as Erasmus, who frequented printing offices in diverse regions. By the eighteenth century, to be sure, it had become a francophone rather than a Latin construct. Yet it remained populated by writers who represented a "third force" (as described in the previous chapter). It proved most compelling to those French-speaking expatriates and refugees who found employment in printing offices established outside France. As had been true of the English Marian exiles, the émigrés had a special reason for welcoming Gutenberg's invention: it provided them with opportunities to continue preaching and teaching abroad even when barred from their pulpits at home.

Whereas the *Grub Street Journal* emanated from London, the journal entitled *Nouvelles de la République des Lettres* was not issued from Paris, let alone from Versailles. It was the first of a swelling stream of review journals that were issued as spinoffs from a far-flung book trade run by publishers in the Dutch Netherlands. These publishers and booksellers employed former preachers and teachers to serve as editors and reporters. The Huguenot exodus from France supplied the lion's share of writers and introduced the word *refugee* into the French vocabulary, but editors were also supplied by disaffected Swiss émigrés, many from Calvinist Geneva.

The new journals departed from earlier literary traditions by abandoning Latin for French. They thus played a role in the emergence of French as the lingua franca of the eighteenth-century republic of letters. (French was acknowledged to be *the* universal language by eighteenth-century Italians, Prussians, and Russians.) But even while helping to propel the spread of French, they undercut the policies of the French crown. Far from reinforcing the linkage between *pouvoir* and *savoir*, between power and knowledge—a linkage which had marked the cultural politics of Bourbon France—the cosmopolitan review journals tended to uncouple *pouvoir* from *savoir*, disconnecting the knowledge industry and literary criticism from French royal power.

From the 1680s until the French Revolution, foreign firms engaged in francophone publication created a relatively autonomous field of operations, one which posed a persistent challenge to the hegemonic claims made by the French crown. In the very first issue of his *Nouvelles* Pierre Bayle had elaborated on the fraternal bonds that linked all men of letters and learning. We are all, he wrote in his preface, equally children of Apollo. He also contrasted the constraints imposed on authors by royal officials and censorious churchmen in France with the freedom enjoyed by expatriates abroad. He thus fixed an invidious comparison between state controls and cosmopolitan freedom into a permanent mold.

Within the context supplied by a far-flung cosmopolitan book trade, the praise of printing had flourished before it became common in France. According to Hans-Jürgen Lüsebrink, Turgot's great tribute to printing in his address of 1750 to the Sorbonne[34] represented a departure from previous trends. Of the many accounts of printing consulted by Lüsebrink, those which were written before the mid-century tended to be purely descriptive, confined to outlining with more or less detail the various technical processes that the craft of printing entailed. Accounts written after the 1750s, however, elaborate on the praiseworthy consequences of the invention and describe how it enhanced rational faculties, demolished error, destroyed prejudices, and in general served as a motor of progress which the ancients had lacked.[35]

These findings, which are based on surveying entries in a large number of eighteenth-century French dictionaries and encyclopedias, provide Lüsebrink with a background for his fascinating account of the "fetishism of printing" during the French Revolution. But the revolutionary apotheosis of Gutenberg, like Turgot's address, represented the culmination of a more venerable and more cosmopolitan tradition than can be ascertained by studying reference works published within the Bourbon kingdom.

The émigré editors, engravers, publishers, and literati looked back to the earlier days of the Latin Respublica Litterarum as if to a golden age.[36] Indeed, they contributed to perpetuating and revivifying Erasmian traditions. When the collected works of Erasmus, which had been either expurgated or banned in Catholic regions, were published in the late seventeenth century, they were issued from Amsterdam under the direction of Pierre Bayle's rival as a leading editor of the cosmopolitan francophone press, Jean LeClerc.

Now Erasmus, who "Stemm'd the wild Torrent of a barb'rous Age, / And drove those Holy Vandals off the Stage,"[37] was also admired by Alexander Pope. The Augustan poet owned numerous volumes of Erasmus's work and courted the displeasure of other English Catholics by attacking Erasmus's ignorant and monkish opponents.[38] As noted elsewhere, Erasmus had celebrated the divine art for creating a library without walls. He had also taken full advantage of print in carving out his own career. But that did not prevent him, especially as he grew older and after religious warfare erupted, from expressing disillusionment with the proliferation of bad new books that threatened to put good old authors in the shade. Pope went much further than Erasmus in denouncing "swarms of new books" and rarely if ever celebrated Gutenberg's invention. But he was by no means singleminded about the uses of print.

In this regard the dramatic contrast provided by juxtaposing two (divine and diabolic) images is more than a little misleading. The Marchand engraving and the Grub Street print represent two extreme poles. The fluctuations that took place in between are not so easily pictured but need attention nonetheless. On both sides of the Channel, reactions were more mixed and nuanced than any two images or literary fictions might suggest. Just as the image of playful putti in a printing shop gives no hint of Marchand's low opinion of those who actually produced his book, so too the caricature of Curll in his hellish "literatory" does not do justice to the complex attitudes of the Scriblerians toward the printed word. Some of the complexities of Swift's views of print were noted in the previous chapter. Here I want to take up the case of Swift's fellow Scriblerian.

There were "two Popes: the Pope who loved print and the Pope who hated it. The Pope who hated print loathed . . . Grub Street scandal, party pamphlets . . . scholarly editions, boring poems, most plays, critics and

booksellers. . . . But the other Pope . . . was fixated on print," loved its looks
and played with all its devices.[39] The latter figure also ran his own press and
promoted his own editions and poems to the point where he became "the
most proficient literary entrepreneur of his era."[40]

This "other Pope" was described almost a century ago by a discerning
bibliographer: "If Pope is not the greatest among English poets, he is the
greatest advertiser and publisher among them."[41] The description has been
cited repeatedly and documented more fully since the 1920s by many authorities who specialize in Pope studies.

Nevertheless the anti-print Pope continues to dominate general treatments of the eighteenth-century literary scene. As Marcus Walsh notes in two
pertinent articles, the idea that an "anarchic proliferation of books produced
. . . a sense of apocalyptic horror and revulsion has achieved the status of an
orthodoxy."[42] Studies that approach Pope's career from different vantage
points tend to reinforce each other on this point. The apocalyptic finale(s) of
The Dunciad are almost always cited in its support.

Some authorities stress the role of political contingency in shaping Pope's
negative stance. The Hanoverian succession ("Dunce the second succeeding
Dunce the first") and Walpole's long ministry deprived the poet of patrons
in high places and forced him to experience the "stigma of print" even while
watching a succession of lesser poets (or Dunces) win glittering prizes they
did not deserve. The infuriating spectacle led him to take gloomy satisfaction
in depicting, in *The Dunciad*, the final triumph of Chaos and Darkness:

> Lost is his God, his country, ev'ry thing;
> And nothing left but Homage to a King!
> The vulgar herd turn off to roll with Hogs,
> To run with Horses, or to hunt with Dogs;
> But, sad example! never to escape
> Their Infamy, still keep the human shape.[43]

According to one critic, Pope was drawing on Virgil's account of how
the death of patronage under an uncaring and alien monarch paved the way
for the barbarian onslaught that brought chaos and death.[44] Another critic
points to more recent precedents entailing religious warfare and civil discord:
Pope was engaged in "defining a print 'crisis'" that had been "underway for
more than two centuries," writes Harold Weber. His portrayal of disorder
was expressed in a language that had previously been used by the state when

confronted by swarms of oppositional pamphlets.[45] Yet another interpretation cites Edmund Spenser's poetic image of "Error's Vomit," "full of books and papers," with "deformed monsters . . . blacke as inke" as a precedent for Pope's "phobic reaction."[46] The most influential poet in this connection was Pope's eminent predecessor and fellow Catholic, John Dryden. Dryden had made "dullness" a fashionable literary topic[47] and had conveyed his disgust with the democratizing effects of print upon sacred texts by means of power-ful metaphors:

> While crowds unlearn'd with rude Devotion warm,
> About the Sacred Viands buzz and swarm,
> the Fly-blown Text creates a crawling Brood:
> And turns to Maggots what was meant for Food.[48]

In addition to poetics and politics, Pope was clearly affected by the eco-nomics of the printed book trade:

> Contemporary opinion was . . . concerned with the new influence
> of the booksellers . . . [that] had the effect of turning literature itself
> into a mere market commodity. . . . [According to] Defoe in 1725:
> 'Writing . . . is becoming a very considerable branch of the English
> Commerce. The Booksellers are the Master Manufacturers. . . . The
> . . . Writers, . . . and all other Operators with Pen and Ink are the
> workmen. . . . ' Defoe did not condemn this commercialization but
> most . . . did so in emphatic terms. . . . What Pope and his friends
> were really alarmed about was the subjection of literature to the
> economic laws of *laissez-faire*.[49]

Ian Watt's pioneering "marxisant" commentary has been elaborated by oth-ers, most notably by Laura Brown, who asserts that "the attack on the capital-ization of the printing industry . . . is the main explicit enterprise of *The Dunciad*."[50] Brown does not deny that Pope was himself deeply involved in the enterprise he attacked. She appreciates that his relation to the printing industry was "problematic and ambivalent."[51] "He understood the industry better than his publishers, besting them in commercial and contractual agree-ments . . . and was a commercial innovator on his own behalf." In contradic-tion to his lifelong claim that he cared nothing for profits, Pope made an effort to meet the demand for cheaper, smaller-scale editions.[52] He was himself so deeply involved in the printing industry and so conflicted about it that his poem embodied all the cultural contradictions of a rising capitalist order:

> Despite its attack on the commodification of literary culture, then, *The Dunciad* represents one of the period's most detailed expressions in poetic form of the workings of capitalist ideology, and it enacts that ideology's deepest and most essential contradiction.[53]

> The fetishization of the commodity, the early energies of a new mode of production and the power and violence through which it is institutionalized—these are the . . . paradoxes of Pope's major poems.[54]

Yet another influential theorist argues that the decline of patronage or the rise of capitalism were less consequential for *The Dunciad* than the anesthetizing effects of the medium of print itself. According to Marshall McLuhan, Pope "has not received his due as a serious analyst of the intellectual malaise of Europe." The poet understood that print had conferred upon Dunces an "unlimited" power . . . to shape and befog the human intellect."

> It is to *The Dunciad* that we must turn for the epic of the printed word . . . here is the explicit study of the plunging of the human mind into the sludge of an unconscious engendered by the book . . . the increasing separation of the visual faculty from the interplay with the other senses leads to the rejection from consciousness of most of our experience, and the consequent hypertrophy of the unconscious. This ever-enlarging domain Pope calls the world "of Chaos and old Night."[55]

McLuhan's views have received support from Alvin Kernan. The latter also takes *The Dunciad* not as a mock epic but as a truly prophetic one. Having fallen into the hands of unscrupulous entrepreneurs such as Curll, Kernan argues, print was far from being a "mystic art" that stimulated imaginative faculties. It had become a "dullish mechanical, undiscriminating, repetitive, mass medium" that privileged mediocrity and squeezed out talent. "Pope would not have found fault with Marshall McLuhan's generalization that print plunged 'the human mind into the sludge of an Unconscious engendered by the book.'" The apocalyptic finale of Book IV pointed to "the death of literature"—the title used for Kernan's subsequent book.

> a flood of printer's ink was a darkness that spread across the land, staining, as in his [Pope's] memorable image of Fleet ditch running into the silver Thames, the white page, darkening the minds of the people and their rulers, obliterating polite letters, and finally extinguishing all light, to leave the land in ancient night and ignorance.[56]

As a black stain upon the land,

> Print spreads through and eventually corrupts not only the book but all polite letters . . . makes simple fools into hack writers . . . turns honest mechanics into greedy printers and simple tradesmen into booksellers without scruples, taste, or morality.[57]

In view of Pope's account of how Curll was tricked into taking an emetic, one might argue that "scruple, taste and morality" were no less lacking among eighteenth-century poets than among their contemporary booksellers.[58] But that is beside the point. The point is that the relevance of the medium of print to the several dark endings of *The Dunciad* is far from clear. Two of the finales to Book IV concern the aftermath of a barbarian onslaught, the return of a "Saturnian age of lead," and the enthronement of the anti-Minerval queen.

> As one by one, at dread Medea's strain,
> The sick'ning stars fade off th'ethereal plain;
> . . . .
> Thus at her felt approach, and secret might,
> Art after Art goes out, and all is Night.
> . . . .
> Lo! thy dread Empire, CHAOS! is restor'd
> Light dies before thy uncreating word:
> Thy hand great ANARCH! lets the curtain fall;
> and Universal Darkness buries all.[59]

However one stretches relevant metaphors, it is hard to see how a dying light and the onset of "Universal Darkness" were intended to evoke images of inky floods staining white pages.

The poem attacks numerous institutions (schools and universities, the Inns of Court, the Grand Tour) as well as presumably dull and dunce-like authors. An ostensibly corrupt and venal prime minister was no less a target than the second-rate poet or greedy bookseller. There is no need to exclude any of the numerous explanations offered for the poet's disaffection. After all, politics, patronage, and book production are not mutually exclusive phenomena.

But it is doubtful, in my view, that the underlying target of the poem was the medium of print. *The Dunciad*'s only explicit reference to the invention appears in the prolegomena of 1729:

> We shall next declare the occasion and the cause which moved our Poet to this particular work. He lived in those days, when (after Providence had permitted the Invention of Printing as a scourge for the Sins of the learned) Paper also became so cheap, and printers so numerous, that a deluge of authors cover'd the land.[60]

Although a "deluge of authors" does entail a flood, it still fails to evoke a "spreading black stain." Moreover, as others have noted, the description of the invention of printing as a "scourge" comes not from the author but from "Martinus Scriblerus," the fictitious product of an elaborate spoof.[61] This parodic figure was not a poet but a pedant. Weren't pedants (in Pope's view) incapable of understanding any poem's true meaning?

To connect a flood of printer's ink with the onset of "Universal Darkness" seems out of keeping with other works produced by Pope. See, for example, his eulogy on Newton mentioned below. Farfetched also is the attribution of post-Freudian (or Jungian) notions of a collective unconscious to an Augustan poet. The attribution of cosmic world historical significance to Pope's apocalyptic finale(s) seems to me to reflect late twentieth-century angst rather more than eighteenth-century attitudes.

A more plausible interpretation of *The Dunciad*'s finale is the one that singles out the phrase "the curtain's fall."[62] The fall of a curtain leaves spectators in the dark only temporarily. It signifies the end of one performance— not the end of the world. As is noted by the poem's editor, far from envisaging any cosmic catastrophe, Pope had designed *The Dunciad* to be the opening salvo in a prolonged paper war: "Speedily will be Published The Progress of Dulness, an Historical Poem, by an Eminent Hand, the Price is

1s6d." Having stirred up angry authors and profiteering booksellers, Pope managed to make publication day a veritable media event.[63]

In this regard, Pope anticipated the tactics employed by Richardson, who accomplished the same feat with the publication of *Pamela*. As author, promoter, and copublisher, Richardson manipulated the novel's reception in such a way as to prolong its popularity and extend its readership. The Scriblerians had, similarly, profited from "the texts they attacked and provoked." Thus Pope's original publication in 1728 initiated a prolonged cycle. When "the Empire of Dulness struck back," it did so by generating enough printed material to fill four albums to be exploited by Pope when preparing his variorum edition.[64]

In the case of *Pamela*, the initial event was skillfully designed to maintain the illusion that an actual correspondence was being placed before the reader. Richardson posed as editor, not author, of the epistolary interchange. He invited his actual readers to become contributors by inserting blank pages in the printed text; the real letters that they sent in were published in subsequent editions.[65] The translations, sequels and parodies that ensued encouraged more interactive reader response and further suspension of disbelief. Plays were written and staged (one by Voltaire, two by Goldoni), poems appeared in newspapers, paintings, engravings, and wax figures were produced and race horses were named. As had been foreshadowed by Don Quixote and Robinson Crusoe, "a literary character emerged as a commodified subject,"[66] to carry on an existence that was detached from the pages of the original narrative but, paradoxically, remained attached to the name of *Pamela*'s creator. The proliferating publicity redounded to the benefit of the author-printer. Richardson's artful "self-effacement," together with his capacity to elicit real tears from real readers, led to his glorification as the "divine Richardson." His death elicited a eulogy from Diderot, who had never met him but who had gasped and sobbed when reading his novel.[67]

The selling of *Pamela* and the sanctification of its author set the pattern for subsequent reactions to characters in novels by authors such as Rousseau and Goethe (and their nineteenth-century successors). The fan mail that was generated, together with all the other commemorative objects, suggests that a "sacre de l'écrivain" (sanctification of the author) occurred well before the coming of the steam press and the roman-fleuve.[68] As noted below, such media events had political as well as literary repercussions—witness the remarkable resonance of the actions of John Wilkes. Benjamin Franklin, who had brought out an edition of *Pamela* in 1742,[69] would be accorded an apotheosis akin to that received by the "divine Richardson."

However popular were the works of Swift and Pope, their attacks fell short of wounding their targets. The much-maligned booksellers found ways of profiting from the publicity that was generated by their opponents. Among others, the "unspeakable Curll" had a special propensity for "turning writers into people who were written about."[70] It was "a blessed age for the mutual felicity of booksellers and authors," noted Swift in *The Tale of a Tub*.[71] Swift may have intended it ironically but, in fact, the counterpoint between original text and controversial context did redound to the benefit of all parties. Said "Bookweight," a bookseller in Henry Fielding's *The Author's Place*, "I love to keep a controversy warm. I have had authors who have writ a pamphlet in the morning, answered it in the afternoon, and compromised the matter at Night."[72]

The pessimistic outlook of the Scriblerians seems to be especially compatible with our own postmodern temper. But it was less compatible with prevailing literary currents during the age of the Whig ascendency. Despite Swift's biting satires, mathematicians, Baconians, and Royal Society publications continued to gain adherents as the century wore on. Pope himself contributed to the apotheosis of Isaac Newton: "Nature and Nature's Laws lay hid in night; / God said, 'Let Newton be!' and all was light."[73]

A prevailing "culture of improvement" provided a favorable environment for tributes to Gutenberg's invention.[74] "He that first invented printing, discovered the use of the Compass, or made public the right use of *Kin Kina* [quinine]," wrote John Locke in his *Essay on Human Understanding*, "did more for the propagation of knowledge, for the supply and increase of useful commodities, and saved more from the grave, than those who built colleges, workhouses and hospitals."[75]

Tributes to Gutenberg's invention were often coupled with disdainful comments. Locke himself wrote to Anthony Collins in an uncomplimentary vein about printers and booksellers:

> Books . . . infect all who trade in them . . . with something very perverse and brutal. Printers, binders, sellers and others that make a trade and gain out of them have universally so odd a turn and corruption of mind, that they have a way of dealing peculiar to themselves, and not conformed to the good of society, and that general fairness that cements mankind.[76]

But not all adverse remarks were aimed at mercenary booksellers. They were also directed at the superstitious priest-ridden age of scribes or "transcribers" (as Palmer called them):

> Before Printing, Old-wives tales were ingeniose: and since Printing came in fashion . . . the ordinary sort of People were not taught to reade. Now-a-dayes Bookes are common, and most of the poor people understand letters; and the many good Bookes and varieties of Turnes of Affaires, have put all the old Fables out of dores; and the divine art of printing and Gunpowder have frightened away Robin-good-fellow and the Fayries.[77]

Joseph Addison, who introduced the term Republic of Letters to English readers,[78] described printing as "this great invention of these latter Ages," an invention that enabled books to achieve immortality: "There is no other Method of fixing those Thoughts which arise and disappear in the Mind of Man, and transmitting them to the last Periods of Time; no other Method of giving a Permanency to our Ideas, and preserving the Knowledge of any particular Person when . . . his Soul [is] retired into the world of Spirits."[79] Not only did printing preserve the thought of long-dead authors, it brought fame to the greatest master printers and glory to the countries that nurtured them. "Elzevir and Aldus were more celebrated than any Dutch Pensioner or Venetian doge. They made Holland and Venice the envy of the greatest of monarchies. Printing was an Art that enhanced the reputation of the People among whom it flourished."[80] To avoid the implication that printing was especially compatible with republics and perhaps less so with monarchies, Addison added a note about Louis XIV installing a press in the palace of the Louvre and commented: "The politest Nations of Europe have endeavored to vie with one another for the Reputation of the finest Printing. Absolute governments, as well as Republicks, have encouraged an Art which seems to be the noblest and most beneficial that ever was invented among the Sons of Man."[81] Despite his welcoming the support provided by royal patrons, Addison did not care much for the use of printing to glorify monarchs. "Had the philosophers and great men of antiquity," he wrote, "been possessed of the Art of Printing," there is no question but that they would have taken advantage of it to "diffuse good sense though the Bulk of a People."[82] The early success of *The Spectator* led him to reflect in a self-congratulatory vein on his success in achieving this goal: "It was said of Socrates, that he brought philosophy down from heaven to inhabit among men; and I shall be ambitious to have it said of me, that I brought philosophy out of closets, libraries, schools and colleges to dwell in clubs and assemblies, at teatables and in coffee houses."[83]

In keeping with this celebrated pronouncement, John Gay asserted that Addison and Steele had rescued learning "out of the hands of pedants and fools" and discovered "the true way of making it lovely to all mankind."[84] Recent studies have pointed out that, for Addison and Steele, "all mankind" actually consisted of a restricted male elite.[85] Those who gathered at tea tables and coffee houses remained at a considerable distance from the inhabitants of Gin Lane. *The Spectator* preached the virtues of moderation and politeness in the hopes of restraining the unbridled enthusiasm that had characterized displays of religiosity. It reflected a preference for oligarchy over democracy. Nevertheless, copies of the journal found their way into a wider public domain and were read with profit by autodidacts, such as Benjamin Franklin.

Addison himself expressed occasional doubt that learning had indeed been rescued from fools. He shared with earlier writers a sense of disenchantment, in view of all the worthless stuff that came off the groaning press. Reworking one of Juvenal's satires on "the itch of writing," he inveighed against numerous periodical writers who employed the art of printing for unworthy purposes: "it is a melancholy thing to consider that the art of printing which might be the greatest blessing to mankind should prove detrimental to us and that it should be made use to scatter prejudice and ignorance through a people instead of truth and knowledge."[86]

Like Joseph Addison, Samuel Johnson expressed misgivings about writers who contributed to "the scattering of prejudice and ignorance." In particular, he objected to radical journalists who encouraged the political participation of a disenfranchised "nation out of doors." Although he was himself responsible (from 1738 to 1744) for providing readers of the *Gentleman's Magazine* with disguised reports of parliamentary proceedings, he was "implacably opposed" to the "disquieting influence exerted later by Wilkes, 'Junius,' and the American rebels."[87]

Johnson's melancholy reflections on the art of printing, however, had less to do with partisan politics than with the fate of heavy scholarly tomes. "No place affords a more striking conviction of the vanity of human hopes, than a publick library, for who can see the wall crouded on every side by mighty volumes, the works of laborious meditation and accurate enquiry, now scarcely known but by the catalogue . . . without considering how many hours have been wasted in vain endeavors."[88] Here Johnson seems to share the complaints of the Scriblerians concerning overproduction: "A lumber-house of books in every head, / For ever reading, never to be read!" Else-where, however, he appeared to be a true believer in the benefits of Guten-berg's invention—to the point where Macaulay would later chastise him for asserting with "arrogant absurdity that there could have been no civilization before the invention of printing."[89] He was alerted to the problems posed by proliferation when he was hired by the bookseller Thomas Osborne to help catalogue the 50,000 volumes, formerly in the Harleian Library, recently purchased by Osborne. In addition to attracting potential purchasers by issu-ing a catalogue, Osborne hoped to recoup part of his investment by reprint-ing selected pamphlets contained in the collection and issuing them as the multivolume *Harleian Miscellany*. Johnson had a hand in selecting the articles to be reprinted and wrote the introduction to the collection. As might be expected, his introduction emphasized the importance of fugitive pieces.[90]

His praise of pamphlets was clearly not disinterested. Nevertheless, it provided a marked contrast to the phobic reaction of seventeenth-century writers who objected to the disorder created by "swarming pamphleteers." It also contrasted with the reaction of Sir Thomas Bodley, who famously ex-cluded printed plays, pamphlets, and other "baggage books" and "riffe raf-fes" from his Oxford library.[91] Johnson not only welcomed the proliferation of small tracts and fugitive pieces, but also argued that they constituted a national treasure. Collecting and preserving evidence of conflicting opinions was a way of demonstrating the special English virtue of maintaining a free press.

> There is, perhaps, no Nation, in which it is so necessary, as in our own, to assemble, from Time to Time, the *small* tracts and *fugitive* Pieces, which are occasionally published: For, besides the general Subjects of Enquiry, which are cultivated by us, in common with every other learned Nation, our Constitution . . . gives Birth to a Multitude of Performances, which would either not have been writ-ten, or could not have been made publick in any other Place.[92]

Johnson's contribution to the *Harleian Catalogue* was no more disinter-ested than his introduction to the *Miscellany*. The *Catalogue* was "an advertis-ing instrument, and praise for the authors of the books for sale was required."[93] But Johnson's enthusiasm for most of the authors he was listing seemed to go beyond the call of duty. The longest tributes were devoted to Francis Bacon and J. J. Scaliger, the most extravagant being reserved for the latter. It culminated in a familiar citation from Daniel Heinsius concerning "a bottomless pit of erudition, the sea of knowledge, the sun of learning, the divine offspring of a divine father, a godlike man, indeed Nature's greatest work."[94] Granted that a positive approach was built into the task of helping with a bookseller's advertisement, Johnson was still able to exhibit personal preferences by singling out certain works for special notice. In keeping with the prevailing views of his compatriots, he exhibited antipapist views, sympathizing with printers (such as Etienne Dolet) who were martyred and with authors whose works were put on the *Index*. But unlike many of his contemporaries, he also favored the often scorned translators, redactors, abstractors, epitomizers, and (of course) lexicographers.[95]

The task of cataloguing left him not with a sense of being overwhelmed by proliferating disorder, but rather with a "sense of awe for the achievements of scholarship and printing in the previous three centuries."[96] He also saw an opportunity to make use of the vast range of materials that would come to fruition later on. While working on the collection, he encountered almost all the books that he would later use for compiling his *Dictionary* and that he would also use when helping his friend, Thomas James, produce a multivolume medical reference work. (James's work was translated into French by the future encyclopedist Diderot.) After the *Dictionary* was completed, he thought of ways to fulfill Comenius's early vision of a "pan-sophia" and dreamt of setting up a universal review journal to be called *The Bibliothèque*, which would abridge and abstract "for popular consumption in England all the important books produced in Europe."[97]

Whereas Johnson expressed admiration for bottomless pits of erudition and the scholarly achievements recorded over the course of three centuries, Diderot and d'Alembert tended, rather, to discount the Latin learning of earlier scholars and to regard their heavy-handed displays of erudition with the same impatience as had been exhibited by Fontenelle. They all seem to have borrowed the same themes from Montaigne's "On Pedantry." In a sense they were biting the hands that fed them, given the debt owed to previous learned compilers. Although Diderot knew enough Latin and Greek to profit from consulting the tomes of Alsted and Brucker, he was scarcely complimentary. "Those Germanic compilations, bristling against all reason and taste, with Hebrew, Arabic, Greek and Latin . . . are very big already, are growing bigger still, will ever grow bigger and will be all the worse for it."[98]

D'Alembert praised Fontenelle for teaching scholars to "throw off the yoke of pedantry."[99] He condemned the "multitude of erudite men immersed in the learned languages to the point of disdaining their own. . . . [they] gloried proudly in practicing a science that was . . . often ridiculous and sometimes barbarous."[100]

Depreciation of the Latin learning of Renaissance scholars was coupled with pleased amazement at the advancement of learning in recent years. D'Alembert's tribute to Bacon for recognizing the worthlessness of scholastic philosophers was followed by a paean to the new philosophy: "Think of the progress that has been made . . . in the sciences and the arts! Think of the many truths that were unveiled today which were not dreamed of then!"[101] That previous works of reference had failed to incorporate remarkable advances in such fields as mathematics, physics, and even *belles lettres* showed the need for a new encyclopédie—an updated reference work upon which posterity could build.

Johnson's views, in part at least, had reflected the demands of his job. He had, after all, been hired by a bookseller to advertise a collection of books for sale. The collection consisted largely of learned Latin tomes. To have questioned its value would have been counterproductive. Expressing awe and admiration was more likely to attract prospective purchasers. The encyclopedists' repudiation of outdated reference works and enthusiasm for recent progress was no less self-serving. To impress prospective subscribers with the desirability of a new encyclopedia, the obsolescence of previous ones needed to be made clear. The theme of improvement was built into *L'Encyclopédie.* It would be odd indeed to find a publisher or editor informing potential purchasers that their new reference work was inferior to previous ones.

Nevertheless, d'Alembert (like Johnson) was also expressing personal convictions. He was fully cognizant of the remarkable advances in the mathematical sciences that had occurred under the aegis of such masters as Descartes, Pascal, Leibniz, and Newton. "Progress in the "physico-mathematical sciences," he wrote in his *Discours préliminaire,* "may be considered the most incontestable monument of the success to which the human mind can rise by its efforts."[102]

Diderot was no less alert to advances in mathematics,[103] but was especially intent on improvements in the mechanical arts, such as the invention of printing itself. In the article on "Art," he cited Francis Bacon ("a philosopher whom I can never tire of praising because I can never tire of reading him")[104] on the three inventions unknown to the ancients. As Giles Barber

notes, Diderot "made technology carry his ideology."[105] He had a good word
for booksellers: "the most noble of all commercial professions"[106] (booksellers
had helped free Diderot from imprisonment in Vincennes). With regard to
printing, he put in a good word for the often neglected typefounders such as
Garamond and Granjon, who were, he wrote, too often eclipsed by the great
fame of printers such as the Estiennes and Elseviers.[107] His enthusiasm for
new instruments knew no bounds. He went so far as to chide Montaigne for
failing to be enthusiastic about improvements in machines of war.[108] He
was also insistent on the dignity of labor and the need to valorize artisanal
labor.[109]

Both editors also were grudging in acknowledging their chief precursor,
Ephraim Chambers. He was chided, perhaps unfairly, in d'Alembert's *Discours préliminaire* for relying too much on book learning and not investigating workshop routines: "everything was lacking on the subject of the
mechanical arts."[110] Enthusiasm for artisans and their work was accompanied
by a devaluation of the liberal arts:

> The liberal arts have sung their own praise long enough; they should
> now raise their voice in praise of the mechanical arts and free them
> from the degradation in which they have so long been held by preju-
> dice . . . . The artisans have thought they deserved disdain because
> they were in fact disdained; let us teach them to think better of
> themselves.[111]

Of course, there was one mechanical art that was especially well suited
to "singing its own praise." *L'Encyclopédie* famously devoted a great many
pages of text along with many plates[112] to "Imprimerie," "Imprimeur," and
"Caractères d'imprimerie" (printing, printers, and typestyles). The article on
printing provided a step-by-step description of the "mechanical exercises"
entailed in handpress printing; following the example set by Moxon, it offered a long and detailed self-reflexive section, composed in the printing shop
by the *prote*, or foreman, who was supervising the printing of *L'Encyclopédie*.
The rest of the article, together with the essay on "Imprimeur," was written
by Diderot's chief collaborator, the Protestant savant and chevalier, Louis de
Jaucourt (1704–79).[113]

In the rest of the "Imprimerie" article, Jaucourt referred the reader to
the numerous histories of printing that were circulating in his day and singled
out for special notice the *Annales Typographiques* of Michael Mattaire. He

Figure 4.5. Two plates from *L'Encyclopédie*, ed. Diderot and d'Alembert (1751–1772). Courtesy of the Folger Shakespeare Library.

paused over Gutenberg and early printing in Mainz. After mentioning a few of Gutenberg's successors, he offered an impassioned tribute to the preservative powers of the new medium.

In the accompanying article on "Imprimeur,"[114] he provided biographical sketches of some forty-odd celebrated early printers. This often neglected prosopographical section is worth pausing over. As was the case with Prosper Marchand's earlier commemorative volume, the treatment of early printers is strongly inflected by the author's anticlerical, antipapist sentiment. We are told about Etienne Dolet's being burned in Paris because of his religious views, about how Jean Crespin left Paris for Geneva to be free to profess his Calvinist views, and about André Wechel's lucky escape from the violence of the St. Barthomew's Day Massacre. There is also an anti-Trinitarian comment in a passage on de Colines's edition of the Greek New Testament.

Most space and praise in the article "Imprimeur" are lavished on members of the Estienne dynasty, who are dubbed "les rois de l'imprimerie." Robert Estienne receives special commendation despite (or because of) his leaving Paris, after arousing the displeasure of the Sorbonne, and moving to Calvinist Geneva: "We owe more to him alone that to all the other savants and artists who worked in France since the days of Francis 1er." His editions of the Greek New Testament contained not a single typographical error. This seemingly impossible perfection had been obtained because the master printer had posted his proofs on college doors and promised to pay any student who spotted an error.

That such perfection was more imaginary than real is suggested by the findings of the acerbic classical scholar Richard Bentley, who claimed to have found some 2,000 instances of corrupt readings in Estienne's biblical editions.[115] But the entry provides a good example of how the scholar printers of the Renaissance were idealized to the point of becoming the objects of a veritable cult.[116] John Aubrey might assert that "all the old Fables had been banished out of doors by the divine art of printing."[117] But if old fables were banished (only to reemerge as children's fairy tales), new ones about the divine art had been created. Commemorative volumes on the history of printing depicted a heroic age that perpetuated the self-congratulatory rhetoric of early printers.

Satirists were quick to poke fun at the cult. Pope produced a dreadful doggerel that playfully put his printer Lintot on the pedestal occupied by the great ones of the past:

Some Colineus praise, some Blaeu / Others account them but so-so.

Some Stephens to the rest prefer / And some old Elzevir.

Others with Aldus would besot us / I for my part admire Lintotus.[118]

In *The Tatler* of April 1710, Addison referred to Tom Folio, a learned idiot, who frequented book auctions and was employed to stock the libraries of great men. "He has a greater esteem for Aldus and Elsevier, than for Virgil and Horace. If you talk of Herodotus, he breakes out into a panegyric upon Harry Stevens."[119] Yet Addison himself rated Aldus and the Elseviers higher than Dutch stadtholders or Venetian doges.

Neither satirists nor scholars did much to undermine the golden age myth which placed the era of the scholar printers at a distance from the eighteenth century, when an iron age of commercialism presumably dawned.[120] Disgust with sharp dealing and unmitigated greed was expressed on all sides. In Great Britain especially, there was a swelling chorus of complaints about a subjugation of literature to commerce which was associated with the new ascendancy of booksellers.[121]

But the Continent was not far behind. Malesherbes wrote about the distance between the heroic age of Plantin and the Estiennes, when publishers were scholars, and his own age, when they had become purely mercenary.[122] Of all those who engage in commerce, Pierre Bayle wrote in 1689, no group is so universally despised for bad faith as the publishers.[123] Prosper Marchand found the cutthroat competition so disgusting, his executor tells us, that after leaving France for The Netherlands and gaining an entry to the local guild, he gave up printing and publishing altogether.[124] Yet the record also shows that when Bayle was forced out of his teaching post, he relied almost entirely (even more than had Erasmus) on the patronage and hospitality of a publisher-bookseller. Marchand also lived out his life as a houseguest of the much maligned species.

Furthermore, horror stories about greed and knavery were not uncommon in earlier eras. "He sets more store by his own good than by the general good, is more concerned for gold than for honor and thinks of nothing but profit."[125] This complaint was directed at the pioneering atlas publisher, W. J. Blaeu, in the so-called golden age of Dutch publishing. The Elseviers, often described as the last representatives of the golden age, not only received fawning dedications as friends of learning, immortals, and demigods, but were also accused of harsh dealings with old acquaintances and, in one instance, of letting the widow of an associate starve.[126] As with all golden ages, even the era of Aldus contains disillusioning evidence when viewed close-up. As references to "iron" and "golden" ages suggest, at least some complaints about the cupidity of booksellers were formulaic, echoing classical precedents that were far removed from eighteenth-century printing and publishing practices.

> Like Martial, most Roman writers knew that the profits of their writing ended up in the pockets of the booksellers, who often combined retail trade with a copying business—and so were, in effect, publishers and distributors too . . . Horace . . . made the obvious comparison: booksellers were the rich pimps . . . and authors . . . were the hardworking but humiliated prostitutes.[127]

There is much to suggest, furthermore, that the cultural and intellectual functions of publisher-booksellers in the age of print were enhanced and not diminished as the centuries wore on. A proliferation of reading societies went together with subscriptions to periodicals, the maintenance of bookshop libraries, and regular gatherings of literary coteries in back rooms.

James Raven calls attention to several eighteenth-century London booksellers who acted as the "conduits of intellectual debate."[128] A prime example was Jacob Tonson (1656–1739), the grandson of a Puritan bookseller, who published Dryden and Congreve, championed Milton and Shakespeare, and served as a "Chief Merchant to the Muses." Raven also cites Maria Edgeworth's poetic eulogy to the publisher bookseller Joseph Johnson (1738–1809). Johnson was stigmatized as a literary middleman "whose only interest in literature could be measured by guineas."[129] Yet he carried on the venerable Continental tradition of using his shop as a gathering place for dissenters, exiles, and radicals. Fuseli, exiled from Zürich, was housed above the bookshop and given work as a translator. Joseph Priestley and Mary Wollstonecraft were frequent visitors. Joel Barlow belonged to a second generation of Americans who used the place as a hospitality center. Tyson's book-length biography of Johnson shows how his shop combined the functions of a business establishment and a cultural center.[130] Similar dual functions were performed by the Société Typographique de Neuchâtel, the Swiss establishment run by Frédéric-Samuel Osterwald and his son-in-law Jean-Elie Bertrand. Robert Darnton's studies, based on the voluminous commercial correspondence conducted by the STN, convey the impression that this enterprise was a purely mercenary one. Osterwald and his son-in-law "wanted to make money rather than to spread *lumières*."[131] Yet both men were also occupied with intellectual and scholarly pursuits. Osterwald's son-in-law was a professor of *belles lettres*, rector of the local college, and editor of the *Journal Helvétique*. Osterwald himself may have been viewed as a harsh master by his printing workers, but, to the numerous men of letters whom he entertained for weeks on end, he was known to be a generous host and helpful patron.[132]

Despite evidence to the contrary, however, the contrast between the avaricious eighteenth-century publisher-bookseller and the generous sixteenth-century master printer was ubiquitous. It was prominent in *L'Encyclopédie*, where relevant articles seemed to celebrate advances in almost all the arts save that of printing. As Roger Chartier notes, there is something paradoxical about finding a paean to progress that contained so many complaints about recent signs of decline. Instead of expressing satisfaction at how far things had progressed, relevant articles in *L'Encyclopédie* seem to be shot through with discontent about all the backsliding that had occurred. Chartier cites complaints about the decline of calligraphy, the mishandling of texts, the failure of authors to make a fair copy, and, especially, the intrusion of greed. He singles out a sentence in the "imprimeur" article to drive his point home: "Once printing was glorious, but now it is only a mercenary craft."[133]

Nostalgia for the lost golden age, however, stopped short of glorifying the age of the scribe. The same article contained a comment about an inferior text that was selected to be printed by the first Paris press: "not even the art of printing could vanquish all traces of barbarism right away."[134] Diderot and d'Alembert regarded medieval times as "hopelessly obscurantist and priest-ridden," and the best thing that could be said about their own century, they thought, was that "it resembled the Middle Ages so little."[135]

Eighteenth-century nostalgia, such as it was, did not take the same form as did a later romantic medievalism. The idealized depictions of early printers who had sacrificed their fortunes (even their lives) while turning out perfect error-free editions served primarily as a means of expressing dissatisfaction with real eighteenth-century printers and publishers. (One recalls the contrast between Marchand's presentation of sixteenth-century printers in heroic guise and his complaints about the real printers who delayed getting his book done on time.) In fact, printing, like bookselling, had always been a mercenary craft, and the actual behavior of many celebrated figures of the past had left much to be desired. As is so often the case, the best of the past was held up against the worst of the present.

The divine powers attributed to the mystic art repeatedly clashed with the realities of a commercial enterprise on earth. But for all that, Gutenberg's invention was assigned a prominent position in the world historical schemes that were set forth by encyclopedists and philosophes.

In his article on "l'imprimerie," Jaucourt himself had offered an impassioned tribute. "By means of print, human thoughts could be preserved and transmitted to the end of time, long after human bodies were turned to dust and their souls had flown to a spirit world." The same theme was sounded in Turgot's address to the Sorbonne on 11 December 1750:

> What new art is suddenly born as if to wing to every corner of the earth the writings and glory of the great men of the past and those still to come. How slow progress has been up to now! For two thousand years, medals made of characters impressed on bronze were familiar to everyone; and then, after countless centuries, it occurs to an obscure individual that characters can be impressed upon paper. All at once the treasures of antiquity are rescued from the dust, pass into every hand, penetrate to every part of the world, bring to light talents hitherto wasted in ignorance and call forth genius from the depths.[136]

Such tributes to printing as "the art which preserves all other arts" provoked a characteristic retort from Rousseau when he set out to create a sensation by attacking ideas of progress. In his contrarian *First Discourse*, he noted that "impious writings" had died with their authors in antiquity because the "art of perpetuating the extravagances of the human mind had not been invented. But, thanks to typography, and the use we make of it, the dangerous dreams of Hobbes and Spinoza will remain forever." A footnote to "typography" attributed disastrous consequences to the invention: "Considering the awful disorders printing has already caused in Europe and judging the future by the progress that this evil makes day by day, one can easily predict that sovereigns will . . . banish this terrible art from their States." The paragraph concludes by praying to God to deliver us from the Enlightenment and fatal arts of our forefathers and give back to us ignorance, innocence, and poverty.[137] Rousseau knew how to make a sophisticated audience sit up and take notice!

Politics in a New Key: The Atlantic Revolutions

The preservative powers of print were prominent in eighteenth-century discourse about arts and letters. The use of the press was praised for protecting learning and letters from the fate suffered by the destruction of the Alexandria Library and for encouraging a cumulative advance in the arts and sciences. It was also regarded with less favor for overloading libraries and vulgarizing learning.

Other aspects of printing came to the fore when writers addressed the political scene. It became apparent that the increasingly widespread use of printing was changing the conditions that had shaped both classical and medieval political institutions. Until mid-century few had dissented from Montesquieu's assertion that the democratic and republican institutions of antiquity were unsuited to large realms: "It is natural to a republic to have only a small territory."[138] Diderot reluctantly agreed: since a democratic government supposes a concert of wills and since a concert of wills supposes men assembled in a rather restricted space, only small republics are feasible.[139] On this point at least Rousseau was in agreement.

After the mid-century, however, the argument was made, most notably by the framers of the American Constitution, that the principle of representation made it possible for republics to grow larger than Montesquieu had envisaged.[140] Destutt de Tracy observed that

> Representation, or representative government, may be considered as
> a new invention, unknown in Montesquieu's time; it was almost
> impossible to put it into practice before the invention of printing,
> which so much facilitates the communication between the constit-
> uents and the representative, and renders it so easy for the former to
> control, and the latter to account for his conduct; and above all,
> which averts those sudden storms, so often excited by the force of
> an impassioned and popular eloquence. It is by no means surprising,
> that it should have remained undiscovered until about three hun-
> dred years after the discovery of that art which has changed the face
> of the universe: it was necessary that other great effects should have
> been produced, before such a conception could be matured.[141]

Time-honored, secretive royal practices also began to be questioned. In the early seventeenth century James I had written a furious letter denouncing members of the House of Commons who dared to "argue and debate publicly of matters far beyond their reach and capacity."[142] His successor, Charles I, issued a royal proclamation against "the excess of lavish and licentious" speech on matters of state: "take heed not to intermeddle by pen or speech with secrets of empire, either at home or abroad."[143] A century later, Trenchard and Gordon were insisting that "All honest magistrates should have their Deeds openly examined and publicly scanned. Only the wicked Governors . . . dread what is said of them."[144] Toward the end of the century, the idea that official actions should be "publicly scanned and openly examined" was winning acceptance. In Anglo-American circles, Addison's boast of bringing philosophy out of schools and closets was seen to apply to politics no less than to philosophy.

> Even in the Republicks of Greece, those boasted mansions of liberty, I question whether the natural rights of man were so generally understood as they are now among us. In those times, there was no mode of communicating the instructions of wise and learned men but in writing; they were . . . confined within a narrow sphere, and enlightened only a few, whereas among us, by the happy invention of printing, and our noble privelege of the liberty of the press, information reaches unto all.
>
> There never was any extensive society in which knowledge was so generally diffused and in which so great a number of men are in the habit of reasoning and inquiring concerning what is best and most beneficial to the society.[145]

The use of print to proselytize on behalf of a republican cause that had presumably been discredited after the death of Oliver Cromwell was demonstrated by the activities of Thomas Hollis, the wealthy patron of radical Whigs. Hollis financed printers and publishers, rewarded periodical editors for printing articles and letters, and also designed and distributed medals, prints, and books (including presentation copies of canonical works by Milton, Algernon Sydney, and others) to influential figures in England and to agents and consuls abroad. He arranged to have the Thomason Tracts acquired by the British Museum. He also supported the activities of John Wilkes and his printer Almon throughout their prolonged tribulations.[146]

The involvement of disenfranchised readers who were "outside the ranks of office-holders" and who represented the "nation out of doors"[147] was sought by journalists such as "Junius" who voiced the complaints of "the people" against the Crown.[148] Their opponents (who included Samuel Johnson)[149] objected to those "forlorn grubs and gazeteers [who] . . . proclaim themselves free born Englishmen and . . . insist on having a spoke in the wheel of government."[150]

Whether this development was welcomed or deplored, there was general agreement that the conduct of political affairs had become much more difficult to contain within traditional structures.[151] This was made clear by the various episodes that together formed the "Wilkes Affair" (1762–74). As the self-appointed protagonist of an exciting narrative involving defiance of the king, repeated arrests and imprisonment, repeated expulsions by Parliament, mob uprisings, and electoral triumphs, John Wilkes won a special niche in British political history.[152] An early biographer, writing in 1769, observed: "History can furnish no one instance of any private man being so long and so extensively the subject of public attention and discourse as Mr. Wilkes has now been for seven years."[153] Wilkes also left his mark on place names in the American colonies—most notably, perhaps, in Pennsylvania, where the city of Wilkes-Barre still couples his name with that of Colonel Isaac Barré (1726–1802) who, like Wilkes, defended the American cause in Parliament.

In all phases of his long-drawn-out contest with the authorities, Wilkes was aided and abetted by many of London's leading pressmen. His formidable skills as a publicist were first displayed when he was holding a seat in the House of Commons and became co-editor, with Charles Churchill, of a weekly paper, the *North Briton*. It was designed to counter Tobias Smollett's pro-government *The Briton*. In April 1763, an inflammatory article led the royal ministers to issue a general warrant ordering the arrest of "the authors, Printers and Publishers of a Seditious and Treasonable Paper entitled *The North Briton* Number 45."[154] Forty-eight people were arrested, including Wilkes. He was temporarily imprisoned in the Tower and promptly published an account of his arrest that attracted public support. After obtaining a release as a privileged Member of Parliament, he rejected his privileged position and claimed that the general warrant violated the rights of all subjects. He urged the complicit printers and publishers to take legal actions for false arrest and helped them win favorable judgment from both the Court of Common Pleas and the King's Bench. While at liberty he used his private press to republish article no. 45 and also (he was ever the unrepentant libertine) to print obscene verses under the title of an *Essay on Women* (a parody of Pope's *Essay on Man*). When found among his papers along with the reprinted *North Briton*, the *Essay* was read out loud in the House of Lords and was denounced as a "scandalous, obscene and impious libel." *The North Briton* no. 45 was publicly burned. Its author was expelled from the Commons, was declared an outlaw, and went into exile in France. There he was "hailed as a defender of liberty by the *Parlement* of Paris in its struggle against the 'ministerial despotism' of Louis XV. Handkerchiefs 'à la Wilkes' were for a time 'à la mode' in French parliamentary circles."[155]

Wilkes's return to England in February 1768 was preceded by a fanfare of publicity that he orchestrated on his own behalf. It was followed by his announcement of his intention, in the forthcoming general election, to run as a candidate for Middlesex (one of the few counties that had a really democratic franchise). During the protracted campaigns that ensued (he was three times elected and three times rejected by Parliament) he won the support of city politicians and London mobs. Even while he was imprisoned, having been sentenced on the old libel charge, he was elected as an alderman by sympathetic Londoners and took up the cause of permitting publication of Parliamentary debates. Fearing a clash with city mobs, Parliament delayed taking action to suppress publication. It became a "fait accompli"; accounts of the debates soon served as "the very lifeblood of newspapers."[156] Here as elsewhere, Wilkes was associated with using the printed word to force open a hitherto closed political process and to attract the vicarious participation of disenfranchised subjects. After being elected Lord Mayor of London, Wilkes finally regained his seat in Parliament in 1775.

Throughout, his cause was promoted by an outpouring of printed materials, among which the most celebrated were composed by the hard-hitting, anonymous author of the *Letters of Junius*. "Pamphlets, periodicals, newspapers, handbills, ballads, cartoons and verses were all marshaled in the cause. The Number 45 was printed or sewed upon every kind of material."[157] The Wilkes case inaugurated a new chapter in cartoon history.[158] There was even a country dance named the "Wilkes wriggle." The Wilkes marketing technique, writes John Brewer, would have excited the admiration of Josiah Wedgwood.[159] It had been anticipated by Samuel Richardson. Indeed the commodification of literature served as a prelude to the commercialization of politics.

The Wilkes Affair showed how press campaigns, when combined with trials by jury, could energize urban crowds and enable even disenfranchised subjects to carry the day.

> Every measure that can affect the publick happiness is examined and discussed not only by the legislators who are representatives of the people but by the people themselves. They judge, they decide, they publish their sentiments boldly, they defend them with zeal and their concurring voice is a formidable restraint to the exercise of

Figure 4.6. William Hogarth, "John Wilkes, esq.," December 15, 1763. Courtesy of the Bridgeman Art Library.

power, warning the kings and their ministers how dangerous it is to run counter to the general sentiments of the people.[160]

Bourbon France lacked a lively newspaper press, jury trials, and representative assemblies. No meetings of an Estates General had been held for more than a century. Yet, even under an absolutist regime, royal ministers could not entirely disregard all the francophone publications that entered the kingdom from abroad and commanded a following among members of the French reading public. As one contemporary observer pointed out, the term "public opinion" was acquiring a new meaning.[161] In ancient and medieval times, it had been associated with official surveillance. When the authorities sought to determine whether the ruler was being praised or maligned they were in a sense gauging public opinion. The new meaning had little to do with the traditional monitoring of gossip and rumors by the police. It meant going over the heads of duly constituted authorities and appealing to the good sense of a reading public at large. In this second sense, public opinion was envisaged as an "invisible power without any bodyguard"[162] and as "the sovereign judge of all the judges of the earth."[163] It was to this power that dissident subjects increasingly appealed—as did Voltaire when condemning injustice in the Calas case, and as did American colonists when expressing a "decent respect to the opinions of mankind" in the Declaration of Independence.

Unlike the Americans who attributed formidable political powers to the printed word, Voltaire took pains to depreciate it. He argued that Protestant victories owed more to the decisions made by the German princes than to all the printed treatises that the reformers penned. It was the sword, not the pen, that determined the fate of nations: "From five to six thousand pamphlets have been printed in Holland against Louis XVI, none of which helped to make him lose the battles of Blenheim, Turin and Ramillies."[164] He also pointed out that treatises by radical authors such as Locke, Bayle, Spinoza, and Hobbes were read by a tiny minority of reclusive philosophers who had no intention of disturbing the peace.

> Divide the human race into twenty parts. Nineteen of them are composed of those who work with their hands and will never know if there is a Locke in the world. . . . In the remaining twentieth part how few men do you find who read. . . . [of] those who do read, there are twenty who read novels for every one who studies philoso-

phy. The number of those who think is excessively small and they are not aiming at upsetting the world. It is not [the philosophers] . . . who have carried the torch of discord, . . . it is the theologians.[165]

Voltaire had spent time in the Bastille as a young man and steered clear of trouble with officialdom thereafter. He was at home in polite society and avoided direct confrontations by various stratagems. But he certainly was determined to undermine clerical authority and to alert his readers to miscarriages of justice, such as the Calas case. He succeeded on more than one occasion in creating a public stir. Some forty years later, in 1775, Malesherbes, the director of the French book trade, gave an address, upon being admitted to the French Academy, that assigned a more influential role to writers than Voltaire had done. He described this "enlightened century" as a "century when each citizen can speak to the entire nation by means of the printing press." In this century, he went on, "men of letters . . . are in the midst of a dispersed public what the orators of Rome and Athens had been in the midst of a people assembled."[166] The same year, he elaborated on this theme in one of his several "remonstrances" that protested royal actions taken against the *Parlements* (law courts).

> The art of printing has given writing the same publicity that the spoken word possessed in the midst of the assemblies of the nation in the first period. But it has taken many years for the discovery of the art to have its full effect upon men. It has required that the entire nation gain the taste and habit of informing itself by reading. And . . . that enough men become skilled in the art of writing to lend their ministry to the entire public, taking the place of those gifted with natural eloquence who made themselves heard by our fore fathers on the Champs de Mars.[167]

Although the king ordered Malesherbes's *Remonstrances* stricken from the official registry, he could not, for long, prevent their appearance in print.

The expansion of the political arena beyond gatherings that could stand within earshot of a speaker entailed less dependence on speech and more on the printed word. This was all to the good, according to the Huguenot encyclopedist Jaucourt. In his article on "reading," he compared the two media in a manner that harked back to religious disputes between Protestant and Catholic and looked forward to recent media analysis.[168] But his comparison was also characteristic of a writer who regarded his own era as an age of reason. Whereas speech appealed to the passions, the written word called forth reflection and careful thought. Whereas sound was fleeting, a printed work was not; one could go back over a text and review its contents. Orality, whether in the form of reading out loud or declaiming, aimed at evoking an emotional response, in contrast to the thoughtful mood engendered by the silent solitary scanning of a given text.[169]

The political implications of this analysis were spelled out in two other speeches given to the French Academy. One, by Abbé Arnaud in 1771, contrasted zealous Athenians, who were swayed by demagogues, with tranquil French subjects who were readers. "What were the Athenians, a people of listeners and zealots. . . . What are we today, a people of tranquil and intelligent readers . . . we no longer govern by eloquence."[170] The other was an inaugural address given by Abbé Barthélmy on 25 August 1789, shortly before the Academy was dissolved. It similarly compared the ancient republics whose ignorant inhabitants were easily swayed (and misled) by an eloquent orator with the improved situation of his own day, when discussions could be duplicated in print and subjected to reasoned analysis.[171]

Perhaps the most knowledgeable and celebrated writer on this theme was an Anglo-American printer turned publicist who would become a cult figure in pre-revolutionary France. In 1739, Benjamin Franklin had experienced firsthand the power exerted by an eloquent preacher. In that year, he attended a sermon delivered by George Whitefield and was so carried away that he overcame his reluctance to part with money when the collection plate was passed. He realized that Whitefield represented a major marketing opportunity, befriended him, and won the preacher's agreement to publish his collected sermons and journals, thereby indicating the compatibility of speech with print while contributing to the "great awakening."[172] When it came to political oratory, however, Franklin was dismissive: "Here comes the Orator! with his Flood of Words, and his Drop of Reason."[173] In 1749, when he set forth his proposals for educating the youth of Pennsylvania, he noted that "Modern Political Oratory" was chiefly performed by pen and press, and had advantages over the ancients, its effects being "more extensive, more lasting, &c."[174] As an autodidact who had been "educated by print outside collegiate walls," Franklin had not undergone the intensive training in oratory that was given to American students at the time. He was unimpressed by the ostensible advantages of mastering this time-honored classical art and wrote humorously about the longwinded sermons and verbose legal writings that reflected training in oratory: "when you find how little there is in a Writing of vast Bulk you will be as much surprised as a Stranger at the opening of a Pumpkin."[175]

In 1782 he wrote to Richard Price: "The ancient Roman and Greek orators could speak only to the number of citizens capable of being assembled within the reach of their voice. Their *writings* had little effect, because the bulk of the people could not read. Now by the press we can speak to nations; and good books and well written pamphlets have great . . . influence."[176]

Characteristically, Franklin was not satisfied to guess about the number of citizens capable of being assembled within the reach of an orator's voice. He stood with a Boston crowd listening to George Whitefield preach and tested how far back he could stand while still hearing the loud, clear voice of the celebrated open-air preacher. After estimating the space that could be occupied by a large assemblage, he satisfied himself that ancient histories of generals haranguing whole armies were plausible.[177]

The idea that orators had floods of words but only drops of reason ran counter to the views of the Renaissance humanists. Although speech had been set against writing by Plato, the two modes of communication had more often been conjoined. Eloquent oratory had been regarded as indispensable for maintaining domestic peace and concord: "It is eloquence which manages whole assemblies of men by the spoken word. . . . It is through it that Peoples, most fierce and jealous of their liberty, voluntarily take on the yoke and servitude of laws. . . . The splendor and majesty of the oration illustrate the beauty, the excellence, and the dignity of things."[178] But during the religious wars, lawlessness and "enthusiasm" were associated with listening to demagogues. Montaigne described rhetoric "as a tool invented to manipulate a mob . . . used only in sick states where things were in perpetual tempest. . . . Eloquence flourished best in Rome when affairs were in their worst state."[179] Despite contrary evidence supplied by numerous pamphlet wars—by Lutheran *flugschriften*, Marprelate tracts, and "Mazarinades"—distancing and rationality were believed to be fostered by reading texts rather than by hearing speeches.[180]

The favoring of print over oratory was especially welcome to the numerous influential publicists who lacked silver tongues but were talented with their pens. Benjamin Franklin himself was a case in point. He spoke infrequently and briefly, in the belief that speech was best confined to private moments; only print was suitable for public ones.[181]

The feature of print that was most valued by Franklin was its impersonality. For Jaucourt, Malesherbes, and the French academicians cited above, the reader's distance from an author was conducive to thoughtful appraisal and acted as a shield against being swayed by demogoguery. But Franklin understood that distance was also compatible with concealment and disguise, that it lent itself to surreptitious propaganda and agitation. As an apprentice printer, he had become familiar with the virtual clubs and clubmen created by Addison and Steele. As a would-be journalist, he achieved success by masking his identity under a variety of pseudonyms and creating virtual characters such as "Silent Dogood." As a printer, he had published an American edition of the virtual epistolary interchange embodied in *Pamela*. Finally, as a master propagandist, he adopted diverse disguises, placing the same item in different journals under different names, thereby conveying the impression that many different people were voicing the same views.

While in England in the 1760s he ensured that the items he wrote under some forty-odd pseudonyms received maximum exposure. He had them first printed and then reprinted in England and then, after running his own clipping service, had the same items printed and reprinted in American journals.[182] When he served at Versailles during the War of Independence he cultivated the French press no less assiduously. Taking advantage of the anti-British posture of Louis XVI's foreign minister, Vergennes, he orchestrated a pro-American campaign: placing atrocity stories about British aid to Indians, writing a hoax about the sale of Hessians, commissioning a French translation of the American Constitution, and helping to found a French-language newspaper on Anglo-American affairs. He also instigated Mirabeau's celebrated attack on the French nobility.[183] He was among the first to be explicit about the advantages of recycling the same items in order to impress the public mind. "The facility with which the same truths may be repeatedly enforced by placing them daily in different lights in newspapers which are everywhere read, gives a great chance of establishing them . . . it is not only right to strike when the iron is hot . . . it may be very practicable to heat it by continually striking."[184]

Striking and heating are not well designed to encourage the use of cold reason. In fact, it was probably easier to discount what was said at one time by a rabble-rousing orator than what appeared in print under many names at different times in diverse journals. The single speaker was less likely to be mistaken for *vox populi*. As Franklin himself put it, print made it feasible to give the impression that "the discontents were really general . . . and not the fiction of a few demagogues."[185] He was not the only publicist to exploit print in this way. The case of Sam Adams, who wrote under more than twenty-five pseudonyms but rarely spoke in public, has been described as "typical of the colonial resistance."[186]

Where Franklin differed from Sam Adams and others was that, although he hid behind numerous pseudonyms and masked his identity repeatedly, he also managed to impress his own name and face upon a far-flung public. As was true of the "divine Richardson," Franklin profited from the two seemingly incompatible powers of print. As a printer and publicist he produced messages that carried an air of impersonal authority. At the same time, he inspired admiration for his personal achievements. As the charismatic Dr. Franklin, author of "Bonhomme Richard" (the French "Poor Richard") and inventor of the lightning rod, he posed in striking costumes, had his portrait painted, engraved, and sculpted, and became the object of a French cult. Even John Adams, who disliked Franklin, grudgingly acknowledged his fame: "His name was familiar to kings, courtiers, nobility, clergy and philosophes as well as to plebeians to such a degree there was scarcely a peasant or a citizen, a valet-de-chambre or footman, a lady's chambermaid or a scullion in a kitchen who was not familiar with it and who did not consider him as a friend to humankind."[187]

Adams attributed this unusual celebrity to the many useful contacts Franklin had made as a printer.

> He had been educated as a printer, and had practiced his art on Boston, Philadelphia and London . . . where he not only learned the full power of the press to exalt and spread a man's fame but acquired the intimacy and the correspondence of many men of that profession with all their editors and many of their correspondents. The whole tribe became enamoured and proud of Mr. Franklin as a member of their body and were consequently always ready and eager to publish and embellish any panegyric upon him they could procure. Throughout his life he courted and was courted by . . . printers, editors, and correspondents of reviews, magazines, journals and pamphleteers and those little busy meddling scribblers that are always buzzing about the press in America, England, France and Holland.[188]

According to Larzer Ziff, this explanation of Franklin's fame with its reference to the "whole tribe" wrongly "hints at conspiracy." In Ziff's view,

Adams "held the key to a better answer," when he wrote about Franklin's taciturnity. The latter conversed freely only with close friends. In company he was totally silent. Even in deliberative assemblies he spoke infrequently and briefly. Although a penchant for secrecy went together with rigorous taciturnity (which was cultivated by George Washington, among others),[189] habitual silence can scarcely explain the quality that provoked Adams's envy, to wit, Franklin's extraordinary fame.

His enviable celebrity owed much to the artful way he devised his own self-portrait even while acting as a spokesman for a public at large. That he provoked suspicions of conspiracy probably had less to do with his taciturnity than with his consummate talents as a "press agent."[190] As Ziff notes, "secrecy and deception were built into the conditions of life" that faced Franklin as a young careerist.[191]

Arousing suspicion of conspiracy was endemic to the use of print for political persuasion: "Disguise, dissimulation and deceit were high on the political and literary agenda throughout the late Stuart era."[192] In Bourbon France, ancien régime practices, which included tacit permissions along with arbitrary punishment, encouraged a resort to secrecy, bad faith and "Aesopian language." One recent study, sparked by Robert Darnton's controversial work on the ancien régime literary underground,[193] provides fascinating details concerning a group of French blackmailer-libellistes who operated out of London between 1758 and 1792 and were often gathered in the bookshop of the publisher-bookseller David Boissiere.[194] Darnton retraces the same ground while disagreeing with Burrows in his *The Devil in the Holy Water*.[195] But there's no need to delve into the "most shadowy, most criminal and dangerous aspects of a vast and influential international clandestine publishing industry"[196] to account for suspicions of conspiracy. The activities of numerous less disreputable and more influential writers were also calculated to engender suspicion. One recalls the numerous ruses employed by Voltaire in his dealings with Marc Michel Rey or the elaborate measures taken by d'Holbach to ensure that the authorship of works such as *Système de la Nature* would remain secret.[197] In all countries, moreover, suspicions were bound to be aroused by the conventions of invisible authorship, entailing anonymity and pseudonymity, that characterized writing for the periodical press. "I have been one year the loquacious Tatler and the next the taciturn Spectator . . . have been everything yet nothing, every sex but no sex, have spoken for heaven . . . and howled from hell—all to serve you, my dear public."[198]

The full-blown conspiratorial myths that were produced by counterrevolutionaries targeted certain ostensibly secret societies such as the Masons and Illuminati. These new fraternal orders seemed to flaunt their secret character by advertising their existence even while closing their doors to all save initiates.[199] (Perhaps the first pure media event in European history was the Rosicrucian furor of 1623, when Gabriel Naudé reported that placards had appeared throughout Paris asserting that "the invisible ones had arrived.")[200]

Although the Masons and the Illuminati were (and remain—with the addition of Jews) prime targets for mythologists, there was also a persistent undercurrent in counter-revolutionary literature concerning the undue influence exerted over an undefined "public" by men of letters at large. "Among [American] Tories, it was widely believed that the colonists had been manipulated by 'serpentine demagogues' . . . who 'ingratiated themselves' in the same manner that Satan is represented seducing Eve 'by a constant whispering.'"[201]

This undercurrent surfaced in Burke's *Reflections on the Revolution in France*, which were "shot through with anxieties about the subversive work of newspapers, pamphlets, reprinted sermons, paper currency and a shadowy conspiracy of political men of letters at home and abroad."[202] What could not be done by any direct or immediate action, Burke observed, could be wrought over the long run "through the medium of opinion." The literary cabal "contrived to possess . . . all the avenues to literary fame," and it exhibited "an unremitting industry to blacken and discredit . . . all those who did not hold to their faction."[203] In a later essay "on the policy of the allies" (1793), Burke assigned full responsibility to men of letters: "How many could have thought that the most complete and formidable revolution in a great empire should be made by men of letters, not as subordinate instruments and trumpeters of sedition, but as the chief contrivers and managers, and in a short time, as the open administrators and sovereign rulers?"[204]

Voltaire had argued that a single philosopher such as Locke had very few readers. It was not the single writer who concerned Burke. It was, rather, the many writers who seemed to act in concert and aim in the same direction. "Writers, especially when they act in a body and with one direction, have great influence on the public mind. . . . [They] pretended to a great zeal . . . for the poor and the lower orders, whilst in their satires they rendered hateful by every exaggeration, the faults of the courts, nobility, and of priesthood. They became a sort of demagogues."[205] (Similar views are still being expressed by American conservatives who object to the ostensibly exaggerated depiction of the faults not of a nobility, but of a plutocracy, by an omnipresent "liberal" media.)

Unlike those French academicians who associated speech with demogoguery and writing with reasoned judgment, Burke was convinced that print was no less compatible with arousing emotional responses. As a silent medium, it was more subversive than oratory. It empowered those who lacked a gift for public speaking but were sufficiently skilled with their pens to reach large publics from afar. In this regard he was perceptive. The Atlantic Revolutions saw numerous "tribunes of the people" occupy important positions on the political stage.[206]

Before the American Revolution, probably the most celebrated figure who successfully exploited print while avoiding speech was John Wilkes. In view of the crowds who had gathered on his behalf one might have expected that Wilkes had been a spellbinding orator. But, as Horace Walpole remarked, he was a very poor public speaker: he "was a propagandist whose skills fell little short of genius . . . to ensure as wide an audience as possible he exploited every available political medium."[207] "His eloquence was not in his voice," Garat wrote about Wilkes in his memoirs, "It was in his pen. His tribunal was a journal and there was one moment when it was heard by all Europe."[208] Apart from *Pamela*, the Wilkes Affair was perhaps the most resonant "media event" of the pre-revolutionary era.

During the French Revolution itself, as during its aftermath, the resonance of the printed debate between Edmund Burke and Thomas Paine was also remarkable.[209] The most explicit accounts of how printing entered into the French Revolution would come after the event—as in Hazlitt's assertion: "The French Revolution might be described as a remote but inevitable result of the invention of the art of printing."[210] Nevertheless, the political benefits and drawbacks of print were implicit in the contrast between Burke's dismissal of printed constitutions as "paltry" pieces of paper and Paine's dismissal of ancient charters as "mouldy parchments."

Burke's *Reflections* (as noted below) would cast a long shadow over Romantic conservatism as the decades wore on. At the time, however, the *Reflections* would become notorious among English working-class readers for containing a passage objecting to the democratization of learning. After praising the nobility and the clergy for keeping learning alive "in the midst of arms and confusions" and noting how learning had subsequently served to enlarge the ideas and furnish the minds of elites, Burke lamented the way "learning" had refused to stay in its "proper place." It had become "debauched by ambition," he complained. No longer "satisfied to continue the instructor," it "aspired to become the master." As a result, he prophesied, "learning" will suffer the same fate as "its natural protectors and guardians." It "will be cast into the mire, and trodden down under the hoofs of a swinish multitude."[211]

Among political philosophers, Burke would achieve a long-lived reputation as a founding father of modern conservatism. To English working-class readers of the revolutionary era, he was known for the single taunting phrase: "swinish multitude." A characteristic episode is related by the biographer of Francis Place: In 1792 Thomas Spence, a former schoolmaster from Lancashire, "was in London and was imprisoned for selling Paine's *Rights of Man*. After his release, he published a long series of tracts, of which the best known was the periodical 'Pigs' Meat or Lessons for the Swinish Multitude.'"[212] So many variations were played upon the phrase—so many pamphlets were issued with titles such as "Hog's Wash," "A Salmagundy for Swine" (with "contributions from Brother Grunter"), "the stye," "the swineherds," "the bacon"—that even a sympathetic chronicler such as E. P. Thomson found it tedious to list them all.[213] The long list of periodicals, pamphlets and poems that the taunting phrase inspired extended into the nineteenth century, eliciting contributions from William Cobbett, Hazlitt, and Shelley.[214]

Several of the earliest satirical variations ("Hog's Wash," "Salmagundi") came from the printing shop of Daniel Isaac Eaton. The son of a well-to-do stationer, he was inspired by reading Tom Paine. He repeatedly stood trial and was imprisoned, not for satirizing Burke but, as was the case with Spence, for republishing Paine.[215] Eaton's press was the object of a self-congratulatory verse he ran in his short-lived journal *Politics for the People*:

Thy magic wand, audacious Burke,
Could metamorphize Man to Pork
And quench the Spark divine:
But Eaton's Wonder-working Wand;
By scattering knowledge through the Land
Is making Men of Swine.[216]

One of Eaton's pamphlets seems especially pertinent to the topic of this book. Not unreasonably, he took Burke's many references to "learning" as alluding to the progress of printing. Under the pseudonym of "antitype" he wrote and published a pamphlet in 1794 titled *The Pernicious Effects of the Art of Printing Upon Society, Exposed.*[217]

Given the relevance of its title and the way its contents reflect the attitudes of Paine's many disciples among English radicals it seems worth paraphrasing and citing at some length:

It starts by describing the situation before this diabolical art was introduced among men; a time when no one doubted the wisdom of priests and princes and the "lower orders knew full well (their superiors having taken pains to inform them)" that the existence of society depended on the rule of priests and princes. This was a "golden Age" when "the feudal system prevailed" and the "villains, or lowest class, were what Mr. Burke so elegantly terms the Swinish Multitude." The "Scripture having declared gold to be the root of every evil, they were humanely prevented from possessing any."

In this beautiful scheme, this happy system of social orders, the situation of the lower orders was equal if not preferable to that of the slaves in our West India islands—not withstanding [that] the friends of the slave trade have lately represented the condition of the negroes to be very enviable.

. . . what will my reader think when I inform him that the late government of France was feudal in the extreme; how will he pity and deplore the . . . folly of that deluded nation—no longer blessed with a king, nobles or priests, but left, like a ship in a storm, without a pilot to their own guidance. . . .

Having briefly shown a few of the advantages enjoyed before printing was discovered, or at least generally known, I come now to point out, as is expressed in my title its pernicious Effects . . .

Since Printing has been employed as the medium of diffusing sentiments, government has become more difficult—the governors are insolently called upon to give account of the national treasure, and if they are late or evasive it is astonishing with what boldness some men will dare to revile and insult them.

The lower orders begin to have ideas of rights, as men—to think that one man is as good as another—that society at present is founded upon false principles—that hereditary honors and distinctions are absurd unjust and oppressive . . . —that instruction . . . is a debt due to every individual . . . that laws should be the same for all . . . that freedom of speech is the equal right of all. . . . This with a great deal more such Stuff is called the rights of man—blessed fruits of the art of Printing—the scum of the earth, the swinish multitude talking of their rights! . . . With similar mistaken notions of liberty, even many women are infatuated; and the press—that . . . source of evil—fruitful mother of mischief, has aready favoured the public with several female productions on this very popular subject—one in particular called the Rights of Women . . . in which a share in legislation is claimed . . . gracious heaven to what will this fatal delusion lead.

In those passages that pertain to the rights of man, freedom of speech, and other "blessed fruits of the art of Printing," the pamphleteer's heavy-handed sarcasm temporarily gives way to real enthusiasm. His references to the slave trade[218] and "female productions," along with his own position as an artisan, also suggest the need to qualify descriptions of late eighteenth-century print culture as an exclusive construct associated with the polite society that was frequented by Mr. Spectator and other white, propertied males. Eaton was subjected to seven prosecutions and spent fifteen months in prison. Among other offenses, he published Paine's "aetheistical" *Age of Reason* in 1795. In 1820, as an old man, after returning from a stay in America, he was put in the pillory. Rather like John Lilburne more than a century earlier, he was cheered by the crowd. According to William Cobbett, the populace objected to "a punishment inflicted for a matter of opinion."

Eaton's enthusiasm for "the pernicious art of printing" went together with his evident pleasure at the spectacle of the collapse of the ancien regime in France. In this regard he was only one of the many disciples of Tom Paine who believed that the press, when put to proper use, could serve as a "magic wand" and deal a fatal blow to the rule of kings and priests. The English radicals of the 1790s, such as Godwin, Paine, and Thelwell, were in agreement: print would be the agent of world revolution.[219] Earlier, Thomas Jefferson had famously declared: "The basis of government being the opinion of the people, the very first object should be to keep that right; and were it left to me to decide whether we should have a government without newspapers or newspapers without a government I should not hesitate for a moment to prefer the latter."[220]

English Wilkites and American revolutionaries were not the only ones who believed in the emancipatory potential of the printed word. As many studies document, this belief also animated several of the future leaders of the French Revolution who had spent time across the Channel and overseas.

His observation of the Wilkite agitation in London during his eleven-year stay in Great Britain inspired Marat to adopt the pen name of Junius in the 1790s.[221] Brissot and Mirabeau, the two journalists who first challenged ancien régime controls and demanded a free press in 1789, had previously followed similar itineraries. Both made stops in Switzerland during the Genevan revolution and both frequented the same circles while residing in London.[222]

Mirabeau combined the skills of an orator with those of a publicist. Brissot was uncomfortable as a public speaker. It was as an editor of *Patriote Française* that he made his mark on the French revolutionary scene. He owed his first job as a journalist to his having mastered the English language (a most useful tool for any eighteenth-century French writer in need of employment, as Jean Le Clerc, Abbé Prevost, Diderot, Suard, and others showed). While in London during the early 1780s he encountered a circle of eminent Dissenters, political reformers, and philosophical radicals: Jeremy Bentham, Joseph Priestley, Richard Price, Catherine Macaulay, David Williams, and others.[223] This was the same circle as the one Mirabeau's London publisher, Joseph Johnson, served. It contained the foreigners who would be accorded honorary French citizenship by the National Convention after Louis XVI's fall. The epigraph which would be repeated on every issue of Brissot's revolutionary journal, *Patriote Française*—"a free press is the eternally vigilant sentinel of the people"—was taken from an address given by Dr. John Jebb (1736–86), who had been engaged in organizing the Society for Constitutional Information during Brissot's London stay.

The year immediately preceding 1789 found Brissot traveling in North America. He visited Washington at Mount Vernon, thanks to a letter of introduction from Lafayette. He tried, without success, to persuade George Washington to free his slaves and join the movement for emancipation.[224] During his American journey, Brissot was especially impressed by the remarkable success of Tom Paine's *Common Sense*. He was persuaded that Paine's work would have remained without much effect had it been left in its original pamphlet form. The idea that its success was due to its being repeatedly reprinted in newspapers underlies his often cited remark: "without newspapers the American Revolution would never have succeeded." Brissot's mémoire to the Estates General of 1789 echoed the views that had been expressed by Malesherbes and others concerning the new political mission of the press. Only by means of an unfettered press "could a large and populous modern country recreate the public forums of the classic city states; only through the press could one teach the same truth at the same moment to millions of men and only through the press could men discuss it without tumult, decide calmly and give their opinion."[225]

Such views received the strongest support during the French Revolution in the publications which were issued by a society called the Cercle Social—the subject of an illuminating study by Gary Kates.[226] Cercle members believed that printing had created a forum for public debate in which thousands, even millions of citizens could participate with one another.[227] It owned its own publishing house (the only revolutionary club to do so) and developed an ingenious plan to link newspaper subscription to Club membership. Its numerous publications gave it a national following. Among Cercle Social members, the most famous was the Marquis de Condorcet, a distinguished mathematician sometimes described as the last of the philosophes. He had written a biography of Voltaire and one of Turgot. He succeeded the latter as a "prophet of progress."[228] Like d'Alembert, Condorcet was a gifted mathematician who marveled at the advances that had been made in the sciences after the advent of printing.[229] He was, however, more gifted as a mathematician than as a politician. As was true of so many others, he lacked oratorical skill and associated eloquence with demagoguery. "Let us hasten, then, to substitute reason for eloquence, books for talkers, and finally bring to the moral sciences the philosophy and the method of the physical sciences."[230]

In common with Malesherbes and other French academicians, Condorcet believed that a free press would usher in a new era of rational politics and put an end to the dangerous enthusiasms kindled by rabble-rousing preachers and orators. That reading publics, no less than hearing ones, were prone to be swayed by printed materials aimed at eliciting emotional responses was overlooked. In making this point, Carla Hesse points to the success of popular fiction during the revolutionary decade: "The reading public demanded . . . tales of private passions rather than reasoned discourses on public virtue."[231] The continued success of *Pamela* and her progeny cannot be denied. Yet arousing emotional responses was scarcely confined to fiction. Reasoned discourse tended to be eclipsed by other forms of printed matter, especially by the popular journals of the day.

Nevertheless, Condorcet and his colleagues were convinced that the widespread use of print would insure not only unparalleled scientific progress but also the triumph of rationality in human affairs.

> For Condorcet the scientist who lacked all powers of oratory, the spoken word was identified with passion and prejudice, the written word with science and reason. With the invention of printing, with the development of representative government in large societies, the politics of rhetoric was to give way to the scientific politics of the written word, "the true rhetoric of the moderns."[232]

To Condorcet print spelled the end of political systems based on secrecy and arbitrary power—the end of prejudice, superstition, and indeed of all organized religion. He collaborated with Tom Paine on a journal, *Le Républicain*, which advocated the abolition of the monarchy after the flight to Varennes in 1791. His "Sketch of the progress of the human race" sounded remarkably similar to Eaton's narrative, insofar as both viewed Gutenberg's invention as a magic wand that signaled the end of rule by kings and priests. It was fortunate, Condorcet wrote, that none of Gutenberg's contemporaries had recognized the capacity of printing to unmask priests and dethrone kings, or they would have strangled the new art in its infancy.

Other members of the Cercle also elaborated on the mythology which had developed around the invention of printing and the figure of the publisher. Gutenberg's discovery was described "as the most important event in the history of mankind"; it would doom all political systems that were based on secrecy and arbitrary power. One deputy who served with Condorcet on the Committee of Public Instruction prophesied that the age of the priest was being replaced by the age of the publisher: "It was necessary to have religions before the invention," he claimed, but printing, "the most beautiful gift from the heavens," had freed man from bondage to conflicting confessional creeds. "The Old Regime was the age of the priest; the new would be the age of the publisher."[233]

The glorification of the invention went together with that of the inventor. This story has been well told by Hans-Jürgen Lüsebrink in a fascinating essay on the fetishism of printing during the Revolution.[234] Tributes to Gutenberg reached a climax in Anacharsis Cloots's address to the newly formed National Convention on 9 September 1792. In the name of all printers, Cloots requested that the remains of the inventor be placed in the Pantheon. A paraphrased excerpt runs as follows:

If God invented the sun, man invented the printing press. The divinely created sun dissipates physical darkness, the man-made sun
vanquishes spiritual darkness. Let us celebrate an inventor who was
the first true revolutionary, without whom we would be mute and
isolated on earth, without whom we would never have known either
a Voltaire or a Rousseau or a Pantheon.[235]

This passionate plea for placing Gutenberg's remains in the Pantheon
was delivered by a deputy to the National Convention who was a true cos-
mopolite—a German-Dutch baron named Jean Baptiste Cloots who found
his first names too Christian and substituted the more pagan Anacharsis.
Cloots's petition was received with enthusiasm at first. But Enlightenment
cosmopolitanism soon gave way to a new bellicose nationalism. In October
1793, little more than a year after he delivered his request to honor Gutenberg, Cloots himself was denounced as a foreign agitator and expelled from
the Convention. In March 1794, he was accused of being implicated in a
foreign plot and was guillotined. By then, the idea of placing a German
culture hero in a French national shrine had become untenable.

By then also, the political activities of newspaper editors, such as Marat
and other "friends of the people," made it more difficult than ever to sustain
the notion that print did not lend itself, as had oratory, to exciting emotional
responses and to arousing mob action. On this point John Adams's marginal
comments on his copy of Condorcet's *Esquisse* are illuminating.[236]

> *Condorcet:* Knowledge has become the staple of an active and univer-
> sal trade. A new kind of authority is established, from which is exer-
> cised a less tyrannical empire over the passions but a more firm and
> lasting power over reason.
> *Adams:* The empire of the press, over the passions, in the hands of
> Marat and others was more tyrannical than the government of Cesar
> Borgia.
> *Condorcet:* A public opinion is formed, powerful by the number of
> those who shared it.
> *Adams:* This public opinion is, at times, as great a tyrant as Marat.
> *Condorcet:* Every new error is resisted from its birth . . . before it has
> been propagated.
> *Adams:* There has been more error propagated from the press in the
> last ten years than in an hundred years before.[237]

Later, in 1811, John Adams blamed the French revolutionaries for trying
to force the pace of change in a way that set back the cause of human progress.

> Their precipitation and temerity has, I fear retarded the progress of
> improvement and amelioration in the condition of mankind for at
> least an hundred years. . . . The public mind was improving in
> knowledge and the public heart in humanity. . . . the fragments of
> feudality, the inquisition, the rack, the cruelty of punishments,
> Negro slavery were giving way . . . But the philosophers must arrive
> at perfection per saltum. . . . they rent and tore the whole garment
> to pieces. They have even been compelled to resort to Napoleon.

In 1815, at the bottom of the last page of Condorcet's work, Adams wrote:
"The question now is whether Popes, Jesuits and Inquisitors shall rule the
human race."[238]

On the Continent, it appeared that Adams's question was going to be
answered in the affirmative. Throughout Metternich's Europe a "reunion of
throne and altar" was celebrated. After 1823, there was even a return of the
Jesuits (banned since the mid-1760s) to Bourbon France. Across the Channel
and overseas, however, optimism about the emancipatory potential of Gutenberg's invention persisted. "The press has come like a true Messiah" wrote
Eaton's successor Richard Carlile in 1821, "to emancipate mankind from
kingly and priestly influence."[239] Nevertheless, the belief that the press was
destined to stifle demagoguery and enable reason to triumph over passion
had suffered a lasting blow.

Chapter 5

The Zenith of Print Culture
(Nineteenth Century)

> Everyone seemed to share this faith in a machine that could usher in
> the social millennium just as surely as the power of steam was trans-
> forming the outward face of English life. Each party, naturally, had
> its special brand of truth to disseminate through print.
> —Richard Altick, *The English Common Reader*

The Revolutionary Aftermath

The last chapter showed how earlier tributes to printing were transposed into
a new key by anticlerical philosophes and de-christianizing revolutionaries.
This not to say that the powers of the press were ever devalued by evangelists
and missionaries. "The evangelicals . . . believed that the grace of God could,
and did, descend to the individual man and woman through the printed
page."[1] Bible societies extended their reach around the globe. Although lay
Bible reading was not encouraged in Catholic Europe, all the other forms of
religious publication flourished there.[2]

But whereas Protestants had celebrated printing as a means of freeing
churches from the tyranny of popes, eighteenth-century prophets of progress
(notably Turgot and Condorcet) had incorporated the invention in a different emancipatory metanarrative. They believed its use would free humanity
from subservience to any church that claimed to offer special access to revealed truth. The invention was placed first among new discoveries for having
introduced the prospect of continuous improvement in human affairs. It held

the promise of bringing about an ultimate triumph of reason over revelation, of science over superstition.

This approach, which set press against pulpit, reached a climax during the French Revolution, shortly before the fall of the Girondins, when a leader of the dechristianizing campaign petitioned the government to place the remains of Gutenberg in the Pantheon. The age of the church had ended, proclaimed one of Condorcet's colleagues; the age of the publisher had arrived![3]

As events developed between 1792 and 1815, however, neither the Church nor the publisher prevailed. Both lost ground to the state during the ensuing decades; first under the Jacobin Terror,[4] and then under Napoleon, who "established a rationalized press system almost wholly under the government's control."[5]

Napoleon was fully alert to diverse uses of the press. "Government is nothing unless supported by opinion," he wrote, and (in a Machiavellian vein) "the truth is not half so important as what people think to be true."[6] As a masterful propagandist, he kept a close watch over the books that were sold and the stories that were run in the domestic and foreign newspapers of the day. "Four hostile newspapers," he purportedly said, "are more to be dreaded than a hundred thousand bayonets."[7] In a letter ordering one of his marshals to arrest booksellers in Augsburg and Nuremberg, he wrote: "It is no ordinary crime to spread defamatory writings in places occupied by the French armies, and to incite the inhabitants against them. It is high treason." The letter ordered the guilty booksellers to be shot within twenty-four hours.[8] (Such harsh measures served only to incite inhabitants against the French. The execution of the Nuremberg publisher Johann Palm provoked an outcry.)[9]

Napoleon's regimes took full advantage of the capacity of print to standardize legal codes as well as the contents of school books. The centralized system of education that he established became celebrated for its standardized curriculum. (One minister of education is said to have looked at his watch and announced that at that very minute, every French schoolboy of a certain age was turning the same page of Caesar's *Gallic Wars*.)

Together with the educational system, the French church came under tighter state control. The actions of all churchgoers were closely monitored; a new catechism was designed to inculcate loyalty to the emperor. There was no attempt to stifle romantic effusions of fervent religiosity, such as

Chateaubriand's *Génie du Christianisme* (1802),[10] but there was little tolerance for ultramontanists who expressed allegiance to the Roman pope.

The domination of the Roman church by Napoleon's regimes is suggested not only by his insistence on crowning himself emperor, but also by his usurpation of functions previously performed by the post-Tridentine Office of the Propaganda. During his Egyptian campaign, presses were set up in Alexandria and Cairo, and Vatican experts were put to work supervising printing in Greek and Arabic using the punches, matrices, and types of the former Catholic office. Among the few benefits that came from that ill-fated venture were the discovery of the Rosetta Stone and the monumental multi-volume *Déscription de l'Égypt* compiled by the 160-odd scientists and savants who accompanied the expedition.[11] The *Description of Egypt* proved more useful to Egyptologists than to those who sought to propagate the Catholic faith.

The Napoleonic regimes did little to encourage either a new age of the publisher or a revived age of the church. After Waterloo, however, the rival forces of press and pulpit were newly empowered in France. With the re-union of throne and altar under the returned Bourbons, and especially after the return of the Jesuits to Charles X's France, it appeared that the age of the Church might be extended. At the same time, French printing and publishing also gained ground.[12]

The expansion of the printing trades in Restoration France is sometimes associated with industrialization. But mechanization came gradually in France and was not a prominent feature during the Bourbon regimes.[13] The fluctuating policies of Louis XVIII's ministers entailed a tightening and loosening of press controls that stimulated political controversy.[14] Whether Bourbon France allowed the periodical press more leeway than had Napoleon is open to question, but it is clear that Louis XVIII's regime was less restrictive than were the draconian press laws enforced elsewhere in Metternich's Europe.

The fate of the newspaper press stimulated political agitation and looms large in histories of the period. But the output of books also shaped attitudes toward print in Restoration France. By the 1820s Paris had become the major publishing center of Europe. Out of a population of 816,000, some 30,000 Parisians were engaged in printing and allied trades.[15] "The situation allowed tremendous publishing opportunities for the writings of the philosophes. Between 1817 and 1824, Restoration publishers, often with active Liberal assistance, produced more than two million copies of the works of Voltaire and

Rousseau alone, as well as hundreds of thousands of books by other important Enlightenment figures."[16]

The reprinting of books by the eighteenth-century philosophes, together with their being publicized and advertised in the periodical press, provoked a violent reaction from ultraroyalists and Catholic churchmen—one that undermined attempts at pacification by Louis XVIII, who sought to downplay troubled memories of the revolutionary past. "The tendency to see France (and Europe as a whole) as a battlefield between contesting Manichean forces . . . returned to the fore."[17]

Nineteenth-century views of printing were largely shaped by reactions to the French Revolution and its aftermath. The terms had been set during the earliest phases of the French Revolution in the well-publicized debate between Paine and Burke.[18] In his defense of the Declaration of the Rights of Man of 1789, Paine had attacked Burke for "laboring in vain to stop the progress of knowledge." "Ignorance is of a peculiar nature; once dispelled it is impossible to re-establish it. . . . it has never yet been discovered how to make a man unknow his knowledge, or unthink his thoughts."[19] In Paine's view and in that of his friends and followers, printing had set in motion an irreversible process which was destined to end priestly monopolies of learning and royal monopolies of power.

This belief in an irreversible process was expressed after Waterloo by the diverse political factions in France who belonged to a so-called party of movement. Orleanists, Bonapartists, and republicans, however much they conflicted over the question of regime, agreed that absolutist monarchy belonged to the past. They opposed any return to secretive or arbitrary practices. Printed charters or constitutions were considered indispensable to counter the abuses that had characterized despotic rulers in the past. The same was true of the printed declarations that (according to Paine) Burke had scornfully characterized as "paltry and blurred sheets of paper about the rights of man."[20]

All of the written (printed) constitutions that were proposed by Liberal parties throughout the Continent during the nineteenth century contained a clause that echoed the freedom of the press clause in the 1789 Declaration of the Rights of Man. A Society for the Freedom of the Press was formed in Bourbon France.[21] The cause of a free press became a liberal shibboleth and remains one even now.

At the opposite pole of the Party of Movement was the so-called Party of Order, comprising a spectrum which ranged from Gallican Voltaireans, like Louis XVIII himself, to extreme reactionaries such as Joseph de Maistre. Whatever the printed word had contributed to advances in science, the conservatives argued, mathematical reasoning was inapplicable to the conduct of human affairs.[22] Age-old customs and time-honored political institutions had to be protected against the recurring threat of demolition. The wisdom of the ages (embodied in documents Paine described as "mouldy parchments")[23] was superior to any blueprint devised by a single generation. Moreover, print had brought an unwelcome publicity to affairs of state. Secrecy was indispensable to statecraft. "There are always some things in every constitution that cannot be written and that must be allowed to remain in a dark and reverent obscurity on the pain of upsetting the state."[24]

As early as 1791, the Catholic Church had made clear its opposition to doctrines pertaining to freedom of opinion. When Pope Pius VI denounced the Civil Constitution of the Clergy, he singled out the free-press clause in the Declaration of the Rights of Man and the Citizen for special condemnation. Since God had limited man's liberty by forbidding him to commit evil, the papal argument went, "how can liberty of thought be described as an imprescriptible right?" It was clearly wrong to grant citizens the right to think, write, and even publish with impunity on religious affairs.[25]

This position was reaffirmed by Catholic churchmen during the Restoration. Some traced the roots of evil back to Luther. The circulation of Bibles printed in the vernacular had blighted Christianity ever since the Reformation, according to de Maistre.[26] But vernacular Bibles were not widely circulated in Restoration France, and putting a stop to Bible printing outside Catholic Europe was a lost cause. The reprinting of the works of Voltaire and Rousseau was a different matter. On the eve of his execution, Louis XVI himself purportedly had acknowledged the enormity of the threat, singling out Voltaire and Rousseau as the two men "who have ruined France." The corrosive effects of their views were described in detail by Lammenais. Enlightenment philosophy had paved the way for a Reign of Terror; any further spread of poisonous Jacobinical and atheistical doctrines had to be arrested. In Metternich's Austria "a government that believed that men can read themselves into criminals censored everything."[27]

In Bourbon France, conservatives were appalled by the permissive approach of Louis XVIII's regime, which allowed the Liberal newspapers of the day to publicize and promote the new editions of the philosophes.[28] The "phobic" reactions of earlier authorities when faced with previous pamphlet explosions were manifested again with equal insistence by Catholic churchmen and lay ultraroyalists. Medieval doctrines pertaining to heresy and the need to sever diseased limbs from the body politic were reiterated. Viscount de Bonald, an oracle of the ultras, regarded censorship as "a sanitary institution established to preserve society from the contagion of false doctrines."[29] When Bonald was appointed royal censor in 1826 under Charles X, however, he was (like previous royal officials) powerless to hold back the inundation of "mauvais livres."

Various countermeasures were attempted. There were ceremonial book burnings (whole libraries were put to flames). There was an outpouring of good books to counter the bad, and the creation of Catholic book clubs and lending libraries. But the attacks on the philosophes and demands for public expiation for their sins served only to excite further interest in the poisonous texts. "The more of Voltaire the missionaries obtain for their auto-da-fés, the more [his] works . . . are sought after" and one enterprising publisher brought out a "fireproof edition" of Voltaire.[30]

The publicity that was associated with the writings of Voltaire and Rousseau did not stop short with circulating their works. The two philosophes, who had violently opposed each other when alive, were destined to be forever yoked together—first by the revolutionaries who glorified them together when placing them in the Pantheon, and then by the restored Bourbons who condemned them together as enemies of the regime. A flourishing trade in images, engravings and prints made the faces of the two authors well known. Even street urchins became familiar with their names, to judge from the song mockingly chanted by Gavroche in Les Misérables: "C'est la faute à Voltaire, c'est la faute à Rousseau."

Print was implicated in the attack on the philosophes, not merely because it spread their subversive ideas and made them media celebrities. More fundamentally, it had given rise to public opinion as a new source of perturbation in the political arena. Whereas this development was welcomed wholeheartedly by nineteenth-century liberals, it was roundly condemned by the disciples of Edmund Burke. As the latter had noted, print had enabled men of letters, "sophisters and calculators," to usurp the roles traditionally performed by legitimate rulers. It had encouraged the application of geometrical reasoning to the conduct of human affairs. "Happy if learning not debauched by ambition had been satisfied to continue the instructor and not aspired to be the master!"[31]

The Romantic Movement

Whereas Burke objected to the application of geometrical reasoning to politics, a new generation that came of age under Napoleon objected to "geometrical reasoning" of all kinds and chafed under the disciplines imposed by their schoolmasters. (Turning the pages of Caesar's *Gallic Wars* could scarcely compare with storming the Bastille or conquering Europe on horseback.) Recent rebellion against literary canons that were restricted to work by dead white men had its counterpart in much earlier Romantic objections to the neoclassic rules that had been honored during the previous century by French academies and royal courts. "The same refrain is repeated," wrote Victor Hugo in his preface to *Cromwell*: "'Follow the rules! Copy the Models!' Whom shall we copy then? The moderns? What! Copy copies! God forbid."[32]

According to William Hazlitt, writing about Wordsworth and the so-called Lake School of Poetry, the Romantic rebellion

> had its origin in the French Revolution, or rather in those sentiments . . . which were imported onto this country in translation from the German. . . . Our poetical literature had . . . degenerated into the most trite, insipid and mechanical of all things, in the hands of the followers of Pope and the old French school of poetry. It wanted something to stir it up and found that something in . . . the French Revolution . . . it rose from the most servile imitation to the utmost pitch of singularity and paradox . . . all was to be natural and new . . . classical allusion was considered antiquated foppery . . . capital letters were no more allowed in print than letters-patent of nobility were permitted in real life. . . . Kings and queens were dethroned . . . in tragedy and epic . . . as they were decapitated elsewhere . . . rhyme was looked on as a relic of the feudal system . . . a singularly affected . . . simplicity prevailed.[33]

The phrase "singularly affected simplicity" evokes the writings of Rousseau. Not all of the Romantic rebellion was imported by translation from the German; in France, at least, some of it came from the disciples of Jean Jacques. But the Germans certainly took the lead in rebelling against neoclassic culture and Enlightenment philosophy. Both were stigmatized as francophone products that had been in vogue at the courts of French-speaking rulers in Prussia and Russia before becoming associated with Napoleon's conquests and French occupying forces. The Enlightenment was stereotyped as being "cold, passionless, hyper-rational."[34] The shallow mockery of Voltaire and his successors was viewed as an imported construct that was alien to the deep-rooted volkish culture of the Teutonic peoples.

Catholic apologists had long objected to the deadening effect of print upon the living words of an apostolic tradition. Similar objections were applied by Romantics to the blighting effects of "mechanical literature" upon oral lore and "folk culture." What Baconians and encyclopedists had viewed as useful knowledge would be celebrated by the utilitarians, as noted below. But the Benthamite philosophy was scornfully dismissed by the Romanticists, who preferred poetry to prose and valued the imaginative visionary above the precise engineer. The "unmitigated exercise of the calculating faculty" was condemned and opposed to the "creative faculty."[35] Dry as dust pedants or petty bookkeepers might pride themselves on mastery of facts and figures; deeper truths were available to those who tapped the wellsprings of folk wisdom.

The attempt to apply mathematical reasoning to human society was seen as having failed. Once again Burke led the way with his attack on the calculators, the would-be social engineers who, by using compass and rule, had carved up the French body politic. They had erased the deep-rooted boundaries of French provinces and replaced them with artificially constructed départements. If the French example were followed, Burke declared, "every landmark" in England would be obliterated "in favor of a geometrical and arithmetical constitution."[36] As if confirming Burke's views, French romanticists would express regret at the loss of their old provinces, ancestral lands and time-honored forms of worship. "Nations do not throw aside their ancient customs as people do their old clothes," wrote Chateaubriand. He noted how his compatriots in "this infidel age" were drawn to the sites (often ruins) where their ancestors had lived and prayed.[37]

Whereas eighteenth-century philosophers had marveled at advances in mathematics and the natural sciences, the Romantics elaborated on Goethe's contrast between gray theory and the evergreen tree of life. The anti-intellectual themes that had accompanied Renaissance attacks on Aristotelian and Galenic teachings were replayed. But, unlike sixteenth-century injunctions to study bodies instead of books, the Romantic deprecation of bookish theories was not designed to favor anatomical dissection. "We murder to dissect" (see Wordsworth poem, below). Nor did advances in mathematical sciences inspire paeans to progress, as had been the case with d'Alembert and Condorcet. Indeed, Novalis argued that the pope had acted wisely in trying to suppress publications that favored Copernican theories and other "untimely and dangerous discoveries in the area of knowledge."[38] The book of nature was not to be deciphered by means of printed equations, charts, and tables. Rather, an antibookish nature had to be experienced as Rousseau (and earlier, Petrarch) had experienced it: by going out of doors to wander over hill and dale. "To go into solitude a man needs to retire as much from his chamber as from society. I am not solitary whilst I read and write though nobody is with me. But if a man would be alone let him look at the stars."[39] Readers were urged to abandon their books and to move out of the library and the study to the field and hillside.[40] "Up! up! My Friend and quit your books!" advised Wordsworth:

> One impulse from a vernal wood
> May teach you more of man,
> Of moral evil and of good,
> Than all the sages can.
>
> Sweet is the lore which Nature brings;
> Our meddling intellect
> Mis-shapes the beauteous forms of things:
> We murder to dissect.
>
> Enough of Science and of Art;
> Close up those barren leaves;
> Come forth, and bring with you a heart
> That watches and receives.[41]

To be sure, the vogue for going outdoors to experience "nature in the raw" contributed to fossil-hunting, botanical expeditions, and many other ventures that, once recorded in print, proved immensely fruitful for nineteenth-century scientific investigation.[42] But an enhanced appreciation of the immense variety and fecundity of natural phenomena went together with a distaste for systematic data collection that was unhelpful to the advancement of learning. It could be argued, indeed, that the true Romantic was set against systematic thinking of any kind.

A distinction was drawn between the public that consumed printed materials and the people who were identified with nature, orality, or voice.[43]

Respect and even reverence were reserved for the latter and for "the embodied spirit of their knowledge."[44] Uncontaminated by print and thus favored by Romanticists were young children who were still preliterate and country folk whose cottages were devoid of bookshelves. There was also nostalgia for those golden ages that had preceded Gutenberg's invention. Although the monkish scribe engaged in copying or illustrating manuscripts was valued, it was the medieval minstrel or bard who was most highly regarded. Oral myths and legends were believed to express the true "soul" of one's native land. "The word 'romantic' has been lately introduced in Germany to designate the kind of poetry which is derived from the songs of the troubadours . . . [and] . . . owes its birth to the union of chivalry and Christianity . . . it expresses our religion, it recalls our history; its origin is ancient although not of classical antiquity."[45]

Printed literature that had been praised for succeeding so well in recovering and preserving the writings of classical antiquity was now viewed as a contaminant—making it ever more difficult to hear the poems of bards as they were meant to be heard without the interposition of the printed page: "the forward march of literacy . . . [was] . . . destroying the popular lore of ages. Reading and writing were . . . the nemesis of the oral tradition. The mood was generally elegiac about the death knell of a plebeian culture which, until that time, was thought to have been unchanged for centuries."[46]

Ironically enough, concern about the ostensible death of "plebeian" culture stopped short of penetrating plebeian consciousness. Even while the benefits of print were being questioned by the upholders of a bygone "rich oral tradition," working-class readers had no doubt that Gutenberg's invention represented progress.[47] In fact, the oral transmission of many old ballads was itself something of an urban myth. Many ballads had long been contaminated, first by hand-copying and later by print.

> When ancient songs and popular traditions first started to become
> subject of retrospective analysis . . . enthusiasts failed to appreciate
> the centuries of mutual transaction between oral, scribal, and
> printed sources which . . . lay behind the evolution of their materials.
> The sensibilities of the Romantic era needed to believe in the idea
> of a pure oral tradition of the folk that had perpetuated itself since
> time immemorial, untainted by the influence of the written word
> and unsuspected in the drawing rooms of the polite reading classes.[48]

However unsuspected in drawing rooms, printed ballads were highly visible in taverns and cottages: "They were pasted on the walls of eighteenth-century taverns and cottage kitchens more often than any other form of popular print."[49]

That objections to the contaminating effects of print were somewhat artificial is also suggested by the enthusiastic reception of printed collections of ballads and tales such as Thomas Percy's *Reliques of Ancient English Poetry* (1765).[50] Moreover, there were few complaints about the way print made the newly composed ballad of a "last minstrel" available to numerous readers in 1805. Less than two decades after Burke lamented that "the age of chivalry is gone," that same age was resurrected and portrayed in glowing colors by Sir Walter Scott, who "transposed the fundamental doctrines of Burke" into "the key of fiction"[51] while depicting the sad fate of the medieval bard:

Old times were changed, old manners gone
A stranger filled the Stuarts' throne.
The bigots of the iron time
Had called his harmless art a crime.[52]

The conservative political subtext of his work was noted by many of Scott's contemporaries. Richard Carlile, always on guard against Burkean views, described Scott as "the greatest literary and political and moral enemy his countrymen had ever known."[53] The dangers of generalizing about reader reception are shown by Jonathan Rose's account of working-class readers who found anti-Tory sympathies in Scott's fiction. The portrayal of Rebecca in *Ivanhoe* was viewed by one reader as a "satire on chivalry no less devastating than Sancho Panza."[54] Rose also points to the appeal of Romantic medievalism among later socialists who valued Scott's negative treatment of economic rapacity.

Despite these qualifications, the vogue for Scott's novels was most often regarded as supporting the counter-revolutionary cause. Scott's Tory sympathies were manifested most clearly in the *Quarterly Review*, which he had helped to found. Later in the century, Mark Twain would blame Scott for creating the mindset that characterized Southern slaveholders and accounted for their determination to destroy the Union:

the Revolution broke the chains of the *ancien régime* and of the
Church, and made a nation of abject slaves a nation of freemen; and

Bonaparte instituted the setting of merit above birth, and also so completely stripped the divinity from royalty that, whereas crowned heads of Europe were Gods before, they are only men since . . . only figure heads. . . .

Then comes Sir Walter Scott with his enchantments, and by his single might checks the wave of progress, and even turns it back, sets the world in love with . . . decayed and swinish forms of religion; with decayed . . . systems of government; with the . . . sham grandeurs . . . and sham chivalries of a brainless and worthless long-vanished society.[55]

In the debate between Burke and Paine there was no doubt where Twain's sympathies lay. In 1887, after rereading Thomas Carlyle's *French Revolution*, he realized that he'd become a sans-culotte who sided with Marat against the monarchy, the aristocracy and the Catholic church.[56] (Carlyle's influential chapter on the Revolutionary newspaper press is noted below.) In his anti-Scott fiction, Twain had his Connecticut Yankee introduce newsprint into King Arthur's court. The role of the printing press in general had long been on the author's mind. As a young man, Sam Clemens had been an apprentice in the local printing office in Hannibal and then in the composing room of the *Philadelphia Inquirer*. He had stood before Benjamin Franklin's wood-bed press at the Patent Office in Washington, D.C., and marveled at the progress exemplified by the difference between 125 and 20,000 sheets per hour.[57] Although they occupied opposing political positions, Twain and Scott had one thing in common: both made money for numerous publishers and booksellers while failing miserably when they became involved in publishing concerns themselves. (Balzac shared a similar experience.)

Whatever political influence Scott exerted, his novels exemplified the contradictions that were inherent in Romantic medievalism. He confessed that he loved "the sound of the press thumping, clattering, and banging in my ear."[58] As an omnivorous reader while still in his youth, he had taken full advantage of Edinburgh's circulating library system.[59] At the age of twelve he had pored over the collection of ballads, songs, and poems contained in Percy's *Reliques*. As a teenager, he read Goethe in German, Dante and Ariosto in Italian, and medieval romans in old French. The idea of writing chivalric romances first occurred to him when reading Cervantes in the original Spanish as a teenager.[60]

Cervantes figures in *Waverley*, the first novel in the Waverley series.

There Scott seeks to disabuse the reader from confusing his approach from that of the Spaniard.

> The reader may perhaps anticipate . . . an imitation of the romance of Cervantes. . . . My intention is not to follow [Cervantes] in describing such a total perversion of intellect as misconstrues the objects actually presented to the senses, but that more common aberration from sound judgment, which apprehends occurrences indeed in their reality, but communicates to them a tincture of its own romantic tone and coloring.[61]

Yet Scott does little to show how his protagonists' sound judgment is distorted when they get caught up in battles. They engage with real historical figures, not with windmills. When the reader is told about medieval crusades or Jacobite uprisings, it is not the protagonist but the author who provides the "romantic tincture." Edward Waverley is depicted as a dreamy youth who prefers reading to hunting or fishing. He shares with Don Quixote a capacity to be lost in the world of books and is especially excited by the "heart stirring and eye dazzling descriptions of war and tournaments like those to be found in Froissart." Then he leaves the library and his bookish reveries to venture into the Scottish highlands. There he gets caught up in an actual historical drama, the 1745 Jacobite uprising. It unfolds in a "picturesque and romantic setting"[62] and is presented in a heart-stirring and eye-dazzling manner. No windmills appear on the scene. Indeed, we are told in a postscript that "the most romantic parts of this narrative are precisely those which have a foundation in fact."[63]

The difference between Scott and Cervantes provoked another outburst from Twain:

> the power of a single book for good or harm is shown by the effects wrought by *Don Quixote* and those wrought by *Ivanhoe*. The first swept the world's admiration for medieval chivalry-silliness out of existence; and the other restored it. As far as our South is concerned, the good work done by Cervantes is pretty nearly a dead letter, so effectually has Scott's pernicious work undermined it.[64]

Cervantes repeatedly reminded his readers of "the disjunction between the literary materials of the past" and the printed books his readers had on hand.[65] Part two of *Don Quixote* describes a visit to a Barcelona printing shop, where the Don sees proofs of a sequel that was falsely attributed to Cervantes by an unscrupulous writer, Avellaneda, who had tried to capitalize on the success of part one.[66] In *Waverley* Scott also introduces a visit to the printing shop, where Waverley's tutor tries in vain to get his huge manuscript published and is turned down by a bookseller and his solicitor. But Scott's scene is designed, not to remind the reader that the book in hand was produced in a printing shop, but rather to contrast the ignoble behavior of mercenary townsmen in the lowlands with the gallantry and hospitality of Highlanders.

Scott was keenly aware of the difference between living in the Middle Ages and writing about them in an age of print. He alerted his readers to the difference in numerous prefaces and annotations. Translating "ancient manners into modern language," conveying an ordinary conversation while avoiding use of "obsolete words," and employing nineteenth-century orthography and typography were discussed in a way that alerted his readers to the problems of resurrecting medieval society in the early nineteenth century. But the numerous prefaces and annotations which provided glimpses of the machinery behind the scenes were all addressed to "Dr. Dryasdust." The actual narratives were artfully designed to enable less pedantic readers to live vicariously in an imagined past.

The *Waverley* novels were not only especially well suited to the political climate in the American South; they also appealed to readers throughout Europe. "Between 1805 and the year of his death 1832, Scott's writings spread over Europe and beyond in ways never known previously. . . . The Germans were the first to take him up in 1810, then came the French, Italians, Swedes, Poles, Danes and the Dutch, the Bohemian Czechs, the Hungarians, Serbians, Turks and Greeks."[67]

To say that Scott's fiction was held in high regard by French publishers during the Bourbon and Orleanist regimes is to understate the case. Between 1816 and 1851 French language editions of his complete works were reissued twenty times, and individual French versions of his novels were printed or reprinted over seventy times (Emma Bovary, like Mark Twain's Southerners, was captivated by Scott.) Not only did francophone editions proliferate, but also numerous French authors were commissioned to produce new novels "à la Scott."[68] The French publishers of the 1820s who commissioned authors to produce novels "à la Scott" anticipated by a century and a half a marketing strategy that American book historians place in the 1970s, when they discern the shift from creating an audience for an existing text to creating a text for an already constituted reading public.[69]

One particular commission of this kind deserves special attention here because of its bearing on attitudes toward print. In November 1828, Victor Hugo signed a contract with the French publisher Gosselin for a "roman à la mode de Walter Scott." He had reviewed *Quentin Durward* in French translation[70] and decided to set his novel in the same era, inserting the year 1483 as a subtitle: *Notre Dame de Paris, 1483.*[71] The writing went too slowly for the impatient publisher, who had been financially pressed by the business downturn in 1826–27. The author seized upon the Revolution of 1830 as an additional excuse for his tardiness and then insisted on revising the first edition by adding a long chapter-length digression dealing with Gutenberg's invention and its effects.[72]

Scott's preface to the novel *Quentin Durward* was written in a Burkean vein. Readers were informed that *Quentin Durward* was set in an age when the feudal system was in decline. The high spirit of chivalry "founded on generosity and self-denial" had been abandoned by Louis XI. A mercantile class was coming to the fore, mercenary soldiers were displacing former knights, and the crafty king was selecting lowborn ministers to counterbalance the power that had been wielded by the nobility.

Hugo elaborated on the idea of the fifteenth century as a transitional interval and the 1480s as time of change. But he chose the Cathedral of Notre Dame rather than Louis XI's court as the locale within which to place his historical turning point. The archdeacon of the cathedral is described in the act of explaining the iconography of Notre Dame to the protagonist: "I shall teach you to read . . . the marble letters of this alphabet, the pages of the granite book." After pointing to the cathedral he turned to the printed book on his desk (a 1474 edition of Peter Lombard's *Sentences*):[73] "Alas," he says, "this will destroy that" ("Ceci tuera celà"). "Trifles overcome the greater things. The rat of the Nile destroys the crocodile. The book shall overthrow the building."[74]

Ceci tuera celà. These words have received a new lease on life, owing to concern about the fate of the book in an age of electronic communications. As Umberto Eco observed: "no conference or collection of essays on the future of the book would be complete without someone citing them."[75] I myself repeated them some thirty years ago while citing from Frances Yates's classic study of the art of memory.[76] More recently, the same passage from Hugo appeared in a review of a book entitled *Print Is Dead.*[77]

When writing about the advent of printing, Hugo had in mind a more grandiose vision of the past than was suggested by *Quentin Durward*. It was not merely the waning of the Middle Ages, Hugo suggested, but the entire course of human history that was changed by Gutenberg's invention. He had learned from reading Chateaubriand to think of the Gothic cathedral as representing something more than a medieval cultural artifact.[78] It was the last of a long series of monuments inscribed with glyphs and letters, going back to the pyramids. (Hugo's vision of vast tracks of time, containing monuments that preserved records when all else had been buried under desert sands, seems to be especially indebted to Volney's *Les ruines*.)[79] The monuments of the past had not merely performed the didactic functions of encyclopedias. They had embodied the collective spirit of entire communities. They represented the people's art.

Unlike Burke, who deeply distrusted the democratizing tendencies that accompanied the spread of print, Hugo shared with Michelet and Lamartine and other "men of 48" adherence to a democratic mystique. It glorified the collective will of the people, even while remaining wary of violent mass movements. (As noted above, similar attitudes were expressed by the English Romantic poets.) It has been suggested that Hugo's ambivalent view of "le peuple" was embodied in the person of Quasimodo, who was fundamentally good-hearted but was also capable of terrible violence—not to mention the fact that he was deaf, dumb, and deformed.[80]

Hugo's ambivalence about "the people" was manifested when he wrote about print. When knowledge was detached from monuments, he wrote, it became more accessible to a public but lost its organic connection to whole communities. During the entire course of civilization, from the Hindustani pagodas to the cathedral of Cologne,[81] architecture had served as the great "scripture of humanity." All human thought had been embodied in stone structures until the fifteenth century. Then everything changed.

Humanity discovered a way to preserve itself that was not only more durable than architecture but much easier to construct. "L'invention de l'imprimerie est le plus grand événement de l'histoire."[82] As was true of many Romanticists, Hugo could present the invention in this way—drawing a stark contrast between printed book and stone monument—only by ignoring the prolonged circulation of hand-copied rolls and codices. The printing of texts on paper, he wrote, detached human knowledge from granite and marble (as if writing on papyrus, parchment, and vellum had not done something of the sort in preceding centuries). Thought was dematerialized, was given wings, and flew like flocks of birds to the four corners of the world. Echoing Turgot and at the same time anticipating Marx's description of the disruptive effects of capitalism ("all that is solid, melts into air"), Hugo wrote that "la pensée . . . se mêle à l'air."[83]

The tendency to dematerialize printed output was common in the 1830s and '40s. Lamartine wrote that printing was not just "paper, ink and type." It was also "thought and sentiment."[84] Echoing the eighteenth-century poem cited at the beginning of Chapter 4, he hailed printing as a mystic art that enabled armchair travelers to make contact with invisible worlds of the past and the present. Similarly, Thomas Carlyle marveled at how "poor bits of rag-paper with black ink on them" constituted "the *purest* embodiment a Thought of man can have."[85]

In another passage, however, Hugo decided that leaden types and printed papers did constitute material objects after all. He mused over the increasing problem of overload, envisaging a great pile of printed papers that already amounted to an edifice a thousand stories high; a pile that kept increasing and was becoming so huge that it would reach from the earth to the moon[86]—a second tower of Babel, a monstrous structure whose topmost layer was lost in the clouds of the future.[87]

Print not only gave rise to a kind of sorcerer's apprentice predicament— the frightening prospect of a cumulative and never-ending output—-but it also had the unfortunate effect, in Hugo's view, of encouraging duplication and imitation. Under its aegis, the arts became increasingly lifeless and academic, consisting as they did of copies of copies of copies.

As already noted in this chapter, in his preface to *Cromwell*, Hugo made clear his distaste for the time-honored rules that were taught in the academies and that were set forth in standard manuals and texts. His deliberate flouting of the neo-classic "three unities" caused a sensation when his dramas were presented on stage.[88] Insofar as print was associated with mathematical precision and with the observance of classical canons, it had (in Hugo's view) a deadening effect. Buildings designed by academically trained professionals, in accordance with classical rules, were no longer in harmony with local communities. Architecture became subject to "cold geometry." Every country had the same imitation of St. Peter's.[89] One might have expected the poet to praise the great sculptors of the Italian Renaissance and the free-standing figures that they produced. But Hugo's Romantic rebellion extended to classical rules pertaining to proportion and symmetry: "The beautiful has only one type; the ugly a thousand!"[90] Stone gargoyles expressed folklore in a way that imitations of classical models did not. The removal of statuary from stone portals disconnected human figures from the grand narrative in which they had been embedded. Like the sculpture that had been removed from façades, Hugo wrote, neoclassic architecture itself was severed from the communities it served and lost its capacity to embody the living spirit of the times. "The magnificent art which Vandals produced, the academies have murdered."[91]

Hugo's love of Gothic architecture had come to the fore when, as a nineteen-year-old, he had attended the coronation of Charles X at Rheims. Although the elaborately staged event had entailed "going by the book" and had been carefully reconstructed from old accounts, the medieval setting provided by Rheims Cathedral was real enough. The experience elicited enthusiastic tributes from both Hugo and Lamartine.[92]

Hugo had attended the carefully scripted ceremony with his friend Charles Nodier (1780–1844), a bibliophile and librarian.[93] Nodier had grown up in Strasbourg, had been a member of a local Jacobin club and had studied under the tutelage of the terrorist and de-Christianizer Euloge Schneider. As a young man, he had composed an extravagant tribute to printing. After the Restoration, however, he worried about being denounced as a former Jacobin. In his position as librarian of the Arsenal, he also became concerned about the unceasing proliferation of printed materials. Rather like the contrarian friar mentioned in the first chapter, but perhaps more in the spirit of Rousseau's denunciation of progress, Nodier, who had once been enthusiastic about the invention, ended by claiming that, far from emancipating humankind, printing had set back the advancement of learning.[94] He pointed to the early replication of late medieval scholastic works—works that were disdained by Renaissance humanists—to substantiate print's retrograde effects.[95] As a bibliophile (and cofounder of the *Bulletin du Bibliophile*) who valued fine editions, Nodier also viewed the growth of a mass readership with disdain: "literacy has not introduced a single sensible idea into the human intellect."[96] His elitist views would win him a sympathetic hearing from fin-de-siècle aesthetes.[97] Nodier has been described as an "anti-Hugo."[98] Yet Hugo had cited with approval Nodier's comment concerning "the subjection of imagination to hard and fast rules."[99] Nodier's nightmarish vision of the towering pile that kept growing higher was also in keeping with the views of his companion at the coronation of Charles X.

The reconstructed ceremonies, complete with holy oil and doves, that marked this coronation in Rheims Cathedral were intended to evoke memo-

ries of a cherished medieval past. But the former Comte d'Artois was too well
remembered for his more recent counter-revolutionary actions as an émigré
leader to attract many followers who were not committed royalists. Among
republicans and Bonapartists, the ceremonies proved counterproductive, pro-
voking satirical verse such as Béranger's famous song, "Crowning Charles the
Simple."[100] Much as the publication of the works of Voltaire and Rousseau
had alarmed Catholics and royalists, so did the elaborate pageantry alarm
the opponents of absolutism and ultramontanism. The latter were already
dismayed that the leader of the counterrevolution had been next in line for
the throne. Now, it seemed that the new king would reinstate forms of government that were unsuitable to a "modern" age. The return of the Jesuits
and the recrudescence of ultramontanist policies also awakened antipapist
sentiment and led to increasing hostility on the part of Gallican bishops.
They joined anticlerical financiers and liberal deputies in contributing to a
campaign that made "amazing progress between 1825 and 1830 using cartoons, songs, satirical poems, pamphlets, plays, newspapers and public dem-
onstrations." Coins were circulated representing Charles X in clerical garb,
the works of Voltaire and Rousseau were distributed, revivals of *Tartuffe* were
accompanied by antireligious demonstration. Every occasion was taken to
recall the Inquisition, Galileo, and massacres of Saint Bartholomew's Eve.[101]

Discontent came to a head in 1829 when an edict was promulgated that
affected the entire Parisian publishing industry. After an election had gone
against the ultras, four *ordonnances* were issued aimed at overturning the
results. The first one closed down the newspaper and periodical press,[102]
thereby inflaming everyone with a stake in the printing industries. Unem-
ployed printers, journalists, editors, and publishers combined forces to help
bring down the government. Prominent among the street fighters were journeymen typographers who had been thrown out of work and were recruited
by members of republican clubs. (Stendhal, who was correcting proofs for
The Red and the Black, looked out his window and observed the printers,
who were to have been working on his book, protesting in the streets. As
noted above, Victor Hugo used the disturbances as an excuse for failing to
meet the deadline his publisher had set for a novel "à la Walter Scott.")

While the bloused printing workers were fighting, frock-coated journal
editors joined Lafayette, Talleyrand, business leaders, and disaffected deputies
to force the abdication of the last Bourbon king. The coronation of Charles
X had followed a medieval French script; the accession of Louis-Philippe
followed an early modern English one. The so-called Glorious Revolution

that had unfolded in England during 1688–89 had been studied by Guizot, Thiers and other French publicists-turned-politicians.[103] The July Days of 1830 were significantly labeled "Les Trois Glorieuses." Charles X was ousted, as James II had been, and his Orleanist cousin was installed, as William and Mary had been.

The events of 1830 resulted in the accession of the citizen king, who had fought on the side of Revolutionaries against émigrés and had shared the anticlerical views of the followers of Voltaire. Interestingly enough, Louis-Philippe also agreed with Condorcet, Paine, and other Girondins about Gutenberg's invention. Writing in the 1800s while traveling in America, he described the advent of printing as the most decisive of all historical events. It had undermined feudalism and advanced equality, he wrote: "the European governments are operating under a delusion if they think that they can hold back the irreversible changes printing is bringing in its wake."[104]

Once he was made king, however, Louis-Philippe could endure the attacks of republicans and ultraroyalists alike for only a few years before he felt obliged to reinstitute press controls. He became the target not only of actual assassination attempts but also of a press campaign that successfully assassinated his character. Long after the July Monarchy had ended, he would be immortalized, not as the patriot who had fought at Jemappes, but as a stupid and stubborn ruler who refused to expand the franchise and who, together with his ministers, embodied a heartless plutocracy.

That the printed image was no less important than the printed word in journalistic politics had been demonstrated for several centuries, starting with antipapist *flugschriften*. But few caricatures were as deeply impressed on the national memory as those that exploited the new technology of lithography in Orleanist France. November 1830 saw the inauguration of a new journal, *La Caricature*, whose editor assembled a group of gifted caricaturists (Grandville, Gavarni, Descamps, Daumier). "When Philipon founded his two journals it was with the deliberate purpose of propagandizing through pictures, and his writers and draftsmen dedicated their talents to 'warfare everyday' . . . as Thackeray observed 'a most curious contest speedily commenced between the state and M. Philipon's little army.'"[105]

It was Philipon himself who first depicted Louis Philippe's head as a pear (the French word means nitwit). Much as Lutheran caricatures had helped to delegitimize popes and cardinals, so too did "Philipon's little army" stigmatize the Citizen King and his ministers. (The pertinence of cartoons designed by Grandville, Daumier, and others in the 1830s to the American

Figure 5.1. "Ah! tu veux te frotter à la presse!" ["So you want to meddle with the press!"]. Honoré Daumier, *La Caricature*, October 30, 1833. Courtesy of Princeton University Library.

political scene in the 1960s is remarkable. Witness their revived appearance and seeming relevance in the *New York Review of Books*.) Little wonder that "Philipon and Daumier spent months in prison"![106] However many prison terms were entailed, Orleanist press laws proved difficult to enforce. As was the case in Georgian England since the days of John Wilkes, trials by jury often resulted in the vindication of the accused and invariably led to publicity that was unfavorable to the beleaguered government.

LES POIRES,

Faites à la cour d'assises de Paris par le directeur de la CARICATURE.

Si, pour reconnaître le monarque dans une caricature, vous n'attendez pas qu'il soit désigné autrement que par la ressemblance, vous tomberez dans l'absurde. Voyez ces croquis informes, auxquels j'aurais peut-être dû borner ma défense :

Ce croquis ressemble à Louis-Philippe, vous condamnerez donc ?

Alors il faudra condamner celui-ci, qui ressemble au premier.

Puis condamner cet autre qui ressemble au second.

Et enfin, si vous êtes conséquens, vous ne sauriez absoudre cette poire, qui ressemble aux croquis précédens.

Ainsi, pour une poire, pour une brioche, et pour toutes les têtes grotesques dans lesquelles le hasard ou la malice aura placé cette triste ressemblance, vous pourrez infliger à l'auteur cinq ans de prison et cinq mille francs d'amende ! !
Avouez, Messieurs, que c'est là une singulière liberté de la presse !

Figure 5.2. Louis-Philippe turned into a pear. Charles Philipon, *Le Charivari*. Courtesy of the City Museum of Paris, Musée Carnavalet/ Bridgeman Art Library.

Commemorating Gutenberg After Four Hundred Years

Elsewhere on the Continent, censorship was enforced more successfully than in Orleanist France. The struggle against the tight controls dominated centennial celebrations of the invention of printing. "Who can measure what you have wrought with your presses, O Gutenberg? You believed you were freeing thought from its narrow confines. Why, then, are people clamoring for freedom of the press?" So ran a contribution to an album compiled in Leipzig in 1840 containing tributes to the inventor of printing by celebrated German writers, including the brothers Grimm. The Leipzig celebration also occasioned several musical compositions by Felix Mendelssohn. (An intriguing metamorphosis: the original lyrics to the tune that now accompanies the carol "Hark the Herald Angels Sing" began with "Gutenberg der Deutsche Mann.")[107]

Many other albums were compiled in other German towns. Some coupled Gutenberg with Enlightenment culture heroes associated with discovery and progress such as Columbus, Galileo, and Newton. Others stressed Protestant themes, linking Gutenberg with Luther and the spread of the Gospel. Several invoked the Biblical creation of light. One, compiled in Braunschweig, contained a poem by Frederick Engels "On the Invention of Printing," which elaborated on the theme (sounded by Turgot many decades before and by Hugo more recently) that printing gave wings to thought. Unlike Hugo, however, Engels did not romanticize inscriptions incised on ancient monuments: "Less mighty are the pyramids so high, the work of slaves who toiled in abject fear." In Engels's poem, Gutenberg is praised as an honest craftsman (Diderot would have approved). His invention spurred intellectual progress, represented by Galileo and Newton. Only repression by official censors barred the way to further achievements. Censorship deliberately blinded the intellect as falcons are blinded that had been bred to soar.[108]

Pleas for press freedom characterized most German commemorations of the invention in a way that differentiated them from prior centennial observances:

> German printing, like Germany itself, is a gagged giant. Today anniversaries are being celebrated everywhere, just as one invites people to make merry to cheer up a sick child on her birthday. . . . the sick girl smiles sadly at all the trouble people have taken. There is one present she is longing for, but it is precisely the one thing that is

missing. . . . She yearns for him who can give her health. But health
is freedom. Will people give the sick German press for its birthday
the health which is its freedom?[109]

Demands for press freedom were coupled with more traditional expressions of civic pride. Competition over which town could claim Gutenberg as
a native son had long been simmering in printing histories.[110] Older civic
loyalties, however, were overlaid by new nationalist rivalries and radical politics. Competition gained momentum in 1823, when the Dutch held a festival
honoring Coster and erected a statue of him in Haarlem. The German town
fathers of Mainz reacted in 1824–25 by placing plaques on various houses
where Gutenberg presumably had stayed, and by erecting a statue to their
first printer in 1835. Two years later, a more impressive monument was commissioned, financed by subscription and designed by the Danish sculptor
Bertel Thorvaldsen. It was erected in Mainz in 1837 amid elaborate commemoration ceremonies.

French activists in Alsace reacted by making claims for their side of the
border. They pointed out that Strasbourg had housed the inventor and his
first experiments with print before his move to Mainz.[111] Undaunted by official cold shoulders, they obtained support from Lamartine and the editors
of the *National*, organized a successful subscription, and commissioned the
designing and casting of a large bronze statue. The task was entrusted to
David d'Angers, the republican sculptor par excellence,[112] who completed the
monument in 1840. On 24 June "Gutenberg Day" was proclaimed throughout France. Foreign dignitaries, together with French literati and publishers,
gathered in Strasbourg to inaugurate the monument. Printing workers assembled around a bronze and gold press and sang verses that started with an
invocation to the press: "moteur du monde, ô levier d'Archimède!"[113] The
statue that was unveiled showed Gutenberg standing beside a small replica of
a wooden handpress. He holds a page from Genesis on which is written "Et
la lumière fut" (and there was light). At its base, bas reliefs illustrate a grand
vision of what Gutenberg had wrought. There is a cavalcade of great men:
Luther, Copernicus, Francis Bacon, Descartes, Boerhave, Galileo, Newton,
and Kant. To represent Asia, Mohamet II is shown reading *Le Moniteur,* and
a Chinese emperor is coupled with Confucius. Africa is represented by an
image of Wilberforce with liberated slaves represented by broken chains.
America is shown by the Declaration of Independence, and portraits of
Franklin, Washington, Jefferson, and Simón Bolívar.[114]

The elaborate inauguration ceremonies lasted for three days. Speeches invoked Enlightenment ideals and glorified the great Revolution. There was also a playlet whose script survived in the form of a brochure that was sent to subscribers in advance. In it, the dying inventor addresses Peter Schoeffer:

> I have not built any majestic edifice nor, as did Friar Bacon, have I presented the world with a homicidal invention. . . . My work will be a product of civilization that will extend the limits of science and will make it accessible to all.
>
> [So far, nothing out of the ordinary. What follows is unexpected and seems to anticipate the events of '48.]
>
> In giving ideas a means of diffusing themselves, is it certain that I am working for the good of humanity? The torch that spreads light, may it not, in careless hands, become the torch that sets off a fire?[115]

In both French and German regions, the ceremonies and monuments that commemorated Gutenberg served as an appropriate prelude to the revolutions of 1848.[116] As disciples of Gutenberg, German printing workers had played a leading role in revolutionary societies such as the League of the Outlawed and the League of the Just.[117] But the signal came from France. The adage "when Paris sneezes, Europe catches cold" was especially appropriate after the new telegraph wires linked together the capital cities of Europe. The February Revolution that created France's Second Republic set in motion a European-wide sequence.

The coronation of Charles X had entailed an elaborate reenactment of medieval coronation ceremonies; 1830 saw a reenactment of England's Glorious Revolution. In the 1840s the great French Revolution itself provided contemporary politicians and publicists, many of them editors and journalists, with the scripts they sought to follow.

Lamartine's *Histoire des girondins* became a bestseller on the eve of '48. It resurrected Condorcet's colleagues as martyrs to a great cause, one which Lamartine passionately espoused.[118] The February Revolution of 1848 saw the Orleanist regime overthrown. Men of letters took control of the French capital. The staffs of two journals headed the provisional government; Victor Hugo was made mayor of his *arrondissement*, and Lamartine became foreign minister.

With men of letters in command, freedom of the press was once again proclaimed—only to give way to new press controls under Napoleon III. After the collapse of the Second Republic, men of letters went into exile. Lamartine would write a brief biography of Gutenberg that cast the German inventor in the role of a misunderstood genius, devoted to serving the people, who were robbed of the fruits of his labor by greedy entrepreneurs[119]—a portrait that owed not a little to Lamartine's self-image during his own later years.

Only after the collapse of the Second Empire and the installation of the Third Republic did the struggle over press laws end in favor of the anticlerical Liberals. In the 1880s, also after numerous setbacks, Liberal parties elsewhere on the Continent were victorious. The last decades of the nineteenth century saw the movement for a free press finally prevail. It provided a triumphant climax in Liberal grand narratives but, as noted below, it also served as a prelude to fin-de-siècle disillusionment.[120]

Tories and Radicals in Great Britain

On the Continent, Enlightenment doctrines which favored printing as an instrument of progress were associated with the struggle against a counter-revolutionary reunion of throne and altar. Across the Channel, contestation took a somewhat different form. To be sure, during the French Revolution, English Anglicans and Tories had already adopted tactics that were similar to those used on the Continent after 1815. There was the same concerted effort to fight fire with fire, not only literally—Tom Paine was burned in effigy on several occasions (and shot and guillotined as well)[121]—but also metaphorically by means of printed output.

> The obvious course for the government was to try to silence the press that spread the inflammatory alien doctrine of "natural rights." Hence . . . the frequent arrest and fining or jailing of radical booksellers; and the State Trials in 1794 of Hardy, Tooke, and Thelwall, three doughty disseminators of Jacobin literature. . . .
>
> But these were at best negative measures, and they had the disadvantage, among others, of advertising the very literature they were designed to wipe out. The heart of the crisis lay not in the circulation of radical propaganda . . . but in the existence of crowds of

readers, who after all could be deprived of their literacy by no device short of extermination.[122]

An appropriate antidote was provided by Hannah More (1745–1833), who emerged as a champion of the established order. Although she was associated with the Evangelical movement, her doctrines found favor with other Anglicans. Her *Village Politics* (1793), written at the request of the bishop of London, was designed as an answer to Paine's *Rights of Man*. The series of tracts she produced has been aptly described as "Burke for Beginners":[123]

> As she wrote . . . in 1795, "Vulgar and indecent pennybooks were always common, but speculative infidelity brought down to the pockets and capacity of the poor, forms a new era in our history." . . . to counter such phenomena . . . the series known as Cheap Repository Tracts [was launched]. [Of the] 114 titles in 1795–8 . . . More contributed at least 50. By March 1796 two million tracts had been sold. They gave rise to the Religious Tract Society which continued the work . . . More's critique of radicalism was wide-ranging. Some of the Tracts dealt directly with the new pestilential philosophy; one was an answer to Voltaire's *Candide* and another to Paine's *Age of Reason*.[124]

The anti-Paine tract described one Mr. Fantom who "fell victim to the wrong kind of reading" and "got hold of a famous little book written by the NEW PHILOSOPHER whose pestilent doctrines have gone about seeking whom they may destroy: these doctrines found a ready entrance into Mr. Fantom's mind."[125] In this view, books act as guided missiles—or perhaps poison-tipped arrows—that gain entrance to unguarded minds.

As Patrick Brantlinger suggests, the political philosophy underlying "Burke for beginners" publishing campaigns entailed a "profound distrust" of "the democratizing potential of the printed word." As had been the case with earlier efforts to combat the spread of the Lutheran heresies, Tory propagandists "were caught in a dilemma: they had to use what . . . they considered to be monster-producing instruments . . . reason, representation, writing, literacy—to oppose those very instruments. The only way to combat the false publications of the philosophes and Jacobins was through more publication . . . Anti-Enlightenment texts [were] . . . both poison and antidote."[126]

To avert the dangerous consequences of enabling the wrong people to read, measures were taken to limit freedom of choice in reading materials. Hannah More noted with pleasure that shops were not only provided with uplifting materials but were also pressed to get rid of the more impious works they had on hand.[127] She had few qualms about sugar-coating her pills. The *Cheap Repository Tracts* were "decked out with rakish titles and woodcuts," and "sent out, like sheep in wolves' clothing, to be sold by hawkers in competition with their 'old trash.'"[128] Judging by their contents, however, intended readers were assumed to be more sheep-like than wolf-like.

The strategy of treating artisan readers as beginners was not entirely successful. Charles Knight, who later became the publisher for the Society for the Diffusion of Useful Knowledge, criticized the tracts for talking "to thinking beings, and for the most part to very acute thinking beings, in the language of the nursery."[129] (Knight's observation was not without irony, since one of his own publications was later attacked for insinuating that poor men were not qualified to understand the measures of government.)[130]

The felt need to counter pro-Jacobin sentiment subsided during the interval that saw England at war with Revolutionary France and the threat posed by French armies overshadowing domestic strife. After Waterloo, however, domestic unrest reappeared. As in France, "the names of Voltaire and Rousseau became objects of universal desecration." In 1815 *The Times* sought to demolish Voltaire's statue and "grind to powder the vain, obscene, heartless, atheistical" philosophe.[131] When the opposition press gained strength, new measures were devised by the government to restrain output. In lieu of the Continental resort to rigorous censorship, new heavy duties on paper and periodicals were imposed.[132]

The praise of printing was revitalized as Whig leaders, philosophical radicals, and working-class pamphleteers combined to campaign against the Tory measures. The stark contrast between ignorance and knowledge which had been drawn by Tom Paine in *Rights of Man* was repeatedly evoked in the campaign. Francis Bacon's aphorism "Knowledge is Power" was transformed into a battle cry by the utilitarians and their working-class opponents alike.[133] When Henry Hetherington, the founding father of the first union of printing workers and a future Chartist leader, was editing the *Poor Man's Guardian* he defiantly substituted for the official red stamp of the government a black one, inscribed with "Knowledge is Power." The objectionable taxes were described as "taxes on knowledge"—a phrase that was stretched to encompass duties that impeded the distribution of printed materials by the postal service and mail coaches.[134]

Scenes from the early 1790s were replayed as Paine's works were re-printed and their publishers placed on trial. Tory reactions to the republica-tion of Paine's works resembled the reactions of Ultras and Catholics to the printing of works by Voltaire and Rousseau in Bourbon France. Whereas works by Voltaire and Rousseau loomed large on the political scene long after their authors' deaths, Paine himself had overseen the first printings and reprintings of the *Rights of Man*. "The success of the Second Part of *Rights of Man* was, in a true sense, phenomenal. . . . [According to an English correspondent,] '. . . the book is now made as much a Standard book in this Country as *Robinson Crusoe* & the *Pilgrim's Progress*.'"[135] Paine died as a relatively obscure immigrant in America a decade later. After his death, the republication of his anti-Christian tract, *Age of Reason*, "which made infidel-ity accessible to the masses for the first time"[136] became a cause célèbre.

In 1818, a tinsmith turned bookseller and radical journalist named Rich-ard Carlile brought out a thousand-copy edition of the *Age of Reason*. Despite his advertising this title in the newspapers and on placards, he sold only one hundred copies in the first month.

> But then the Society for the Suppression of Vice started a prosecu-tion; the news got into the Sunday papers; and in another month the edition was sold out. A second edition, of 3,000 copies, was printed, and in six months two-thirds of it was gone. The publicity given Carlile's trial helped sell 10,000 copies of the verbatim pro-ceedings of the first day. Since *The Age of Reason* had been read into the record during that day, as the basis of the case against him, it was incorporated into these pamphlets and thus given additional distribution. . . . the more he was persecuted, the more both his business and his cause flourished. While he was in prison, his wife continued his bookselling business and was promptly arrested in turn. In his *Republican*, he wrote: "I take this opportunity of repeat-ing my thanks to the Vice Society for the extensive circulation they are again giving my publications."[137]

No wonder Carlile described the printing press as a "multiplication table" and "the art of printing" as "a multiplication of the mind."

> The Printing-press may be strictly denominated a multiplication Table as applicable to the mind of man. The art of Printing is a

multiplication of mind. . . . Thus it is evident that a compression of sound moral truths within pamphlets, as the smallest and cheapest forms of giving effect to this multiplication of mind, is most conducive to the general good, and future welfare, of mankind.[138]

My whole and sole object, from first to last, from the time of putting off my leather apron till this day, has been a Free Press and Free Discussion. When I first started as a hawker of pamphlets I knew nothing of political principles . . . but I had a complete conviction that there was something wrong somewhere, and that the right application of the printing press was the remedy.[139]

Carlile, like Daniel Eaton, was prosecuted and imprisoned almost as often as had been John Lilburne. He proved to be fearless, as had Lilburne, about courting imprisonment in order to win publicity.

The seventeenth-century figure of John Lilburne served as a ghostly presence at many early nineteenth-century trials. The plight of "free-born John" was echoed in Cruikshank's caricature of the "free-born Englishman" who was shackled by the restraints on the press contained in the infamous Six Acts of 1819. William Hone, another artisan pamphleteer, and a needy bookseller whose *Register* was sponsored by Francis Place, became celebrated for being repeatedly acquitted of the charge of blasphemy after undergoing three separate trials. The story of Hone's conversion to radical politics may be apocryphal but seems worth retelling as indicative of the long reach of the printed word. When he was a boy, Hone had hung around the cheesemongers' shops in the hopes of finding occasional printed pages to read. (As had been the case in ancient Rome, according to poets and satirists, the remnants of old books were used to wrap groceries.) While looking over scraps of wrapping paper, Hone happened upon an account of John Lilburne's career, and it impressed him so much that he decided to become a political activist.[140] When put on trial, he defended himself by repeating the words Lilburne had used in his (Lilburne's) own defense. Olivia Smith suggests that Hone so identified himself with Lilburne that it affected not just what he said but also how he saw himself and viewed his judges and prosecutors.[141] If the story is true, Lilburne's constant resort to the medium of print paid off more than 150 years later.

Unlike Hone, who adhered to the faith of John Bunyan, Richard Carlile was a defiant atheist, a "showman for free thought and a driving force in the militant rationalist tradition."[142] When in jail in 1818 he wrote that solitary

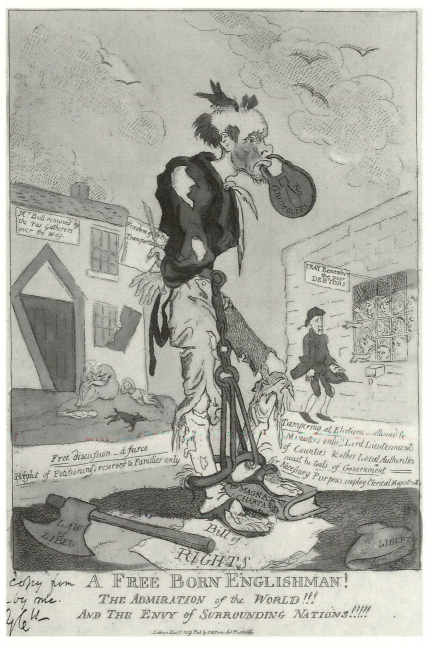

Figure 5.3. "A Freeborn Englishman." George Cruikshank, 1819. Courtesy of Princeton University Library.

confinement was not a real hardship: "I have no disposition or inclination to make converts by preaching. I leave that to priests. . . . My business is with the Press."[143] In the conduct of his business, he proved to be a shrewd journalist who knew how to turn a skirmish into an atrocity story, by describing, for example, how a poor woman's infant was drenched in his mother's blood during the so-called "massacre" at Peterloo.[144]

Many other publicists and pamphleteers played significant roles in supporting the removal of the taxes on knowledge and in publicizing anti-Burkean views. But there were few who were so confident and single-minded about the emancipatory powers of print. A Marxist critic complains that Carlile's preoccupation with the evils of kingcraft, lordcraft, and priestcraft was the same in 1830 as it had been in 1819 and left no room for new economic theories concerning the abuses of capitalism.[145] She had been anticipated by Hetherington, who complained that Carlile "does not strike at the root of evil which exists. . . . Were there no property, there would be no Kings, Priests, and Lords."[146] As a disciple of Tom Paine, Carlile agreed with Paine's friend, Condorcet, and proclaimed: the press "has come like a true messiah to emancipate the great family of mankind" from kingly and priestly influence.[147]

Steam Presses, Railway Fiction

It is worth noting that the press Carlile hailed as a "true messiah" was still likely to be a handpress. By the second decade of the nineteenth century, the iron handpress, which had been invented by Lord Stanhope around 1800, had been redesigned and was being produced in large numbers.[148] It was sturdy enough to withstand larger print runs and served as a valued weapon of working-class defiance. Indeed, it was repeatedly reproduced in caricatures by Cruikshank and others to represent a weapon wielded by freeborn Englishmen who refused to bow down to the crown, church, government, magistrates, soldiers, and tax collectors.[149] William Heath's cartoon of 1829 shows the Stanhope iron-frame press wearing a liberty cap and driving away obscurantism and privilege.[150]

Nevertheless, it was not the iron handpress but the more novel iron steam-driven one that dominated the nineteenth-century imagination.[151] After the introduction of iron cylinder presses harnessed to steam, first used by the London *Times* in 1814, the celebration of printing would acquire many

Figure 5.4. The Stanhope Press. William Heath, May 30, 1829. Courtesy of Princeton University Library.

of the characteristics that marked enthusiasm for other aspects of the "technological sublime."

> The steam engine loomed over the intellectual landscape as the chief symbol of a new age. . . . New technologies, from steam presses to railway bookstalls, postage stamps and telegraph lines, were altering not only the terms of debate, but its fundamental forms. . . .
>
> . . . . From the perspective of intellectual and literary life, the most significant changes involved printing and publishing. Innovations ranging from paper-making machines to machine-stamped bindings, from improved mechanisms of distribution to sales at railway bookstalls, transformed processes that had altered little since the sixteenth century. In terms of output and innovation, the industry was small compared with textiles, iron or the railways. But print culture, reporting on itself, occupied a central place in public awareness of industrial revolution.[152]

The phrase "print culture reporting on itself" is worth pausing over. A self-reflexive aspect had characterized Gutenberg's invention from the start: witness those self-congratulatory printers' prefaces commenting on the novelty of the divine art. This aspect came to the fore again when nineteenth-century publishers sought to impress their readers with the improvements that resulted from use of the steam press.

In addition to turning out periodicals, encyclopedias, and almanacs, and serving as publisher to the Society for the Diffusion of Useful Knowledge (SDUK), Charles Knight (1791–1873) wrote numerous works of his own that paid tribute to Gutenberg's invention and celebrated the recent mechanization of all facets of the industry.[153] In *Knowledge Is Power: A View of the Productive Forces of Modern Society* (1855) he described how advances in printing and papermaking had proved "injurious to no-one and beneficial to all."[154] Similarly, Knight's chief rival, Robert Chambers, publisher of *Chambers Encyclopedia*, the *Edinburgh Journal*, and other successful ventures, opined: "Nothing, in our opinion, within the compass of British manufacturing industry presents so stupendous a spectacle of moral power, working through inert mechanism, as that which is exhibited by the action of the steam press."[155]

"Everyone seemed to share . . . faith in a machine that could usher in the social millennium just as surely as the power of steam was transforming the outward face of English life. Each party . . . had its special brand of Truth to disseminate through print."[156] Printing ceased to be described as a divine art and was repeatedly hailed as a "mighty engine" (or a locomotive) of progress by nineteenth-century commentators. It was coupled with other steam-run machines, especially the railway engine. Not only did more rapid transport speed up the dissemination of printed materials, but train rides also encouraged reading and railway kiosks promoted book sales.

Indeed, a new category of reading matter, a subspecies that came to be known as "railway fiction," became profitable for entrepreneurial publishers such as W. H. Smith. To be sure, railway fiction was more likely to be condemned than praised by contemporary critics, consisting as it did of "tales of horror, sentimental novelettes of adventure and banditry, and soppy senti-mental fiction of high life."[157] It dismayed later Victorians such as Matthew Arnold and John Ruskin, who hoped to elevate popular taste. Arnold's aes-thetic sensibilities were offended by the "hideous and ignoble . . . tawdry novels which flare in the bookshelves of our railway stations."[158] As an educa-tor and school inspector, he promoted mass literacy. "Yet, . . . he looked upon that goal with some trepidation, and he hoped for a better result than universal novel-reading."[159]

However ignoble were some of the end products, the connection be-tween rail transport and printed output inspired many lofty pronouncements on the spirit of the age. Just as the railroads and steam engines suppress distance, Lamartine wrote, so too did print suppress time, linking Homer and Cicero to the Homers and Ciceros of the future in a silent, continuous conversation.[160] Numerous commentators attributed an acceleration of all historical processes to the advent of the printing machine. ("The Printing Machine" was the title of one of Charles Knight's monthlies.) After citing this pertinent passage from Charles Babbage: "Until printing was very gener-ally spread, civilization scarcely advanced by slow and languid steps; since that art has become cheap, its advances have been unparalleled, and its rate of progress vastly accelerated," Altick adds: "No sentiment was more fre-quently or grandiloquently repeated during the first half of the century."[161]

The progress that was believed to have been vastly accelerated, however, differed little from the progress that had been celebrated in the previous century. Along with enthusiasm for the new machinery went a determination to use it on behalf of earlier goals, such as the dissemination of Bibles or the advancement of learning or ending arbitrary rule. Chambers's *Edinburgh Journal* was accused by the Tory-Anglican journal *John Bull* of being "established for the purpose of conveying the poison of French philosophism into the hearts of the British people."[162]

"French philosophism" continued to attract enthusiastic adherents. In *Sartor Resartus* (1833–34), Thomas Carlyle reasserted the views of Condorcet in his own inimitable style: "He who first shortened the labor of Copyists by the device of Movable Types was disbanding hired armies, and cashiering most Kings and Senates, and creating a whole new Democratic world: he had invented the Art of Printing."[163] Charles Dickens, in an 1843 address to a gathering of printers, described printing as the only product of civilization that was necessary to the existence of free men. The press, he said, was "the fountain of knowledge and the bulwark of freedom, the founder of free States and their preserver."[164]

Enlightenment values were especially prominent in the publications of the Society for the Diffusion of Useful Knowledge, which was founded in 1829 under the aegis of Henry Brougham, the future Lord Chancellor, with the aim of improving educational opportunities and encouraging self-help among factory workers and other disadvantaged members of a growing urban populace.[165] It has become celebrated less for its virtuous intentions than for the satire it inspired. Few historians fail to introduce it without some mention of the "steam intellect society," the satiric invention of Thomas Love Peacock.[166] In a manner reminiscent of Swift's satires on the Royal Society but in a more good-natured vein, Peacock described how a cook burned down the house while studying the Society's sixpenny tract on hydrostatics.

The belief that the steam press was ideally designed to implement social progress rested on the assumption that ignorance and superstition were responsible for the worst social ills. Once taxes on knowledge were removed, information would become freely available to those artisans and skilled mechanics who were the "natural teachers of the poor" and who would be able to teach the semiliterate.[167] The sentiment that mankind had come closer to realizing the "heavenly city of the eighteenth-century philosophers" made the struggle against Tory taxes seem especially urgent. If only the press were free of constraints, wrote James Mill in 1821, "something better than the dreams of the Golden Age would be realized upon earth."[168] James Mill's son, John Stuart, was inspired "above all by Condorcet's *Life of Turgot*." In striking contrast to John Adams's acid comments about the French "prophets of progress," he described the book as "one of the wisest and noblest of lives, delineated by one of the wisest and noblest of men."[169]

Benthamites and Malthusians really believed that ignorance was chiefly responsible for the misery of the laboring poor and that education was the appropriate remedy for the nation's ills. Once they could be properly informed about the principles of legislation and population, workers would come to understand the need for family planning and exhibit more self-control. Even alcoholism could be eliminated, it was argued, once the public's thirst for news could be requited without working men having to go to taverns to look at newspapers.[170]

In the 1830s, after the defeat of the Tories by a coalition of Whigs, Liberals and Peelites, the heavy duties were reduced. A legal penny press came into existence in 1836. The middle-class supporters of the Useful Knowledge society were pleased. The society's publisher, Charles Knight, launched the *Penny Encyclopedia* and a new journal, the *Penny Magazine.*

Working-class spokesmen, however, felt cheated. The new laws made "'the rich man's paper cheaper, and the poor man's paper dearer,' said the *Northern Star* in 1838."[171] They were "cruel laws that prevent the free circulation of thought through the medium of a cheap and honest press."[172] Class divisions over the maintenance of some "taxes on knowledge" became prominent and intruded on the larger political scene.

> The campaign against the "taxes on knowledge" was intensified . . . .the crusade for the unobstructed circulation of news and political opinion became not a by-product but a direct cause of new agitation in the broader political sphere . . . an organization founded specifically to pay the fines of convicted editors and printers, William Lovett's London Working Men's Association, . . . became the fountainhead of the Chartist movement. . . . the repeal of all the taxes on knowledge—stamp tax, advertisement duty, paper duty— was an integral, not an incidental, part of the radical prescription for improving the condition of England.[173]

A repeal of "all taxes on knowledge" was eventually enacted, but by that time the Chartist movement had, so to speak, run out of steam. The output of artisanal iron handpresses had been dwarfed by that of entrepreneurial publishers, who could invest in new papermaking and printing machines in order to publish on a massive scale. Machine printing made publication possible at a price far beyond the reach of those without substantial capital. The process was ideal for those with large-scale financial backing. Working-class protests were soon "drowned in the sea of useful knowledge pouring from the steam press factories."[174]

Working-class protests were not alone in being drowned. The sea of useful knowledge kept getting larger, engendering increasing concern about being overwhelmed by the sheer quantity of reading matter (i.e., Hugo's tower that never stopped growing). "This future universal inundation of books," wrote Isaac d'Israeli, "this superfluity of knowledge, in billions and trillions, overwhelms the imagination."[175] As earlier chapters suggest, the feeling of being victimized by the overproduction of printed matter had been experienced by previous generations. Nineteenth-century commentators felt no less certain than had their forebears that they were confronted by an unprecedented situation. They had good reason to feel that way. Improvements in printing technology had made it possible for presses to churn out ever larger quantities of printed materials. For the most part, it was the flooding of markets with useless, not useful, materials, which was viewed as the greatest threat. Charles Knight (echoing Morhof) noted that all great instruments of power, printing being one of the greatest, may be abused as well as used. Fortunately, he wrote hopefully, the more works representing wholesome enjoyment are issued, the more will printing's detrimental effects be curbed.[176]

Publishers such as Knight and Chambers, utilitarian philosophers such as Bentham and Mill, and politicians such as Henry Brougham wholeheartedly embraced the new printing machines as a means of promoting useful knowledge, improving the lot of workers, and encouraging self-help. But much of what was deemed useful knowledge in publications such as Knight's was regarded as "nonsensical tittle tattle about forks and spoons, and smock frocks, bridges, waterfalls, and a thousand other things," that were "utterly useless" to the poor.[177]

> Knight's journal offered useful knowledge in the form of pirated descriptions of tea-growing in China, the origin of Somerset House, the entrance of Fingal's cave—dear me how instructive!—or how many humps there are on the back of a dromedary; how a caterpillar grows from chrysalis to butterfly; how a kangeroo jumps . . . useless Tory frippery as patronizing as it was hypocritical.[178]

Disillusioned artisans who felt cheated by reforms that stopped short of removing all taxes on knowledge were not the only ones who objected to the output of the Society for the Diffusion of Useful Knowledge. As Peacock's satire suggests, the utilitarians came under attack from other quarters on other grounds. Poets and fiction writers had been exiled from the republic of letters by Jeremy Bentham. "None of Jeremy Bentham's crotchets is better remembered than his exclusion of poetry, in fact all imaginative literature, from his ideal republic."[179] Bentham's crotchet is so well remembered partly because it inspired memorable satire and also because it called forth such an effective outpouring of indignation from those he had banished. They objected to the overly rational approach used by the members of the "steam intellect" society while seeking with great success to inspire imaginative and sympathetic responses from their readers.

"It seems to me," wrote Carlyle in 1840,

> the Unbelieving century with its unblessed products is already past: a new century is already come . . . go thy way! . . . hollow Formulism, gross Benthamism. . . . An unbelieving Eighteenth Century is but an exception . . . I prophesy that the world will once more become *sincere*; a believing world with *many* Heroes in it, a heroic world. . . .
>
> We will rejoice greatly that Skepticism, Insincerity, Mechanical Atheism with all their poison dews are going, and are as good as gone.[180]

Probably the most telling example of the sense of cultural impoverishment that was attributed to the use of print by utilitarians was offered by Carlyle's contemporary, John Stuart Mill. After a youth spent under the tutelage of his utilitarian father and having been thoroughly saturated with useful knowledge, Mill reports in his *Autobiography* that he fell into a prolonged depression during the winter of 1826–27.[181] He then came to the realization that by concentrating entirely on intellectual concerns he had neglected to consider his emotional needs, and found in Wordsworth's poetry "a medicine for my state of mind."[182] Wordsworth's poems expressed "not merely outward beauty" but "inward joy." They provided a source of "sympathetic and imaginative pleasure that could be shared in by all human beings."[183] After this breakthrough, Mill's reading took a new direction:

> The influences of European, that is to say, Continental thought, and especially those of the reaction of the nineteenth century against the

eighteenth, were now streaming in upon me. They came from various quarters: from the writings of Coleridge . . . from what I had
read of Goethe, from Carlyle's early articles, . . . though for a long
time I saw nothing in these (as my father saw nothing in them to
the last) but insane rhapsody.[184]

Although Mill was in partial agreement with the Romantic reaction, he continued to value the eighteenth-century philosophes and marveled at the
"blind rage" that was expended against them.[185]

The most objectionable aspects of utilitarianism—the aspects that provoked blind rage—were captured by Dickens and immortalized in his depiction of Thomas Gradgrind. As Raymond Williams notes, Gradgrind should
not be confused, as he often is, with Josiah Bounderby, the other villain in
Hard Times, who represented the aggressive, money-making, power-seeking,
hard-driving employer.[186] Gradgrind is instead a follower of Jeremy Bentham
(who had himself espoused the doctrines of Helvetius, author of "Man the
Machine"). Gradgrind would weigh and measure any part of human nature
with a rule and a pair of scales. "All I want is facts. Stick to the Facts, Sir."
Much as Swift satirized excessive reliance on mathematical measurement, so
too did Dickens satirize the way would-be reformers and social engineers,
such as Edmund Chadwick, reduced human behavior to statistical averages.
In "condemning Thomas Gradgrind, . . . we are invited also to condemn the
kind of thinking and methods of enquiry and legislation which promoted . . .
social and industrial reform."[187] Dickens "pitted the individual person against
the system." His description (again in *Hard Times*) of War Office thinking
during the Crimean War seems painfully relevant to Pentagon planning during the Iraq War. (The average temperature during a year in Crimea led the
bureaucrats to put soldiers in light clothing on a night when they would have
been "frozen in fur.")

Gradgrind was determined to destroy any poetic or imaginative impulse
in the youngsters under his charge. His counterparts in real life were responsible for the content of the schoolbooks that provoked Matthew Arnold when
he served as school inspector in 1860.[188] He represented all that is unsympa-
thetic about the purported distancing effects of print—about the tendency
to envisage human beings as dots on graphs, to reduce human behavior to
statistical averages, and to act in accord with pseudosciences such as "eugen-
ics." One is reminded of Foucault's condemnation of Bentham and his social
engineering device, the Panopticon. The indictment of print by Lewis Mum-

ford also comes to mind. "Through the habit of using print and paper thought lost something of its . . . organic character and became abstract, categorical, stereotyped."[189]

Gradgrind may be viewed as a byproduct of the printing machine. But so too could the novels that were turned out by his creator. Much as Romantic poetry supplied what had been missing in J. S. Mill's unimaginative upbringing, Victorian fiction supplied the imaginative and emotional dimensions that utilitarian publications had lacked. In view of opinions such as Mumford's, we need to be reminded that the printing machine was especially conducive to the production of fiction. In this regard it would be a mistake to depict Charles Knight as a prototype for Gradgrind, despite his many services to the SDUK. Knight took pains to disassociate himself from the Benthamites: "those who address themselves to the imagination," he wrote, "poets, novelists, painters, musicians," are *not* "unprofitable laborers."[190] He dedicated one of his books "To Charles Dickens, One of the most earnest laborers in that Popular Literature which elevates a People, this volume is affectionately inscribed."[191]

Charles Dickens was only one of numerous novelists and poets, on both sides of the Channel, who were elevated to the status of culture heroes after printing was mechanized. The Romantic cult of the hero was just as much a product of the steam press as was useful knowledge. Carlyle's "man of letters with his copy rights and copy wrongs"[192] was a byproduct of those same impersonal market forces that all claimed to despise. Indeed, Carlyle's essay inspired the 39-volume series devoted to English men of letters issued by Macmillan (1878–92).[193]

> What becomes of the Goddess Fame side by side with Printing
> House Square? . . . Is Achilles possible side by side with powder and
> lead? Or is the Iliad at all compatible with the printing press and
> the steam press? Does not singing and reciting and the muses neces-
> sarily go out of existence with the appearance of the printer's
> bar . . . ?[194]

There is more than a little irony in Marx's question, "What becomes of the Goddess Fame?" As many studies have demonstrated, the nineteenth-century steam press did little to diminish the status of artist or author and much to elevate it. "Mr. Dickens collected around him at Birmingham such an audience as never before waited upon an author."[195] Singing and reciting profited from the printed publicity that filled large concert halls and filled also the purses of a new group of intermediaries who acted as publicity agents. Much as impresarios promoted their performers and advertised their virtuosity, so too did publishers try to persuade the public that authors were men of genius. Scientists and inventors were promoted alongside novelists and poets. "Publishers . . . encouraged . . . a heroic role for the man of knowledge because familiar names sold books."[196] Successful authors had their names and faces replicated in myriad contexts, even stamped on cards for family games of "books and authors."

Where Richardson and Rousseau had pioneered, scores of later poets and authors followed.[197] In the 1820s and '30s, Wordsworth became the object of a pilgrimage. His house in the Lake District was thronged with tourists, Keats among them. They came by on what Charles Lamb called "gaping missions."[198] William St. Clair describes how Byron's image achieved its iconic status: Byron portraits were "copied, recopied, reversed, exaggerated and added to by unnumbered, mostly unskilled, pirate engravers, becoming ever more Byronic with every re-engraving. . . . Lightning flashed round his head. Grecian columns lurked in the background . . ."[199] (The reference to lightning evokes the earlier cult of Benjamin Franklin, where copies and recopies similarly fixed the image of "Le Bonhomme Richard" in a lasting mold.) Paul Bénichou's classic study places the "sacre de l'écrivain" between 1750 and 1830.[200] The sanctification of the author persisted, reaching its apogee later on. One thinks of the people waiting on the dock to learn about the death of Little Nell or the worshipful crowds walking behind Victor Hugo's hearse.

Nineteenth-century literati, however, continued to wax nostalgic for bardic poets, scribal arts, and noble patrons. As in former epochs, enthusiasm for technological advance was countered by nostalgia for a world that was lost. After the mechanization of printing had gotten underway, use of the wooden handpress was regarded less and less as an instance of mechanical reproduction, and more and more as a tool that lent itself to the production of aesthetically pleasing objects. Profit-seeking early printers who pioneered in double-entry bookkeeping, marketing techniques, and strike-breaking were forgotten, to be replaced by idealized master artisans who were celebrated for the beauty of their products.[201]

The enhanced appreciation of the early printer had been manifested in those nineteenth-century jubilee celebrations (noted above) that elevated Gutenberg to the status of a Western culture hero. It reached a climax toward the end of the century, when William Morris added handpress printing to the rest of his multifaceted arts and crafts movement. Morris was a passionate utopian socialist who inveighed against "the present system of commercialism and profit mongering."[202] Among other ugly products he associated with the reign of "plutocracy" were the cheap machine-made books and papers of the day. His decision to take up handpress printing was triggered by a slide lecture given in November, 1888, by his neighbor, Emery Walker.[203] Walker's account of the "horrors of Victorian typography," in contrast to examples of fifteenth- and sixteenth-century masterworks by Nicholas Jenson and other Renaissance printers, inspired Morris. With Walker's help, Morris set up the Kelmscott Press (1891) and issued deluxe volumes that combined Gothic revival designs with Renaissance typography. In keeping with the views of Victor Hugo, Morris believed that "the only great art is popular art shared by all the people."[204] For Hugo, however, the truly popular art of medieval communities had been embodied in the Gothic cathedrals that presumably had been displaced by the invention of printing. Morris detached the handpress from the commercial concerns that had once sustained it, ignored its novelty as a duplicating machine, and embraced it as an expression of an imagined medieval zeitgeist. "Each Kelmscott Press book was intended to be, not a Victorian railway novel done in the Gothic style, but a miniature cathedral . . . inspired by the Ruskinian tradition of craftsmanship as an act of worship."[205] In the late eighteenth century, the handpress had been celebrated by working-class leaders as a popularizing and democratizing instrument. By the end of the nineteenth century, it was being used to issue deluxe volumes of value to a relatively small elite.

The idealization of early printers was also manifested in the growing passion for collecting books. Altick refers to a "secular bibliolatry indulged in and celebrated by men like Dibdin and the elder d'Israeli."[206] The acquisition of early printed books became subject to the rules that governed all other collecting manias. Fierce competition among bibliophiles and book dealers led to increased market value. Books printed before 1500, which were assigned the status of incunabula,[207] were especially highly prized and highly priced.

Dismay at the onset of an iron age of commercialism had been common enough in the age of the wooden handpress, as the preceding chapter notes. In the days of Swift and Pope, when artisans were still manning wooden presses and papermaking had not yet been mechanized, it was the ascendancy of booksellers that led literati to express dissatisfaction. Complaints aimed at booksellers in the eighteenth century were not dissimilar from those aimed at press barons and publishers in the new era of railway fiction. Nineteenth-century literati set the best of the past against the worst of the present, exaggerated the role of the aristocratic patron, ignored the greed and knavery of early printers, and downplayed the market forces which had affected writers before industrialization.

In Great Britain, the place of the avaricious bookseller had been taken by the entrepreneurial owner of a chain of newspapers, railway stalls, and circulating libraries. W. H. Smith and Charles Mudie reigned as the self-styled arbiters of public taste. They dominated reading markets, encouraged anonymous reviewing, and determined the reputation of authors. They dictated the size of novels, insisting on a three-volume format (that "triple-headed monster, sucking the blood of English novelists")[208] so that lending libraries could receive triple payments for a single work.[209]

The literary system on the Continent was somewhat different from that which pertained in Great Britain, but complaints about living in an iron age were no less vociferous. The most celebrated essay on this theme was "On Industrial Literature" (1839) by Sainte-Beuve.[210] Perhaps the most damning description of print culture in the early industrial age was provided by Balzac's *Illusions perdues*. The novel opens with mention of the Stanhope press. The first chapter introduces us to a printing shop that symbolizes the world turned upside down after 1789. We are introduced to a shrewd, albeit ignorant, provincial printer, formerly an illiterate pressman, who makes a fortune during the Terror by employing his natural masters, a count and an abbé, as hired hands. The old villain is too much of a skinflint to equip his presses properly. He accumulates money by hoarding and starving the members of his household. (The portrait is not dissimilar from that drawn by Erasmus of Aldus's miserly father-in-law, the publisher Asola, who starved the writers Aldus lodged.) The scene then moves to the great city of Paris, which is depicted as a kind of hell, with market forces viewed in a lurid light. The miserly artisan with his wooden handpress has been left behind in the provinces. In Paris, the iron laws of capitalism prevail. Publishers investing in meretricious best sellers protect their investments by bribery and blackmail. They arrange for corrupt critics to praise worthless books and denounce or ignore praiseworthy ones. They force poor authors to choose between slavery to the system and starving on their own.

Balzac's portrayal of conniving publishers and desperate Grub Street authors is often taken at face value as a realistic rendering of the literary marketplace in nineteenth-century Paris.²¹¹ (The same thing is true of George Gissing's much later portrayal of literary London in *New Grub Street*.) No doubt, book reviewing was subject to bribery and corruption, especially during the interval when anonymous reviewing was customary. But patronage was scarcely dispensed evenhandedly in earlier eras. Was currying favor with powerful princes and prelates less humiliating than trying to win favorable notice in a newspaper review? Even now most writers have to depend on agents or patrons for their work to receive favorable notice (or any notice) from reviewers and be deemed acceptable for publication. As César Grana suggests, an author's complaint of being abused by self-seeking intermediaries has a paradoxical aspect: it implies merely that a work isn't selling well.²¹²

When appraising Balzac's work, some allowance needs to be made for the partisan politics of the day. As a royalist who sympathized with the counter-revolutionary cause, as the author of *Les chouans*—a novel à la Scott—which glamorized the counter-revolution in the Vendée, Balzac was predisposed to view the social landscape of the 1830s in a bleak light.²¹³ His depiction of a noble and a priest working for an ignorant employer provided a vivid fictional embodiment of Burke's dystopian vision of the world turned upside down. The long history of friction between authors and publishers also needs to be taken into account. Is there any era from the sixteenth century to the present that lacks complaints about cold-blooded, calculating, profit-seeking printer-publishers who wring the last penny from starving writers while hastily marketing inferior goods?²¹⁴

It is noteworthy that Robert Darnton finds that Balzac's portrayal fits the eighteenth-century publishing scene, although Darnton's conniving publishers and desperate Grub Street characters belong to a prerevolutionary and preindustrial age.²¹⁵ There is little to differentiate Darnton's description of the cutthroat business of publishing from Balzac's except that Darnton's publishers (with one late exception)²¹⁶ operate outside French borders, whereas Balzac's are especially intent on receiving favorable notice in the Parisian daily press. It is also intriguing to find references in *Illusions perdues* to a distant golden age of handpress printing when Aldus Manutius, Plantin, and the Elseviers plied their trade. Not all illusions had been lost in the 1830s.

Chapter 6

The Newspaper Press: The End of Books?

> The newspaper is in all literalness the bible of democracy. The book
> out of which a people determines its conduct. It is the only serious
> book that most people read. It is the only book they read every day.
> —Walter Lippmann, *Liberty and the News*

Winning favorable reviews in the daily press, by fair means or foul, was a
major concern of the Parisian literati described in *Illusions perdues*. Mention
of the daily press points to a phenomenon that certainly loomed large in
nineteenth-century views of printing and that deserves separate treatment.
Up to this point we have been concerned with the "huge froth-ocean of
Printed Speech we loosely call literature"[1] without distinguishing between
diverse genres. When considering such issues as attitudes toward censorship,
distinctions between books, pamphlets, and periodicals seem to be of minor
consequence. To be sure, printers were less likely to be prosecuted for costly
volumes aimed at elites than for cheap papers and pamphlets, which presumably stirred up the rabble. "A three guinea book," said William Pitt the
younger to his colleagues, "could never do much harm among those who
had not three shillings to spare."[2] Yet efforts to control all printed output
characterized the authoritarian regimes of the past and the totalitarian ones
of the twentieth century. Thus after Waterloo, the reprinting of books by
Voltaire or Tom Paine was subject to prosecution. Nineteenth-century liberals objected to an *Index of Prohibited Books* as well as to censorship of periodicals and newspapers. Even today, civil libertarians may feel uneasy about
allowing the free circulation of the *Protocols of the Elders of Zion* or *Mein
Kampf*. A difficult book, not a readable pamphlet, led to a death sentence
being imposed on Salman Rushdie.

Furthermore, in the nineteenth century as in earlier eras, distinctions between books and periodicals were themselves very blurred. Eighteenth-century journals were initiated as spinoffs from book publishing.[3] Separate issues were also collected and bound as books. (This practice still continues in most libraries even now.) Nineteenth-century novels were published in installments and often serialized in newspapers.[4] Journals carried book reviews, which were, and still are, a significant element in determining book sales.

Nevertheless, even a sketchy account such as this one must make room for the special niche occupied by journalism when surveying views of printing. The difference between book and periodical press had been underlined—before the coming of steam—by a French revolutionary journalist, Pierre-Louis Roederer, who wrote an essay on "the different means of communication of ideas among men in society" (1796). Newspapers, Roederer wrote,

> contained only the latest and most pressing news; they had more readers than books or other forms of printed matter that customers had to seek out in bookstores, because, thanks to hawkers and postmen, newspapers sought out their audiences. Journals had a greater social impact than other media because they were read by all classes and because they reached their audience "every day, at the same time . . . in all public places," and because they were the "almost obligatory diet of daily conversation."[5]

Roederer's observation that, unlike other kinds of printed materials, newspapers reached their audience "every day at the same time" points to the attribute of simultaneity that was a special feature of the daily newspaper. The attribute of periodicity was also significant, as shown by Pierre Rétat's study of a journal entitled *Les Révolutions de Paris*. It had been issuing sporadic bulletins called "occasionels" until 14 July 1789. On that date, it turned itself into a regular weekly. As the issues piled up, its readers were encouraged to think of Bastille Day as the beginning of a new and continuously unfolding narrative in the history of mankind.[6] Periodicity entailed continuity. "A newspaper and its readers are a sort of association," wrote Mme. de Staël, while reflecting on the revolutionary experience; "the newspaper is a continuing action."[7]

As these comments suggest, and the previous chapter makes clear, the increased significance assigned to the newspaper press owed much to the French Revolution. The Revolutionary press seemed especially explosive largely because so many new papers did burst onto the scene. Five hundred new papers appeared in Paris between 1789 and 1791 to serve a population of 600,000.[8] (The Goncourts described the French press as springing fully armed like Minerva from the head of Zeus.)[9] It also seemed explosive because it appeared in a context of relative dearth. Before 1789, Parisians had had relatively little experience with domestic partisan journalism and had largely relied on the biweekly products of foreign presses (such as the *Gazette de Leyde*) for their political news.[10] This was in striking contrast to the experience of eighteenth-century Londoners. Paris saw its first daily newspaper in 1777—some 80 years after London's.[11] The difference between the English experience and that of populations across the Channel was a source of considerable satisfaction to patriotic English writers.

"The liberty of the English press had, in a sense, been secured by the cessation of licensing in 1695."[12] In his *History of England*, Macaulay made much of this event: "The lapse of what he called the Licensing Acts was the day on which the emancipation of our liberties was accomplished. . . . [It] did more for liberty and for civilization than the Great Charter or the Bill of Rights."[13] James Raven cites this statement to illustrate Macaulay's propensity for Whiggish "mythologizing" and, in this instance, for creating "a watershed where there was none."[14] Yet Macaulay had made it clear that contemporaries, far from considering the vote as a watershed, regarded it as insignificant. He pointed out that the vote to allow licensing to lapse attracted little attention and that members of the House of Commons "knew not what they were doing, what a revolution they were making, what a power they were calling into existence. . . . The Licensing Act is condemned not as a thing essentially evil, but on account of the petty grievances, . . . the jobs, the commercial restrictions . . . which were incidental to it."[15]

Whether or not historians should consider the end of licensing as a watershed, the "liberty of the free-born Englishmen to write and publish for the common good" soon became a significant ingredient in English exceptionalism. "Many writers regarded the rest of Europe as shackled and unenlightened." In his history of printing (1749), Joseph Ames used an unfortunate metaphor to honor the "period when Britain roused herself from amid various superstitions and sat down on the seat of liberty, where she now remains." An obituary for William Caslon in 1778 praised Caslon for improving "the art of letter founding," an art obviously and essentially important to a nation whose "great and glorious characteristic is the freedom of the press."[16]

The celebration of "freedom of the press" in eighteenth-century Britain did not, of course, exclude negative views of particular newspapers and newsmen. Indeed, little enthusiasm was expressed for actual journals and even less for the practices of actual journalists, who were, for the most part, disdained as hired hands. Negative reactions to print journalism may be traced back to its earliest appearance in early sixteenth-century Venice, where Pietro Aretino, the so-called "scourge of princes," had pioneered in exploiting printed publicity for the purposes of blackmail. "In a certain sense," Burckhardt wrote, Aretino "may be considered the father of modern journalism."[17] It is fair enough to describe Aretino as the father of modern pornography given the enormous success of his "Postures."[18] But it might be more appropriate to describe him as an antijournalist, since he had no desire to inform the public and sought to profit from withholding rather than from disclosing any news. Later manifestations of his tactics were on view in eighteenth-century London, where an enclave of unscrupulous French writers sought rewards for their silence from special agents sent by the French king.[19]

Aretino's immediate followers, who were known as "poligraphi," came closer to serving as prototypes for later newsmen. These "low-born adventurers of the pen" produced lively sketches of Venetian society that were accompanied by satirical commentary.[20] They were especially prone to elaborate on anticlerical themes, providing humorous anecdotes long favored by college students with organs of publicity that had not been available before.[21] "Increasingly the arts of a corrosive journalism would be directed at the shortcomings of the clergy both high and low."[22]

Less entertaining forms of journalism also had their start in sixteenth-century Europe, especially in Antwerp in the 1540s when the price lists of merchants ceased to be copied by hand. Lists of commodities to be sold, goods available for purchase, the rates at which money was lent, shipping news, and so forth; all were conveyed in printed form by Antwerp papers after the mid-sixteenth century. This encouraged an expansion of the business that was conducted by the Antwerp Exchange and increased profits for local printers and publishers.[23]

As was true of merchants, royal officials found it useful to substitute printer for copyist. "Princes who had employed the cumbersome method of manuscript to communicate with their subjects switched quickly to print to announce declarations of war, publish battle accounts, promulgate treaties or argue disputed points in pamphlet form."[24] Royal entries, in particular, lent themselves to printed propaganda. Well illustrated festival newsletters were printed and distributed as rapidly as possible. They transposed actual performances for local communities into virtual events that were vicariously experienced.[25] The regency of Louis XIII saw the founding of the first royally sponsored newspaper in Europe, the controlled weekly *Gazette*. Well before then, Amsterdam had succeeded Antwerp as the leader of the business press and had pioneered in other forms of journalism. It was in early seventeenth-century Amsterdam that the first newspapers took form.[26]

The New Tydings out of Italie, the first newspaper sold in England (December, 1620) came from an Amsterdam publisher, but soon the London syndicate of Bourne and Butter had set up business on their own. The two pressmen rapidly achieved unwonted celebrity as figures of fun in Ben Jonson's comedy *The Staple of News* (1626). As the play's title suggests, news could already be regarded as one more commodity to be bought and sold in London's shops.[27] The play showed Jonson's ambivalent attitude toward print. Pride in having authored his monumental printed *Werkes* in 1616 went together with anxiety about the new medium that was threatening to displace the theater as a public forum. D. F. McKenzie has dramatized (so to speak) the underlying message of Jonson's play: "*The Staple of News* marks the end of theatre as the only secular mass medium, the end of the play-house as the principal forum of public debate. . . . The dramatic poet, as rhetor in the truest sense, had lost his vocation as a journalist."[28]

Another authority suggests that it may be premature to take Jonson's play of 1626 as marking the point where dramatist gives way to journalist. Jonson, she argues,

> was the only playwright of the time to pay much attention to print. The early theatre was quite sure of its place and function. But with the abolition of the Star Chamber in 1641 and the closing of the theatres in 1642, the stage neither could be nor was needed to be the locus of popular discourse. . . . The press was given an opportunity to take over many functions that the stage had once performed. Pushed aside by journalism, the stage ceased to be the center of news, the source of public information, and the focus of debate.[29]

It may be premature to take *The Staple of News* as marking the end of the playhouse as a principal forum for debate. Yet it may also be premature to assign the same significance to the closing of theaters in 1642. The theater rapidly regained its vitality during the Restoration. Thereafter, the effects of a controversial play were more likely to be amplified than muffled by printed news reports. In later centuries, public debate continued to be generated by dramatists such as Ibsen or Shaw, whose plays were sufficiently newsworthy to be given extended life in printed form. Indeed, theatrical productions continued to command public attention, not in spite of, but because of the coverage they received from the press. Here as elsewhere, coexistence rather than supersession held sway.

Still, it is clear that the pamphlet wars of the 1740s temporarily occupied the center of the British political stage. In the aftermath of the Civil War, the tattoo of "paper bullets" subsided, but journalism continued to be a source of anxiety to royal officials. In 1663, Roger l'Estrange, who became Surveyor of the Press (1665–79) and editor of two journals supporting Charles II, famously declared:

> a Public Mercury should never have my vote, because I think it
> makes the multitude too familiar with the actions and counsels of
> their superiors . . . and gives them not only an itch, but a kind of
> colourable right and license to be meddling with the Government.[30]

During the eighteenth century, the trade of the journalist provoked numerous comments that were, for the most part, unfavorable. The term "journalist" was subject to considerable semantic confusion, since it was used to designate both the respectable editors of journals for savants (Pierre Bayle, Jean LeClerc) and the disreputable scandal-mongers who followed "Aretino's métier." Most eighteenth-century commentators were contemptuous. Defoe, who was himself scarcely in good repute, affected to despise the "street scribblers who daily and monthly abuse mankind with stories of great victories when we are beaten."[31] The philosophes were also dismissive:

> Voltaire said journalism was discredited by the "multitude of papers
> which . . . greedy booksellers have published and. . . . which obscure
> writers fill with incorrect extracts, stupidities and lies". . . . Diderot
> remarked . . . Newspapers were invented "for the solace of those
> who were either too busy or too lazy to read whole books." . . .
> Rousseau thought journalism a labourer's task and a periodical "an
> ephemeral work without merit and without utility which cultivated

men . . . despise and which serves only to give women and fools vanity without instruction."[32]

Nevertheless, the philosophes were indebted to an expatriate journalist named Pierre Rousseau, who stimulated public interest in the *Encyclopédie* and the encyclopedists by means of his *Journal Encyclopédique* (1756–58). It was published in several locales outside France but eventually gained admittance within the realm. The journal was devoted to extracts and anecdotes about the multivolume work in progress and kept it in the public eye when the enterprise was foundering in Paris—providing yet another example of the symbiosis between book and journal.[33]

Most eighteenth-century literati affected to disdain journalists. The political activists who participated in the French Revolution often preferred calling themselves "publicistes."[34] When they did accept the role of journalist, they assigned themselves a higher calling as "tribunes of the people" and wrote in a self-congratulatory vein: "Here I am a journalist, and it is a rather fine role. No longer is it a wretched and mercenary profession, enslaved by the government. Today in France it is the journalist who holds the tablets, the album of the censor, and who inspects the senate, the consuls, and the dictator himself."[35] In this regard, as in many others, the events of 1789–99 made a deep and lasting impression upon the nineteenth-century French political scene: "The Revolution established a tradition by which, in 1830 and 1848, journalists played a leading role in overthrowing governments."[36]

By the 1830s, however, journalism itself was being "revolutionized"— transformed by the improvements in papermaking and print technology that signaled the end of the age of the wooden handpress. The two key dates are 1814, when *The Times* of London came off an iron rotary press powered by steam, and 1836, when Émile Girardin inaugurated *La Presse*, which doubled the circulation and halved the costs of previous Paris newspapers. This publication gave the French term "la presse" its special journalistic significance. Girardin ostensibly moved "beyond ideology" and sought to provide "publicity of facts and not polemic of ideas."[37] The celebrated duel that saw Girardin kill Alexis Carrel, the editor of the *National*, has often been taken to signify the end of one era in French journalism and the beginning of another.[38] From then on, it is said, the political pamphleteer-cum-journalist would be overshadowed by the entrepreneurial press baron. As is the case with all such developments, it would be a mistake to think in terms of supersession. *La Presse*, which was aimed at expanding its readership, providing "objective" reports and avoiding trouble with the authorities, scarcely put an end to more partisan "journaux d'opinion."[39] Moreover, the political pamphlet was never superseded and would resurface again and again after the daily press had become a fully capitalized industry. One of the more memorable products of 1848 was Marx's *Communist Manifesto*. Moreover, the political pamphlet could be transformed into a front page "open letter" in a newspaper, as was the case with Émile Zola's *J'accuse*.[40]

In Great Britain, as elsewhere, the newspaper that was produced on steam-driven presses figured prominently in the excitement over the "technological sublime." It was described by Robert Owen as "the most powerful engine for good or evil that has been brought into action by human creation."[41] Charles Knight reflected on the new global reach of the steam-driven printing machines: "Visit, if you can, the interior of that marvellous human machine, the General Post Office, on a Friday evening from half past five to six o'clock. Look with awe upon the tons of newspapers that are crowding in to be distributed through the habitable globe. Think silently how potent a power this is for good or evil."[42]

In the aftermath of the French Revolution and with the industrialization of printing processes, observers began to view the newspaper press as a separate estate of the realm. Probably the most influential phrase-maker on this theme was Thomas Carlyle, who elaborated on the way the dream of the Girondins had been realized. "Journalists are now our true kings and clergy," he wrote. "The true Church of England lies in the editors of our newspapers."[43] He attributed to Edmund Burke the idea that newspaper reporters constituted a new Fourth Estate:

> Burke said that there were three estates in parliament, but in the reporters' gallery yonder there sat a fourth estate more important far than they all. It is not a figure of speech or a witty saying; it is a literal fact very momentous to us in these times. . . . Whoever can speak, speaking now to the whole nation, becomes a power, a branch of government with inalienable weight in law-making.[44]

It is uncertain whether Burke ever did point to the reporters' gallery and say this. But the phrase *was* repeatedly employed by liberal politicians: Macaulay, Brougham, and others during the 1830s.[45] Later in the century, Oscar Wilde offered an amusing version:

Figure 6.1. The "fourth estate" (Press Gallery in the House of Commons),
1867. Courtesy of the Bridgeman Art Library.

In the old days men had the rack. Now they have the press. That is
an improvement certainly. But still it is very bad, and wrong, and
demoralising. Somebody—was it Burke?—called journalism the
fourth estate. That was true at the time, no doubt. But at the present
moment it really is the only estate. It has eaten up the other three.
The Lords Temporal say nothing, the Lords Spiritual have nothing
to say, and the House of Commons has nothing to say and says it.
We are dominated by Journalism.[46]

The concept was still current in Anglo-American parlance a century later;
witness the title of Douglas Cater's book published in 1959: *The Fourth*

Branch of Government.[47] Cater prefaced his treatment with an epigraph from James Reston: "The nineteenth century was the era of the novelist. The twentieth century is the era of the journalist." The observation seems wide of the mark. From the days of Daniel Defoe to those of Norman Mailer and George Orwell, novelist and journalist have coexisted; on more than one occasion the same person has assumed both roles.

Not only were newspapers assigned a distinctive political status in nineteenth-century discourse, but also they were often placed in a different category from books. As noted above, the explosion of newspapers in revolutionary Paris had led Roederer to reflect on the difference between the two kinds of printed materials. Carlyle's influential passages on journalism appeared in his *History of the French Revolution*, where he described how Marat, Brissot, and others were launched on their political careers.

> Great is Journalism. Is not every Able Editor a Ruler of the World, being a persuader of it; though self-elected, yet sanctioned by the sale of his Numbers? . . . They made the walls of Paris didactic, suasive, with an ever fresh Periodical Literature wherein he that ran might read: Placard Journals, Placard Lampoons. . . . What unutterable things the stone-walls spoke, during these five years! But it is all gone: To-day swallowing Yesterday, and then being in its turn swallowed of tomorrow, even as Speech ever is. Nay what, O thou immortal Man of Letters, is Writing itself but Speech conserved for a time? The Placard Journal conserved it for one day; some Books conserve it for the matter of ten years; nay some for three thousand.[48]

These passages caught the attention of Louis Blanc when he was writing his multivolume history of the French Revolution. Blanc was in exile in England, working in the British Museum. He had been a participant-observer in the February Revolution of 1848, serving on the staff of one of the two journals that dominated the provisional government of the Second Republic. Books were suited to quieter times, he wrote, paraphrasing Carlyle, but we are now in an era when today devours yesterday and must be devoured by tomorrow. The age of books is closed; the age of the journal is on hand.[49] As is noted below, the age of the book would be closed over and over again, yet somehow remains open even now.

The supersession of the book by the journal was echoed by others. John

Stuart Mill, when reflecting on the tyranny exerted by public opinion, observed, much as Burke had done, that "the masses" were no longer taking their opinions from "dignitaries in Church or State." Unlike Burke, however, Mill also wrote that people were no longer taking their opinions from books. "Their thinking is done for them by men much like themselves . . . through the newspapers."[50] After the century's end, Oswald Spengler would assert that the age of the book was flanked "on either hand by that of the sermon and that of the newspaper."[51]

The idea that newspapers had a predominant influence on the thinking of contemporaries appealed to press barons and editors. A former London *Times* editor writing in the *Edinburgh Review* announced that journalism had become "truly an estate of the realm, more powerful than any of the other estates." *Times* leader writers elaborated on the theme. An editorial of February 1852 described the newspaper as "daily and forever appealing to the enlightened force of public opinion; anticipating if possible the march of events, standing upon the breach between the present and the future, and extending its survey to the horizon of the world." Thus newspaper editors advertised their craft much as had early printers.

An American journalist had already assumed a self-congratulatory posture in the mid-1830s: "What is to prevent a daily newspaper from being made the greatest organ of social life?" asked James Gordon Bennett in 1835. He went on: "books have had their day—the theatres have had their day—. . . religion has had its day. . . . A newspaper can be made to take the lead in all these great moments of human thought."[53] As a journalist, Bennett claimed to be the true successor to the great dramatists, novelists, and poets of the past: "Shakespeare is the greatest genius of the drama, Scott of the novel, Milton and Byron of the poem, and I mean to be the genius of the newspaper press."[54]

Such extravagant claims provoked extravagant ripostes from novelists. James Fenimore Cooper, who was unhappy at receiving negative reviews, lashed out at the "profoundly evil influence" of newspapers, in a manner that evokes very recent complaints about new media. "The entire nation," Cooper wrote, "breathes an atmosphere of falsehoods."[55] In his *American Notes* (1842), Charles Dickens wrote about the "corrupt control of every phase of American life by the press" in a manner that verged on paranoia. The ubiquitous newspaper constituted "an evil eye in every house . . . its black hand in every appointment in the state, from president to postman . . .

it is the standard literature of an enormous class, who must find their reading in a newspaper or they will not read at all."⁵⁶

Thackeray's approach to the English press was more modulated. His treatment of the "Corporation of the Goosequill . . . the Press . . . the fourth estate" in *Pendennis* was full of irony. But he also conveyed the awe that was inspired among his contemporaries when passing a London newspaper office at night with its lights ablaze: "Look at that! There she is—the great engine— she never sleeps. . . . Her offices march along with armies and her envoys walk into statesmen's cabinets. They are ubiquitous."⁵⁷ According to John Gross, this celebrated passage determined the career choice of several later journalists: "Thackeray's occasional flights of enthusiasm seem to have made a stronger impression on the succeeding generation than his muted satire. Over the next fifty years more than one hardened newspaperman was to reveal that it had been a boyhood reading of *Pendennis* which had fired him with his first romantic dreams of a Fleet Street career."⁵⁸

The image of the never-sleeping newspaper office with couriers upon every road may have been inspiring to a later generation of journalists. But the image of a never-sleeping all-powerful machine with tentacles reaching all over the world also tended to excite the paranoid imagination, much as had been the case with the "tribe of printers" or the "cabal of men of letters" mentioned above. Paranoia about the media also entered into the shaping of modern antisemitism, which made much of the apparent prevalence of Jews in journalistic enterprises.⁵⁹ As is well known, a polemic published in 1864 that contained, among other things, a diatribe against the manipulation of the press by the regime of Napoleon III, was copied almost verbatim in the 1890s into an account of secret manipulations on the part of the "elders of Zion."⁶⁰

Maurice Joly's *Dialogue in Hell Between Machiavelli and Montesquieu* (subtitled *The Politics of Machiavelli in the Nineteenth Century*) was first published in Geneva in 1864.⁶¹ It was smuggled into France but quickly seized by the police, along with its author, who was sentenced to fifteen months in prison. Of the few copies that survived, one found its way to a member of the Russian secret service, who incorporated passages into the *Protocols of the Elders of Zion*, a composite text that appealed to Henry Ford and is even now in vogue in the Middle East. Joly's so-called satire is worth consideration in its own right as expressing opposition to Napoleon III's authoritarian regime.⁶²

In the twelfth dialogue, Machiavelli boasts of his solution to the problem posed for rulers who had to contend with parliamentary governments and the existence of an opposition press. He will "neutralize the press" by using "the press itself." He will make sure that papers supporting the government will outnumber those in the opposition. At the same time he will secretly control all the unofficial organs of opinion, taking care to disguise their indebtedness to his regime.

> I expect a loyal organ in every camp, in every party. I shall have an aristocratic organ . . . a republican organ . . . a revolutionary organ . . . an anarchistic organ. . . . Like the God Vishnu, my press will have a hundred arms, and these arms will stretch out their hands throughout the country delicately giving form to all manner of opinion. Everyone will belong to my party without knowing it. . . . Those who think they are marching under their own banner will be marching under mine. . . .
>
> [I can] shape public opinion the way I want on all questions of domestic or foreign policy. I can stimulate the imagination of my people or put them to sleep . . . admit to something as a fact or deny it . . . I plumb public opinion and assess whatever reaction I provoke. . . . It will be said that I am a man of the people, that there is a secret and mysterious sympathy that unites me with their will.[63]

Thus the sovereign would gain mastery over public opinion, obliterate distinctions between the state and civil society, and exert mind control over his ostensibly independent subjects.

Whereas Joly was concerned with the emperor's control of the French press, Anthony Trollope was concerned with the uncontrolled power of the British press. "[From] Mount Olympus . . . issue forth fifty thousand nightly edicts for the governance of the subject nation. . . . From here issue the only known infallible bulls for the guidance of British souls and bodies. . . . Here reigns a pope . . . self-nominated, self-consecrated" as pontiff, never wrong, "ever vigilant and all knowing"[64]: "from the palaces of St. Petersburg to the cabins of Connaught; nothing can escape him."[65] Readers (or viewers) of *The Warden* will be familiar with inhumane and amoral behavior attributed to the reporter for *The Times*, or *The Jupiter*, as it is called in Trollope's novel. The power attributed to the newspaper by the novelist is that of a pope issuing a bull. It is accountable to no one—except, perhaps, for the advertisers who hinged rates to circulation figures.

The emergence of an independent newspaper press, which provoked so much comment in the nineteenth century, was linked to the replacement of government subsidies by commercial advertising—a phenomenon well advanced in England before it caught on in France[66] and one that Tory ministers regarded with dismay. "In 1795 the publisher of *The Times* agreed to support the government for a pension of 600 pounds. His successor in 1815 would have laughed at such a proposal." Lord Liverpool complained to Castlereagh:

> No paper of any character . . . will accept money from
> Government. . . . their profits are so enormous in all critical times,
> when their support is most necessary, that no pecuniary assistance
> . . . would really be worth their acceptance. The truth is they look
> only to their sale. They make their way like sycophants with the
> public.[67]

To become sycophants of the public meant independence from government manipulation, but it also meant increased deference to commercial interests. As early as 1823, William Hazlitt noted that *The Times* was timid about espousing causes that were out of favor with ordinary businessmen. "The greatest engine of temporary opinion in the world . . . is the mouthpiece, oracle and echo of the Stock Exchange. . . . It takes up no falling causes, fights no uphill battle, advocates no great principle. . . . It is 'ever strong upon the stronger side.'"[68]

The symbiosis between journalism and advertising, which has become so important in determining the fate of newsprint since the advent of online publication, elicited a famous bon mot from a twentieth-century German critic: "A Newspaper is a business undertaking which produces advertising space as a commodity, which becomes saleable only by means of non-advertising space."[69] By then, Hazlitt's views had become left-wing orthodoxy. Trollope's mighty *Jupiter* would be viewed as more worthy of disdain than of awe as a servile organ of corporate wealth.[70]

In the early Victorian era, the intrusion of commercial interests was especially galling to fiction writers, partly because it was so visible. It was not just that sales depended on favorable reviews by critics who could be bought. It was also that, when published in serial form, writers had to compete for space with other, less reputable commodities. In his preface to *Mlle. de Maupin* (1832), Theophile Gautier expressed savage indignation at seeing his work advertised along with elastic belts, crinoline collars, patent-nipple nursing bottles, and recipes for toothaches.[71]

In addition, Gautier complained that the public's appetite for scandal was whetted by police reports and accounts of sensational trials. "The reader refused to be caught save by a book baited with a small corpse in the first stage of putrefaction. . . . Men are not as unlike fishes as most people seem to think."[72] Of course, disgust at the "degrading thirst after outrageous stimulation" was not peculiar to fiction writers in the 1830s. When Wordsworth had commented on the degradation of popular tastes he was concerned not with newsprint but with the attractions of city life.

> The human mind is capable of being excited without the application
> of gross and violent stimulants; and he must have a very faint per-
> ception of its beauty and dignity who does not know this. . . . To
> enlarge this capability is . . . [especially important] at the present
> day . . . [given] the increasing accumulation of men in cities where
> the uniformity of occupations produces a craving for extraordinary
> incident which the rapid accumulation of intelligence hourly grati-
> fies.[73]

Although many writers expressed disgust at the vulgar sensationalism of others, few could afford to abandon the hope of creating a sensation themselves.

Literati were not alone in expressing concern about the effects of sensational journalism. Much as early printers had denounced each other for sharp dealing, so too did newspapers hurl accusations at each other: "squirt of filthy water," "slop pail of corruption"; such epithets scarcely dignified the trade.[74] Moralists persisted as they had for centuries, deploring the public preference for the salacious over the edifying tale. And as is the case even now with regard to crime and violence on television, doctors expressed concern about the state of the nation's mental health and sounded alarms about the effects of sensational journalism on the national psyche.[75] The key passages in a book published in 1863, entitled *Mental Hygiene*, by an American physician named Isaac Ray, begin with the observation, regarding the "art of printing," that "at no period since its invention have its benefits and evils been more widely diffused." Ray went on: "the details of a disgusting criminal trial, exposing the darkest aspects of our nature, finds an audience that no courtroom less than a hemisphere could hold."[76]

The point was pertinent not only to sensational journalism but also to sensational fiction. When the printed word came under attack for "rotting the minds of readers," and for "promoting vice and subverting cultural standards,"[77] it was no less likely to be located in a novel than in a newspaper. This takes us back to the "huge froth ocean of literature." The reading public did not have to rely only on newspapers to learn about the details of criminal trials. Indeed the darkest aspects of human nature could be examined in greater detail and exposed at greater length in novels than in daily newsprint. News about criminal trials was transcribed into the key of fiction by literary artists, such as Stendhal or Dostoevsky, as well as by the slapdash producers of penny dreadfuls. Reading aloud from the *Police Gazette* achieved lasting resonance when Dickens put words in the mouth of Betty Higben in *Our Mutual Friend*: "I ain't much at reading writing hand tho' I can read my Bible and most print. And I do love a newspaper . . . Sloppy is a beautiful reader of a newspaper. He do the Police in different voices." Compressed into this brief passage is a remarkable concatenation of varied media: voice, handwriting, print, Bible, newspaper, all culminating in a multivocal performance with newsprint (*The Police Gazette*) serving as a playscript. The passage would obtain a new lease on life when it was selected by T. S. Eliot as his original title for *The Waste Land*, all of which suggests that newsprint is deeply embedded in "the huge froth ocean" of printed materials.

When dealing with nineteenth-century views, later complaints about later mass media seem close at hand: the ubiquity of sex, intrusive commercials, sycophancy to mass taste, and semi-hypnotic power over readers' minds. In this regard, it is not surprising that the utilitarian valorization of print brings satire to mind. Confidence in the capacity of the printed word to diffuse useful knowledge has persistently been undermined by the diffusion of seemingly useless and often repellent printed matter. Nevertheless, concern about low literacy rates, inadequate supplies of books, ill-equipped schoolrooms, and overcrowded schools is no less alive today than it was in Victorian times. Ignorance and superstition are still regarded as plaguing inner-city populations. Campaigns to teach reading by one means or another are still being conducted under a slogan that was coined in the seventeenth century: "Knowledge is Power."[78] In this regard, attitudes toward print have changed remarkably little, despite the obsolescence of nineteenth-century printing machines and the advent of new electronic media.

On the other hand, attitudes did undergo a marked change in at least one respect. As the next (and final) chapter suggests, by the 1900s the spread of literacy and the ubiquity of newsprint were seen to have had disappointing results. Gutenberg's invention was less likely to be celebrated for its contributions to a peaceful knowledge industry and more likely to be condemned for promoting hysteria, unreason, and world wars.

Chapter 7

Toward the Sense of an Ending
(Fin de Siècle to the Present)

There are false dusks in literature as well as false dawns.
—John Gross, *The Rise and Fall of the Man of Letters*

The last decades of the nineteenth century saw newspaper publishers throughout Europe take advantage of diverse innovations, such as wood pulp paper and typesetting machines, that speeded up production and cheapened output. Under the aegis of parliamentary governments, the movement for a free press finally achieved success; "freedom of the press" was pledged in the preambles of almost all the constitutions that marked the end of the era of absolute monarchy. Throughout the Continent, educational reforms were also enacted, with the aim of achieving mass literacy.[1]

In many liberal narratives, these developments were viewed as bringing to a triumphant conclusion the trends that had been initiated by the invention of printing. "The combined operations of a broad electorate . . . and cheap newspaper were widely deemed to have created the perfect mechanism for the governance of society."[2] According to W. H. Stead, "the telegraph and the printing press together had converted Great Britain into a vast agora, or assembly of the whole community, in which discussion of the affairs of State is carried on from day to day within the hearing of the whole people."[3]

Outside liberal circles, however, these same developments were viewed in a less favorable light. "The advance of literacy to near universality by 1900 was often cited as indisputable evidence of social progress. But mass literacy continued to seem threatening to many observers."[4] "More people were reading than ever before; but in the opinion of most commentators they were reading the wrong things for the wrong reasons and in the wrong way."[5]

With daily papers (and evening ones) rolling off gigantic machines, print was increasingly seen as a "mass medium." As such it was viewed as an instrument wielded by powerful press lords who sought to increase circulation (and advertising revenues) by exciting emotional responses. Advertisements had once been welcomed as an innocuous way of rendering the press independent of government control.[6] They would be condemned later as exemplifying the cynical manipulation of the reading public by "hidden persuaders."

> The newspaper world appeared more and more to be the mirror of the worst aspects of the capitalist world. . . . Concentration of ownership became the order of the day . . . the editor declined in power and prestige as the business managers came into their own. The press lost the mystique of being regarded as an estate: it was now described . . . as an industry.[7]

Suspicions of bad faith extended to journalists. With regard to news stories, some recent critics note that "telling stories" may be defined as telling lies: "Journalists and those who rely on them are not our guides but our great misleaders."[8] G. M. Young, writing in the 1930s, commented: "What failed in the late Victorian age and its . . . Edwardian epilogue was the Victorian public, once so alert, so masculine and so responsible. The English mind sank toward that easily excited, easily satisfied state of barbarism and childlike ignorance which the press ever more easily excited and satisfied."[9] The notion that the press might contribute to barbarism and childlike ignorance presented a sharp contrast to the expectations of the earlier prophets of progress, later members of the SDUK, and optimistic Victorians. Young's lament over the decline of a public that had once been not only alert and responsible but also masculine seems worth pausing over.

The coupling of effeminacy with literacy was an old topos, going back to an era when warriors had left the reading of books to monks and old men. In his essay on pedantry, Montaigne had sounded a similar note with regard to the fate of Rome: "the pursuit of knowledge makes men's hearts soft and effeminate more than it makes them strong and warlike. Rome was more valiant before she was learned."[10]

In the later nineteenth century, similar views were voiced by nationalists and militarists. This entailed a marked change from eighteenth-century attitudes. Proponents of the Enlightenment had belittled the possibility of new barbarian invasions; any victory over the West required educated opponents who had mastered the advances in arts and sciences that had been propelled by printing. Barbarians who had achieved such mastery, wrote Gibbon, had ceased to be barbarians.[11] Even earlier, typography and literacy had been regarded as incompatible with barbarism. Thus, when Germans claimed cultural superiority as the inventors of printing they did so to repudiate Italian accusations of barbarism.[12]

But barbarians were reevaluated in the later nineteenth century. Constantine Cavafy (1864–1933) captured this cultural reversal in a memorable poem depicting the disappointment of civilized officials when barbarian invaders failed to appear: "night has fallen and the barbarians have not come. / . . . And now what's going to happen to us without barbarians? / They were, those people, a kind of solution."[13]

As had been the case with Montaigne and Machiavelli, the martial vigor of the pre-literate Germanic tribes inspired admiration. Tacitus's *Germania*, again, became a key text; victories over the enfeebled, sedentary, luxury-loving Romans were celebrated anew. Youth movements such as the German *Wandervogel* were organized to counter the sedentary habits of schoolboys with back-to-nature expeditions aimed at mastery of rugged native landscapes and indoctrination into a pre-literate, masculine, volkish national past.[14] Antisemitic stereotypes attributed a soft, flabby, and sedentary lifestyle to the bookish Jew in contrast to the masculine, muscular Aryan. Observers in 1933 witnessed the book-burnings of works by Jews and other "decadent" authors, along with the elimination of the same works from libraries and bookshops.[15] The elimination of Jewish books served as a prelude to measures in the next decade aimed at eliminating the Jews themselves. Needless to say, the commemoration of the 500th anniversary of Gutenberg's invention in Mainz was a very muted affair.[16]

Concern about the loss of vitality engendered by too much book reading was by no means confined to Nazi Germany. (In fact this particular theme had a long history associated with the idea that vital fluids were lost by masturbation, a practice famously encouraged by "reading with one hand.")[17] In the early nineteenth century the spread of literacy had alarmed conservatives, who recalled mob violence during the French Revolution and who feared that exposure to radical propaganda would lead to working-class uprisings. In the later nineteenth century different alarms were sounded concern-

ing the ill effects of sedentary habits. "Reading has become a downright
vice—a vulgar detrimental habit like dram-drinking . . . a softening, demoral-
izing, relaxing practice which, if persisted in, will end by enfeebling the minds
of men and women, making flabby the fibre of their bodies and undermining
the vigour of nations."[18] "Civilization!" exclaimed one of Gissing's characters:

> Do you call it civilizing men to make them weak, flabby creatures,
> with ruined eyes and dyspeptic stomachs? Who is it that reads most
> of the stuff that's poured out daily by the ton from the printing
> press? Just the men and women who ought to spend their leisure
> hours in open-air exercise: the people who earn their bread from
> sedentary pursuits and who need to live as soon as they are free from
> the desk or counter, not to moon over small print.[19]

The waning of literacy and the gradual disappearance of books in Morris's
utopian romance, *News from Nowhere*, were taken as signs of health.[20] Contrasts between the fat and flabby bookworm (once described as a "sissy" and
depicted wearing eyeglasses) with the energetic muscular "jock" persist even
now as the stock in trade of comic strips and situation comedies.

Some commentators worried that the spread of literacy was leading to a
decline of martial (and masculine) vigor. But others took the opposite view,
holding the mass circulation of printed materials responsible for repeated
outbreaks of irrational war fever. "The ability to read and write made the
urban population the potential victim of nationalistic indoctrination, which
would begin in school, would be continued in the army and, after the return
to civilian life, would be emphasized in the press."[21]

In his *Outline of History*, H. G. Wells asserted that "mass literacy with
its untrained appetite for mindlessly chauvinistic, war mongering journalism,
[was] a main cause of the disastrous war-making of the twentieth century."[22]
Toward the middle of the twentieth century, the final volume in a Harvard
series devoted to "the rise of modern Europe" described how mass literacy
and popular journalism went together with bellicose nationalism, imperialist
adventures, and ever more destructive wars.[23]

American critics of the way the Hearst newspapers drummed up support
for the Spanish American War were joined by English opponents of the
"jingoism" that accompanied the Boer War. It was "a biased enslaved and
poisoned press" that had been the chief engine for manufacturing the "war

spirit," according to J. A. Hobson's account of the Boer War. With the 1900 Boxer Rebellion in mind, G. M. Trevelyan declared that the "yellow peril" was not nearly so dangerous to Western civilization as the "white peril" made up of the masses of the great cities who were also readers of the *Daily Mail.*[24]

The dangerous effects of a "white peril" were reaffirmed in 1951 by Marshall McLuhan:

> The headline is a primitive shout of rage, triumph, fear, or warning, and newspapers have thrived on wars. . . . Any kind of excitement or emotion contributes to the possibility of dangerous explosions when the feelings of huge populations are kept inflamed even in peacetime for the advancement of commerce. Headlines mean street sales. It takes emotions to move merchandise. And wars and rumors of wars are the merchandise and also the emotion of the popular press. . . . When people have become accustomed for decades to perpetual emotions, a dispassionate view of anything at all is difficult to achieve.[25]

Wars between Protestant and Catholic powers had gone together with the emergence of a cosmopolitan "third force." Despite official alarms about paper bullets and printed poison, printing had been regarded, in the early modern era, as a peaceful art. It was associated with the advancement of learning and contrasted with infernal war machines. News from the Republic of Letters had been issued by émigrés and exiles who evaded both Catholic and Calvinist censorship. Their journals reflected a cosmopolitan ethos that cut across boundaries associated with any one church or dynastic state. In the later nineteenth century, however, nationalist sentiment prevailed. Cosmopolites were scorned as traitors; press and cannon, together, fought under the same flag. (The denunciation of cosmopolites had been anticipated in the French Revolution, when the Dutch-German baron who had petitioned to pantheonize Gutenberg was denounced as a foreign conspirator and guillotined.) Delegates at the Frankfurt Assembly of 1848 had exhibited the same chauvinistic and bellicose posture as that manifested by Jacobins in the 1790s.[26] In France, however, Lamartine, as foreign minister, took care to announce that the Second Republic meant peace. In England at mid-century, the proponents of free trade, who had pushed through the repeal of the so-called Corn Laws, were confident that the peaceful merchant bearing goods was going to replace the bloody warrior bearing arms.[27]

But of course merchants, however peacefully inclined, were not unwilling to traffic in arms. Moreover, as the above passage from McLuhan suggests, "wars and rumors of wars" meant profits for newspaper publishers. By the century's end, the transfer of allegiance from the universalistic ideals that were associated with the Enlightenment to nationalist causes seemed to be ubiquitous, affecting not only the so-called masses but also, most emphatically, intellectual elites. The prelude to World War I saw Marxists who ostensibly embraced the cause of international working-class solidarity transformed into patriotic Frenchmen and Germans.

After World War I, Julien Benda (1867–1956) would accuse Europe's intellectuals of betraying the cosmopolitan ideals to which they had previously been attached. "The men of science, the artist, the philosopher are attached to their nations as much as the day-labourer and the merchant . . . All Europe, including Erasmus, has followed Luther."[28] As a pacifist, Leo Tolstoy would reverse the equation of printing with knowledge and refer to the diffusion of printed materials as a powerful engine of ignorance.[29]

In fact, the uses of print had always been multifarious. The printed tables and charts that were indispensable to the mathematical sciences had served to enhance rational decision-making and had circulated across dynastic state boundaries. To be sure, religious censorship still had to be surmounted (Galileo remained on the *Index of Prohibited Books* until the twentieth century.) But by and large the exchange of scientific data was (relatively) peaceful. ("There are no sects among geometers," wrote Voltaire.) No doubt, Newton and Leibniz quarreled over credit for the invention of calculus. The invention of printing itself remained a bone of contention between the Dutch and the Germans. But rancorous priority disputes went together with the widespread adoption of maps, charts, tables, and all manner of useful mathematical tools. Linguistic and political divisions had been surmounted by the adoption of a uniform metric system and legal codes throughout the Continent. (To be sure, it required a revolution in France and Napoleonic conquests to implement these seemingly "rational" reforms, and they never have been accepted in the English-speaking world.) International cooperation was marked among practitioners of the medical and mathematical sciences, as shown by the nineteenth-century German doctors and scientists who abandoned their native idiosyncratic Fraktur typestyle when printing their books and periodicals so as to assure they could be read by a non-German public.[30] Later agreements on patents and postal services conventions were also indicative of the trend toward cosmopolitan interchange and the rationalizing of previously disordered systems. Similarly, the vogue for written constitutions indicated a felt need to provide more uniform and impersonal guidelines for the governance of diverse nations.

But distancing and rationality had never characterized the use of print by pamphleteers, patent medicine salesmen, or caricaturists. Nor had they been manifested in advertising copy or printed fiction. *Pamela* and her progeny had always been designed to touch the human heart. Insofar as vernacular Bibles were authorized by Protestant rulers, they encouraged the illusion that God spoke in English or German, thereby splintering the linguistic unity of Latin Christendom and contributing to patriotic, populist trends.[31] Well before the development of a newspaper press, printed materials had been a conduit for propaganda and agitation. During World War I, American newspapers whipped up outrage by carrying images of Belgian babies being stabbed by Germans with bayonets. But the exploitation of atrocity stories had a very long history—going back to the earliest accounts of the deaths suffered by Christian martyrs, not to mention those that were described in horrendous detail by John Foxe and other sixteenth-century martyrologists. Images of innocents being massacred and Sabine women being raped were circulating in prints long before the development of photogravure sections.

The fallacy of holding a so-called free press responsible for war fever is suggested by the bellicose attitudes that flourished in Germany and Italy (and the Bolshevik USSR) during the prelude to World War II, when freedom of the press had been curtailed and censorship instituted by the new totalitarian regimes. Nor had the cause of peace been advanced when rigorous censorship had prevailed in early nineteenth-century France under Napoleon. The cause of peace had been favored by the press in England and France during the late 1930s. But ensuing events only made it clear that pacifist sentiment, however strongly encouraged by the press, was ineffectual and, indeed, only gave aid and comfort to determined enemies bent on conquest.

Cosmopolitan concerns had been reflected in the abandonment of the Fraktur typestyle by nineteenth-century German scientists and technicians. The final conversion of German typestyles, however, told a different story. For some time, the Nazis

> were inclined to enforce the use of gothic type as the genuine typographical expression of the Nordic soul. When, however, the vistas of . . . world domination began to fire their minds, Hitler shrewdly realized the advantages of appealing to the non-German world. On

3 January 1941, it was decreed that "the so called gothic type" was a Jewish invention ("Schwabacher-Judenlettern") and that therefore Antiqua was henceforth to be the "normal type" of the German people.[32]

Around the turn of the century, the daily newspaper was held responsible for generating war fever. It was also believed to signify the end of the book. As we have seen, nineteenth-century historians of the French Revolution had initiated this theme when writing about the explosion of journals in the streets of Paris.[33] It was incorporated into later world historical schemes. In the *Decline of the West* (1918), Oswald Spengler wrote:

> Democracy has by its newspaper completely expelled the book from the mental life of the people. . . . The people read one paper, "its" paper, which forces itself through the front doors by millions daily, spellbinds the intellect from morning to night, drives the book into oblivion with its more engaging layout, and if one or another speci-men of a book does emerge into visibility, forestalls and eliminates its possible effects by "reviewing" it.[34]

In the course of the century after the *Decline of the West*, similar prognos-tications multiplied, giving rise to a sequence of (premature) obituaries that are discussed below. These prophecies had been anticipated in 1894. The end of both newspaper and book, indeed the end of all printed matter, was the topic of a journal article translated from French and published in *Scribners* in 1894. It was entitled "The End of Books." Instead of heralding a decline of the West, however, the article seemed to anticipate future progress in communications, including the invention of "talking" books. It had a playful rather than an elegiac air.[35]

Its author, Octave Uzanne, was a fin-de-siècle aesthete, a disciple of Baudelaire, and an independently wealthy connoisseur of fine printing.[36] As a youth he frequented the Arsenal library, a rendezvous for a côterie of erudite book lovers who were disciples of the former Arsenal curator, Charles No-dier.[37] Along with many other aesthetes, Uzanne represented a latter-day manifestation of the earlier Romantic rebellion against soul-less machines, the cash nexus, and so-called bourgeois values. As was true of Ruskin, Wil-liam Morris, and the pre-Raphaelites, he rejected industrialism, plutocracy, and the popular press of the day.[38] Whereas Morris and his friends sought to revive the ethos of fifteenth-century artisans, to the point of imitating their working routines and replicating their tools, Uzanne rejected the "tired fonts" of previous printers and sponsored newly designed art nouveau type styles in keeping with his avant-garde aesthetics. He sought to exploit the most recent communications technologies while turning them against the purposes for which they were developed. Thus he used photolithography and other new techniques, not in order to meet the demands of a burgeoning market, but rather to produce deluxe volumes in ever more original and singular formats for aesthetic effect and for the exclusive benefit of a select clientele. (It is intriguing to note how the two opposite approaches to fin-de-siècle book printing for niche markets, represented by Morris and Uzanne, resulted in works that were unmistakably of the same decade—together they represented a composite hybrid style one might describe as late Victorian eclectic.)[39]

Although Morris and Uzanne were united in their distaste for pulp paper and mass production, they adhered to opposite political positions. Morris embraced the idea of communal ownership and upheld socialist doctrines. Uzanne was an elitist, an anti-Dreyfusard, and a right-wing precursor of poets and essayists such as Pound, Yeats, Charles Maurras, or T. S. Eliot.[40] In reacting against their common enemy, the "printing machine," William Morris looked back to a golden age of hand-produced books; Uzanne looked forward to a future that had been rendered bookless.

In the "End of Books," Uzanne describes how a group of savants and scientists met in London to discuss their visions of the future. The essay begins with a physicist who predicts the end of the world in ten million years. It goes on to discuss the fate of art "in an age of mechanical reproduction."[41] As described by a painter who has founded a "School of Aesthetes of To-Morrow," the whole universe having been completely saturated with pictures, "painting will die. . . . Art will then be a closed aristocracy" and "a few holy men . . . amidst the silence and incomprehension of the masses will produce masterpieces at last worthy of the name."[42] After the painter finishes, the author responds to a request for his prediction about books.

> If by books you are . . . referring to our innumerable collections of paper, printed, sewed, and bound in a cover announcing the title . . . I do not believe (and the progress of electricity and modern mechanism forbids me to believe) that Gutenberg's invention can do otherwise than sooner or later fall into desuetude. . . .

Printing, which Rivarol . . . called the artillery of thought, and
of which Luther said that it is the last and best gift by which God
advances the things of the Gospel—printing, which changed the
destiny of Europe, and which . . . has governed opinion through the
book, the pamphlet, and the newspaper—printing, which since 1436
has reigned despotically over the mind of man, is . . . threatened
with death by the various devices for registering sound which have
been lately invented . . .

. . . the art in which Fust and Scheffer, Estienne and Vascosa
[sic], Aldus Manutius and Nicholas Jenson successively excelled, has
attained its acme of perfection . . . our grandchildren will no longer
trust their works to this somewhat antiquated process, now become
very easy to replace by phonography, which is yet in its initial
stage.[43]

Challenged to explain the technical details that might make it possible to
transform readable texts into hearable ones, Uzanne envisaged a "pocket apparatus run by an electrical current kept in a simple opera glass case and
suspended by a strap on the shoulder." When walking, hearers would be able
to "[reconcile] hygiene with instruction" and "[nourish] their minds while
exercising their muscles." Today's joggers with their iPods come to mind,
and so do families watching TV: Uzanne described how stories could be
illustrated by taking advantage of the "the Kinetograph of Thomas Edison
(whom I have recently visited in New Jersey)" in order to project photo-
graphs "on large white screens in our own homes." An illustration in the
Scribners article is titled "Reading on the Limited" and depicts a "Pullman
Circulating Library." Top-hatted, whiskered gentlemen and corseted ladies
are depicted sitting in a Pullman car holding cylinders to their ears. The
contrast between their Edwardian costumes and the action in which they are
engaged is amusingly incongruous, for they appear to be receiving messages
over cell phones or perhaps iPods.

Uzanne appeared to be prescient; yet his conception of talking books
had been anticipated several centuries earlier in seventeenth-century moon
voyage fantasies. Perhaps the most celebrated work in this genre was Cyrano
de Bergerac's *States and Empires of the Moon*, which had borrowed the talking-book theme from Francis Godwin's *The Man in the Moon* (1638).[44] Marjorie Hope Nicolson, writing in the 1940s, saw in the talking-book theme
an anticipation of "recordings for the blind." Roger Chartier's more recent

Figure 7.1. "The Author Making Cylinders of His Own Works"; and
"Manufacturing Books," from Octave Uzanne, "The End of Books,"
'Scribner's Magazine Illustrated', July–December 1894. Illustrations by Albert
Robida. Courtesy of the University of Maryland, Baltimore County.

Figure 7.2. "The Author Exploiting His Own Works"; and "Reading on The Limited," from Uzanne, "The End of Books." Courtesy of the University of Maryland, Baltimore County.

interpretation stresses miniaturization.[45] Chartier suggests that Cyrano was influenced by the triumph of the small-format book, which had dominated Parisian publishing in the second half of the seventeenth century.[46] Of course, reduction in the sizes of large books had found favor with printers earlier—at least since the days of Aldus Manutius. Moreover, tiny books had been produced even earlier, in the age of the scribe. Whatever its sources, Cyrano's fantasy did seem to point to future developments.

> An entire "book" fits into a tiny box the size of a diamond or large pearl. Thanks to a mechanism of springs similar to those of a clock, these miraculous books produce sound: they are made for the ear, not for the eye. The "readers" of the Other World have only to rewind the mechanism and place the needle on the desired chapter to listen to their talking books. . . . [Moon people are] "never without reading material . . . they can carry thirty books in their pockets. . . . [and one can wear them] attached to his ear like earrings."[47]

Uzanne, who was a connoisseur of French literature, may well have been familiar with Cyrano's work. During his trip to Edison in New Jersey, he may have recalled those seventeenth-century earrings. He obviously lacked foreknowledge of all the innovations that would lead to the development of the cell phone and iPod. He was prescient enough to foresee the rise of a recording industry, but like many of his contemporaries, he was misguided in assuming that the phonograph signified the end of the printed book.

An anonymous commentator in *The Bookworm*[48] took issue with Uzanne's prophecy. He started by satirizing the notion that books would be displaced by "little wax cylinders." If this occurred, "authors would have to acquire the rudiments of elocution. . . . The squeaky-voiced romanticist, no matter how enthralling his story to the eye, will have small chance . . . the poet with a speech impediment will starve . . . But after all," he concluded, "there is no call to be grieved by M. Uzanne's forecast. No phonogram, however entrancing its tones may be, can ever affect the dominion of the printed page."[49] The dominion of the printed page would persist another hundred years before the unanticipated development of electronic media did indeed begin to affect it.

As indicated by previous references concerning the end of the age of the book, the last two centuries have witnessed—the death not of the sermon, nor of the novel, nor of literature (I will pass over the death of the author and of God)—not a succession of deaths but, rather, a sequence of premature obituaries. In an essay collection entitled *The Future of the Book*, Geoffrey Nunberg and Paul Duguid take note of this phenomenon, which they attribute to the mistaken doctrine of supersession. This doctrine, they observe, underlies expectations (false ones it seems at the moment) that photography would put an end to painting, movies would kill the theatre and television would kill movies.[50] To be sure (the essayists do not point this out but it is worth noting), the doctrine is not always at odds with reality. The age of the hand-copied book, like that of the horse and buggy, did come to an end. Yet, hand-copied books were still being produced in Western Europe for several centuries after Gutenberg.[51] Moreover, there are many non-Western regions which still offer employment to scribes. Even in the West, as Curt Bühler noted many years ago, the scribe long outlived the manuscript book and was not superseded until the advent of the typewriter.[52] One thinks of all those clerks plying quill pens in nineteenth-century law offices, not to mention Thackeray's coupling of the steam press with the "Corporation of the Goose-quill."[53] And although the manual typewriter may now be on the verge of obsolescence, its keyboard, transferred to the word processor, has received another lease on life.

As noted in a previous chapter, the advent of printing was seen to outmode not the manuscript book but the Gothic cathedral in Victor Hugo's oft-cited work.[54] Commentators rarely pause over the ironic implications of Hugo's making this pronouncement while living, as he did, in the midst of a Gothic revival. This revival did not merely consist of building nineteenth-century structures such as the Houses of Parliament. It also entailed completing thirteenth-century cathedrals such as the one at Cologne, which was finished in 1880.[55] Nor did the building of Gothic cathedrals cease after the Gothic revival had waned—witness the Cathedral of St. John the Divine in New York City and the National Cathedral, which my children watched being completed near our home in Washington, D.C.

Of course, there are significant differences between medieval cathedral building and that of more recent centuries, just as there are between the experience of nineteenth-century readers of Hugo's original novel and that of recent viewers of Disney's *Hunchback of Notre Dame*. To complicate matters (and these issues are remarkably complex), one must also allow for the difference between the way Hugo's novel would have been received in a French-language version as against a translated one; by a nineteenth-century reader as against a twentieth-century one; by a working-class reader as against a middle-class one.[56] To such coarse-grained distinctions one must add the more subtle ones entailing the idiosyncratic reception of each individual reader. As Roger Chartier richly documents, each individual appropriates a given text in a distinctive way. Finally, as bibliographers remind us, one must also allow for the way the presentation of the same text varies from one edition to another.

For printed editions often do supersede one another. David Hume thought the fact that he was able continually to improve and correct his work in successive editions was the chief advantage conferred on an author by the invention of printing.[57] The third edition of Newton's *Principia* was judged to be superior to the previous two. To be sure, later editions may also be inferior to earlier ones; witness the successors to the fourteenth edition of the *Encyclopedia Britannica*. Furthermore, even when defective early editions are superseded by improved later ones, the early editions, however defective, are often regarded as being especially valuable to rare book collectors. (Indeed, defects may even enhance the value of a printed product, as in the case of a mistake in printing a postage stamp.)

It is characteristic of our culture that markets for antiques flourish alongside demand for the latest designs. Even the horse and buggy has reemerged as a fashionable acquisition, along with the antique car. Very soon, it will be the turn of the manual typewriter—but never, I suspect, of an old floppy disk. Indeed, the survival value of a 500-year-old book is greater than that of a 10-year-old floppy which is the wrong size to fit into today's machines. The operating systems of computers represent a genuinely novel phenomenon, resulting as they do from "planned obsolescence . . . the deliberate malfunctioning of consumer goods within a given period of time and . . . the regular release of new styles into consumer markets. (Think of the mountains of discarded personal computers that now reside permanently in landfills because their processors and hard drives cannot accommodate software released even just a few years ago.)"[58]

The doctrine of supersession is much too coarse-grained to make room for such complications. It makes no more allowance for revivals than it does for survivals and thus encourages us to overlook a significant characteristic of our own era—namely the coexistence of a vast variety of diverse styles and artifacts reflecting different spirits of different times. What applies to the ever more eclectic mélange of styles and artifacts also pertains to media. That is to say, we confront an ever more complex mixture of diverse media: painting, woodblock, engraving, lithograph, photograph, film, television, radio, DVD, iPod, phone, fax, word processor, copying machine, and so on and so forth—none of which have yet been superseded, all of which confront us in a bewildering profusion at the present time.

None of this was foreseen by Uzanne. In a self-congratulatory vein, he went on to recount the enthusiastic reception of his venture into futurology. His forecast of the end of the book was welcomed by one of his listeners, who cried:

> Either the books must go or they will swallow us up. I calculate that
> . . . from eighty to one hundred thousand books appear every year
> . . . the majority of which . . . propagate only prejudice and error.
> Our social condition forces us to hear many stupid things every day.
> A few more or less do not amount to any great suffering . . . but
> what happiness not to be obliged to read them, and to be able at
> last to close our eyes upon the annihilation of printed things![59]

The annihilation of printed things was a playful conceit for Uzanne and his circle of dandies and bibliophiles. It acquired more ominous significance among the protofascist youth who would later become followers of Benito Mussolini, as is shown by the following sections of Marinetti's Futuristic manifesto, which was published in *Le Figaro*, 20 November, 1909:

> Article 9: We want to glorify war—the only cure for the world—
> militarism, patriotism, the destructive gesture of the anarchists, the
> beautiful ideas which kill, and contempt for woman. . . .
> Article 10: . . . demolish museums and libraries, fight morality, femi-
> nism and all opportunist and utilitarian cowardice. . . .
> Article 11: . . . deliver Italy of its gangrene of professors, archaeolo-
> gists, tourist guides and antiquarians. . . .
> Heap up the fire to the shelves of libraries. Divert the canals to flood
> the cellars of museums.[60]

The hatred of museum culture was related to the frustration experienced by would-be avant-garde artists who sought to make a name for themselves but found it increasingly difficult to find room for yet another contribution to the rapidly growing "tradition of the new." Ironically, Futurism would receive notice along with other similar movements, largely owing to its novel typographical designs.[61] It would end up being classified as yet one more early twentieth-century aesthetic movement, destined to be lumped together with Vorticism, Expressionism, Cubism, and the rest, and fated to be incorporated into an ever-expanding museum culture.[62]

The rejection of museum culture by avant-garde artists was accompanied by a rejection of bestselling fiction by the leaders of the so-called modernist movement in literature. "The claim of modernist fiction to high cultural status entails rejecting or demoting ordinary novels as commercial, mass-cultural detritus."[63]

"On or about December, 1910, human nature changed." This celebrated pronouncement from Virginia Woolf's 1917 essay, which attacked Arnold Bennett, John Galsworthy, and others, is cited by Brantlinger to indicate the great divide that separated "modernist, high culture fiction from the ordinary novels of the past." Woolf's essay, Brantlinger writes, indicated the way "the vast majority of fiction" was assigned to a "debased" mass culture by a select minority that placed its own work in the "domain of 'great art.' "[64]

Woolf's choice of the year 1910 was based on the opening date of the first post-Impressionist exhibition in London, which was organized by her friend, Roger Fry. Oddly enough, this same exhibition had won the praise of Arnold Bennett, who condemned Londoners for scorning the Post-impressionists.[65] In the field of fine arts, Bennett's "modernist credentials" have been described as "impeccable." Moreover, his literary work has recently been reappraised; his later work shows that he was "on the brink of a new modernist aesthetic."[66] The "great divide" seems increasingly less great as time goes on.

Virginia Woolf's essay actually had less to do with the popular success of Bennett, Galsworthy, and the others than with their inadequate treatment of the characters they depicted. Although the houses these fictive beings lived in, and the clothes they wore, were described in careful detail, Woolf complained, they had been deprived of the pulsating inner life that marked them as truly human. It was this inner life, "spasmodic, obscure and fragmentary," that Woolf, together with her fellow artists, hoped to reproduce. In his reply to Woolf's attack, Arnold Bennett defended "ordinary novels that achieved commercial success as coming closer to the lived experience of most readers than did the rarefied works that came from private presses." Arnold wrote, "There is a numerous band of persons in London who spend so much time . . . in practicing the rites of the religion of art that they become incapable of real existence. Each is a Stylites on a pillar. . . . They never approach normal life. They scorn it. They have a horror of it."[67]

Among other aspects of normal life for a novelist such as Bennett were negotiations with printers and publishers. With a private income and a private press at her disposal, Virginia Woolf was insulated from such difficulties.[68] Her favorite authors also usually left them out of their work. Printers, publishers and, indeed, all traces of a book trade vanished from the fictionalized self-portraits rendered by Joyce and Lawrence (in sharp contrast to the fiction of Balzac and Gissing).

> When Joyce or Lawrence portray themselves as aspiring young novelists they "focus entirely on the development of the Artist and dispense entirely with commercialism. Stephen Dedalus and Paul Morel are Artists. . . . They have nothing to do with publishers, editors, agents. They are not even shown writing books."[69]

One recalls the eighteenth-century poem that presented a rarefied view of printing as a mystic art and nineteenth-century essays that "dematerialized print and paper." Virginia Woolf herself described her Edwardian opponents as "materialists" while depicting her "Georgian" friends as "spiritualists." In many respects, this particular instance of the so-called "great divide" between mass and elite seems to be yet another manifestation of the long-lived, unresolved conflict experienced by all authors since Gutenberg's day: between aspiring to serve the muses and competing in the marketplace of print.

It is also possible that the thesis of an early twentieth-century "great divide" between the mandarins and the mass public has been overdone. John Gross argues persuasively that the splintering of Victorian culture in the late nineteenth century was a temporary affair. The division between elite and popular that he describes was manifested first of all in fin-de-siècle periodical literature well before Virginia Woolf's transformative year.

> In the 1890s big papers grew bigger and brasher while small papers grew more exclusive, more stylized, more flamboyant. If it was Northcliffe's decade it was also Aubrey Beardsley's, a decade of côteries and collectors' items, ornate periodicals and exotic reviews. . . . The little magazine . . . was as much an expression of the *fin de siècle* spirit as the limited edition; both were symptoms of the splintering-up of Victorian culture, of a process of fragmentation which might

well have been expected to go even further in the years which followed.[70]

According to Gross, the process of fragmentation did not go further;
subsequent decades saw Victorian attitudes revived.

> There are false dusks in literature as well as false dawns, and the
> mauve and yellow Decadence was one of them. . . . [These years]
> led on to a period dominated by writers who were closer to the Early
> Victorians than to their immediate predecessors in their readiness to
> enter the public arena as preachers, debaters, entertainers. . . . Shaw
> and Wells, Bennett and Chesterton put their trust in a popular audi-
> ence; they might promulgate minority opinions, but not the idea of
> a minority culture.[71]

But what was true of Shaw and Wells was not true of T. S. Eliot or James
Joyce. The "little" magazine that embodied the "fin de siècle" spirit gained a
new lease on life as the chief vehicle for "modernist movements" in the 1910s
and 1920s.

> It's not easy to name a modernist writer from the 1910s to the 1920s
> who didn't publish in some little magazine or other. *Poetry, Others,
> Broom, The Dial, The Little Review, The Egoist,* and *transition* are
> the stuff of legend. The little magazine, more than the book or the
> anthology, was the preferred medium for the exchange and circula-
> tion of literature during this period. What the quartos are to Shake-
> speare scholars, the little magazines are to modernists: an
> indispensable material resource that makes it possible to see into the
> culture and politics of literary production.[72]

The persistence of the "little magazines" was not the only indication that
Shaw, Wells, and others had not really erased divisions between the mandarins and the rest. After the modernists came the postmodernists, who were
even less comprehensible to the lay reader. "Readerly engagement could only
deteriorate into tedious labor, frustrated incomprehension and, more often
than not, anger at the author's pose of superiority and command."[73]
   One other point is worth noting in connection with early twentieth-
century developments. Avant-garde movements, such as Futurism in the vi-

sual arts and "modernism" in literature, were self-proclaimed phenomena that were announced by manifestos. An entirely different development, one that was unheralded and available to a mass reading public, may also have contributed to a new aesthetic style—namely, the layout of the front page of daily newspapers:

> The newspaper's form denies form, overturns the consecrated canons of text structure and coherence . . . [it] is built by addition of the discrete, theoretically disconnected elements which juxtapose themselves only in response to the abstract requirements of "layout"—thus of a disposition of space whose logic, ultimately, is commercial.[74]

Indeed, the newspaper press in its later incarnations offers a corrective to the often cited view that associates the printed word with linear, sequential modes of thought. This view not only ignores the inventive powers of literary artists from Laurence Sterne to James Joyce, who exploited the resources of print while subverting straightforward narratives, but it also ignores ordinary paratextual devices such as tables of contents and indexes. More important, perhaps, are the various nontextual printed materials that furnished "jobbing printers" with a livelihood. The extent to which print is conducive to nonlinear reading practices is well documented in a recent article on nineteenth-century timetables.[75] The front page of the modern newspaper was unexceptional in this regard. But it was perhaps unique in the way it sought to excite interest in a story, or, rather, in several different stories, while at the same time interrupting narrative flow. When Woolf wrote of capturing a "fragmentary and spasmodic" stream of consciousness, she was referring to an inner life. But the outward form of the daily newspaper was no less fragmentary and spasmodic.

Aptly described by Marshall McLuhan as a "mosaic of unrelated items unified only by a dateline,"[76] the front page conveyed a simultaneous presentation of disconnected items in a way that influenced generations of artists and poets, beginning with numerous early twentieth-century works of art that employed collage techniques or experimented with providing diverse perspective renderings of the same object within the same canvas.

Experiments with the juxtaposition of disconnected items marked the publications of Marshall McLuhan himself—witness *The Mechanical Bride* and *The Gutenberg Galaxy*. Despite the obvious connection, *The Gutenberg*

Galaxy justified its nonlinear presentation with reference to the field theories of modern physics. Given its unconventional format and its substitution of headlines for chapter titles, the influence of the newspaper may be more to the point. Its author's special training, not in electromagnetic theory but in English literary studies, also needs to be taken into consideration. To be well versed in literary criticism in the 1960s was to be predisposed against histori-cal narratives, regardless of other trends. Other antihistorical influences were also at work, for example, Catholic theology. McLuhan's treatment seems to me to owe rather more to St. Augustine than the author was prepared to admit. The linear sequential approach of the chronicler is, after all, relevant only to the corrupt and transitory City of Man. The City of God exists outside historical time; all the events that unfold on earth are simultaneously present in the mind of God.

That Catholic theology is not without significance in recent media analy-sis is shown not only in the work of McLuhan, who was a Catholic convert, but also in that of Walter Ong, who was a Jesuit priest. Unlike the Lutherans, who hailed printing as God's highest act of grace, Catholic scholars are more likely to remind us that God produced the Incarnation—his truly highest act of grace—in the age of scribes.

> God entered human history . . . at the precise time when . . . his
> entrance would have the greatest opportunity to endure and
> flower. . . . The believer finds it providential that divine revelation
> let down its roots into human culture . . . after the alphabet was
> devised but before print had overgrown major oral structures and
> before our electronic culture further obscured the basic nature of the
> word.[77]

One wonders whether preachers who use the so-called electronic church would agree that the Word is now being obscured.

For Father Ong, in any event, the age of the scribe was especially privi-leged for having contained the Incarnation. As we have noted, the same age was seen to contain other blessings in the aftermath of the French Revolution. Stained glass and illuminated parchments were celebrated even while the colorless and soulless world machine of Enlightenment deists was con-demned. This Romantic indictment of the age of reason provided a subtext for *The Gutenberg Galaxy: The Making of Typographic Man.* Arguments that were aimed at rationality and science were transferred by McLuhan to printing and its effects—with anomalous results. After all, the printed word achieved an unrivalled preeminence when the Romantic movement was at its height. How McLuhan's favorite literary artists escaped being contaminated by the all-enveloping effects of typography remains to be explained. Isaac Newton's presumably impoverished "single vision" is attributed to print culture, whereas William Blake's prophetic imagination is not. Yet surely print played as important a role in the work of the eighteenth-century poet and engraver as in that of the seventeenth-century mathematical physicist.[78]

As many critics have already noted, the enveloping effects of print are especially apparent in the idiosyncratic formulations of McLuhan himself. He was an omnivorous reader and crammed his text with citations taken from a vast variety of other books. Despite his affinity with nineteenth-century Romanticists, he lacked the historical imagination of a Carlyle or a Michelet and made no effort to resurrect the multidimensional, rich texture of life as it was lived in the past. Typographic man suffered from the very ailment his creator attempted to describe: emerging as an unconvincing and abstract construct assembled by means of scissors and paste.

Scissors and paste have by now become outmoded and blocks of text are moved more easily by punching keys. But the views held by previous generations cannot be deleted as easily as can words upon a screen. As noted in the preface, the new media seem to give rise to many of the same concerns that had been associated with the old. "The activity of novel reading which . . . had seemed so dangerous to the mental heath of the reading public . . . now seemed benign and even healthful to those who looked on the movies as toxic. Exactly the same arguments would be repeated, of course, about television."[79] The term "couch potato" was new, the phenomenon itself was not—witness previous comments about sedentary bookworms. Like the activity of novel reading, print journalism began to seem benign when compared with television sound bites and "infotainment." Indeed, all the products of print technology, whether resulting from the use of hot type or cold, are beginning to be viewed with the sort of nostalgia that was first lavished on the age of the scribe and then on the early days of the wooden handpress—as the best of the past continues to be set against the worst of the present.

Concern about being overwhelmed by the sheer quantity of reading matter has recently been treated as an entirely new phenomenon. "Having lived our professional lives in a culture of scarcity," wrote Roy Rosenzweig, "historians find that a world of abundance can be unsettling."[80] One commentator believes that present-day information overload is so unsettling it has given rise to a new childhood ailment: ADD (Attention Deficit Disorder). "Extreme expressions of the culture's malaise, symptoms and disorders mirrored the time's order." In the twenty-first century, "'when the sum of information available in any given minute is larger than it has ever been in history,' we've conceived 'a condition in which attention is at a deficit.'"[81]

From the present vantage point, previous generations may appear to have lived in a culture of scarcity. They did not anticipate the abundance of information provided in a digital era, where the world appears to be "overgrown with data, options and demands" with a "billion Web sites and millions of blogs, tens of thousands of books in the store and hundreds of television channels."[82] Tens of thousands of books may appear to be relatively insignificant when placed beside a billion web sites. But these figures vastly underestimate contemporary book production. According to Ian Donaldson, writing in 1998, the number of books issued annually from the world's presses is estimated to be in excess of 2 billion.[83] Donaldson added: "Copyright libraries throughout the world have long been unable to handle the avalanche of material that arrives weekly at their doorsteps."[84]

As previous chapters suggest, the sense of being overwhelmed by an avalanche was manifested by commentators long before the digital era had arrived. Literati who worried about their works being squeezed on crowded bookshelves, librarians who had to keep confronting disorder as new volumes poured in and bibliographers trying to keep track of new titles would have been astonished at the thought that they were living in a culture of scarcity.

The fate of the book has long been subject to two contradictory concerns: anxiety about scarcity and loss on the one hand; worry about glut and overload on the other. Concern about scarcity and loss predominated throughout the age of scribes, when the complete destruction both of individual manuscripts and of entire libraries had repeatedly been experienced by scholarly communities. The loss of works by the Greek dramatists and the destruction of the Alexandrian Library were catastrophes from which there was no recovery. Such disasters were associated with the gnawing tooth of time from which no artifact could ever be secure.

Such concern about total oblivion needs to be differentiated from anxiety about the reception of a given work. Variations on this latter theme were sounded by both ancients and moderns alike. Thus the complaints of classical poets who envisaged their works, once inscribed on papyrus or parchment, falling out of favor and being used to wrap fish, line pastry dishes, or wipe behinds were echoed by later writers who lived in the age of print. They elaborated on the ease with which soft paper, unlike stiffer parchment or vellum, could be used for nonliterary purposes.

> Such jokes about the recyclable nature of books are themselves tire-lessly recycled throughout much English Augustan satire. Dryden Oldham, Pope, [and] Swift . . . constantly envision a world in which books are dismembered, dispersed, and humiliatingly used for pur-poses other than those for which they were first intended.[85]

This sort of gallows humor expressed anxiety about the fleeting nature of fame and the fickle nature of readers. It needs to be distinguished from aware-ness that all scrolls and codices were at the mercy of the "great Engines of Destruction . . . such as Swords, and Fire, and the devouring Moths of Antiquity."[86]

Concern about the recyclable nature of inscriptions on papyrus or paper is different from concern about their total oblivion.[87]

> Horace, like Pope, like Byron, is pondering the nature of poetic fame, and he recognizes that his own poems may merely serve in the end to wrap frankincense, perfumes, pepper, and similar commodi-ties. Yet as Pope is well aware, Horace's lines about this very possibil-ity have actually survived. Byron, in recalling Pope recalling Horace . . . consciously places himself in a classic tradition of poets whose work has in fact, despite their own disclaimers, stood the test of time. To speak about the likelihood of one's book being used as waste paper may be in part a talismanic act, designed to ward off ill fortune and avert the result the writer most deeply fears.[88]

Indeed, recycling always held the promise of possible retrieval, as was the case with palimpsests, where one might recover faint inscriptions under scraped parchment, and as was the case with those Italian humanist book-hunters who claimed to rescue ancient works that were being dismembered and abused by ignorant monks. A memorable nineteenth-century example has been noted above, on how the use made of a cheesemonger's wrapping shaped William Hone's career.[89]

After the advent of printing, there was less concern about total destruc-tion, although the fate of Alexandria continued to haunt later generations. Scarcity did remain troublesome to scholars who tried to track down hard-to-find books. But the chief problem confronting most authors who lived after print was (and still is) overabundance. The fear of loss, expressed by most writers, was not related to destruction by "sword, fire, or devouring" insects. It was rather, as Jonathan Swift made clear, the fear of getting lost in a crowd. "There are so many books," lamented Robert Burton in the sixteenth century, that the "very Presses are oppressed."[90] Previous chapters have cited other comments in other centuries to the same effect.

With regard to a sense of overload, each generation in turn, notes Ann Blair, has been absolutely certain that its situation was completely unprecedented.[91] Given the cumulative effects of printing technology, each was probably correct! "For those who believed true understanding required . . . a comprehensive and therefore impartial view, for those who strove for wisdom through unity and coherence, the explosion and fragmentation of knowledge was disconcerting and alarming."[92] Even before the great leaps forward in productivity during the last two centuries, each generation was in possession of more printed (and hand-copied) materials than the one before.

In his introduction to a group of essays devoted to information overload in the early modern era, Daniel Rosenberg wonders "how and why a phenomenon so patently old can periodically and convincingly be re-experienced as a fundamental symptom of the new?"[93] Perhaps prolonged exposure to classical and medieval learning had led literate elites to be forever on guard against loss and forever surprised by confrontation with the opposite problems posed by the relentless accumulation that affected all written materials after printing.

There is a peculiar diachronic aspect to print culture which is strongly biased in favor of accumulation and against subtraction. "For contemporaries, the copiousness of the press was one of its most defining characteristics."[94] Not only did the output of new books increase with each improvement in the technology of printing and papermaking, but also the reprinting and the collecting of old books (and journals and ephemera) never ceased. New volumes are, even now, being added every year to the Loeb Classical Library. Indeed, old materials that had once seemed lost forever are constantly being unearthed and restored. The retrieval of once buried or lost papyrus rolls, the piecing together of fragmented scrolls, the deciphering of incised glyphs and symbols goes on even now at an ever accelerated pace. Furthermore, thanks to photocopiers that are placed in libraries and the printers that accompany most home computers, texts are being replicated at a rate that defies calculation. As I've noted elsewhere, Chronos, the God of Time, was once feared for his all-devouring, monstrous appetite. A monstrous capacity to disgorge would seem to be more threatening to all the generations that have lived in the age of print[95]: "She spewed out of her filthy maw, / a flood of poison horrible and black / . . . Her vomit full of books and papers was."[96]

Of course, the boy who cried wolf was eventually proved right. Simply because predictions of the death of the book have proved false in the past, that does not mean they may not prove true in the future. It is always possible that the codex form will be abandoned and that print itself will be superseded. Printed encyclopedias have already been largely displaced by digital ones. Heavy, costly textbooks are being replaced in some U.S. schools by lighter, cheaper, and easily revised digital "flexbooks."[97] The often-predicted paperless office has not yet materialized, but it has progressed far enough to raise alarms about the replacement of government papers by emails and the consequent erosion of official record-keeping.[98]

On the other hand, copying machines are doing a thriving business, and online bookstores continue to sell printed books alongside new reading machines, such as the Kindle. Not only are old printed books still being borrowed from libraries, and not only are new ones purchased from Amazon, but their contents are also being given a new lease on life in electronic form. Novels by Jane Austen, Victor Hugo, and the rest, far from being superseded, are recycled repeatedly in diverse new media, thereby exciting enough interest to get reprinted and resold in book form.

Given these contraindications, along with the increased output of books worldwide, coexistence seems more likely than supersession for some years to come. Coexistence is scarcely an unusual phenomenon. It accounts for the mixed-media environment that we take for granted at present. Yet, when the advent of new media comes up for discussion, the very possibility of coexistence tends to be discounted.

Here is a typical scenario, taken from *The Gutenberg Elegies*, first published in 1994:

> we are in the midst of an epoch-making transition as consequential for culture as was . . . Gutenberg's invention. . . . Ten, fifteen years from now the world will be nothing like what we remember, nothing much like what we experience now . . . our relationship to the space-time axis will be very different from what we have lived with for millennia.[99]

Fifteen years have passed; many new developments have occurred. But the same book, *The Gutenberg Elegies*, is still available in hardback and also in paperback in bookstores both real and virtual. It is unlikely that people lived with any one "space-time axis" for millennia. It is more likely that diverse groups in diverse locales using diverse systems of measurement experienced "space-time" in diverse ways. Whatever the case, it is certain that Western Europeans have lived with printed materials for much less than one millennium. During the centuries that ensued after Gutenberg's invention, moreover, the experience of "space-time" scarcely remained unchanged. Indeed, the feeling of being "in the midst of an epoch-making transition" serves to link our generation with several that have gone before.

To go back no farther than the 1830s, Alfred de Musset described how his generation experienced the aftermath of the French Revolution and the Napoleonic wars: "behind them, a past forever destroyed . . . before them . . . the first gleams of the future; and between these two worlds . . . a troubled sea filled with wreckage . . . the present, in a word."[100] In the nineteenth century, as noted above, new media were expected to drive out the old. Just as the printed book had superseded encyclopedias "in stone," so too the newspaper was expected to supersede the book.

Hindsight suggests that nineteenth-century observers were right to assign special significance to the newspaper press. It restructured the way readers experienced the flow of time and altered the way they learned about affairs of state. It created a forum outside parliaments and assembly halls that allowed ordinary readers and letter-writers to participate in debates. It provided ambitious journalists, from Marat to Mussolini, with new pathways to political power. It gave a tremendous boost to commercial advertising. It served to knit together the inhabitants of large cities, for whom the daily newspaper would become a kind of surrogate community.

Not only did it knit together city-dwellers, but also, according to many Victorians (as noted above), it created solidarity on a nation-wide scale, functioning as a grand national agora. More recently, the anthropologist Benedict Anderson has elaborated on this concept:

> the newspaper is merely an "extreme form" of the book, a book sold on a colossal scale, but of ephemeral popularity. Might we say: one-day best-sellers? The obsolescence of the newspaper on the morrow of its printing—curious that one of the earlier mass-produced commodities should so prefigure the inbuilt obsolescence of modern du-

rables—nonetheless, for just this reason, creates this extraordinary mass ceremony: the almost precisely simultaneous consumption. . . . We know that particular morning and evening editions will be overwhelmingly consumed within this hour and that, only on this day, not that . . . The significance of this mass ceremony—Hegel observed that newspapers serve modern man as a substitute for morning prayers—is paradoxical. It is performed in silent privacy. . . . Yet each communicant is well aware that the ceremony he performs is being replicated simultaneously by thousands (or millions) of others of whose existence he is confident, yet of whose identity he has not the slightest notion. Furthermore, this ceremony is incessantly repeated . . . throughout the calendar. What more vivid figure for the secular, historically clocked, imagined community can be envisaged?[101]

Anderson's description seems especially appropriate to the interval when print was the sole medium for transmitting the news of the day, although even then it is somewhat abstracted from real life, given the divergent routines of flesh-and-blood newspaper readers. By the time he was writing, electronic media (radio and/or television) were already providing newscasts at various times to listeners who might be engaged in driving to and from work or taking time out at irregular intervals from domestic routines. Not only were the recipients of the day's news often out of sync with each other, but many of them were no longer engaged in the act of reading.[102] Now, of course, the clockwork "mass ceremony" has been more severely disrupted by online publication.

Nineteenth-century observers were right to sense that journalism had significant transformative effects. But they were wrong in assuming the advent of the newspaper signified the end of the book. At present, indeed, it appears that they got hold of the wrong end of the stick: the end of the newspaper seems more imminent than that of the book. Oddly enough, the chief mark of success for an aspiring politician these days is not getting one's name in a newspaper, or on television, or in any number of diverse online publications. It is receiving a large advance for agreeing to serve as the ostensible author of an old-fashioned printed book. With regard to newsprint, the possibility of supersession cannot be ruled out. Online publication offers such an efficient means of conveying both news and advertisements that the heavy equipment and labor-intensive delivery systems required to get the daily newspaper into print and at the doorsteps of subscribers seem fated to go the way of so-called rust-belt industries. But although the Internet is poised to supersede most daily papers (as well as postal services and department stores), it continues to facilitate the browsing and purchasing of printed books.

Perhaps one reason for the difference between the likely fate of the newspaper and that of the book has to do with the preservative powers of print. Journalism is, by its nature, an ephemeral phenomenon: what is more obsolete than yesterday's news? When Anderson plays with the notion of the newspaper as a best-selling book, he underlines its obsolescence on the morrow of its printing and suggests that it prefigures the built-in obsolescence of other ostensibly durable commodities. Given its ephemeral character, the news appears to be well suited to being conveyed by machines that are themselves designed to go out of date. To be sure, yesterday's news is of intense interest to historians. The failure of librarians to preserve newspapers that constitute invaluable documentation has elicited anguished appeals from Nicholson Baker, among others.[103]

Be that as it may, rapid obsolescence is a nightmarish concept for authors who are appealing to "Prince Posterity." They are likely to feel more comfortable entrusting their work to the duplicative powers of print than running the risk of having it vanish into cyberspace. Recent Kindle readers have been unpleasantly reminded of this possibility. Their digital editions of George Orwell's *Animal Farm* were erased before their eyes, dropping into the "memory hole" that Orwell had imagined in *1984*.[104] It is true that some postings on the Internet that have been deliberately deleted (e.g., for advocating hate crimes) are nevertheless subject to being "cached and preserved" by archival tools like the "Wayback Machine" and by amateur online archivists.[105] The latter, however, tend to "evade responsibility for the tricky issue of long-term maintenance."[106] The preservative powers of "virtual" archives are still untested compared to those that have enabled five-hundred-year-old printed products to survive. Here, as elsewhere, coexistence should not be ruled out. Being online and in print are by no means incompatible. One author (cited in the *Times Literary Supplement* in 2008) "makes the text of all of his books available for free online, and believes, with justification, that the additional exposure boosts sales of the physical book."[107] Readers who will be alive to witness the future centennial celebration of Gutenberg's invention in 2040 will be in a better position than the present author to provide an informed opinion on such issues.[108]

My first chapter contained mention of a rhetorical model used by humanists who paid tribute to diverse innovations, including the art of printing. The model was derived from Virgil's fourth *Eclogue*, which had been taken by Christians to indicate pagan foreknowledge of the coming of the Christ child. Insofar as it described a birth that signified the advent of a new age, it seemed applicable to Gutenberg's invention. Here was an infant art, still in swaddling clothes or in a cradle, that, like the infant Hercules, miraculously sprang to life full-blown. The providential nature of the invention was reasserted by early Protestants, who believed it heralded emancipation from the rule of the papal anti-Christ. The idea that the invention signified the coming of a new age was reiterated by those eighteenth-century prophets of progress who (prematurely) heralded the victory of science over superstition, and of reason over revelation.

With the coming of iron and steam, the age of the handpress came to an end. Renaissance tributes to a divine art were replaced by tributes to a mighty engine of progress. At the same time, concern about commodification never abated and was, indeed, only intensified as the centuries wore on. The villainous role assigned to Gutenberg's financier and to profiteering early printers was subsequently transferred to unscrupulous booksellers. In the nineteenth century, fictions pertaining to profiteering publishers were freshly composed by new Napoleons of the pen. The American literary scene in the 1980s has been characterized as a "particularly fraught historical moment" when conditions threatened to upset "the precarious balance between the commercial and the literary."[109] It is difficult to find any interval after the late fifteenth century that lacked expressions of concern about maintaining a balance, if not between the "literary"[110] and the commercial, at least between serving the muses and marketing products for profit. Nor were ambivalent reactions confined to issues pertaining to the marketplace of print. Enthusiasm about the advancement of learning went together with anxiety about overload—an anxiety that never abated and also intensified as the centuries wore on. The welcome accorded diffusion of information and the spread of literacy was countered by dismay at degradation and vulgarization. The pamphlet press was hailed for giving voice to popular protests and condemned for unleashing civil war. Newsprint was acclaimed for creating a vast national agora and condemned for generating war fever.

At present, the idea of a printer's devil is as quaint as a classical allusion, a black-faced newsboy, or the use of hot type itself. Yet ambivalence about communications technologies seems just as strong today as ever it was in the past. Witness reactions to recent on-demand digital devices that promise universal access to a world-wide library without walls. Hailed as an awesome and magnificent venture, Google's project has also been described as "the most massive and brazen copyright violation ever attempted."[111] Enthusiastic approval of the replacement of so-called dead-tree editions by the Kindle e-reader has been countered by alarms over the way "Amazon and other e-media aggregators . . . are seizing the opportunity to codify, commodify and control access."[112]

Whatever the future holds, Western attitudes that have survived over millennia are likely to persist, however many new electronic instruments are devised. Premature obituaries on the end of the book and the death of print are themselves testimony to long-enduring habits of mind. In the very act of heralding the dawn of a new age with the advent of new media, contemporary analysts continue to bear witness, however inadvertently, to the ineluctable persistence of the past.

Notes

PREFACE

1. Michael Warner, *The Letters of the Republic* (Cambridge, 1990), xii.

2. Harold Nicolson diary entry, cited by Clarence Tracy, "Johnson and the Common Reader," Roy M. Wiles Memorial Lecture, 17 March 1976 (Hamilton, 1976), 4.

3. Neil Postman, *Amusing Ourselves to Death* (New York, 1985).

4. See Jason Scott-Warren on the "sensationalist culture of cheap print" in Jacobean England, *Early Modern English Literature* (Cambridge, 2005), 90.

5. Isaiah Thomas, *History of Printing in America*, 2 vols., 2nd ed. (Albany, 1874), 1: 330–31. In the version given by Warner, 182 n.64, John Buckner is confused with Buckner's printer, William Nuthead; 1682 is described as fourteen years after 1671. Warner extrapolates from the Virginia case that "most seventeenth-century colonists were quite content, insofar as we can tell, to do without a press" (17). David Hall, *Cultures of Print* (Amherst, 1966), 99, says that Berkeley "was not hostile to printing *per se*" because he encouraged a London printer to issue an edition of the "Virginia statutes." Hall attributes the absence of a printing office in the Chesapeake region to economic conditions: there was not enough work there for printers to do. But then why did the colonial governors find it necessary to prohibit establishing a press?

6. James Raven, *The Business of Books* (New Haven, 2007), 132, 377.

7. Compare the controversies provoked by plans to commemorate the 500th anniversary of 1492 with the celebratory activities of 1892.

8. See, e.g., essays by Geoffrey Roper, Kai-Wing Chow, Vivek Bhandari, Tony Ballantyne, and Jane McRae in *Agent of Change*, ed. Sabrina A. Baron, Eric N. Lindquist, and Eleanor F. Shevlin (Amherst, 2007). Also Cynthia Brokaw, "Book History in Premodern China," Christopher A. Reed, "Gutenberg and Modern Chinese Print Culture," both in *Book History* 10 (2007): 253–315. The collaborative two-volume *Books Without Borders*, ed. Robert Fraser and Mary Hammond (Basingstoke, 2008), aims at providing a non-Western, transnational framework for book history (albeit not for print culture).

9. Gary Marker, *Publishing, Printing, and the Origins of Intellectual Life in Russia* (Princeton, 1985); Peter Kornicki, *The Book in Japan* (Leiden, 1998); Mary Elizabeth Berry, *Japan in Print* (Berkeley, 2007).

10. Anindita Ghosh, Review of Rochelle Pinto, *Between Empires: Print and Politics*

in Goa (Oxford, 2007), *American Historical Review* 114 (June 2009): 744–45. See also Swapan Chakravorty and Abhijit Gupta, eds., *Print Areas: Book History in India* (Delhi, 2004).

11. Michel de Montaigne, "On Carriages," in *The Complete Essays of Montaigne*, ed. Donald Frame (Stanford, 1957). On Chinese views of Gutenberg, see Reed's essay, cited above.

12. Citation from William Hazlitt (on Thomas Holcroft), Roy Porter, *The Enlightenment* (London, 2000), 484.

CHAPTER 1. FIRST IMPRESSIONS

Epigraph: Gabriel Harvey, *Pierces Supererogation* (1593), in *Works of Gabriel Harvey*, 3 vols., ed. Alexander B. Grosart (New York, 1966 [1884]), 2: 218.

1. See Stuart Atkins, "Motif in Literature: The Faust Theme," in *Dictionary of the History of Ideas*, ed. Philip Wiener et al. (New York, 1973), 3: 244–53; E. M. Butler, *The Fortunes of Faust* (Cambridge, 1979). Many other references are given by Henri-Jean Martin in "Comment on écrivit l'histoire du livre," *Le livre français sous l'Ancien Régime* (Paris, 1987), 267–68 n.26 (hereafter Martin, "Comment"). The Abbot Trithemius (who talked about Fust with the latter's son-in-law, Peter Schoeffer, and also recorded his distrust of the necromancer, Dr. Faustus) provides a link between the two figures.

2. Prosper Marchand, *Dictionnaire historique, ou mémoires critiques . . .* , ed. J. N. S. Allemand, 2 vols. (The Hague, 1758), 1: 249. See also relevant selections from Voltaire cited in Martin, "Comment," 269 n. 61.

3. Stephen Jones, *New Biographical Dictionary* (London, 1811), 205–6.

4. Daniel Defoe, *History of the Devil* (London, 1727), 378; italics mine.

5. Adrian Johns, *The Nature of the Book* (Chicago, 1998) and David McKitterick, *Print, Manuscript and the Search for Order* (Cambridge, 2003) both stress the multiformity of handpress output.

6. "Any sufficiently advanced technology is indistinguishable from magic," according to Arthur C. Clarke, *Profiles of the Future* (New York, 1962), quoted in *New York Times*, 31 October 2002, E9.

7. Pierce Butler, *The Origin of Printing in Europe* (Chicago, 1940), 130 describes this as "the classic Gutenberg legend."

8. Theo L. DeVinne, *The Invention of Printing* (New York, 1878), 416–17 n.1.

9. "Fust and Schoeffer," in E. C. Bigmore and C. W. H. Wyman, *A Bibliography of Printing with Notes and Illustrations*, 2 vols. (London, 1881), 1: 246.

10. Alexandra Halasz, *The Marketplace of Print* (Cambridge, 1997), 21–23.

11. R. D. Dunn, ed., "Fragment of an Unpublished Essay on Printing by William Camden," *British Library Journal* 12 (1986): 147. Halasz, 22, interprets this particular imputation of criminality to Camden's defensive posture as an elitist scholar who opposed the development of a "popular press."

12. Elizabeth L. Eisenstein, *Grub Street Abroad* (Oxford, 1992), 23–24.

13. Peter Beal's fascinating account of seventeenth-century attacks on scribes and scriveners, as "greedy," "covetous," "pharisees" and "vipers," seems pertinent, but it is relevant to the notarial role of scribes in drawing up wills and other legal documents (bonds, mortgages, indentures) rather than to their role as producers of handcopied books. See Beal, *In Praise of Scribes* (Oxford, 1998), 7ff.

14. Johann Amerbach, *The Correspondence of Johann Amerbach*, trans. and ed. Barbara Halporn (Ann Arbor, 2000), 74.

15. I owe thanks to Alberto Manguel for sending me a page of hand-colored panels in comic strip form describing the history of printing and depicting Fust as a usurious Jew who robbed the poor inventor. It is taken from an illustrated popular encyclopedia series produced by Pellerin et Glucq (Gaston Lucq) ("Histoire de l'imprimerie," Imagerie d'Épinal 3820, Pellerin & Cie, n.d.). According to a Département des Vosges archivist, the first edition came out in 1905 and a new one appeared more recently. I would guess that it reflects the views of anti-Dreyfusards and later of Vichy supporters.

16. David Hume, *Enquiry Concerning the Principles of Morals*, ed. Tom L. Beauchamp (Oxford, 2006), 73.

17. See, e.g., the letter of Conrad Leontorius to Johann Amerbach (November 1497) deploring the way the "divine art of printing" was being undermined by ignorant and corrupt printers. Letter no. 145, Amerbach, *Correspondence*, ed. Halporn, 217.

18. Paul Needham, "*Haec sancta ars*: Gutenberg's Invention as a Divine Gift," *Gazette of the Grolier Club* 42 (1990): 104–5.

19. In addition to Needham's citation, see Martin Davies, "Juan de Carvajal and Early Printing," *The Library* 6th ser. 18 (1996): 193–215. David McKitterick takes this same letter to indicate that printing was regarded as "not necessarily either better or worse" than hand-copying, but his interpretation seems to be idiosyncratic; *Print, Manuscript*, 31.

20. Mary Rouse and Richard Rouse, "Nicolaus Gupalatinus and the Arrival of Print in Italy," *La Bibliofilia* 88 (1986): 225. The Rouses regard the physician's enthusiasm as exceptional, point to the seeming indifference of members of the Lucca town council, and conclude that "in the early years, [the] superiority [of the press] was neither apparent nor real" (245). Wasn't it apparent to the physician?

21. See, e.g., Asa Briggs and Peter Burke, *A Social History of the Media* (Cambridge, 2002), 17, where "triumphalist accounts" are countered by "catastrophist narratives," although the only such narratives cited come from the seventeenth-century English Civil War (with *Macaria* misattributed to Samuel Hartlib, instead of to Gabriel Plattes, and an Andrew Marvell citation misconstrued.)

22. David McKitterick offers rich documentation in his *Print, Manuscript*.

23. Martin Lowry, *The World of Aldus Manutius* (Ithaca, 1979), 24.

24. François I temporarily banned printing in January 1535, but soon rescinded the ban. On the Virginia governors, see Isaiah Thomas, *History of Printing in America*, 2 vols., 2nd ed. (Albany, 1874), 1: 330–32.

25. Georgius Alexandrinus, quoted in Rudolph Hirsch, *Printing, Selling, and Reading* (Wiesbaden, 1967), 48 n. 20. See also use of same phrase by Curt Bühler, *The Fifteenth-Century Book* (Philadelphia, 1960), 50. Relevant also is Squarciafico's dream about whether printing was more to be praised than blamed. See Leslie Alfred Sheppard, "A Fifteenth Century Humanist: F. Filelfo," *The Library* 4th ser. 16 (1936): 1–27.

26. Brian Richardson, "The Debates on Printing in Renaissance Italy," *La Bibliofilia* 100 (1998): 136. Richardson's article contains less evidence of actual debates than of imaginary dialogues composed by mid-sixteenth-century "poligraphi" such as Domenichi and Doni.

27. Brian Richardson, *Printing, Writers and Readers in Renaissance Italy* (Cambridge, 1999), 3.

28. Lowry, *Aldus*, 35.

29. Mary A. Rouse and Richard H. Rouse, *Cartolai, Illuminators, and Printers in Fifteenth Century Italy*, UCLA Occasional Paper 1 (Los Angeles, 1988), 21.

30. Hugh H. Davis, review of Silvia Rizzo, *Il lessico filologico degli umanisti, Renaissance Quarterly* 28 (Autumn 1975): 353.

31. Bühler, 40. Bühler goes on to mention the interest expressed by Francesco Filelfo in July, 1470 in acquiring printed books which Filelfo described as being equivalent to "the work of a skilled and exact scribe" (41).

32. See reference to a "typewritten manuscript" by Felicia R. Lee, "In Brief," *New York Times*, 19 June 2004, A9.

33. Silvia Rizzo, *Il lessico filologica degli umanisti* (Rome, 1973), 7, 69.

34. Armando Petrucci, *Writers and Readers in Medieval Italy*, trans. and ed. Charles M. Radding (New Haven, 1995), 200.

35. Bühler, 16; Cora Lutz, "Manuscripts Copied from Printed Books," in *Essays on Manuscripts and Rare Books* (Hamden, 1975), 129–39.

36. David Shaw, "*Ars formularia*: Neo-Latin Synonyms for Printing," *The Library* 6th ser. 11, 3 (1989): 221.

37. Richardson, "Debates," passim.

38. Sheila Edmunds, "From Schoeffer to Vérard: Concerning the Scribes Who Became Printers," in *Printing the Written Word*, ed. Sandra Hindman (Ithaca, 1991), 24–27, 33. To illustrate her point, Edmunds notes ambiguity in the archaic term "trucker." She questions Bühler's assertion (Bühler, 48) that "countless scribes" took up printing, and also cites Hirsch, *Printing, Selling*, 18 as saying that this was the "usual" route to the new occupation. But Hirsch only says this was the most "obvious" (not "usual") transfer and in a footnote (n.21) cites Carl Wehmer, who pointed to uncertain terminology in 1955. Hirsch also notes that some printers actually called themselves scribes. The vocational shift of scribe-into-printer is downplayed by the Rouses, who are mainly concerned with the manuscript book dealers who became printed book sellers.

39. Hellmut Lehmann-Haupt, *Peter Schoeffer of Gernsheim and Mainz* (Rochester, 1966).

40. Edmunds, 27.

41. Alfred Pollard, *An Essay on Colophons with Specimens and Translations*, intro. Richard Garnett (Chicago, 1905), 13–17, 24–25. On colophons issued from Gutenberg's and later Schoeffer's printing shop in Mainz in the 1460s and '70s see Lotte Hellinga, "Analytical Bibliography and the Study of Early Printed Books with a Case Study of the Mainz *Catholicon*," *Gutenberg Jahrbuch* (1989): 14–96, 65–70; also Nicholas Barker, "A Contemporary Panegyrist of the Invention of Printing," in *Incunabula*, ed. Martin Davies (London, 1999), 187–215.

42. Michael Warner, *Letters of the Republic* (Cambridge, 1990), 8. Warner is not upholding a thesis of continuity but rather trying to prove that the "latent" logic of the new medium was a retrospective construct and entirely foreign to a fifteenth-century mentality.

43. Colophon of Wendelin of Speier (in his 1470 edition of Sallust) in Pollard, 37. All subsequent rhymed translations from Latin are taken from Pollard.

44. Florencio, cited in Marc Drogin, *Anathema!* (Totowa, 1983), 7.

45. Richard Garnett, introduction to Pollard, xvi.

46. When William Caxton did refer to hardship it was not that he was tired from so much physical labor but rather that he had learned a new craft "at my grete charge and dispense" so that "euery man" could obtain a copy of his book "attones [at once]." From Caxton's translation of Raoul Le Fevre's *Recuyell of the Histories of Troy* (Bruges, 1473–74) quoted in Needham, 116–17.

47. Pollard, 14–15.

48. Ibid., 55–56.

49. Ibid., 35. The reference to a buyer's eyes failing to read a "blurred" manuscript, like Aeneas Sylvius's comment about not needing glasses (mentioned above), points to a significant coupling of hand-copying with blurred vision and printing with clear-sightedness.

50. George Hoffman, "Writing Without Leisure: Proofreading as Work in the Renaissance," *Journal of Medieval and Renaissance Studies* 25 (1995): 21. Hoffman does not take note of the possible benefits of harsh criticism among competitors and the relatively rapid reporting of errors that was a concomitant of printing. See discussion of editions of Pliny, below.

51. Martin Davies, "Making Sense of Pliny in the Quattrocento," *Renaissance Studies* 9, 2 (1995): 242–43. Davies cites the verdict of contemporary scholars that Johannes de Spira's edition of Pliny's *Historia Naturalis* issued in Venice in the summer of 1469 was a disaster and notes that it had no influence on subsequent editions—unlike the more influential (albeit defective) Roman edition of 1470, edited by de Bussi.

52. On the anxiety of classical poets about their work withstanding "the gnawing tooth of time," see Ian Donaldson, "Jonson, Shakespeare and the Destruction of the Book," in *Jonson's Magic Houses* (Oxford, 1997), chap. 12. For further discussion of this theme, see Chapter 7 below.

53. Johannes Trithemius, *In Praise of Scribes* (*De Laude Scriptorum*), trans. and ed. Klaus Arnold (Lawrence, 1974), 35.

54. The term "divine" was increasingly used and abused during the Renaissance to designate especially talented artists and poets. Montaigne was scornful of the way the term was overused by self-promoting publicists such as Aretino. See Patricia Emison, *Creating the "Divine" Artist from Dante to Michelangelo* (Leiden, 2004), 143. The most effective use of the epithet on a title page—one that has stuck to the title ever since—was the 1555 edition of Dante's *Commedia*, edited by Ludovico Dolce and printed by Giolito. A. J. Butler, "Dante," *Encyclopædia Britannica*, 11th ed., 814.

55. Selected early prefaces about printing are presented in English translation by Pierce Butler, *Origin*, 93–99. In some cases the printer also served as editor and preface writer. Josse Bade, for example, contributed some 250 prefaces to the books he published. See Isabelle Diu, "Medium typographicum et respublica literaria: le rôle de Josse Bade dans le monde de l'édition humaniste," in *Le livre et l'historien*, ed. Frédéric Barbier et al. (Geneva, 1997), 111–24. How tributes to printing were inserted by glossators into early glossed printed editions of Horace is noted by Evelyn B. Tribble, *Margins and Marginality* (Charlottesville, 1993), 59–60.

56. Victor Schölderer, "Printers and Readers in Italy in the Fifteenth Century," Annual Italian Lecture of the British Academy Brochure, *Proceedings of the British Academy* 35 (1949): 15 n.1. See also editor's preface to Augustine's *De Arte Praedicandi* (Strasbourg, c. 1467–68) cited in Malcolm B. Parkes, *Scribes, Scripts and Readers* (London, 1991), xxi. The editor regarded printing primarily as a means of producing identical copies of a text he had corrected, thus, Parkes states, eliminating the accumulation of errors inherent in manuscript transmission."

57. See, e.g., Johns, *Nature of the Book*.

58. That Johann Heynlin, who served on the faculty of theology at the Sorbonne before moving to Basel, was fascinated by the invention of printing and the promise it held for education is documented by Barbara Halporn, who also sketches Heynlin's role as a mentor of the distinguished Basel printer, Amerbach, *Correspondence*, ed. Halporn, 3, 52. In a 1492 letter to Amerbach urging the printer to undertake the ambitious project of publishing the collected works of Augustine, Ambrose, Jerome, and Gregory, Heynlin asserts that printers deserve greater praise than do scribes because they supply more "weapons" to those who are fighting for the holy faith. Letter 224, 311–15.

59. Guillaume Fichet, letter to Robert Gaguin, Jan 1, 1471, inserted in some copies of Gasparinus Barzizius Pergamensis, *Orthographia* (Paris, 1471). Needham, *"Haec sancta ars,"* 115 n. 11 gives the Latin version and refers in his text to "the Latin vegetal Gods" who purportedly invented agriculture as "Liber and Ceres," 111. Most other translations use the more familiar Bacchus instead of Liber—both names served as the Latin equivalent of Dionysius, who was often coupled with Persephone (in Latin: "Ceres"). On Fichet and Heynlin, see Anatole Claudin, *The First Paris Press, an account of the books printed for G. Fichet and J. Heynlin in the Sorbonne, 1470–1472* (London, 1898). Also see references given by Martin, "Comment," 265 n.2 and Elizabeth L. Eisenstein, *The Printing Press as an Agent of Change*, 2 vols. (Cambridge, 1979), 1: 250 n.254 (hereafter Eisenstein, *Press as Agent*).

60. Richardson "Debates," 136n. cites a pertinent article by Carlo De Frede that offers additional evidence of the enthusiastic reception of printing by Italian humanists: "Entusiasmi umanistici . . . per l'inventione della stampa," *Richerche per la storia della stampa* (Naples, 1985), 7–54.

61. Ian Thomson, "The Scholar as Hero in Ianus Pannonius' Panegyric," *Renaissance Quarterly* 44, 2 (1991): 207.

62. 1475 colophon to edition of Justinian in Pollard, 24. See Hellinga, "Analytical Bibliography," for discussion of all Schoeffer's Mainz colophons.

63. Luigi Balsamo, "Technologia e capitali," in *Studi offerti a Roberto Ridolfi* (Florence, 1973), 91–92, cited in Richardson, "Debates," 137.

64. Alex Keller, "A Renaissance Humanist Looks at 'New' Inventions: The Article on 'Horologium' in Giovanni Tortelli's *De Orthographia*," *Technology and Culture* 11 (1970): 345–65. The verses in praise of printing are discussed by McKitterick, 173. On later treatment of post-classical inventions, see the introduction to Polydore Vergil, *On Discovery*, trans. and ed. Brian P. Copenhaver (Cambridge, 2002), xi, and the series of engravings, *Nova Reperta* (Chapter 3 below). Vergil deprecated Tortelli's list for containing nothing comparable to Gutenberg's invention.

65. Bishop of Brescia, Preface to Gregory the Great, *Moralia, sive Expositio in Job* (Rome, 1475), item 135 in *Le livre*, Catalogue of the Bibliothèque Nationale Exhibition (Paris, 1972), 46 (my translation of the French citation).

66. Preface to *De Arte Praedicandi*, cited in Parkes, *Scribes, Scripts*, xxi.

67. On the 2,000 letters of indulgence issued from Mainz to help the king of Cyprus hire soldiers to fight against the Turks, see Albert Kapr, *Johann Gutenberg*, trans. Douglas Martin (Aldershot, 1986), 190–91. That printing was viewed as a providential invention to demonstrate Western superiority over the Turks is noted by Geoffroy Atkinson, *Les nouveaux horizons de la renaissance française* (Paris, 1935), 57.

68. *Rudimentorum Novitiorum* (Lübeck, 1475) cited in *Landmarks of Mapmaking*, ed. Charles Bricker, Gerald Roe Crone and R. V. Tooley (Amsterdam, 1968), 60.

69. Eberhard König, "New Perspectives on the History of Mainz Printing," in *Printing the Written Word*, ed. Hindman, 150.

70. Needham, 106–7.

71. The responsibility of the Ottoman Turks (rather than Persians or Arabs) for this prohibition is stressed by Leila Avrin, *Scribes, Script, and Books* (Chicago, 1991), 330. The reasons for the persistent refusal of the authorities to countenance the printing of any Arabic texts remain somewhat mysterious. See Halil İnalcik, *The Ottoman Empire*, trans. Norman Itzkowitz and Colin Imber (London, 1973), 174; Juan R. I. Cole, "Printing and Urban Islam in the Mediterranean World, 1890–1920," in *Modernity and Culture from the Mediterranean to the Indian Ocean*, ed. Leila Tarazi Fawaz, C. A. Bayley, and Robert Ilbert (New York, 2001), 1–28; Francis Robinson, "Technology and Religious Change: Islam and the Impact of Print," *Modern Asian Studies* 27, 1 (1993): 229–51.

72. At least seven monastic presses were established in German regions before the 1470s; Hirsch, *Printing, Selling*, 54. On other regions see references in Eisenstein, *Press as Agent*, 1: 15n.

73. Obtaining manuscripts from monasteries was essential for almost all early printers who were engaged in publishing patristic texts. Johann Amerbach's collaboration with members of monastic communities is noted in *Correspondence*, ed. Halporn, 308.

74. Barbara Halporn, "Libraries and Printers in the Fifteenth Century," *Journal of Library History* 16 (1981): 135.

75. P. S. Allen, *The Age of Erasmus* (Oxford, 1914), 159–60. Allen cites the examples of Erasmus carrying off a manuscript from Louvain and Aldus Manutius receiving codices from all over Europe whose owners requested that they be printed but never asked for their return. Opposite evidence indicating alarm about errors being duplicated in print is discussed below.

76. Johannes Trithemius, *In Praise of Scribes*, chap. vii, 63. In addition to Arnold's introduction, see his biography, Klaus Arnold, *Johannes Trithemius*, ed. Theodor Kramer (Würzberg, 1971) and also Noel Brann, *The Abbot Trithemius 1462–1516* (Leiden, 1981), esp. 144–74.

77. That Trithemius was borrowing from St. Jerome the *topos* of durable parchment versus perishable papyrus is noted in Eisenstein, *Press as Agent*, 1: 14–15.

78. Johannes Trithemius, entry under year 1450 in *Annales Hirsaugienses* (written in 1514 but not published until 1690), 2 vols. (St. Gall, 1690), 2: 421.

79. Needham, 113–14 provides the Latin citation.

80. Richard Tottel, "The Printer to the Reader," *Tottel's Miscellany (1557–1587)*, ed. Hyder E. Rollins (Cambridge, 1928), lines 14–15.

81. Arthur Marotti, *Manuscript, Print, and the English Renaissance Lyric* (Ithaca, 1995), 292.

82. That de Bussi argues against this view indicates that it did exist—contrary to the view attributed by P. S. Allen to those lenders of manuscripts who assumed they would be printed error-free.

83. Since this preface was published in 1468, it refutes Bühler's statement that printed books did not become cheaper than manuscripts until around 1480 (Bühler, 62 n. 155). According to Brian Richardson, *Printing, Writers*, 114, when de Bussi indicated that a printed book cost one-fifth the price of a hand-copied one, he had actually *under*estimated the drop in cost.

84. M. D. Feld, "Sweynheim and Pannartz, Cardinal Bessarion . . . and Two Early Printers' Choice of Texts," *Harvard Library Bulletin* 30 (1982): 282–335, argues (unconvincingly) that de Bussi chose the texts that were published in Rome between 1468 and 1472 on the advice of Cardinal Bessarion, who had a secret plan "to promote and distribute pagan literature" (334). That so-called "pagan" works had been infused with Christian significance for a millennium is overlooked.

85. Pollard, 92–93.

86. Richardson, *Printing, Writers*, 82.

87. Rudolf Hirsch, "Bulla super Impressione Librorum, 1515," *Gutenberg Jahrbuch* (1973): 248.

88. That printing was encouraged by Catholic authorities, who have been persis-

tently misrepresented as keeping people in darkness and ignorance, and that English print-ers were first restrained not by Catholics but by a schismatic king (Henry VIII), is vehemently argued by a nineteenth-century English Catholic, William Eusebius Andrews, *A Critical and Historical Review of Fox's Book of Martyrs*, 2 vols. (London, 1853), 1: 10. As with futile attempts to dispel the "Black Legend," Andrews's "debunking" of Foxe had little effect on the popular belief (among non-Catholics) that the Church was set against printing from the start.

89. See the citation of a speech given in 1792 by a French revolutionary (Martin, "Comment," 17). As was true of all Catholic institutions, the Sorbonne did not turn against printing per se, but rather against printers who propagated "heretical" views. It was the French king François I, not a Sorbonnist, who took the drastic action (soon rescinded) in January 1535 of forbidding all printers throughout the kingdom to print on pain of death.

90. Vespasiano, cited in Jacob Burckhardt, *The Civilization of the Renaissance in Italy*, trans. S. G. C. Middlemore (from the 15th ed.), 2 vols. (New York, 1958), 1: 204. See also my comments on Vespasiano in Eisenstein, *Press as Agent*, 48–49.

91. Bühler, 104 n.66.

92. Martin Lowry, *Nicholas Jenson and the Rise of Venetian Publishing* (Oxford, 1991), 70.

93. See references in Eisenstein, *Press as Agent*, 1: 48. On Burckhardt's use of Ves-pasiano's memoirs see Helene Wieruzowski, "Burckhardt and Vespasiano," in *Philosophy and Humanism*, ed. Edward P. Mahoney (New York, 1976), 387–405.

94. Stephen Botein, "'Meer Mechanics' and an Open Press," *Perspectives in American History* 9 (1975): 127–225.

95. Richardson, "Debates," 144 n.30.

96. George Hoffman, "Writing Without Leisure," 18.

97. On Regiomontanus, Charles Estienne, and others, see Elizabeth L. Eisenstein, "The Early Printer as a Renaissance Man," *Printing History* 3 (1981): 6–17.

98. All three German printers who set up the first Paris presses in the Sorbonne and later on the Rue Saint Jacques were graduates of universities. Jeanne Marie Dureau, "Les premiers ateliers français," in *Histoire de l'édition française*, ed. Henri-Jean Martin and Roger Chartier, vol. 1, *Le livre conquérant* (Paris, 1985), 163–75. In the 1580s, Montaigne's printer Simon Millanges of Bordeaux was a former professor of grammar at the Collège de Guyenne. George Hoffmann, *Montaigne's Career* (Oxford, 1998), 64.

99. How both masters and journeymen sought to dignify their work is well docu-mented by Natalie Zemon Davis, *Society and Culture in Early Modern France* (Stanford, 1975), chaps. 1, 7.

100. Diu, "Medium typographicum," 122–24. But Badius appears as a respected "humanist scholar" in Cynthia Brown, *Poets, Patrons and Printers* (Ithaca, 1995), 46.

101. Lowry, *Aldus*, 28.

102. Cited in John L. Flood, "Nationalistic Currents in Early German Typography," *The Library* 6th ser. 15 (1993): 129.

103. See Gilbert Redgrave, *Erhard Ratdolt and His Work at Venice* (London, 1899).

104. Marjorie Plant's contrary opinion that "the mechanically-made book had to survive years of contempt before it came to be recognized as fully respectable" is based on Vespasiano's now discredited account, *The English Book Trade*, 2nd rev. ed. (London, 1965), 22.

105. Emison, 11.

106. Lowry, *Aldus*, 23. The term "upper levels" needs qualifying insofar as clerks, secretaries, and most professionals depended on patronage and were regarded as being closer to servants than to elites.

107. Julia H. Gaisser, *Catullus and His Renaissance Readers* (Oxford, 1993), 35.

108. Michael Kline, *Rabelais and the Age of Printing* (Geneva, 1963), 8.

109. John Monfasani, "The First Call for Press Censorship: Niccolò Perotti, Giovanni Andrea Bussi, Antonio Moreto, and the Editing of Pliny's *Natural History*," *Renaissance Quarterly* 41, 1 (1988): 1–31.

110. Davies, "Making Sense of Pliny," 248 n.33.

111. Anthony Grafton, "Printers' Correctors and the Publication of Classical texts," in *Bring Out Your Dead* (Cambridge, 2001), 150–51 describes Perotti as subjecting "the art of printing to a withering critique."

112. Davies, "Making Sense of Pliny," 250.

113. Charles G. Nauert, Jr., "Humanists, Scientists, and Pliny: Changing Approaches to a Classical Author," *American Historical Review* 84 (February 1979): 78.

114. Leslie Alfred Sheppard, "A Fifteenth-Century Humanist: F. Filelfo," *The Library* 4th ser. 16 (1936): 1–27.

115. Ian Donaldson, "The Destruction of the Book," *Book History* 1, 1 (1998): 5 cites Horace and Martial.

116. See section on "hue and cry against the scribe" ("Haro sur le scribe!") in Pascale Bourgain, "L'édition des manuscrits," in *Histoire de l'édition française*, ed. Henri-Jean Martin and Roger Chartier (Paris, 1982), 1: 50–51.

117. Richardson, *Printing, Writers*, 103. On the much more complex workforce faced by authors after printing see Adrian Armstrong, *Technique and Technology* (Oxford, 2000), 211. George Hoffman, "Writing Without Leisure," 21 also describes the numerous intermediaries who had a hand in getting the author's manuscript into printed form and notes the complaints made by sixteenth-century authors (among others, Montaigne) about the mutilation of their texts.

118. Hirsch, *Printing, Selling*, 47. An often overlooked example is that of Montaigne and his printer. Their close collaboration is shown by Hoffman, *Montaigne's Career*.

119. Burton, *Anatomy of Melancholy*, 1: xl, xli–xliv, cited in Johns, *Nature of the Book*, 138.

120. H. S. Bennett, *English Books and Readers, 1603 to 1640* (Cambridge, 1970), 59–60.

121. The thesis put forth by J. W. Saunders, "The Stigma of Print," *Essays in Criticism* 1 (1951): 137–64, which was echoed for many decades, has been called into question

by (among others) Nita Krevans, "Print and the Tudor Poets," in *Reconsidering the Renaissance*, ed. M. A. DiCesare (Binghamton, 1992), 301–13; Marotti, *Manuscript, Print*; Steven May, "Tudor Aristocrats and the 'Stigma of Print'," *Renaissance Papers* 10 (1980): 11–18; and Wendy Wall, *The Imprint of Gender* (New York, 1993).

122. Ernst Curtius, *European Literature and the Latin Middle Ages*, trans. Willard R. Trask (New York, 1953), 83–85 describes how the "modesty formula" was used in ancient Rome and applied not just to writings but also to orations. See also references to Quintilian and Galen in Krevans, "Print and the Tudor Poets," 305.

123. Wall, *Imprint of Gender*, 21.

124. Gilbert Tournoy, "Juan Luis Vives and the World of Printing," *Gutenberg Jahrbuch* (1994): 130.

125. Richardson, *Printing, Writers*, 84, 89–91.

126. See James Sutherland, Introduction to Pope, *The Dunciad Variorum with the Prolegoma of Scriblerus*, Facsimile of 1729 ed., ed. James Sutherland (London, 1943), xxi.

127. Cited in Wall, *Imprint of Gender*, 175. Daniel's views of print are discussed by John Pitcher, "Editing Daniel," in *New Ways of Looking at Old Texts*, ed. W. Speed Hill (Binghamton, 1993), 59.

128. Thomas Browne, "To the Reader," *Religio Medici* (1643), in *Prose of Sir Thomas Browne*, ed. Norman Endicott (Garden City, 1967), 5.

129. Marotti, *Manuscript, Print*, 209 notes that there was no English equivalent to the early and prestigious Italian editions of Petrarch's poetry or the collections of French verse published by Anthoine Vérard. Mary Beth Winn, *Anthoine Vérard, Parisian Publisher 1485–1512* (Geneva, 1997) shows how Vérard made good use of both patronage and marketing.

130. Peter C. Herman, "Authorship and the Royal 'I': James VI/I and the Politics of Monarchic Verse," *Renaissance Quarterly* 54, 4, part 2 (2001): 1517 n.69.

131. May, "Tudor Aristocrats," 15–17.

132. Ibid., 12. The term "publique eie" comes from Arthur Marotti, "Malleable and Fixed Texts: Manuscript and Printed Miscellanies and the Transmission of Lyric Poetry in the English Renaissance," in *New Ways of Looking*, ed. Hill, 159–73 citing from a 1648 edition of the collected poems of Richard Corbett. Marotti notes that Tottel's *Miscellany* of 1557 had set the pattern for printing poetry collections.

133. Cited in Marotti, *Manuscript, Print*, 228.

134. Cited in Bennett, *English Books and Readers*, 193.

135. That preachers in England were themselves hesitant about appearing in print, often prefacing their works with polite self-deprecation and blaming patrons for twisting their arms, is noted by Alexandra Walsham, *Providence in Early Modern England* (Oxford, 1999), 54–55. Note the contrast with Savonarola, for example.

136. The diverse factors that inhibited poets from printing verse—its association with ballads and ephemera, etc.—are outlined by Marotti (*Manuscript, Print*). He also notes that the eventual publication of Sir Philip Sidney's poetry made the practice more acceptable. See also H. R. Woudhuysen, *Sir Philip Sidney and the Circulation of Manuscripts, 1558–1640* (Oxford, 1996), 384.

137. Marotti, *Manuscript, Print*, 321–33. See also Joseph Loewenstein, "The Script in the Marketplace," *Representations* 12 (1985): 109.

138. Tribble, *Margins*, 8.

139. Loewenstein, cited in Tribble, *Margins*, 67.

140. Eisenstein, *Press as Agent*, 155–56.

141. Donaldson, *Jonson's Magic Houses*, 199, 211. See also Joseph Loewenstein, *Ben Jonson and Possessive Authorship* (Cambridge, 2002).

142. See, e.g., Halasz, passim.

143. Donaldson, "Destruction," 4–5. For further discussion of these antecedents, see Chapter 7, below.

144. Cited in Andrée Hayum, "Dürer's Portrait of Erasmus and the *Ars Typographorum*," *Renaissance Quarterly* 38, 4 (1985): 661.

145. "Festina Lente" (1508 edition), Erasmus, *The Adages of Erasmus*, trans. and ed. Margaret Mann Phillips (Cambridge, 1964), 174–76.

146. Erasmus, "Opulentia Sordida," in *The Colloquies of Erasmus*, trans. and ed. Craig Thompson (Chicago, 1965), 488–99. See also Lowry, *Aldus*, 77.

147. Raymond B. Waddington, "*Meretrix est stampificata*: Gendering the Printing Press," in *Books Have Their Own Destiny*, ed. Robert Barnes et al. 136.

148. Hoffman, "Writing Without Leisure," 21.

149. Successive versions of "Festina Lente" are provided in *The Adages*, ed. Phillips, 174–76, 182–85. Unfortunately the abridgment *Erasmus on His Times* (Cambridge, 1967), 10 has just one easily overlooked footnote to indicate that a passage was added in 1526. As a result, the complaint about "rascally printers" has sometimes been misattributed to the "Festina Lente" of 1508.

150. Elizabeth Armstrong, *Before Copyright* (Cambridge, 1990) offers an overview of the European scene.

151. Cited in Hirsch, *Printing, Selling*, 45.

152. Pollard, 108–9.

153. John Day, "Preface to the Reader," in *The Tragidie of Ferrex and Porrex* (1570), cited in Douglas Brooks, *From Playhouse to Printing House* (Cambridge, 2000), 29–31. In this preface to the second edition of *Gorboduc* by Thomas Norton and Thomas Sackville, Day was attacking the first edition by William Griffiths.

154. Pollard, 74.

155. Sebastian Brant, *The Ship of Fools* (*Narrenschiff*), trans. [into rhyming couplets] and ed. E. H. Zeydel (New York, 1962), no. 47.

156. Richardson, "The Debates," 144 mentions that the shops were "dirty and noisy." Lowry, *Aldus*, 28 refers to the printer's grubby ground floor and drunken assistants, and Robert Darnton, *The Business of Enlightenment* (Cambridge, 1987), 242 describes shops and printers alike as "dirty, loud and unruly." But Laurie Maguire, "The Craft of Printing," in *A Companion to Shakespeare*, ed. David Scott Kastan (London, 1999), 448 suggests that the drunken, disorderly theme is often overdone.

157. Lisa Jardine, *Worldly Goods* (New York, 1996), 136–47.

158. "From Cicero and Martial all the way to Petrarch there was but a single cry condemning the ineptitude, the ignorance, the stupidity of these corruptors of texts. Everyone was persuaded that the scribes of their own era were even worse than those of earlier times." Bourgain, "L'édition des manuscrits," 1: 50–51.

159. Cited in Anthony Grafton, "The Importance of Being Printed," *Journal of Interdisciplinary History* 11 (1980): 265–86, 274.

160. The first recorded strike of printers' journeymen was in Basel in 1471, according to Sigfrid Henry Steinberg, *Five Hundred Years of Printing* (London, 1961), 48. On a strike in Padua in 1477, see Giovanni Mardersteig, *The Remarkable Story of a Book Made in Padua in 1477*, trans. Hans Schmoller (London, 1967).

161. Di Strata's polemics against printing are used by Brian Richardson in his "Debates." They are also cited as if they expressed more than an idiosyncratic view by, among others, Richard and Mary Rouse, Julia Crick, and Alexandra Walsham.

162. Fra Filippo di Strata's manuscripts were discovered and described in Italian periodicals of 1909 and 1911 and then rediscovered by Martin Lowry, who discusses them in *Aldus*, 26–67 n.73. Lowry has published one piece under the title *Polemic Against Printing*, ed. and intro. Martin Lowry, trans. Shelagh Grier (Birmingham, 1986).

163. Richard de Bury, *Philobiblon*, ed. Michael Maclagan, trans. E. C. Thomas (Oxford, 1960), chap. 16, 147.

164. Martin Elsky, *Authorizing Words* (Ithaca, 1989), 210.

165. Browne, *Religio Medici* (1643), in *Prose of Sir Thomas Browne*, 32.

166. Lowry, *Aldus*, 31 cites the preface to Jacopo Filippo Foresti's *Supplementum Chronicarum* (Venice, 1483), an early "Book of Knowledge" which ran through numerous editions. There the author boasts that young men no longer need feel inferior to their elders since they could now easily become just as knowledgeable.

167. Cited in J. G. Ebel, "Translation and Cultural Nationalism in the Reign of Elizabeth," *Journal of the History of Ideas* 30 (1969). 593, 598. I cite this in my discussion of popularization and translation in Eisenstein, *Press as Agent*, 361–62.

168. It is unclear to which order Fra Filippo belonged. He is described by Lowry as a Dominican in *Aldus*, 26 but as a member of a Benedictine community in the introduction to the *Polemic Against Printing* and in *Nicholas Jenson*, 38.

169. Richardson, "Debates," 140.

170. Myron Gilmore, *The World of Humanism 1453–1517* (New York, 1952), 207.

171. Filippo di Strata, *Polemic*. Wall, 169, had singled out this citation for discussion before Waddington used it as the title of his article (see n. 147 above). The metaphor of the press as a "sexually gendered apparatus" is elaborately treated by Margareta de Grazia, "Imprints: Shakespeare, Gutenberg, Descartes," in *Alternative Shakespeares*, ed. Terence Hawkes (New York, 1996), 2: 63–94.

172. Lowry, *Aldus*, 27, suggests that Fra Filippo was "not without friends" in high places in Venice, but there is no evidence that anyone ever seriously considered banning printing from the Republic. Lowry also takes the fact that 60 of 159 Senate members voted against one printer's petition in 1492 to indicate that "some opposition to the press may have lingered on for a surprising length of time."

173. Paul Grendler, *Critics of the Italian World* (Madison, 1969), 4–10.

174. But Caxton's first products had been printed in the Netherlands; Wynken de Worde, his foreman and successor in London, was a Dutch immigrant. A German printer from Cologne set up the first Oxford press two years after Caxton. Of those who engaged in the early sixteenth-century English book trade, two-thirds were foreign-born. James Raven, *The Business of Books* (New Haven, 2007), 14, 40.

175. See prefatory letter by Guillaume Fichet likening Germany to a Trojan horse for having discharged her printers on the world, Claudin, *The First Paris Press*, 5.

176. Bühler, 58, points to the appeal of printed place names to local pride.

177. Pollard, 69–70.

178. Allen, *Age of Erasmus*, 265.

179. Christopher S. Wood, *Forgery, Replica, Fiction* (Chicago, 2008), 64.

180. Ingrid Rowland, "Revenge of the Regensburg Humanists, 1493," *Sixteenth Century Journal* 25, 2 (1994): 308. See also Barbara M. Hallman, "Italian 'Natural Superiority' and the Lutheran Question," *Archiv für Reformationsgeschichte* 71 (1980): 134–48; and Flood, "Nationalistic Currents."

181. Letter from Franciscus Barbarus to Poggius, in *Two Renaissance Book Hunters*, trans. and ed. Phyllis Walters Goodhart Gordan (New York, 1974), 199.

182. Allen, *Age of Erasmus*, 264.

183. Pollard, 33.

184. Conrad Leontorius to Johann Amerbach (19 November 1494), Letter 33, in Amerbach, *Correspondence*, ed. Halporn, 68.

185. From *Varia Carmina*, Basel, 1498, reprinted in Brant's *Narrenschiff*. Barbara Halporn, "Sebastian Brant's Editions of Classical Authors," *Publishing History* 16, 34 (1984): 34.

186. Wood, 65.

187. Eusebius, *Chronicon*, updated by Matteo Palmieri, ed. Johannes Lucilius Santritter (Venice, 1483). The same date was given in the *Nuremberg Chronicle* of 1493, the *Cologne Chronicle* of 1499, and Jacob Wimpheling's *Epithoma Germanorum* (1505). In the latter work, the date is assigned to Gutenberg's inventing the press in Strasbourg before moving to Mainz. John L. Flood, "On Gutenberg's 600th Anniversary: Towards a History of Jubilees of Printing," *Journal of the Printing Historical Society* n.s. 1 (2000): 6.

188. Adrian Wilson, trans., in *The Making of the Nuremberg Chronicle* (Amsterdam, 1976), 181.

189. See Donald F. McKenzie, "Speech-Manuscript-Print," in *Making Meaning*, ed. Peter D. McDonald and Michael F. Suarez (Amherst, 2002), 237–58 for an insightful account of the spectrum of reactions to print.

190. "Before and After Gutenberg: A Conversation with Roger Chartier," in *The Book and the Computer*, http://www.honco.net /os /chartier.html, accessed 25 May 2002.

191. On the two instances of resistance in sixteenth-century France and seventeenth-century colonial Virginia, see n.24 above.

192. Grafton, "Printers' Correctors," 150.

193. See Lewis Spitz, *The Religious Renaissance of the German Humanists* (Cambridge, 1963), 84–85, and Hajo Holborn, *Ulrich von Hutten*, trans. Roland H. Bainton (New Haven, 1937), 42.

CHAPTER 2. AFTER LUTHER: CIVIL WAR IN CHRISTENDOM

Epigraphs: Christopher Ness cited in Sharon Achinstein, *Literature and Dissent in Milton's England* (Cambridge, 2004), 245; Roger L'Estrange, Preface to *Mercurius Politicus,* cited in Joad Raymond, *Invention of the Newspaper: English Newsbooks, 1641–1649* (Oxford, 1996), 187.

1. Sleidan's 1542 address as cited and translated by Gerald Strauss, "The Course of German History," in *Renaissance,* ed. Anthony Molho and John A. Tedeschi (DeKalb, 1971), 684. Born John Philippson in the town of Schleidan in Lorraine, Sleidan joined the faculty of the University of Strasbourg in 1540 and stayed there until his death in 1556. His *Commentaries on Government and Religion in the Age of Charles V* (1555) was translated into many languages. Donald Kelley, "Johann Sleidan and the Origin of History as a Profession," *Journal of Modern History* 52 (1980): 573 describes Sleidan as "one of the greatest of all modern historians."

2. As historiographer of the Schmalkaldic League and author of *De quatuor summis imperiis* (Geneva, 1559), later translated as *The Key of History* (London, 1631), Sleidan linked the fate of the Holy Roman Empire, the last of "the four world monarchies," to the end of the world.

3. Katharine R. Firth, *The Apocalyptic Tradition in Reformation Britain* (Oxford, 1979), 33. William Lamont, *Godly Rule* (London, 1969), 22–23, 174 contrasts Calvin's belief that God's future plans were unknowable with the views of Luther and of later Calvinists. Ernst R. Tuveson, *Millennium and Utopia* (New York, 1964), 222, n.81 says Calvin differed from all other reformers in his rejection of scriptural prophecies.

4. Walter Klaasen, *Living at the End of the Ages* (New York, 1992), 117.

5. Andrew Penny, "John Foxe, the *Acts and Monuments* and the Development of the Prophetic Interpretation," in *John Foxe and the English Reformation,* ed. David Loades (Aldershot, 1997), 262. Penny is citing from V. Norskov Olsen, *John Foxe and the Elizabethan Church* (Berkeley, 1973).

6. Klaasen, *Living at the End,* 20.

7. "Table Talk #5488" (1542), trans. and ed. T. G. Trappert, from *Luther's Works,* ed. Jaroslav Pelikan and H. T. Lehmann, 55 vols. (Philadelphia, 1964), 54: 427. This same metaphor is cited in Gerald Strauss, *Luther's House of Learning* (Baltimore, 1978), 32, along with an account of Melanchthon's gloomy eschatology.

8. Tyndale also worked on his Old Testament translation in the printing house of Martin de Keyser in Antwerp, where Miles Coverdale may have also worked as a proofreader before he completed the translation and published the Tyndale-Coverdale Bible in Cologne in 1535. (De Keyser had adopted the pseudonym Hans Lufft, thus paying homage

to the Lutheran Wittenberg printer.) Stanley L. Greenslade, "English Versions of the Bible, 1525–1611," in *The Cambridge History of the Bible* (Cambridge, 1963), 142–43, 148. Other relevant false addresses are given by Bennett, *English Books and Readers, 1475 to 1557*, 2nd ed. (Cambridge, 1969), 209–10.

9. That Bale had spent his first period of exile in the 1540s after Thomas Cromwell's fall, in Switzerland and Germany, "never far from a printer," is noted by William Haller, *The Elect Nation* (New York, 1963), 61. John N. King, "The Light of Printing: William Tyndale, Foxe, Day and Early Modern Print Culture," *Renaissance Quarterly* 54 (Spring 2001): 52–85, also notes that Bale was "a habitué of printing shops in Antwerp and Wesel" before he established a bookshop near St. Paul's Cathedral during Edward VI's reign (54).

10. Haller, *Elect*, 78–79 cites, among other titles, the two tracts of 1558 by John Knox and Christopher Goodman that became classics of resistance theory.

11. On the "troubles of Frankfurt" see Firth, 70. Also John Mozley, *John Foxe and His Books* (London, 1940), 46–50. Mozley notes that Foxe disapproved of Calvin's burning of Servetus (27 October 1553) but also avoided too close an association with Lutheran printers and tried to make contact in 1558 with Zwingli's printer, Froschauer, in Zürich (48, 56).

12. Foxe had an introduction from Peter Martyr to meet Sleidan in 1555. Firth, 71.

13. Matthäus Judex, *De Typographia Inventione* (Copenhagen, 1566).

14. Some of the new passages on printing in the second edition (1570) of the *Actes and Monuments* that were derived from Judex are noted by Susan Felch, "Shaping the Reader," in *John Foxe and the English Reformation*, ed. Loades, 58–59. Judex's treatise is cited in a footnote to *The Actes and Monuments of John Foxe* (based on the 1583 4th ed.), rev. Josiah Pratt, intro. John Stoughton, 8 vols. (London, 1877), 3: 718 (hereafter Foxe, *A and M*). See n.23 below concerning other editions. Judex also figures in Robert Kolb, "The Book Trade as Christian Calling," in *Books Have Their Own Destiny*, ed. Barnes et al.: 61–72.

15. Mario Carpo, *Architecture in the Age of Printing*, trans. Sarah Benson (Cambridge, 2001), 85–86.

16. See Haller, *Elect*, 75, on the influence of Martin Bucer in Cambridge, Peter Martyr in Oxford, and Zwingli's disciple Heinrich Bullinger in Zürich.

17. When Foxe first left England for the continent he visited Erasmus's birthplace in Rotterdam and later may have worked for Erasmus's Basel printer, Froben (Mozley, 40, 51). His admiring reference to Erasmus and Froben in the *Actes and Monuments* is noted below.

18. This Basel firm provoked both the Genevan Calvinists and Counter-Reformation authorities. It was blacklisted by the Council of Trent in 1559. See Martin Steinmann, *Johannes Oporinus* (Basel, 1967), 97ff. Foxe may have encountered Matthias Flacius Illyricus in Oporinus's shop when the latter was preparing publication of his *Catalogus Testium Veritatis* (1556). Assorted figures associated with the "radical" Reformation who lodged at some point with Oporinus are noted in Eisenstein, *Press as Agent*, 446.

19. The so-called Magdeburg Centuries were printed between 1559 and 1574. Greg-

ory Lyon, "Baudouin, Flacius and the plan for the *Magdeburg Centuries*," *Journal of the History of Ideas* 64 (2003): 253–72.

20. C. L. Oastler, *John Day, the Elizabethan Printer* (Oxford, 1975), 26–29. That Foxe met Day through their common patron William Cecil and that the former actually lived for some time in Day's printing house is documented by Elizabeth Evenden and Thomas Freeman, "Foxe, Day and the Printing of the *Book of Martyrs*," in *Lives in Print*, ed. Robin Myers, Michael Harris, and Giles Mandelbrote (London, 2002), 32. Oastler's study has been supplanted by Evenden's D.Phil. thesis, published as *Patents, Pictures and Patronage* (Aldershot, 2008).

21. "The Benefite and Invention of Printing" is the title of the section in the one-volume 1583 edition of Foxe's *Actes and Monuments* that is cited here (707, paragraph 3). The title has been rearranged in the more accessible nineteenth-century edition of 1877, Foxe, *A and M*, 3: 718, to read: "The Invention and Benefit of Printing." The need to check later editions against earlier ones is shown by Thomas Freeman, "Texts, Lies, and Microfilm: Reading and Misreading Foxe's 'Book of Martyrs,'" *Sixteenth Century Journal* 30 (1999): 23–47.

22. See above, Chapter 1, passage cited from Trithemius's *Praise of Scribes*.

23. Foxe, *A and M*, 3: 720.

24. Foxe, *A and M*, 3: 719–21.

25. Foxe, *A and M*, 3: 720.

26. Haller, *Elect*, 69.

27. Foxe's printer, John Day, had printed an English translation of Sleidan's *Commentaries* in 1562. Evenden and Freeman, "Foxe, Day," 34.

28. This is most fully discussed and documented in two essays by Margaret Aston: "Lollardry and the Reformation: Survival and Revival," *History* 49, 166 (1964): 149–70; "John Wycliffe's Reformation Reputation," *Past and Present* 30 (1965), 23–51. Both are reprinted in Margaret Aston, *Lollards and Reformers* (London, 1984). See also Leslie Fairfield, *John Bale* (Lafayette, 1976), passim.

29. Patrick Collinson, "John Foxe and National Consciousness," in *John Foxe and His World*, ed. Christopher Highley and John N. King (Aldershot, 2002), 10–37, esp. 13–14.

30. Mozley, 118. Mozley suggests that Jean Crespin had begun his martyrology with Hus in 1554 but was persuaded by Foxe's Latin *Commentarii* (1554) to begin with Wycliffe instead. (Yet Wycliffe was not, like Hus, truly martyred, but rather died in his bed.)

31. Firth, 236.

32. See several works cited in Jesse Lander, "Foxe's Books of Martyrs: Printing and Popularizing the *Acts and Monuments*," in *Religion and Culture in Renaissance England*, ed. Claire E. McEachern and Deborah K. Shuger (Cambridge, 1997), 70. Lander stresses how the output of different editions destabilized the text and agrees with Firth and others that Timothy Bright's post-Armada abridged edition of 1589 was mainly responsible for the "triumphalist" aspects of the narrative.

33. Aston, "John Wycliffe's Reformation Reputation," 26.

34. Cited in ibid.

35. Ibid., 26, 23. Foxe's treatment of the purported Lollard leader John Oldcastle as a proto-Protestant martyr is also relevant. See discussion (illustrated by a woodblock) by Kristen Poole, *Radical Religion from Shakespeare to Milton* (Cambridge, 2000), 18; also Douglas Brooks, *From Playhouse to Printing House* (Cambridge, 2000), 103.

36. King, "Light of Printing," 59.

37. The importance of Cecil's patronage is brought out by Evenden and Freeman, "Foxe, Day," 27–30.

38. Frances Yates, *The Art of Memory* (Chicago, 1966), 347.

39. Oastler, 26.

40. Foxe, "Epistle or preface to the Christian Reader," *The Whole Works of W. Tyndall, John Frith and Doct. Barnes* (London, 1572–73), cited in Aston, *Lollards and Reformers*, 239.

41. James V. Mehl, "Printing the Metaphor of Light and Dark," in *Books Have Their Own Destiny*, ed. Barnes et al.: 83–92 points out that these dichotomies were employed before Luther by pre-Reformation German humanists writing about printing.

42. Aston, *Lollards and Reformers*, 239 (italics mine).

43. Evenden and Freeman, "Foxe, Day," 34.

44. Oastler, 27.

45. See citation in Chapter 1 above.

46. Oastler, 27.

47. Oastler, 28 gives estimates of expenses and returns.

48. See Evenden and Freeman, "Foxe, Day," 36, 49.

49. Lander, "Foxe's Books," 73, however, finds Turner's comment, "not a few poor men complained of the price," to be more significant.

50. On this controversial issue, see Elizabeth Evenden and Thomas Freeman, "Print, Profit and Propaganda: The Elizabethan Privy Council and the 1570 Edition of Foxe's 'Book of Martyrs,'" *English Historical Review* 119 (November 2004): 1289ff, cxix, 484.

51. Haller, *Elect*, 221. John Day printed the canons that ordered "Bishops to make [the work] available in hall or chamber for the use of strangers and servants." Haller also notes that a "cheaper abridged edition"—a quarto of 792 pages—was published in 1589, after Day's death, by Timothy Bright (223). This was the post-Armada triumphalist edition referred to in n.32, above. Another full edition (the last to appear during Elizabeth's reign) came out in 1596.

52. David Kastan, "Little Foxes," in *John Foxe and His World*, ed. Highley and King, 117–33.

53. Ibid., 123–25 discusses several duodecimo and even one 64-mo version. See also Haller, *Elect*, 228. On the later fate of the work, the essayists in *Foxe*, ed. Loades disagree. Eirwen Nicholson, "Eighteenth Century Foxe," 143–77 is skeptical about diffusion. He says it is assumed but not demonstrated that there was a widespread dispersal of the work in the seventeenth and eighteenth centuries, whereas Damien Nussbaum's account, "Appropriating Martyrdom," 178–91 gives the opposite impression. So does Lois Schwoer-

er, *The Ingenious Mr. Henry Care, Restoration Publicist* (Baltimore, 2001), 71, n.264. She mentions the abridgements and selections that were circulating in the 1670s and the enthusiastic announcement of a forthcoming 1684 edition in Henry Care's *Weekly Pacquet* 5, 44 (22 June 1683). Linda Colley, *Britons* (New Haven, 1992), 25 notes that the work was sold serially in installments in the eighteenth century. She also mentions the other means (almanacs and popular festivals) by which Foxe's version was diffused.

54. See below concerning *Animadversions*.

55. Marsha S. Robinson, *Writing the Reformation* (Aldershot, 2002).

56. Colley, 19, cites pertinent passages from David Cressy. See also Odai Johnson, *Rehearsing the Revolution* (Newark, 2000), 1.

57. For a nuanced account of Foxe's readers and his appeal to illiterate listeners, see Evelyn Tribble, "Godly Reading: John Foxe's *Actes and Monuments* (1583)," in *The Reader Revealed, Catalogue of the Folger Library Exhibition*, comp. and ed. Sabrina Alcorn Baron (Washington, 2001), 39–45.

58. Henri Hauser, *La naissance du protestantisme* (Paris, 1962), 58.

59. According to Andrew Penny, "John Foxe . . . and the Development of the Prophetic Interpretation," in *Foxe*, ed. Loades, 257, Foxe left the final act of the drama "open ended." Tom Betteridge's chapter in the same volume, "From Prophetic to Apocalyptic: Foxe and the Writing of History," gives a different impression of the 1570 edition.

60. Betteridge, 229.

61. Loades, Introduction to *Foxe*, ed. Loades. (The shifting date of Judgment Day evokes the clock on the cover of the *Bulletin of the Atomic Scientists*, where the hands read closer to midnight (and doomsday) depending on the editors' opinion of current events.)

62. In addition to Haller, *Elect*, 227ff, see Damian Nussbaum, "Appropriating Martyrdom" in *Foxe*, ed. Loades, 178–91.

63. Nussbaum, "Appropriating Martyrdom," 177.

64. Alexandra Walsham, " 'Domme Preachers,' " *Past and Present* 168 (August 2000): 122. The most influential work refuting triumphalist English Protestant historiography while documenting the depth and vigor of popular Catholicism under the Tudors is Eamon Duffy, *The Stripping of the Altars* (New Haven, 1992). See especially "The Coming of Print," 77–87.

65. Duffy, 74.

66. Ibid., 80.

67. Alexandra Walsham, "Unclasping the Book? Post-Reformation English Catholicism and the Vernacular Bible," *Journal of British Studies* 42 (April 2003): 142. The unmythical aspects of counter-Reformation opposition to vernacular Bibles are made clear in later sections of the article.

68. Alison Shell, *Catholicism, Controversy and the English Literary Imagination, 1558–1660* (Cambridge, 1999), 13.

69. Among other issues, there was disagreement over the dangers of unsupervised lay literacy. Lutheran and Henrician concerns are often cited to equate "Protestant" views with Catholic ones. But the Calvinists took a different approach; see Francis Higman, *Lire et découvrir* (Geneva, 1998), 579ff.

70. Joad Raymond, *Pamphlets and Pamphleteering in Early Modern Britain* (Cambridge, 2003), 25.

71. This is discussed more fully in connection with pamphlet warfare during the English Civil War, below. The "dialogic character" of pamphleteering is discussed by David Zaret, *Origins of Democratic Culture* (Princeton, 2000), 250. Raymond, *Pamphlets*, 262 n.186 agrees with Zaret but questions the wisdom of separating petitions from pamphlet culture as a whole.

72. Mark Edwards, *Printing, Propaganda, and Martin Luther* (Berkeley, 1994), 58; see also Higman, *Lire et découvrir*, 522ff, and David V. N. Bagchi, *Luther's Earliest Opponents* (Minneapolis, 1991), chap. 9. Catholic ambivalence about using a mass medium is noted on 250–51.

73. Walsham, "Unclasping," 156.

74. Ibid., 159.

75. Ibid., 158. See also Robert Preus, *The Inspiration of Scripture* (Edinburgh, 1957), 17–18.

76. According to Martin Elsky, *Authorizing Words* (Ithaca, 1989), 132–33, writing was upheld against speech by ancient Hebrews. He suggests that the Hebrew tradition entailed thinking of the "Word" not as being spoken but as being embodied in written characters. The Hebrew word for God (illustrated on Foxe's frontispiece) when presented without vowel points—JHWH—must not be spoken.

77. John Bossy, *Christianity in the West, 1400–1700* (Oxford, 1985), 98; also see above, Chapter 1, on Savonarola et al.

78. From Erasmus, Colloquy: *Pietas Puerilis*, cited in *La Réforme et le livre*, ed. Jean-François Gilmont (Paris, 1990), 481 n.5. This collection of separate essays on diverse regions is useful for comparing Catholic and Protestant approaches.

79. See Eisenstein, *Press as Agent*, chaps. 3–4. The Lutherans held that the "essence of scripture was unaffected by the means used to transmit it." Preus, *Inspiration of Scripture*, 17–18.

80. The terms appear in II Corinthians as cited in Michael Camille, "Seeing and Reading: Some Visual Implications of Medieval Literacy and Illiteracy," *Art History* 8, 1 (March 1985): 32.

81. Walsham, *Providence*, 52.

82. These considerations led some authorities to argue that the debate over transmission did not divide Catholics from Protestants but divided Christians of "every confession." Gilmont, *La Réforme et le livre*, 483.

83. Adam Fox, *Oral and Literate Culture in England, 1500–1700* (Oxford, 2000), 406–7. Fox cites several Protestants who stressed oral/literate divisions in antipapist writings.

84. Duffy, 532.

85. Bossy, 98–99.

86. On the recent recirculation of this citation, which comes from the seventeenth-century French Oratorian priest Bernard Lamy and was picked up by Jacques Derrida and

then by Alvin Kernan, see Marcus Walsh, "The Superfoetation of Literature: Attitudes to the Printed Book in the Eighteenth Century," *British Journal for Eighteenth Century Studies* 15 (1992): 153.

87. Louis Bredvold, *The Intellectual Milieu of John Dryden* (Ann Arbor, 1966 [1934]), 100.

88. On Hardouin, see Anthony Grafton, *Bring Out Your Dead* (Cambridge, 2001), chap. 10.

89. Robert R. Palmer, *Catholics and Unbelievers in Eighteenth-Century France* (Princeton, 1939), 65–76.

90. Francis M. Higman, *Censorship and the Sorbonne* (Geneva, 1979), 26–27.

91. Walsham, "Unclasping," 150.

92. Andrew Pettegree, "Illustrating the Book: A Protestant Dilemma," in *John Foxe and His World*, ed. Highley and King, 133–49. Of course, Lutherans had made full use of woodcut cartoons for antipapal propaganda. See Robert Scribner, *For the Sake of Simple Folk* (Oxford, 1994), passim.

93. See H. Outram Evennett, *The Spirit of the Counter-Reformation*, ed. John Bossy (Cambridge, 1968), 25.

94. The Commission for the Propagation of the Faith had been convened by Pope Gregory XIII five decades before the office. The Sacred Congregation for the Propagation of the Faith was instituted with a papal bull by Clement VIII. See pertinent passages by Donald Kelley, *The Beginning of Ideology* (Cambridge, 1981), 245ff.

95. Robert McCune Kingdon, *Geneva and the Coming of the Wars of Religion in France, 1555–1563* (Geneva, 1956), passim.

96. See proclamation of 1530, cited in Harold Weber, *Paper Bullets* (Lexington, 1996), 135.

97. Weber, *Paper Bullets*, 137–39.

98. Zaret, *Origins*, 141.

99. See Duffy, 524–65. Also Lucy E. C. Wooding, *Rethinking Catholicism in Reformation England* (Oxford, 2000), chap. 4. I owe this reference to Alexandra Walsham, whose own articles cited above are also pertinent.

100. Gedeon Borsa, "Le livre et les débuts de la Réforme en Hongrie," in *La Réforme et le livre*, 388.

101. Cited in John Elliott, *Europe Divided 1559–1598* (London, 1968), 31–32.

102. "Heresy was regularly referred to as a disease or poison," Nancy L. Roelker, *One King, One Faith* (Berkeley, 1996), 194.

103. Bishop John Jewel (1522–71), cited in Walsham, "Unclasping," 142.

104. Eisenstein, *Press as Agent*, 347–48.

105. Higman, *Lire et découvrir*, 581–84. The difference between Lutheran and Calvinist approaches in England is brought out by Ruth Bottigheimer, "Bible Reading, Bibles, and the Bible for Children in . . . Germany," *Past and Present* 139 (1993): 66–89.

106. John H. Salmon, *Renaissance and Revolt* (Cambridge, 1987), 155. The entire chapter on "Gallicanism and Anglicanism" is relevant. On Sarpi, see also Eisenstein, *Press as Agent*, 412–13.

107. Mack P. Holt, *The French Wars of Religion, 1562–1629* (Cambridge, 1995), 150–52. See also John H. Salmon, ed., *The French Wars of Religion* (Boston, 1967).

108. A short-lived, secret "Greenstreet Press" was set up by the two Jesuits, Campion and Pearsons, in England in 1580. Bennett, *English Books and Readers, 1558 to 1603*, 80. Walsham, "'Domme Preachers,'" 72–123ff argues against making too much of Catholic/Protestant divisions and points to the "astonishingly rich culture of print" engendered by English Catholicism.

109. The exceptions were the "inner light" sects, such as the Quakers, who did not assign a high value to the printed word. In their view, Scripture consisted of dead letters unless informed by the Holy Spirit. The Quakers did value print as a means of proselytizing, however, and used it to advantage in publicizing the name (Quaker) that their opponents had contemptuously assigned to them. See Kate Peters, *Print Culture and the Early Quakers* (Cambridge, 2005), passim.

110. Joseph Black, "The Rhetoric of Reaction: The Martin Marprelate Tracts (1588–89), Anti-Martinism and the Uses of Print in Early Modern England," *Sixteenth Century Journal* 28 (Fall 1997): 724. See also Black, ed., *The Martin Marprelate Tracts* (Cambridge, 2008).

111. Poole, 30.

112. Paul Arblaster, review of *News, Newspapers and Society in Early Modern Britain*, ed. Joad Raymond (1999), *Sharp News* 110, 3 (Summer 2001): 6.

113. Black, Introduction, "Martinism and Anti-Martinism, 1590–1700," to *The Marprelate Tracts* provides a helpful overview regarding this long-lasting resonance.

114. Jason Scott Warren, *Early Modern English Literature* (Cambridge, 2005), 88–89.

115. Works of John Hall, cited in Walsham, "Unclasping," 21.

116. Cited in D. M. Wolfe, Introduction, *Complete Prose Works of John Milton* (New Haven, 1953), 8 vols., 1: 31.

117. Jesse Lander, *Inventing Polemic* (Cambridge, 2006), 108.

118. Cyndia S. Clegg, *Press Censorship in Elizabethan England* (Cambridge, 1997), 181.

119. John Milton, "Animadversions upon the Remonstrants . . . ," (July, 1641), *Complete Prose Works*, ed. Wolfe, 1: 653–79. Both Michael Fixler, *Milton and the Kingdoms of God* (London, 1964), 37–38 and William Haller (on whom Fixler relies) take Milton's accusation at face value. But an editorial note by Rudolf Kirk (678–79 n.7) asserts that Laud, when on trial, said he had no intention of prohibiting a new edition and had only insisted that it should be done "without abridgement or alteration." In any event, the successive editions of Foxe had scarcely "crept into the world by stealth."

120. Bacon, *An Advertisement Touching the Controversies of the Church of England*, cited in *Areopagitica: A Speech of Mr. John Milton for the Liberty of Unlicenc'd Printing to the Parliament of England* (1644), in *John Milton: Selected Prose*, ed. Constantinos A. Patrides (Columbia, 1985), 230.

121. William Haller, *The Rise of Puritanism* (New York, 1957), 325.

122. Christopher Hill, *The Century of Revolution, 1603–1714* (New York, 1982), 83.

123. Richard Overton's poem prefixed to *Vox Borealis* (1640–41), cited in Black, "Rhetoric," 724. On previous Marprelate pamphlets and the "explosion" of the 1640s, see Raymond, *Pamphlets*, 267–68.

124. The proceedings that inspired Overton to launch his "Marprelate" campaign involved both Milton and Overton being referred to the Committee on Printing of the House of Commons for violating regulations. Sabrina Baron, "Licensing Readers, Licensing Authorities," in *Books and Readers in Early Modern England*, ed. Jennifer Andersen and Elizabeth Sauer (Philadelphia, 2002), 222–23. The "Martin Mar-Priest Press" operated by Overton and William Larner is noted by Fred Seaton Siebert, *Freedom of the Press in England, 1476–1776* (Urbana, 1952), 197–98. See *Tracts on Liberty in the Puritan Revolution*, ed. William Haller, 3 vols. (New York, 1954), 1: 97ff.

125. David R. Como, "Secret Printing, the Crisis of 1640, and the Origins of Civil War Radicalism," *Past and Present* 196 (2007): 45.

126. Raymond, *Pamphlets*, 204–5. The reference to fairies alludes to Aubrey's claim that printing had put an end to such superstitions. See below, Chapter 4.

127. Haller, *The Rise of Puritanism*, 280.

128. Pauline Gregg, *Free-Born John* (London, 1961), 39–43, 312.

129. In addition to Raymond, see the extensive treatment by Jason Peacey, *Politicians and Pamphleteers* (London, 2004).

130. Raymond, *Pamphlets*, 162.

131. Blair Worden, "Puritan Propaganda," *Times Literary Supplement*, 21 February 1997, 26. Although it has been generally accepted, this view of 1641–42 was sharply criticized by the late Donald McKenzie, who asserted that the idea of an "explosion in print" lacked solid evidence and the "many effects claimed for the lapse of licensing in 1641 are largely illusory" (*Making Meaning*, 130). McKenzie's critique was reiterated by Robert Darnton, review article, *New York Review of Books*, 29 May 2003, 43–45. More recently, David Cressy, *England on the Edge* (Oxford, 2006), 281ff, has provided solid evidence of an unprecedented "media storm" starting in 1640. In any event, contemporary observers did not think the "explosion" was at all illusory.

132. Weber, *Paper Bullets*, 135, cites from royal proclamations of the 1530s and '40s that employ metaphors of poison and plague and that "demonize" the press.

133. Thomas Browne, "To the Reader," *Religio Medici* (1643), in *Prose of Sir Thomas Browne*, ed. Norman Endicott (Garden City, 1967), 5.

134. Peacey, citing comment of 1641, 315.

135. John Taylor, a royalist pamphleteer writing in 1644, cited in Raymond, *Pamphlets*, 27.

136. Poole, 113.

137. See Chapter 1, above.

138. At the same time, the use of vernacular Scriptures and liturgies contributed to the disunity—indeed the balkanization—of Latin Christendom. See Eisenstein, *Press as Agent*, chap. 4, 358–60.

139. Preface to *The Book of Common Prayer* (1559). How the printing of the Book of

Common Prayer was hailed for ensuring uniformity is stressed by John Wall, "The Reformation in England and the Typographical Revolution," in *Print and Culture*, ed. Gerald P. Tyson and Sylvia S. Wagonheim (Wilmington, 1986), 208–22.

140. It was deemed objectionable for containing "vestiges of papist ceremonies." Clegg, *Press Censorship in Elizabethan England*, 183.

141. John Lilburne, *England's Birthright Justified* (1645), cited in Siebert, 200.

142. Poole, 105.

143. Ann Hughes, "Approaches to Presbyterian Print Culture: Thomas Edwards's *Gangraena* as Source and Text," in *Books and Readers*, ed. Andersen and Sauer, 99. Since writing this article, Hughes has completed a definitive study: *Gangraena and the Struggle for English Revolution* (Oxford, 2004). It combines book history analysis with an exhaustive account of the contents and reception of the work.

144. Poole has an interesting discussion of Edwards's determination to bring a semblance of order into discursive chaos by classifying and categorizing each and every splinter sect (114–17). His taxonomic approach to proliferating sects was akin to that taken by natural philosophers and polymaths who were also confronted by a bewildering proliferation of data during the second century of printing. See Chapter 3, below.

145. Hughes, "Approaches," 100.

146. Richard Atkyns, *Original and Growth of Printing* (Whitehall, 1664), 2.

147. To strengthen his argument for royal control, Atkyns invented a myth about the royal origins of English printing. See Johns, *The Nature of the Book*, 338–43.

148. Atkyns, *Original and Growth of Printing*, 7.

149. Was this drawn from Ben Jonson's comedy, *The Staple of News* (1626), where the gullibility of readers was similarly mocked?

150. Atkyns, "Epistle to the King," *Original and Growth of Printing*, B2.

151. Ibid., B1–2.

152. Statutes at Large (1661) cited in Weber, *Paper Bullets*, 133–34. Another measure was taken "against Tumultuous Petitioning." During the 1640s riots had accompanied presenting petitions to Parliament. The "Act Against Tumultuous Petitioning" limited the number of people allowed to participate to a maximum of ten. On printing and petitions see Zaret, *Origins*, passim.

153. C. V. Wedgwood, "Good King Charles's Golden Days," in *The Restoration of the Stuarts* (Washington, D.C., 1960), 15.

154. The first issue of the *Intelligencer* (1663) in James R. Sutherland, ed., *The Restoration Newspaper and Its Development* (Cambridge, 2004), 97.

155. See Preface, above.

156. Philip Knachel, *England and the Fronde* (Ithaca, 1967).

157. Jeffrey Sawyer, *Printed Poison* (Berkeley, 1990), 15; Luc Racaut, *Hatred in Print* (Aldershot, 2002).

158. Cited in Laurence Hanson, *Government and the Press 1695–1763* (Oxford, 1937), 5, 7.

159. *Lords Journals*, 15, 545, cited in Richard T. Vann, ed., *Century of Genius* (Englewood Cliffs, 1967), 7.

160. Charles Blount and John Milton, *A Just Vindication of Learning: Or, An Humble Address to the High Court of Parliament in Behalf of the Liberty of the Press*, by "Philopatris" (London: [s.n.], 1679). In *The Harleian Miscellany*, ed. William Oldys. (London, 1810), 8: 290–300.

161. Raymond, *Pamphlets*, 263.

162. "To the High Court of Parliament: The Humble Remonstrances of the Company of Stationers" (1643), cited in Raymond, *Pamphlets*, 266.

163. Cited in Raymond, *Pamphlets*, 267.

164. See Lander, *Inventing Polemic*, 190–94.

165. See Eric Nelson, "True Liberty: Isocrates and Milton's *Areopagitica*," in *Milton Studies 40*, ed. Albert C. Labriola (Pittsburgh, 2002), 201–22; David Norbrook, "*Areopagitica*, Censorship and the Early Modern Public Sphere," in *The Administration of Aesthetics*, ed. Richard Burt (Minneapolis, 1994), 15; also Joseph Loewenstein, *The Author's Due* (Chicago, 2002), 171.

166. *Areopagitica*, ed. Patrides, 236.

167. Ibid., 236, 237. In another treatise, Milton eloquently elaborated on Foxe: on how England had this grace and honour from God to "blow the first Evangelick Trumpet to the Nations" and how the "darke Ages . . . had almost swept all the Starres out of the firmament of the Church and how the bright and blissful Reformation strook through the black and settled Night of Ignorance." But once again he passed by the section Foxe devoted to printing. "Of Reformation touching Church-Discipline in England" (1641), in *Milton's Works*, ed. Wolfe, 1: 524–26. That Milton used the seventh English edition of *Actes and Monuments* (1631–1632) for these passages is noted by Wolfe, nn.24, 30.

168. *Areopagitica*, ed. Patrides, 205.

169. Ibid., 201; on Sarpi, see 205.

170. Ibid., 207.

171. See, e.g., passages in *Areopagitica* about the new Purgatory of the *Index* as if St. Peter had "bequeathe'd them the keys of the Presse out of Paradise" (206); how Spanish licensing "gags the English Presse" (215); the travails of an author who has to submit his work to the "hasty view" of an inferior licenser and then, if he wants to add something, causes all sorts of problems to his printer (224); the aftermath of the defeat of the bishops when "all presses were to be open (as was the peoples birthright) but now the liberty of Printing must be enthralled again" (230). See also the list of references to printing procedures in Raymond, *Pamphlets*, 270.

172. The purpose of licensing "was to extinguish, if it were possible the light of the Reformation, little differing from that policie wherewith the Turk upholds his Alcoran by the prohibition of printing." *Areopagitica*, ed. Patrides, 234. Here as elsewhere, the fact that *secular* authorities in diverse European regions favored licensing to cope with printed output is ignored.

173. Raymond, *Pamphlets*, 267–68.

174. See below, Chapters 4 and 5.

175. *Areopagitica*, ed. Patrides, 218. Another passage (233) indicates a blurring of

distinctions between handwriting and printing. Milton says: "Christ preached in publick yet writing is more publick than preaching." Writing a letter to a friend or to any single recipient may be *less* public than preaching to an assembly.

176. Lois Schwoerer, "Liberty of the Press and Public Opinion," in *Liberty Secured?* ed. James R. Jones (Stanford, 1992), 214.

177. Blount, "A Just Vindication," chapter VII, 290–300.

178. Andrew Marvell, *The Rehearsal Transpros'd* (London, 1672), "Printed by J. D. for the Assigns of John Calvin and Theodore Beza at the sign of the King's Indulgence, on the South-side the Lake-Lemane; and sold by N. Ponder in Chancery-Lane, 1672."

179. Annabel Patterson, *Marvell and the Civic Crown* (Princeton, 1978), 178–79.

180. Andrew Marvell, *Rehearsal*, 5–6.

181. Compare with *Areopagitica*, ed. Patrides, 206 where licensers are accused of acting as if St. Peter had "bequeath'd them the keys of the Presse . . . out of Paradise."

182. According to Pierre Legouis, *Andrew Marvell* (Oxford, 1968), 198–99, after Marvell printed his pamphlet without a license and with a "burlesque imprint," he ran into trouble not with any licenser but with the Stationers and was rescued by the intervention of Lord Privy Seal Anglesey.

183. *Areopagitica*, ed. Patrides, 200–201. Marvell, *Rehearsal*, 9.

184. That a Marprelate printer described his spilled type as "shott" and other comparisons of type with ammunition are noted by Raymond, *Pamphlets*, 53. In *Invention of the Newspaper*, 185, Raymond also discusses updating the old pen/sword trope. On this trope see also Chapter 3, below.

185. Raymond, *Pamphlets*, 54. See also Leo Braudy, *The Frenzy of Renown* (New York, 1986), 265; Asa Briggs and Peter Burke, *Social History of the Media* (Cambridge: Polity Press, 2002), 18.

CHAPTER 3. AFTER ERASMUS: PROPELLING A KNOWLEDGE INDUSTRY

Epigraph: Thomas Jefferson, Report of the Commissioners for the University of Virginia, 4 August 1818.

1. Cited in Annabel Patterson, *Censorship and Interpretation* (Madison, 1984), 4–6.

2. Justus Lipsius played "the Lutheran in Jena, the Catholic in Italy, the Calvinist fellow traveler in Leiden, and the Catholic once again in Louvain." Anthony Grafton, "Portrait of Justus Lipsius," in *Bring Out Your Dead* (Cambridge, 2001), 241.

3. Peiresc to Dupuy (March 1635) cited in Peter N. Miller, *Peiresc's Europe* (New Haven, 2000), 86.

4. Miller refers to Jacques Auguste de Thou, Isaac Casaubon, Hugo Grotius, Joseph Scaliger, and Justus Lipsius in this connection (109).

5. Eisenstein, *Press as Agent*, 441–47. See also Eisenstein, *Grub Street Abroad*, 20 regarding Jean LeClerc.

6. Henri Estienne, *The Frankfort Book Fair*, ed. James W. Thompson (Chicago, 1911).

7. Polydore Vergil, *De Inventoribus Rerum* (1499; expanded in 1521 ed.), trans., ed., and intro. Beno Weiss and Louis Perez (Nieuwkoop, 1997), book II, chap. VII, 127–30 has passages on printing. That printing is held to flourish "in all parts of the world" indicates that Vergil, unlike Louis LeRoy (see below) was either ignorant of or indifferent to the banning of printing by Ottoman rulers.

8. On Vergil (1470–1555) see Brian Copenhaver, Introduction, Polydore Vergil, *On Discovery*, viii and also the full biography by Denys Hay, *Polydore Vergil, Renaissance Historian and Man of Letters* (Oxford, 1952). That Giordano Bruno drew heavily on Vergil when listing inventions is noted by Frances Yates, *The Art of Memory* (Chicago, 1966), 222. Vergil's influential history of England (*Anglica Historica*) is discussed by F. Smith Fussner, *Tudor History and the Historians* (New York, 1970), 251–54.

9. Frontispieces of Polydorus Vergilius, *De Rerum Inventoribus* (Lugduni, 1546; Amsterdam, 1671). I owe thanks to Ullrich Langer for showing me copies of these editions.

10. Vergil, *On Discovery*, Book II, chap. XI, 262–63.

11. François Rabelais, *Gargantua and Pantagruel*, trans. Thomas Urquhart (London, 1900), chap. 8. See Gargantua's letter on the education of Pantagruel.

12. Ullrich Langer, *Invention, Death, and Self-Definitions in the Poetry of Pierre Ronsard* (Saratoga, 1986), chap. 2, 22–24. On gunpowder, see also Roy S. Wolper, "The Rhetoric of Gunpowder and the Idea of Progress," *Journal of the History of Ideas* 31 (1970): 598; J. R. Hale, "Gunpowder and the Renaissance," in *From the Renaissance to the Counter Reformation*, ed. Charles Howard Carter (New York, 1965), 113–45.

13. See, e.g., Tartaglia, cited in Langer, *Invention, Death*, 23 and Postel, noted below.

14. Ernst Curtius, *European Literature and the Latin Middle Ages*, trans. Willard R. Trask (New York, 1953), 178–79.

15. Cited in Joad Raymond, *Pamphlets and Pamphleteering in Early Modern Britain* (Cambridge, 2003), 50–51.

16. Wolper, "Rhetoric of Gunpowder," 598.

17. For comments by Jean Fernel, Girolamo Cardano, William Barlowe, et al., see Wolper and also George Sarton, *Six Wings* (Bloomington, 1957).

18. William Bouwsma, *Concordia Mundi* (Cambridge, 1957), 271.

19. Bouwsma, 240.

20. Jean Bodin, *Method for the Easy Comprehension of History*, trans. Beatrice Reynolds (New York, 1966 [1945]), 302. The *Methodus* (1565) went through some thirteen editions between 1566 and 1650.

21. John H. Salmon, *Renaissance and Revolt* (Cambridge, 1987), 121.

22. In rejecting German claims to be the last of the great world empires, Bodin noted that Spain had a much larger world empire and so did the Turks, whose sultan owned the richest part of Asia, Africa, and Europe (291–92). He indignantly repudiated the idea that "Karl der Grosse" was a "German" emperor. Charlemagne, he wrote, was French by race, birth, education, language, customs, and institutions (294).

23. Bodin, 302.

24. A long list of "new things" that have come into view in the last hundred years:

"new seas, new lands . . . new inventions, etc." is given in LeRoy's other work, *Considérations sur l'histoire universelle* (Paris, 1567) cited in Paolo Rossi, *Philosophy, Technology, and the Arts in the Early Modern Era*, trans. Salvator Attanasio (New York, 1970), 68.

25. Louis LeRoy, *De la vicissitude ou variété des choses en l'univers* (1575), ed. B. W. Bates, trans. James B. Ross in *The Renaissance Reader*, ed. Ross and Mary McLaughlin (New York, 1972), 98ff.

26. Montaigne, "On Carriages" (1588), *The Complete Essays*, ed. Frame. See Preface, n.11.

27. This was deemed a "rare" work in the late nineteenth century by Falconer Madan, "Early Representations of the Printing Press," in *Bibliographica* (London, 1895), 1: 223–48, 499–503. It has been duplicated repeatedly since then.

28. Edward Rosen, "The Invention of Eyeglasses," *Journal of the History of Medicine* 2 (1956): 13–46, 183–218.

29. Thus Lynn White, *Medieval Technology and Social Change* (Oxford, 1962), 135 n.1, refers to Stradanus (or Jan van der Straet) as having "published" *Nova Reperta*. The most informative account of *Nova Reperta* is similarly focused on its Flemish-born Florentine artist. See Alice B. McGinty, "Stradanus (Jan Van der Straet): His Role in the Visual Communication of Renaissance Discoveries, Technologies, and Values," Ph.D. dissertation, Tufts University, 1974.

30. Anthony Wells-Cole, *Art and Decoration in Elizabethan and Jacobean England* (New Haven, 1997), 115ff.

31. Christopher Plantin, *An Account of Calligraphy and Printing in the Sixteenth Century* (1567), trans. and ed. Ray Nash (Cambridge, 1940), 3–4.

32. Isaac d'Israeli, *Isaac d'Israeli on Books*, ed. Martin Spevack (New Castle, 2004), 48. See also a similar citation from Thomas Hartwell Horne, "Introduction to Bibliography" (1814) in James Raven, *The Business of Books* (New Haven, 2007), 350.

33. Joseph Moxon, Preface, *Mechanick Exercises on the Whole Art of Printing* (London: on the Westside of Fleet-ditch "at the sign of the Atlas," 1683), facsimile edition, ed. Herbert Davis and Harry Carter (New York, 1978), 3–4, 10, 11–12.

34. Silvia De Renzi, ed., *Instruments in Print* (Cambridge, 2000).

35. See discussion of W. J. Blaeu in Eisenstein, *Press as Agent*, passim, and AHR Forum, *American Historical Review* 107, 1 (February 2002): 100.

36. John Headley, *Tommaso Campanella and the Transformation of the World* (Princeton, 1997), 323.

37. Ibid.

38. Johannes Kepler, *New Star* (Prague, 1606) (*Gesammelte Werke* [Munich, 1937], 1: 329ff), trans. and cited in Edward Rosen, "In Defense of Kepler," in *Aspects of the Renaissance*, ed. Archibald R. Lewis (Austin, 1967), 143. The printing operations depicted at the base of the engraving representing Kepler's "House of Astronomy" are illustrated in Elizabeth Eisenstein, *The Printing Revolution in Early Modern Europe* (Cambridge, 1993).

39. "Between 1550 and 1650 Western thinkers ceased to believe that they could find all important truths in ancient books." Anthony Grafton, *New Worlds, Ancient Texts* (Cambridge, 1995), 1.

40. Bacon, *The Proficience and Advancement of Learning Divine and Humane* (1605), in *Francis Bacon: A Selection of His Works*, ed. Sidney Warhaft (Toronto, 1965), 231.

41. Bacon, *The New Organon*, 84, in *Bacon*, ed. Warhaft, 356.

42. J. B. Bury, *The Idea of Progress* (London, 1921), 107; see also Rossi, 98. Fontenelle was the pen name of Bernard le Bovier (1657–1757), secretary of the French Academy of Sciences.

43. Jason Scott-Warren, *Early Modern English Literature* (Cambridge, 2005), 132.

44. Richard F. Jones, *Ancients and Moderns* (Berkeley, 1965), 290 n.23. On 129–31 Jones cites from a preface to an English translation of Descartes's *Passions of the Soule* (1650). The unnamed translator links Descartes with Bacon. Both show that "the too great reverence born to antiquity, is an errour extreamly prejudicial to the advancement of Sciences." Inventions, such as printing and the compass, are mentioned to indicate how knowledge may advance far beyond the "pillars of Hercules."

45. Engraved by Simon van der Passe, this title page probably reflected Bacon's views. See A. D. Burnett, "The Engraved Title Page of Bacon's *Instauratio Magna*: An Icon and Paradigm of Science and Its Wider Implication," Thomas Harriot Seminar Occasional Paper 27 (Durham, 1998).

46. "Plus Ultra" also signified imperial expansion and missionary zeal. It was adopted by Charles V as a Hapsburg motto. See Burnett, 9.

47. Bacon, *The Advancement of Learning* (1605), trans. and ed. J. E. Creighton in *Advancement of Learning and Novum Organum* (New York, 1944), 59.

48. Ibid.

49. Samuel Eliot Morison, *Admiral of the Ocean Sea* (Boston, 1942), 654.

50. Mark Twain, *A Connecticut Yankee in King Arthur's Court* (London, 1889), makes use of this story.

51. Fritz Saxl, "Veritas Filia Temporis," in *Philosophy and History*, ed. Raymond Klibansky and H. J. Paton (New York, 1963 [1936]), chap. 15.

52. Bacon, *New Organon*, 84, in *Bacon*, ed. Warhaft, 357.

53. Bacon, *The New Organon*, trans. Lisa Jardine and Michael Silverthorne (Cambridge, 2000), 69; see also 70.

54. Glanville's *Plus ultra, or the Progress and Advancement of Knowledge since the days of Aristotle* (1668) was written in defense of the Royal Society. It provoked the contrarian physician Henry Stubbe to turn out *The Plus Ultra reduced to a Non Plus . . .* (1670); Jones, *Ancients and Moderns*, 337 n.16.

55. Rossi, 73–74.

56. Bacon, *The Letters and the Life of Francis Bacon Including All His Occasional Works*, ed. James Spedding (London, 1861), 4: 138.

57. *The Fall of Man* (1616) by the Queen's chaplain, Godfrey Goodman, provoked "the first significant defense of modernity in England," according to Richard F. Jones, who cites extensively from George Hakewill's *An Apologie* (1627), 29–39. Hakewill inserted in his work an essay by Henry Briggs, Savilian professor of astronomy at Oxford, who explained the advantages of the Copernican theory and Galileo's telescope. Hakewill also

noted that "all antiquitie can boast of nothing equal to these three" (printing, compass, and gunpowder). On Hakewill, see also Rossi, 92.

58. *Novum Organum*, trans. Creighton, 349.

59. Charles Webster, *The Great Instauration* (London, 1975).

60. Hugh Trevor-Roper's essay on Hartlib, Drury, and Comenius, "Three Foreigners: The Philosophers of the Puritan Revolution," in *The Crisis of the Seventeenth Century* (New York, 1968), 284 notes how Hartlib and Robert Boyle together sponsored a translation of the Gospel into Lithuanian.

61. Webster, 333 uses this phrase to contrast the Baconian approach with that of the more secretive outlook of Paracelsus and Rosicrucians.

62. Webster, 49.

63. Ibid., 70.

64. See Eisenstein, *Press as Agent* on Marcello Malpighi, 664–65; also Rossi, 97.

65. For pertinent citations concerning printing, compass, and gunpowder by Tassoni (1620) and Borel (1655), among others, see Rossi, 87–93n.

66. On Renaudot see Eisenstein, *Press as Agent*, 246, 643; also Howard Solomon, *Public Welfare, Science, and Propaganda in Seventeenth-Century France* (Princeton, 1972), passim.

67. Rossi, *Philosophy, Technology*, 95.

68. On Mersenne's activities as a "publicist manqué" see Eisenstein, *Press as Agent*, 644–45.

69. "Art," Diderot, *Encyclopedia: Selections* (1st ed., 1751–72), trans. and ed. Nelly S. Hoyt and Thomas Cassirer (New York, 1965), 1: 15, xxxvi. On the *Encyclopédie* and Diderot see Chapter 4, below.

70. Rabelais, *Gargantua and Pantagruel*, trans. Urquhart; see Gargantua's letter in *Pantagruel*, chap. 8.

71. Cited in Bury, *Idea of Progress*, 35, from Ramus, Praefat, *Scholarum Mathematicarum* (Basel, 1569).

72. See collection of essays in Marc Baratin and Christian Jacob, eds., *Le pouvoir des bibliothèques* (Paris, 1996), passim.

73. Michael Ryan, review of Baratin and Jacob, eds., *Le pouvoir des bibliothèques*, *Bryn Mawr Classical Review* (23 September 1997).

74. See Archer Taylor, Introduction to Gabriel Naudé, *Advice on Establishing a Library* (Berkeley, 1950). John Evelyn's English translation, *Instructions Concerning Erecting of a Library*, was published in 1661.

75. Cited in Luigi Balsamo, *Bibliography*, trans. W. A. Pettas (Berkeley, 1990), 64.

76. Mark McDayter, "The Haunting of St. James's Library: Librarians, Literature, and 'The Battle of the Books,'" *Huntington Library Quarterly* 66 (2003): 24.

77. "In the Germanies alone, book production was ten times greater in 1763–1803 than in 1721–1763." William Clark, "On the Bureaucratic Plots of the Research Library," in *Books and the Sciences in History*, ed. Marina Frasca-Spada and Nicholas Jardine (Cambridge, 2000), 200.

78. Ann Blair, "Annotating and Indexing Natural Philosophy," in *Books and Sciences*, ed. Frasca-Spada and Jardine, 69. See also the collection of articles edited by Daniel Rosenberg on "Early Modern Information Overload," *Journal of the History of Ideas* 64, 1 (January 2003): 1–73 (hereafter "Information Overload," *JHI*).

79. Richard Yeo, *Encyclopaedic Visions* (Cambridge, 2001), 84.

80. Richard Yeo, "Encyclopedic Knowledge," in *Books and Sciences*, ed. Frasca-Spada and Jardine, 212.

81. Preserved Smith, *A History of Modern Culture*, vol. 2, *The Enlightenment* (New York, 1934), 276. The student goes on to pay tribute to the art of printing and to its inventor "Gutenberg of Mainz" before anticipating *The Dunciad* and complaining about the many dunces who have become famous authors because of the "ease with which they can publish their foolishness." When Pope and Swift contemplated a parodic *History of the Works of the Unlearned*, did they have Leonelo's comment in mind?

82. Cited in Ann Blair, "Reading Strategies for Coping with Information Overload, ca. 1550–1700," in "Information Overload," *JHI*: 11. Blair's forthcoming book, *Too Much to Know*, will be published by Yale University Press in 2010.

83. Roger Chartier, *L'ordre des livres* (Paris, 1992), 77.

84. d'Israeli, *Isaac d'Israeli on Books*, 120–23.

85. Blair, "Reading Strategies," 2.

86. See Chapter 1, above.

87. Yeo, *Encyclopaedic Visions*, xiv.

88. Ibid., 87.

89. Jon Thiem, "The Great Library of Alexandria Burnt: Toward the History of a Symbol," *Journal of the History of Ideas* 40 (December 1979): 513.

90. Louis LeRoy, *De la vicissitude* (1575), cited in Thiem.

91. Thiem, 516.

92. Ibid., 519.

93. On Morhof's *Polyhistor* (1697) and other relevant works, see Anthony Grafton, "The World of the Polyhistors," in *Bring Out Your Dead*, 166–80, esp. 171–72.

94. Cited in Blair, "Annotating," 70.

95. Adrien Baillet, *Jugements des savans sur les principaux ouvrages des auteurs* (Amsterdam, 1725), xi; cited in Blair, "Annotating," 70. On Baillet (1649–1706), whose pretensions were ridiculed by poets and wits, see also Rémy Saisselin, *The Literary Enterprise in Eighteenth-Century France* (Detroit, 1979), 19, 29.

96. (Amsterdam, 1725), xi, cited in Blair, "Annotating," 70. Similarly, Edmund Law justified the "publication of his own book," composed almost entirely of citations, on the basis of his "opposition to the multiplication of books." Cited in Marina Frasca-Spada, "Compendious Footnotes," in *Books and the Sciences*, 173.

97. Yeo, *Encyclopaedic Visions*, 95.

98. Blair, "Reading Strategies," 12.

99. Grafton, *Bring Out Your Dead*, 167. However, Morhof's *Polyhistor* did appear in five editions from 1687 to 1747 and "appealed widely" to German students and scholars. Blair, "Reading Strategies," 14 n.10.

100. See introduction to John Arbuthnot et al., *Memoirs of the Extraordinary Life, Works, and Discoveries of Martinus Scriblerus, written in Collaboration by the Members of the Scribbler's Club*, ed. Charles Kerby-Miller (New Haven, 1950).

101. Thémiseul de Saint-Hyacinthe, *Le chef d'oeuvre d'un inconnu: poème heureusement découvert et mise au jour avec des remarques savantes et recherchées par M. le docteur Chrysostome Mathanasius* (The Hague, 1714). Probably the result of collaboration by Saint-Hyacinthe and his friends, it purported to be about a little ballad discovered by "Dr. Mathanasius." The paratextual apparatus includes a statement by false censors, laudatory verses on Dr. Mathanasius in Hebrew, Greek, Latin, English, Dutch, and French and a 51-page commentary on the first strophe. See Elisabeth Carayol, *Thémiseul de Saint Hyacinthe 1684–1746* (Oxford, 1984); Saisselin, 13–14.

102. See Editor's preface to *Martinus Scriblerus*. In a similar vein was Mencke's Latin satire "On the Charlatanry of the Learned" (Grafton, *Bring Out Your Dead*, 166–77), which was probably known to Pope.

103. See citation from Vives and others in Eisenstein, *Press as Agent*, 472–74. According to Peter Burke, it was relatively unusual to hold that "peasants and artisans know more than many philosophers." Peter Burke, *A Social History of Knowledge* (Cambridge, 2000), 13. But this "primitivist" trend is thickly documented by Hiram Haydn, *The Counter-Renaissance* (New York, 1950), passim.

104. Letter of Tommaso Campanella (1607), cited in Eugenio Garin, *Italian Humanism*, trans. Peter Munz (New York, 1965), 475.

105. See René Descartes, *A Discourse on Method*, trans. John Veitch (London, 1986), Part I, 6–7.

106. Thomas Sprat, *History of the Royal Society* (London, 1667), 113.

107. Rosenberg, "Information Overload," 1–3.

108. See R. Loyalty Cru, *Diderot as a Disciple of English Thought* (New York, 1913), chap. 4, n.94; Richard Yeo, "A Solution to the Multitude of Books," *Journal of the History of Ideas* 64.1 (2003): 64–65; Rosenberg, 1–3.

109. Jean Le Rond d'Alembert, *Preliminary Discourse to the "Encyclopedia of Diderot"* (1751), trans. Richard N. Schwab (Chicago, 1963), 92–93.

110. John Harris, Preface to *Lexicon Technicum, or, An universal English dictionary of arts and sciences* (London: Printed for Dan Brown et al., 1704–1710).

111. Robert De Maria, Jr., *Johnson's Dictionary and the Language of Learning* (Chapel Hill, 1986), 4–5.

112. Yeo, "Solution to the Multitude of Books," 64–65.

113. De Maria, *Johnson's Dictionary*, 6–7.

114. Rosenberg, 7.

115. Henri Basnage de Beauval, *Histoire des ouvrages des savans*, 24 vols. (Geneva, 1969 [1687–1709]). On the learned periodicals that were spinoffs from publishers' book catalogues, see Eisenstein, *Grub Street Abroad*, 14–16.

116. Hans Bots and Lenie van Lieshout, *Contribution à la connaissance des réseaux d'information au début du XVIIIe siècle* (Amsterdam, 1984), 5.

117. See, for example, the Maunsell catalogue, Eisenstein, *Press as Agent*, 1: 106–7.

118. See above, nn. 74–76; below, n.138.

119. Ann Cline Kelly, "Swift's Battle of the Books: Fame in the Modern Age," in *Reading Swift*, ed. Hermann Josef Real and Helgard Stöver-Leidig (Munich, 1998), 91–101.

120. Bury, *Idea of Progress*, 117.

121. Fontenelle (Bernard le Bovier), Preface to *History of Oracles* (1687), trans. and ed. Richard T. Vann, in *Century of Genius*, ed. Vann (Englewood Cliffs, 1967), 11–12.

122. On d'Alembert's *Preliminary Discourse*, see Chapter 4, below.

123. Montaigne, "Of Pedantry," Essay 25, *The Complete Essays*, ed. Frame, 97–106.

124. Yeo, *Encyclopaedic Visions*, 93.

125. Mark Greengrass, Michael Leslie, and Timothy Raylor, eds., *Samuel Hartlib and Universal Reformation* (Cambridge, 1994).

126. William Wotton, *Reflections upon Ancient and Modern Learning* (London, 1694). The Royal Society engaged Wotton (1666–1727), chaplain to the earl of Nottingham, to respond to Sir William Temple's *An Essay upon the Ancient and Modern Learning* (1690). Jones, *Ancients and Moderns*, 267 notes that many of Wotton's arguments draw on the work of Joseph Glanville, whose *Plus Ultra* is mentioned above.

127. Wotton, Preface to *Reflections*, 3. On Gibbon's comments, see Chapter 7, below.

128. The same point had been made in the fifteenth century by de Bussi; see Chapter 1, above.

129. Wotton, chap. 15, 169–83.

130. Yeo, *Encyclopaedic Visions*, 3; see Eisenstein, *Press as Agent*, 458 n.14.

131. This point has been challenged by Adrian Johns, *Nature of the Book*, and by David McKitterick, *Print, Manuscript*. Both stress the difference between early printed editions, which were multiform, and later, more uniform ones. However, this difference was not apparent to early modern observers, who were unfamiliar with twentieth-century output and whose attitudes are the topic of this chapter.

132. Anticipating Voltaire's comment that there are "no sects among geometers," Wotton contrasted the endless debates among rhetoricians to the agreed-on solutions to mathematical problems. See citation in Rossi, *Philosophy, Technology*, 94.

133. Wisdom 11:20.

134. Mark Knights, *Representation and Misrepresentation in Later Stuart Britain* (Oxford, 2005), 37–38.

135. See Chapter 4, below.

136. Marjorie Nicolson, *Science and Imagination* (Ithaca, 1956), 118.

137. Swift, *A Tale of a Tub. Written for the Universal Improvement of Mankind . . . To which is added an Account of a Battel between the Antient and Modern Books in St. James Library. With the Author's Apology and Explanatory Notes*, ed. W. W-tt-n . . . and others (London: 5th ed. 1710). Wotton is described as "the son of Ignorance and Pride" in the *Battel*, 240–42. See also editorial introduction to the modern edition: *A Tale of a Tub to which is added the Battle of the Books and the Mechanical operation of the Spirit*, ed. A. C. Guthkelch and David Nichol Smith (Oxford, 1958) on how Swift turned Wotton's critique into "explanatory notes."

138. For the attack on the "advancement of Universal Knowledge," see *Tale*, 106 n.3; title page of 1710 edition.

139. *Tale*, section VII, "A Digression in Praise of Digressions."

140. *Battel*, 236.

141. Addison's comment (in *The Spectator* no. 262), "The Air-Pump, the barometer . . . and the like Inventions were thrown out to these Busy Spirits as Tubs or Barrels are thrown to a whale that he may let the Ship sail on without Disturbance," is cited by Swift in his Preface to *Tale*, 39 n.1.

142. *Battel*, 238. This attack was provoked by Richard Bentley's plans to include pamphlet collections in the St. James Library in accord with Gabriel Naudé's instructions on how to build a library. On John Evelyn's translation of Naudé's advice in 1661 and Evelyn's support of the Royal Society see Jones, *Ancients and Moderns*, 322 n.123.

143. James A. Downie, *Robert Harley and the Press* (Cambridge, 1979), 12.

144. J. Paul Hunter, *Before Novels* (New York, 1990), 106–7.

145. Preface to *Tale*, 45.

146. Kelly, "Swift's Battle," 96.

147. *Battel*, 246.

148. *Tale*, 145.

149. For background on issues pertaining to ordering the collection of books in the St. James Library, see McDayter, 15–17.

150. Cited in Harold Weber, "The 'Garbage Heap' of Memory: At Play in Pope's Archives of Dulness," *Eighteenth Century Studies* 33 (1999): 7.

151. Kelly, "Swift's Battle," 95.

152. Dustin Griffin, "Critical Opinion: Fictions of Eighteenth Century Authorship," *Essays in Criticism* 43 (1993): 181–94.

153. Kelly, "Swift's Battle," 96 suggests that by binding three pamphlet-like works together and presenting them as a single book, Swift offered a seemingly more substantial and less ephemeral unit.

154. *Tale*, 55.

CHAPTER 4. EIGHTEENTH-CENTURY ATTITUDES

Epigraph: "The Art of Printing. A Poem," by Constantia Grierson (1706–33). Constantia (née Phillips) was the wife of George Grierson (George II's printer in Dublin) and a learned lady, well versed in Latin, Greek and Hebrew. Before her premature death she had helped her husband with the publication of several classical editions. The poem was first published in 1764. The first stanza was republished as an epigraph to an issue of the *London Chronicle* (28–30 June 1785). Thanks are due to Eleanor Shevlin for bringing the poem and its author to my attention and to Richard Sher for showing me the *London Chronicle* epigraph.

1. Note the contrast with Marshall McLuhan's insistence (in keeping with the Catholic position) that print had a "stupefying" effect and led to "the separation of the visual

faculty from the interplay with the other senses." McLuhan, *The Gutenberg Galaxy* (Toronto, 1962), 255. See citation re Pope, below.

2. Marjorie H. Nicolson, *Science and Imagination* (Ithaca, 1956), chap. 4, "Milton and the Telescope," 80–109. The reference to one sense performing the work of three also shares something in common with Addison's poem (*The Spectator*, 1712) about the "solemn silence" in which we move round the "dark terrestrial ball" even while we "utter forth in glorious voice" forever singing in "reason's ear."

3. See Chapter 1, above.

4. Janice Radway, *A Feeling for Books* (Chapel Hill, 1997), 76.

5. *An Essay on the Original, Use and Excellency of the Noble Art and Mystery of PRINTING* (London, Printed for T. Legg . . . at the Pamphlet-Shops of London and Westminster) MCDCCLII, Price Four-Pence).

6. Michael Warner, *The Letters of the Republic* (Cambridge, 1990), 73–74. On epitaphs using the metaphor of the book that preceded Franklin's version, and led Franklin to be accused of plagiarism, see James N. Green and Peter Stallybrass, *Benjamin Franklin* (New Castle, 2006), 17–21. Franklin's version was written in 1728 but was not printed until the 1770s.

7. Thanks go to Calhoun Winton for providing me with a copy of this poem.

8. *The Harleian Miscellany*, 8 vols, ed. William Oldys [1744–46], reprinted in 10 vols. and ed. by Thomas Park (1808–13) (London, 1810) 10: 238–39.

9. David McKitterick, *Print, Manuscript and the Search for Order* (Cambridge, 2003), 171. Louis XVI provides another example of an eighteenth-century royal figure who learned how to run a printing press.

10. Samuel Palmer, *A General History of Printing from the First Invention of it in the City of Mentz to its Propagation and Origins through most of the kingdoms of Europe, particularly the Introduction and Success of it here in England* (London, 1733), 3. According to McKitterick, *Print, Manuscript*, 168–70, it was originally published in monthly parts and intended to encompass sections dealing with technology. Much of it was written not by Palmer but by George Psalmanazar, who was responsible for the chapter—apparently tacked on after Palmer's death in 1732—that repeated Atkyns's story about the fictitious Corsellis who preceded Caxton (iii). On Atkyns see Chapter 2, above.

11. Palmer, *General History of Printing*, 108. See Luigi Balsamo, *Bibliography*, trans. W. A. Pettas (Berkeley, 1990), 122 for the first Latin histories of printing and the original use of the term *incunabula*. Bernard von Mallinckrodt, *De ortu ac progressu artis typographicae* (*On the origin and progress of Printing*) (Cologne, 1639), which commemorated the 1640 bicentennial of printing, defined the period up to and including the year 1500 as "prima typographiae incunabula." The term was taken up by the Dutch bookseller Cornelius van Beughem, who titled his pioneering bibliography *Incunabula Typographiae* (Amsterdam, 1688). It became and remains a significant term for the marketing of old books. Jacqueline Glomski, "Incunabula Typographiae: Seventeenth Century Views on Early Printing," *The Library* 7th ser. 2, 4 (Dec. 2001): 334–48. The authoritative account by Kristian Jensen, "Collecting Incunabula: Enlightenment, Revolution, and the Market—

Rediscovering and Re-Creating the Earliest Printed Books in the Eighteenth Century"
(Oxford, 2008) was unfortunately unavailable before this chapter went to press.

12. I am summarizing the section on "The World of Prosper Marchand" in Eisenstein, *Grub Street Abroad*, chap. 3, which draws on the pioneering studies of Leyden
Library archivist Christiane Berkvens Stevelinck. Anne Goldgar, *Impolite Learning* (New
Haven, 1995), depicts Marchand as a "literary agent" *avant la lettre*, which does not, in
my view, do justice to the many other functions he performed when writing prefaces,
compiling dictionaries, designing illustrations, editing journals and collaborating with
d'Argens on *Lettres juives*. The French term "homme du livre" seems most appropriate.

13. As noted above, in Chapter 1, fifteenth-century chronicles had fixed 1440 as the
birthdate of the infant industry.

14. Natalie Zemon Davis, "Strikes and Salvation in Lyons," in *Society and Culture
in Early Modern France* (Stanford, 1975), 5.

15. See Chapter 1, above.

16. See Eisenstein, *Grub Street Abroad*, 48. Stephen Parks, *John Dunton and the
English Book Trade* (New York, 1976), 83, 100, notes how Dunton's *Athenian Gazette*
published Swift's first poem and also supplied Defoe with his first connection to a periodical. Dunton's defensive references to printing and bookselling as trades practiced by respected scholars such as Scaliger and Stephanus (Estienne) are good examples of how early
printing history was used to legitimate later activities.

17. Dorothy Schlegel, "Freemasonry and the Encyclopédie Reconsidered," *Studies
on Voltaire and the Eighteenth Century* 90 (Oxford, 1972): 1433–60.

18. Picart's frontispiece for *The Journal Literaire* [sic] *(de la Haye)* 9 (1717), is shown
in *Grub Street Abroad*, fig. 10.

19. Margaret Jacob, *The Radical Enlightenment* (London, 1981), chap. 6.

20. Henri-Samuel Formey, *La Belle Wolfienne*, 6 vols. (The Hague, 1741–63. See also
Eisenstein, *Grub Street Abroad*, 138n.

21. This was the motto, derived from Horace, which served as the focal point of
Kant's essay: "Was ist Aufklärung?" On transformations undergone by "Sapere Aude"
from Horace to Wolff, see Franco Venturi, *Utopia and Reform in the Enlightenment* (Cambridge, 1971), 8–9.

22. Eisenstein, *Grub Street Abroad* shows Marchand's sketch instructing the engraver, Fig. 16.

23. Eisenstein, *Grub Street Abroad*, 75–77.

24. Richard Altick, *The English Common Reader* (Columbus, 1998), 62. See also
William St. Clair, *The Reading Nation in the Romantic Period* (Cambridge, 2004), 244.
For a full account, see Dorothy Blakey, *The Minerva Press, 1790–1820* (Oxford, 1939).

25. The point of departure for many studies is the early work by Ralph Straus: *The
Unspeakable Curll* (London, 1927), now outdated by Paul Baines and Pat Rogers, *Edmund
Curll, Bookseller* (Oxford, 2007). See especially the seminal article by David Saunders and
Ian Hunter, "Lessons from the Literatory," *Critical Inquiry* 17 (1991): 479–509. On the
Grub Street Journal, see James Theodore Hillhouse, *The Grub Street Journal* (Durham,
1928), and on the street itself Pat Rogers, *Hacks and Dunces* (New York, 1972).

26. An intriguing connection between illustrators serving Marchand and Pope is furnished by Bernard Picart. Jacob Van der Schley, who did the engravings for Marchand's history of printing, studied with Picart, as did Pierre (or Peter) Fourdrinier, who illustrated the later books of *The Dunciad*. Elias Mengel, "*The Dunciad* Illustrations," *Eighteenth Century Studies* 7 (Winter 1973–74): 161. The above account summarizes parts of my Clifford Lecture, "Gods, Devils and Gutenberg: The Eighteenth Century Confronts the Printing Press," *Studies in Eighteenth Century Culture* 27 (1998): 13.

27. Both versions—pertaining to M. De Vile and Johann Fust—had appeared earlier in Daniel Defoe's *History of the Devil* (see Chapter 1, above). Defoe's help goes unacknowledged in the *Grub Street Journal* text; elsewhere he is denigrated as a two-faced pamphleteer.

28. Alan T. McKenzie, "The Solemn Owl and the Laden Ass: The Iconography of the Frontispieces to *The Dunciad*," *Harvard Library Bulletin* 24 (1976): 25–39. See also Mengel, "*Dunciad* Illustrations," 161–79.

29. The poem's original title was "Progress of Dulness." Dryden (in *Mac Flecknoe*) first made dullness "a fashionable topic" which was then picked up by Swift and later by Pope. Introduction, *The Dunciad*, ed. Sutherland, xxii, xxxix.

30. This epigram was found on the flyleaf of a copy of *The Dunciad* that was attributed by the copyist to the *Daily Gazeteer*, 18 December 1738. P. D., "Epigram on the Frontispiece to 'The Dunciad,'" *Notes and Queries* 2nd ser. 36 (6 September 1856): 182.

31. Dustin Griffin, "Critical Opinion: Fictions of Eighteenth Century Authorship," *Essays in Criticism* 43 (1993): 181–94.

32. Dustin Griffin, *Literary Patronage in England, 1650–1800* (Cambridge, 1996), 41. See also Preface to "Martinus Scriblerus" and Introduction to *The Dunciad*, ed. Sutherland. On Swift's ambition to be made a "historiographer Royal," see Ann Cline Kelly, *Jonathan Swift and Popular Culture* (New York, 2002), 45.

33. Eisenstein, *Press as Agent*, 137n. See also Françoise Waquet, "Qu'est-ce que la république des lettres?" *Bibliothèque de l'École des Chartes* 147 (1989): 473–502.

34. Anne Robert Jacques Turgot, "A Philosophical Review of the Successive Advances of the Human Mind" (11 December 1750), in *Turgot on Progress, Sociology, Economics*, ed. and trans. Ronald L. Meek (Cambridge, 1973), 57.

35. Hans-Jürgen Lüsebrink, "Hommage à l'écriture et éloge de l'imprimerie," in *Livre et révolution*, ed. Frédéric Barbier et al. (Paris, 1989), 134–44.

36. Some sixteenth-century firms (such as the Estiennes) had familial connections with eighteenth-century ones. Eisenstein, *Grub Street Abroad*, 20; also my "The Libraire-Philosophe: Four Sketches for a Group Portrait," in *Le livre et l'historien*, ed. Frédéric Barbier et al. (Geneva, 1997), 539–50.

37. See Pope, *Essay on Criticism*, lines 692–95.

38. George Sherburn, *The Early Career of Alexander Pope* (Oxford, 1934), 86–87, 95–96. That Pope owned and bequeathed to Henry St. John, Viscount Bolingbroke, eleven volumes of Erasmus's works is noted by Marcus Walsh, "The Superfoetation of Literature: Attitudes to the Printed Book in the Eighteenth Century." *British Journal for*

Eighteenth Century Studies 15 (1992): 152. When comparing Erasmus with Pope, Walsh mistakenly conflates Erasmus's tribute to printing in his Adage (about Aldus) of 1508 with the post-Lutheran, disillusioned Adage of the 1520s.

39. James McLaverty, *Pope, Print and Meaning* (Oxford, 2001), 1. (Studies by David Foxon and Maynard Mack are cited for describing that "other Pope.")

40. Breen S. Hammond, *Professional Imaginative Writing in England 1670–1740* (Oxford, 1997), 209.

41. Reginald H. Griffith, *Alexander Pope: A Bibliography*, 2 vols. (Austin, 1927), 2: 285. The same citation appears in two pertinent studies: James Winn, "On Pope, Printers, and Publishers," *Eighteenth Century Life* 6 (January–May 1981): 94; and Laura Brown, *Alexander Pope* (Oxford, 1985), 130. While agreeing that Pope's relation to the printing industry is problematic and ambivalent (131), Brown herself has no hesitation about describing "the main explicit enterprise of *The Dunciad*" in somewhat anachronistic Marxist terms: as "an attack on the capitalization of the printing industry" (130).

42. Walsh, "Superfoetation"; "Text, 'Text' and Swift's *Tale of the Tub*," *Modern Language Review* 85, 2 (April 1990): 290–303.

43. *The Dunciad*, IV, lines 522–28, cited in Louis I. Bredvold, "The Gloom of the Tory Satirists," in *Pope and His Contemporaries*, ed. James L. Clifford and Louis A. Landa (Oxford, 1949), 1–20.

44. Douglas Brooks-Davies, *Pope's Dunciad and the Queen of the Night* (Manchester, 1985), 19.

45. Harold Weber, *Paper Bullets* (Lexington, 1996), 131.

46. Opening Canto of Book I, *The Faerie Queene*, cited in Alexandra Halasz, *The Marketplace of Print* (Cambridge, 1997), 7; see also 21.

47. See n. 29, above.

48. Lines from *Religio Laici* (1682), cited in Louis Bredvold, *The Intellectual Milieu of John Dryden* (Ann Arbor, 1966 [1934]), 125.

49. Ian Watt, *The Rise of the Novel* (Berkeley, 1957), 53–54.

50. Brown, *Alexander Pope*, 130.

51. Ibid., 131.

52. Ibid., 130–31.

53. Ibid., 152.

54. Ibid., 157.

55. McLuhan, *Gutenberg Galaxy*, 255–62.

56. Alvin Kernan, *Printing, Technology, Letters, and Samuel Johnson* (Princeton, 1987), 15–16.

57. Kernan, 13.

58. Ostensibly angry about Curll's unauthorized publication of Lady Mary Wortley Montagu's letters, Pope, "who was too puny" to do it himself, got Arbuthnot and Lintot to give Curll an emetic and then published two pamphlets giving "A Full and True account of a horrid and barbarous revenge by poison on the Body of Mr Edmund Curll, Bookseller" (1716), Sherburn, 169–70. The episode is a good example of a classical author's

indulgence in "grotesquerie" as discussed by Peter Stallybrass and Allon White, *The Politics and Poetics of Transgression* (Ithaca, 1986), chap. 2.

59. *The Dunciad*, Book IV, lines 635–40, 653–57.

60. "Martinus Scriblerus, of the Poem," in *Dunciad Variorum*, ed. Sutherland, 49. See also Arbuthnot et al., *Memoirs of Scriblerus*, ed. Kerby-Miller.

61. McLaverty, 3–6.

62. Catherine Ingrassia and Claudia Thomas, eds., *"More Solid Learning"* (Lewisburg, 2000), 21.

63. Introduction, *Dunciad*, ed. Sutherland, xxii–xxvi.

64. Thomas Keymer and Peter Saybor, *Pamela in the Market Place* (Cambridge, 2005), 13.

65. Roger Chartier, *Inscription and Erasure*, trans. Arthur Goldhammer (Philadelphia, 2007), chap. 7.

66. Deidre Lynch, *The Economy of Character* (Chicago, 1998) cited in Robyn L. Schiffman, "A Concert of Werthers," *Eighteenth Century Studies* 43, 2 (Winter 2010): 208.

67. Chartier, *Inscription*, 123–25. On Richardson's early career as proofreader, hack, and jobbing printer, and on his later transformation into a "literary lion," see also John Brewer, *The Pleasures of the Imagination* (London, 1997), chap. 3, 125–29.

68. On the "sacre de l'écrivain" in the nineteenth century, see Chapter 5, below. For a pertinent article on eighteenth-century literary celebrity that depicts Rousseau's presentation of himself, see Antoine Lilti, "The Writing of Paranoia: Jean Jacques Rousseau and the Paradoxes of Celebrity," *Representations* 103 (Summer 2008): 53–83.

69. The first novel published in America (vol. I in 1742; vol. II in 1744), Franklin's *Pamela* was a disappointing, costly venture that was outsold by imported copies. Green and Stallybrass, 70.

70. Pat Rogers, "Nameless Names: Pope, Curll and the Uses of Anonymity," *New Literary History* 33 (2002): 240.

71. Cited in Keymer, 12.

72. Ibid.; see also Jesse Lander, *Inventing Polemic* (Cambridge, 2006), 230.

73. Marjorie Nicolson, *Newton Demands the Muse* (Princeton, 1966), 37. McLuhan's treatment of Pope as anticipating William Blake's anti-Newtonian views is not easy to reconcile with these celebrated lines. Nicolson persuasively argues that "it was not Newton but the Newtonians whom Pope castigated," 134.

74. McKitterick, *Print, Manuscript*, 172; Asa Briggs, *The Age of Improvement, 1783–1867* (London, 1959).

75. Book IV, chap. xii, paragraph 12.

76. John Locke to Anthony Collins, *Works*, 10 vols. (London, 1801), 10: 291, cited in Richard T. Vann, ed., *Century of Genius* (Englewood Cliffs, 1967), 6.

77. John Aubrey, *Three Prose Works*, ed. John Buchanan Brown (Sussex, 1972), 290. See also Bishop Thomas Sprat, *History of the Royal Society*, 2nd ed. (London, 1702), 340 on how "fairies" and "apparitions" were banished.

78. Alan T. McKenzie, "Giuseppe Baretti and the 'Republic of Letters' in the Eighteenth Century," *Studies on Voltaire and the Eighteenth Century* 193 (Oxford, 1980): 1816.

79. No. 166 (Monday, 10 September 1711), *The Spectator*, ed. Donald F. Bond, 5 vols. (Oxford, 1965), 2: 153–56.

80. No. 367 (Thursday, 1 May 1712); 3: 379–82.

81. Ibid.

82. No. 124 (Monday, 23 July 1711); 1: 507.

83. No. 10 (12 March 1711); 1: 44.

84. Scott Black, "Social and Literary Form in the *Spectator*," *Eighteenth Century Studies* 33, 1 (1999): 34.

85. Brian Cowan, "Mr. Spectator and the Coffeehouse Public Sphere," *Eighteenth Century Studies* 37 (2004): 345–66.

86. No. 582 (Wednesday, 18 August 1714); 4: 591.

87. Edward A. Bloom, "Johnson on a Free Press: A Study in Liberty and Subordination," *English Literary History* 16, 4 (1949): 251–57.

88. *Rambler*, No. 106, cited in Kernan, *Printing, Technology*, 243.

89. Thomas Babington Macaulay, *Miscellaneous Works of Lord Macaulay*, 5 vols., ed. Lady Trevelyan (New York, 1880 [1824]), 4: 449.

90. O. M. Brack, Jr., and Mary Early, "Samuel Johnson's Proposals for the *Harleian Miscellany*," *Studies in Bibliography* 45 (1992): 127.

91. Bodley's insistence that his librarian Thomas James exclude pamphlets figures prominently in Halasz, 1. See also Michael Mendle, "Preserving the Ephemeral," in *Books and Readers in Early Modern England*, ed. Jennifer Andersen and Elizabeth Sauer (Philadelphia, 2002), 201–16.

92. Robert DeMaria, Jr., *The Life of Samuel Johnson* (Oxford, 1993), 107.

93. Ibid., 100.

94. Ibid., 101.

95. Robert DeMaria, Jr., *Johnson's Dictionary and the Language of Learning* (Chapel Hill, 1986), 103.

96. DeMaria, *Life*, 105.

97. DeMaria, *Johnson's Dictionary*, 187.

98. R. Loyalty Cru, *Diderot as a Disciple of English Thought* (New York, 1913), 27. On Brucker's and Diderot's borrowings see also Jacques Proust, *Diderot et l'Encyclopédie* (Paris, 1982 [1962]), 247–48.

99. Jean Le Rond D'Alembert, *Preliminary Discourse to the Encyclopedia of Diderot*, trans. Richard N. Schwab (Indianapolis, 1963), 93.

100. Ibid., 64.

101. Ibid., 108–9.

102. Ibid., 21–22.

103. Arthur Wilson, *Diderot, The Testing Years* (New York, 1957), 90–91 shows that Diderot was unjustly accused of being ignorant of mathematics.

104. "Art," in *L'Encyclopédie ou Dictionnaire Raisonné des Sciences, des Arts, et des Métiers*, par une société de gens de letters, ed. Denis Diderot and Jean Le Rond D'Alembert (Paris, 1751–72), 17 vols. text, 11 vols. plates, 1st ed.; reprinted in *Encyclopedia: Selections*, trans. and ed. Nelly S. Hoyt and Thomas Cassirer (New York, 1965), 8.

105. Giles Barber, Introduction, *Book Making in Diderot's Encyclopédie*, ed. Barber (Farnborough, 1973).

106. Diderot, "Caractères de l'imprimerie," cited in Barber.

107. Ibid.

108. Diderot, "Art," 16.

109. Ibid., 15.

110. D'Alembert, *Preliminary Discourse*, 110. Chambers's unfulfilled plans for a second edition *had* included coverage not only of "Books, Libraries, and Cabinets," but also of "Shops, Garrets, Cellars, Mines and other obscure Places where men of Learning rarely penetrate." Cited in DeMaria, *Johnson's Dictionary*, 5.

111. Diderot, "Art," 15.

112. On interpretations of these plates by Robert Darnton and William Sewall, see my 1996 Clifford Lecture: Eisenstein, "Gods, Devils, and Gutenberg," 11.

113. On Jaucourt's contribution of fifty-five articles, see Barber, Introduction, *Book Making*.

114. All references to "Imprimeur" are taken from an online version: *ARTFUL Encyclopédie* (rev. 2.1–06/2005), a copy of vol. 8, 624–30 of the first edition of *L'Encyclopédie*, translated by me.

115. Adrian Johns, *Nature of the Book* (Chicago, 1998), 425 n.99.

116. On this phenomenon, see Henri-Jean Martin, "Comment on écrivit l'histoire du livre." In *Le livre français sous l'Ancien Régime*, ed. Henri-Jean Martin (Paris, 1987), 16.

117. See Aubrey, *Three Prose Works*, n. 75 above.

118. "Verses design't to be prefixed to Mr. Lintot's Miscellany of 1712," in David Foxon, *Pope and the Early Eighteenth Century Book Trade*, ed. James McLaverty (Oxford, 1991), 25.

119. *The Tatler* no. 158, Thursday, 13 April 1710 ("Harry Stephens" is Henri II Estienne or Stephanus).

120. Journeymen printers had their own version of a longed-for vanished past, when there had been no division between the master printer and his workers. Nicolas Contat, *Anecdotes typographiques* (1762), ed. Giles Barber (Oxford, 1980), 30–31.

121. Watt, 52–55, offers pertinent citations. See below on Joseph Johnson, a publisher-bookseller stigmatized as a literary middleman.

122. Cited in Jean Paul Belin, *Le commerce des livres prohibés à Paris de 1750 à 1789* (Paris, 1913), 72.

123. Otto S. Lankhorst, "Le rôle des libraire-imprimeurs néerlandais dans l'édition des journaux littéraires de langue française (1684–1750)," in *La diffusion et la lecture des journaux de langue française sous l'Ancien Régime*, ed. Hans Bots (Amsterdam, 1988), 9.

124. Prosper Marchand, *Dictionnaire historique, ou mémoires critiques et littéraires, concernant la vie et les ouvrages de diverses personnes distinguées dans la république des letters*, 2 vols. (The Hague, 1758) 1: 2. The passage comes from the "Avertissement de l'éditeur," a sketch of Marchand's life by Jean Nicolas Sebastien Allemand.

125. Comment of Vossius about Blaeu in David W. Davies, *The World of the Elseviers, 1580–1712* (The Hague, 1954), 139.

126. Ibid., 67.

127. Mary Beard, "Scrolling Down the Ages," *New York Times Book Review*, Sunday, 16 April 2009, 27.

128. James Raven, *The Business of Books* (New Haven, 2007), 119.

129. Gerald P. Tyson, "Joseph Johnson, an Eighteenth Century Bookseller," *Studies in Bibliography* 28 (1975): 3.

130. Gerald P. Tyson, *Joseph Johnson* (Iowa City, 1979), describes Johnson's services to an influential circle of dissenters, exiles and radicals. See below on Johnson's role as Mirabeau's publisher.

131. Robert Darnton, *The Business of Enlightenment* (Cambridge, 1979), 40. On Darnton's emphatic reiteration of this point in several of his later articles, see Eisenstein, *Grub Street Abroad*, 25 n. 96.

132. See references in Eisenstein, *Grub Street Abroad*, 26–29. See Michel Schlup's two articles on reading societies in Neuchâtel: "Diffusion et lecture du *Journal Helvétique*, au temps de la Société Typographique de Neuchâtel," in Bots, *La diffusion et la lecture*, 59–71; "La lecture et ses institutions dans la Principauté de Neuchâtel au tournant des Lumières," *Revue Française d'Histoire du Livre* 55/56 (1987): 463–500.

133. "Alors l'imprimerie était glorieuse, aujourd'hui ce n'est qu'un art lucrative," cited in Roger Chartier, "Écriture, publication et lecture," in *L'Encyclopédie: du réseau au livre et du livre au réseau*, ed. Robert Morrissey and Philippe Roger (Paris, 2001), 61. The comment comes at the end of a biographical sketch of Daniel Bomberg, who is depicted as spending a fortune on his celebrated editions of the Hebrew Bible before dying poor. "Imprimeur," *Encyclopédie*, vol. 8.

134. "Imprimeur," 627.

135. Wilson, *Diderot*, 133. See also Wilson's reference to Jaucourt's "Art of Heraldry" article with its dismissal of the "vain and ridiculous study of heraldry and armorial bearings" (136).

136. Turgot, "A Philosophical Review," 57.

137. Jean Jacques Rousseau, "Discourse . . . on the question "Has the Restoration of the sciences and arts tended to purify morals?" (1750) in *The First and Second Discourses*, ed. Roger D. Masters (New York, 1964), 61. The appended footnote that refers to the "awful disorders printing has caused in Europe" also hails the destruction of a press briefly established in Constantinople by Achmet III (1726–30).

138. Montesquieu, *The Spirit of the Laws*, ed. David W. Carrithers (Berkeley, 1977), 176.

139. Cited in Durand Echeverria, *The Maupéou Revolution* (Baton Rouge, 1985), 262.

140. James Madison in the *Federalist Papers* 14, 389n, pointed out that the principle of representation enabled republics to grow larger than Montesquieu had envisaged. On earlier views pertaining to representation in Great Britain, see Mark Knights, *Representation and Misrepresentation in Later Stuart Britain* (Oxford, 2005).

141. Antoine Louis Claude Destutt de Tracy, *A Commentary and review of Montesquieu's "Spirit of Laws"*, trans. Thomas Jefferson (1811; New York, 1969), 19.

142. David Colclough, *Freedom of Speech in Early Stuart England* (Cambridge, 2005), 178.

143. Cited in Jason Peacey, *Politicians and Pamphleteers* (Ashgate, 2004), 327.

144. John Trenchard and Thomas Gordon, "Cato's Letters," cited in Ronald Hamowy, "Cato's Letters, John Locke, and the Republican Paradigm," *History of Political Thought* 11 (1990): 292.

145. William Robertson, Sermon (5 November 1788), cited in Richard B. Sher, "1688 and 1788," in *Culture and Revolution*, ed. Paul Dukes and John Dunkley (London, 1990).

146. William Bond, *Thomas Hollis of Lincoln's Inn* (Cambridge, 1990), passim. See also Caroline Robbins, "The Strenuous Whig: Thomas Hollis of Lincoln's Inn," *William and Mary Quarterly* 3rd ser. 7 (1950): 433–40.

147. Knights, 51–53.

148. *Public Advertiser* (2 January 1769), cited in Geoffrey A. Cranfield, *Press and Society* (London, 1978), 66–67.

149. See above.

150. Tobias Smollett, BRITON no. 15 (September, 1762), cited in Robert R. Rea, *The English Press in Politics 1760–1774* (Lincoln, 1963), 3.

151. For a well-documented discussion of the "alternative structure of politics," see John Brewer, *Party Ideology and Popular Politics at the Accession of George III* (Cambridge, 1976), pt. 3.

152. For a detailed chronology, see Rea, Appendix 1, 225–27.

153. Cited in George Rudé, *Wilkes and Liberty* (London, 1962), 176.

154. Cited in Cranfield, 62.

155. Robert R. Palmer, *The Age of the Democratic Revolution*, 2 vols. (Princeton, 1959), 1: 167.

156. Ibid.

157. Brewer, *Party Ideology,* 171

158. M. Dorothy George, *English Political Caricature*, 2 vols. (Oxford, 1959), 1: 140.

159. Brewer, *Party Ideology*, 173.

160. From William Robertson's sermon, in Sher, "1688 and 1788," 100.

161. Claude Carloman de Rulhière, "De l'action de l'opinion sur les gouvernements" (Reception Address to the Académie Française, 4 June 1787), in *Oeuvres de Rulhière*, 2 vols. (Paris, 1819), 2: 204–5. See also the pertinent study by J. A. W. Gunn, *Queen of the World* (Oxford, 1995).

162. Jacques Necker cited in Paul A. Palmer, "The Concept of Public Opinion in Political Theory," in *Essays on History and Political Theory in Honor of Charles H. McIlwain*, ed. Carl F. Wittke (Cambridge, 1936), 239.

163. Chrétien-Guillaume Lamoignon de Malesherbes cited in Keith M. Baker, *Inventing the French Revolution* (Cambridge, 1990), 189.

164. Voltaire, *Philosophical Dictionary*, "Liberty of the Press," in *The Portable Age of Reason Reader*, ed. Crane Brinton (New York, 1956), 274.

165. Voltaire, Letter 13, "Letters on England," in *Philosophical Letters*, trans. and ed. Ernest Dilworth (Indianapolis, 1961), 58.

166. Malesherbes, "Discours de réception à l'Académie Française (1775)," *Malesherbes* (Paris, 1989), 92 (my translation).

167. Baker, *Inventing*, 188.

168. Chartier, "Écriture, publication et lecture dans l'Encyclopédie" discusses Jaucourt's two entries, "Lecteur" and "Lecture." In *Culture écrite et société* (Paris, 1996), 25–27 Chartier mentions media analysts such as Ong, Goody, et al.

169. See Chartier's analysis of Jaucourt's article on "Lecture." Here, as elsewhere, Rousseau took a contrary position, insisting that speech not writing was the only legitimate medium for use by a body politic. See Warner, *Letters*, 103 and relevant passages in Jacques Derrida, *Of Grammatology*, trans. Gayatri Spivak (Baltimore, 1977), 297–301.

170. Daniel Gordon, "Philosophy, Sociology and Gender in the Enlightenment Conception of Public Opinion," *French Historical Studies* 17, 4 (1992): 895.

171. Cited in Jean Starobinski, "Eloquence Antique, Eloquence Future," in *The French Revolution and the Creation of Modern Political Culture*, vol. 1, *The Political Culture of the Old Regime*, ed. Keith M. Baker et al. (Oxford, 1987), 322.

172. Green and Stallybrass, 66ff.

173. Benjamin Franklin, *Poor Richard's Almanac* (1735), cited in Warner, *Letters*, 189 n.10.

174. Ibid.

175. Larzer Ziff, *Writing in the Nation* (New Haven, 1991), 92, 94. Sandra Gustafson deals with this issue in detail in *Eloquence Is Power* (Chapel Hill, 2000).

176. Letter to Richard Price (1749) cited in Warner, *Letters*, 189 n.10.

177. Benjamin Franklin, *The Autobiography and Other Writings,* ed. L. Jesse Lemisch (New York, 1961), 119.

178. Archbishop du Perron (1580s), cited in Marc Fumaroli, "Rhetoric, Politics, and Society," trans. Ruth B. York in *Renaissance Eloquence*, ed. James J. Murphy (Berkeley, 1983), 255.

179. Montaigne, "De la vanité des paroles," cited in Fumaroli, 257.

180. This analysis does not allow for the "elocutionary revolution" described by Jay Fliegelman, *Declaring Independence* (Stanford, 1993), 28–35. As was demonstrated by Richardson, Rousseau and others, the art of speaking could be mimicked in writing with the aim of communicating not ideas or information but feelings and intentions. Plain writing that imitated plain speaking was a specialty of Tom Paine's.

181. Ziff, 101.

182. Verner Crane, *Benjamin Franklin's Letters to the Press, 1758–1775* (Chapel Hill, 1950), passim.

183. Palmer, *The Age of the Democratic Revolution*, 1: 250; Durand Echeverria, *Mirage in the West* (Princeton, 1957), 45–61.

184. Crane, *Benjamin Franklin's Letters to the Press*, 128.

185. Philip Davidson, *Propaganda and the American Revolution 1763–1783* (Chapel Hill, 1941), 15, cited in Warner, *Letters*, 68.

186. Warner, *Letters*, 67.

187. Ziff, 101.

188. Ibid.

189. On Washington's reluctance to speak and his awkward delivery that was interpreted as sincerity, see Gustafson, *Eloquence Is Power*, 222–23.

190. Bruce I. Granger, "Franklin as Press Agent in England," in *The Oldest Revolutionary*, ed. Joseph A. Leo LeMay (Philadelphia, 1976), 21–32.

191. Ziff, 88.

192. Knights, *Representation*, 65.

193. Robert Darnton, *The Literary Underground of the Old Regime* (Cambridge, 1982). On subsequent controversy see essays in Haydn T. Mason, ed., *The Darnton Debate* (Oxford, 1998).

194. Simon Burrows, *Blackmail, Scandal and Revolution* (Manchester, 2006).

195. Robert Darnton, *The Devil in the Holy Water, Or the Art of Slander from Louis XIV to Napoleon* (Philadelphia, 2009).

196. Burrows, 3.

197. On the "black hole of silence" regarding d'Holbach's authorial activities, see Eisenstein, *Grub Street Abroad*, 128–29.

198. Robert Chambers cited in James A. Secord, *Victorian Sensation* (Chicago, 2000), 367.

199. Eisenstein, *Press as Agent*, 274–78.

200. Didier Kahn, "The Rosicrucian Hoax in France," in *Secrets of Nature*, ed. Anthony Grafton and William R. Newman (Cambridge, 2001), 235–344.

201. Jay Fliegelman citing Peter Oliver, *Prodigals and Pilgrims* (Cambridge, 1982), 157.

202. Kevin Gilmartin, *Writing Against Revolution* (Cambridge, 2007), 4.

203. Edmund Burke, *Reflections on the Revolution in France* (Dublin, 1790), 167–68.

204. Edmund Burke, "On the Policy of the Allies" (1793), *Works of Edmund Burke*, 8 vols. (1889–1900) 3: 456–57. Cited by Seamus Deane, "Burke and the French Philosophes," *Studies in Burke and His Time* 10, 2 (Winter 1968–69): 1121 n.31. Deane points to connections between Burke and the secret society mythologists (Barruel and Robison) without differentiating between their two different views of "conspiracy" as undertaken by "men of letters" in general and by the Freemasons and Illuminati in particular.

205. Burke, *Reflections*, 167–68.

206. One was actually described as a "mute orator." See Elizabeth L. Eisenstein, "Tribune of the People: A New Species of Demagogue," in *The Press in the French Revolution*, ed. Harvey Chisick et al. (Oxford, 1991), 145–60; Eisenstein, "Le publiciste comme démagogue: *La sentinelle du peuple* de Volney," in *La révolution du journal, 1788–1794*, ed. Pierre Rétat (Paris, 1989), 189–97.

207. Brewer, *Party Ideology*, 166.

208. Dominique-Joseph Garat, *Mémoires historiques sur la vie de M. Suard, sur ses écrits, et sur le XVIIIe siècle* (Paris, 1820), 2: 91.

209. On the publication history of Paine's two-part pamphlet, *Rights of Man*, see

Tyson, *Joseph Johnson*, 122–27. Tyson also describes other replies to Burke (by Mary Woll-stonecraft, Joseph Priestley, et al.) that were published by Johnson. On the energetic promotion of Paine's work by the Society for Constitutional Information see Albert Goodwin, *The Friends of Liberty* (London, 1979), 176–78.

210. William Hazlitt, *The Life of Napoleon Buonaparte* (London, 1878), 1: 40; see 41–46 for an enthusiastic account of the press as emancipatory.

211. Burke, *Reflections*, 117.

212. Graham Wallas, *The Life of Francis Place, 1771–1854* (London, 1898), 61.

213. E. P. Thompson, *The Making of the English Working Class* (New York, 1966), 90.

214. Patrick Brantlinger, *The Reading Lesson* (Bloomington, 1998), 54.

215. *The Pernicious Effects of Printing*, discussed below, has a list of "Publications by D. I. Eaton on sale at 74 Newgate Street" placed between title page and texts. The list includes "An Address to the Hon. E. Burke from the Swinish Multitude," "Pearls cast before Swine," and several pamphlets recounting the court cases where Eaton stood trial (for publishing Tom Paine's works, among others). At the end of the list there's an offer to purchasers of Eaton's three trials of "A perfect likeness of D. I. Eaton," noting that "anyone purchasing two of the three may have one gratis."

216. *Politics for the People* 1: 1, cited in Olivia Smith, *Politics of Language* (Oxford, 1984), 80.

217. Printed for Daniel Isaac Eaton (London, 1794). I owe this reference to Margaret DeLacy.

218. A powerful abolitionist pamphlet that attacked the slave trade while urging a boycott of West Indian produce was issued in 1791 by William Fox, in collaboration with the Baptist bookseller Martha Gurney: "On the Propriety of Abstaining from the Use of West Indian Sugar and Rum" is said to have outsold Thomas Paine's *Rights of Man* while mobilizing readers (as consumers) in an effective boycott. Timothy Whelan, "William Fox, Martha Gurney and Radical Discourse of the 1790s," *Eighteenth Century Studies* 42, 3 (2009): 397–411

219. Gilmartin, 4.

220. Christopher Small, *The Printed Word* (Aberdeen, 1982), 79.

221. Gérard Walter, *Marat* (Geneva, 1977) 13, 22–23.

222. The important role played in Mirabeau's career by the exiles from the Genevan revolution and his stormy relationship to the Swiss financier Clavière, who helped Brissot, are discussed by Jean Bénétruy, *L'atelier de Mirabeau* (Geneva, 1962). See also Derek Jarrett, *The Begetters of Revolution* (Totowa, 1973).

223. Jacques-Pierre Brissot de Warville, *Mémoires, 1754–1793*, ed. C. L. Perroud, 2 vols. (Paris, n.d.) 1: 347–49, 363, 366, 372; also Eloise Ellery, *Brissot de Warville* (New York, 1970 [1915]), 24–25.

224. Ellery, 79–80.

225. Brissot, *Mémoire aux États-Generaux*, cited in Jeremy Popkin, "The Business of Political Enlightenment in France," paper presented at French Historical Studies Meeting, Lexington, Kentucky, 15 December 1990.

226. Gary Kates, *The "Cercle Social," the Girondins and the French Revolution* (Princeton, 1985).

227. Ibid., 178–79.

228. Frank E. Manuel, *The Prophets of Paris* (Cambridge, 1962), chaps. 1, 2.

229. See references to improvements in algebra, etc., in Condorcet, *Esquisse d'un tableau historique des progrès de l'esprit humain* (1793), ed. Monique Hincker and François Hincker (Paris, 1966), 193.

230. Cited in Keith M. Baker, *Condorcet* (Chicago, 1975), 298.

231. Carla Hesse, *Publishing and Cultural Politics in Revolutionary Paris* (Berkeley, 1991), 241.

232. Baker, *Condorcet*, 298.

233. Cited in Kates, 180.

234. Lüsebrink, "Hommage à l'écriture et éloge à l'imprimerie."

235. "Discours prononcé à la barre de l'Assemblée Nationale au nom des imprimeurs par Anacharsis Cloots, orateur du genre humain, le 9 Septembre, 1792, l'an IV de la Liberté et le 1er de l'égalité," in *Anacharsis Cloots*, ed. Michéle Duval (Paris, 1979), 391–96. The *Cercle Social* article of 4 October 1792, by Nicolas Boileau (cited in Kates, 180) echoes Cloots's remarks about Voltaire and Rousseau almost word for word.

236. Condorcet died as a prisoner of the Jacobins in April, 1794. After the fall of Robespierre (9 Thermidor), the surviving Girondins returned to favor and his *Esquisse* was published. Three thousand copies were distributed at the National Convention. It was translated into English as *Outlines of . . . the Progress of the Human Mind* (London, 1795). John Adams read it at least twice in 1798 and 1811 and wrote a 4,000-word commentary. Zoltán Haraszti, *John Adams and the Prophets of Progress* (New York, 1964 [1952]), 239–40.

237. Haraszti, 251–53. The views of John Adams in 1765 that are depicted by Michael Warner, *Letters*, 1 are quite different from those conveyed by his later marginalia.

238. Haraszti, 258.

239. Cited in James A. Secord, "Progress in Print," in *Books and the Sciences in History*, ed. Marina Frasca-Spada and Nicholas Jardine (Cambridge, 2000), 371–72.

CHAPTER 5. THE ZENITH OF PRINT CULTURE (NINETEENTH CENTURY)

Epigraph: Richard Altick, *The English Common Reader* (Columbus, 1998), 130.

1. Altick, 99.

2. On the enormous number of volumes comprising the Universal Catholic Library turned out in mid-century by abbé Migne, see R. Howard Bloch, *God's Plagiarist* (Chicago, 1994).

3. Gary Kates, *The Cercle Social, the Girondins and the French Revolution* (Princeton, 1985), 178–79; see Chapter 4, above.

4. There was an interval under the Directory when an opposition press run by the

"last Jacobins" flourished. On its resurgence and the leading role played by publisher René Vatar, see Isser Woloch, *Jacobin Legacy* (Princeton, 1970), 144–48.

5. Jeremy Popkin, *Revolutionary News* (Durham, 1990), 178.

6. Robert B. Holtman, *Napoleonic Propaganda* (Baton Rouge, 1950). See epigraphs.

7. Raymond, *Invention of the Newspaper*, 188. See also Holtman, chap. 3.

8. Napoleon to Marshal Berthier, writing from Saint Cloud, 5 August 1806. Napoleon, *Napoleon Self-Revealed*, trans. and ed. James M. Thompson (Boston, 1934), 154.

9. Holtman, 237.

10. John McManners, *The French Revolution and the Church* (London, 1970), 146–47. See below, n.38, on Chateaubriand.

11. James M. Thompson, *Napoleon Bonaparte* (Oxford, 1952), 97–99.

12. Guillame de Bertier de Sauvigny, *La restauration* (Paris, 1955), 446–47 gives figures for the production of both periodicals and books to show that the Restoration output was much larger than that of the Empire. His account differs from that of James Allen Smith, *In the Public Eye* (Princeton, 1991), 86, who says that the Restoration regime tightened the imperial decrees on the printed word. See also Irene Collins, *The Government and the Newspaper Press in France, 1814–1881* (Oxford, 1959), 9.

13. Martyn Lyons, *Le triomphe du livre* (Paris, 1987), 42–44 notes that despite the fears of Parisian printing workers who tried to smash the newly mechanized royal presses in 1830, industrialization of paper-making and printing came very gradually in France. See also relevant chapters in Roger Chartier and Henri-Jean Martin, eds., *Histoire de l'édition française*, vol. 3, *Du romantisme à la Belle Époque* (Paris, 1982).

14. Press laws were framed in accord with diverse interpretations of Article 8 of the Charter, promulgated by Louis XVIII in 1814. Article 8 is given by Bertier de Sauvigny, 93.

15. Daniel L. Rader, *The Journalists and the July Revolution in France* (The Hague, 1973), 17.

16. Darrin McMahon, *Enemies of the Enlightenment* (Oxford, 2001), 158. See also Lyons, chap. 5.

17. McMahon, 165.

18. See Chapter 4, above.

19. Thomas Paine, *Rights of Man*, ed. Philip Foner (Secaucus, N.J., 1974), pt. 1, 124. (On the first edition written as a response to Burke and published in London, 1791, see Foner, Introduction.)

20. Paine, *Rights of Man*, ed. Foner, 77.

21. Bertier de Sauvigny, 532.

22. See discussion, below, of Burke on traditional French provinces versus newly created départements.

23. Paine, *Rights of Man*, ed. Foner, 282.

24. Joseph de Maistre, *Considerations on France*, trans. Richard Lebrun (Cambridge, 1994), 50.

25. André Latreille and René Remond, *Histoire du catholicisme en France* (Paris,

1962), 3: 83–94, trans. and cited in Frank A. Kafker, James M. Laux, and Darlene Gay Levy, *The French Revolution*, 3rd ed. (Malabar, 1983), 92.

26. Benjamin Thurston, "Joseph de Maistre," Fourth International Symposium on Eurolinguistics, Croatia, 19–22 September 2002, *2000: The European Journal* 2 (2002): 2.

27. Frederick Artz, *Reaction and Revolution* (New York, 1953), 238. See Metternich's letter to Friedrich von Gentz, June 1819 on the need for sweeping censorship laws covering all the German states; such laws were soon to be incorporated in the Carlsbad Decrees. Cited in Mack Walker, ed., *Metternich's Europe* (New York, 1968), 61–69.

28. See McMahon, 164 on Lammenais, "Influence of Philosophic Doctrines upon Society."

29. Cited in Frederick Artz, *France Under the Bourbon Restoration, 1814–1830* (Cambridge, 1931), 83–84.

30. McMahon, 184.

31. See Chapter 4, above.

32. Victor Hugo, Preface to *Cromwell*, trans. G. B. Ives, cited in Eugen Weber, ed., *Paths to the Present* (New York, 1960), 51.

33. William Hazlitt, "Lectures on the English Poets" (1818), in *The Romantic Reader*, ed. Howard Hugo (New York, 1960), 61–82.

34. Jonathan Israel, "Enlightenment! Which Enlightenment?" *Journal of the History of Ideas* 67, 3 (2006): 523–45.

35. Raymond Williams, *Culture and Society, 1780–1950* (New York, 1983), 46.

36. Burke, *Reflections*, 80.

37. Excerpt from Chateaubriand, *The Genius of Christiantiy*, trans. C. I. White (1862), cited in *Romantic Reader*, ed. Howard E. Hugo, 340–41.

38. "Novalis" [Friederich von Hardenberg], *Christendom or Europe* (1799), cited in *Romantic Reader*, trans. Howard Hugo, 338.

39. Emerson, *Nature*, cited in *Romantic Reader*, ed. Howard Hugo, 386.

40. Howard Hugo, Introduction, *Romantic Reader*, 17.

41. William Wordsworth, "The Tables Turned," *Lyrical Ballads* (1798).

42. For an enthusiastic popular account of the Romantic contribution to "science" see Richard Holmes, *The Age of Wonder* (New York, 2008).

43. Patrick Brantlinger, *The Reading Lesson* (Bloomington, 1998), 16.

44. Raymond Williams, 36–38.

45. Mme. de Staël, *Concerning Germany*, cited in *Romantic Reader*, ed. Hugo, 64–65.

46. Adam Fox, *Oral and Literate Culture*, 7.

47. Jonathan Rose, *Intellectual Life of the British Working Classes* (New Haven, 2001), 25.

48. Fox, 6.

49. Sheila O'Connell, *The Popular Print in England, 1550–1850* (London, 1999), 18.

50. On Percy's influential *Reliques*, first published in three volumes in 1765, see Michael Alexander, *Medievalism* (New Haven, 2007), 16–23.

51. D. C. Somervell, *English Thought in the Nineteenth Century* (London, 1963 [1929]), 8–9.

52. Walter Scott, "Lay of the Last Minstrel," lines 19–22. Written in 1802–4, published in 1805, this six-canto poem is in *English Romantic Writers*, ed. David Perkins (New York, 1967), 376–78.

53. Richard Carlile, *Jail Journal*, ed. and comp. Guy. A. Aldred (Glasgow, 1942), 8. On Carlile, see below.

54. Rose, 40.

55. Mark Twain, *Life on the Mississippi* (New York, 1901 [1883]), chap. 46, "Enchantments and Enchanters," 327–28.

56. Justin Kaplan, *Mr. Clemens and Mark Twain* (New York, 1990), 298–99.

57. Ibid., 284.

58. Cited in Lewis Coser, *Men of Ideas* (New York, 1965), 55.

59. Mark A. Weinstein, general preface to *The Prefaces to the Waverley Novels* (Lincoln, 1998).

60. "Scott, Sir Walter," *Encyclopedia Britannica*, 11th ed. (Cambridge, 1911), 24: 469–75.

61. Walter Scott, *Waverley: or 'Tis Sixty Years Since*, 3 vols. in 2 (Philadelphia, 1821), 1: 29.

62. Ibid., 38.

63. Ibid., Postscript, 364.

64. Twain, *Life on the Mississippi*, 330.

65. Walter Reed, *An Exemplary History of the Novel* (Chicago, 1981), 89.

66. See Roger Chartier, *Inscription and Erasure*, trans. Arthur Goldhammer (Philadelphia, 2006), chap. 3.

67. James Campbell, "Coeur de Midlothian," Review of Murray Pittock, ed., *The Reception of Sir Walter Scott in Europe* (London, 2007), *Times Literary Supplement*, 10 August 2007, 32.

68. See Lyons, 131–44 for details along with publication figures. Lyons notes that the vogue lasted well into the middle of the century and describes its influence on the fiction of Balzac, Dumas, et al.

69. Theodore G. Striphas, *The Late Age of Print* (New York, 2009), 115 cites Janice Radway, *Reading the Romance* (Chapel Hill, 1991) in this connection. See Radway's treatment of "category publishing" as an innovation, 29–44.

70. Victor Hugo, "*Quentin Durward . . .* , par Sir Walter Scott," *Muse Française* (July 1823), in Hugo, *Oeuvres complètes*, ed. Jean Massin, 18 vols. (Paris, 1967), 2: 431–38.

71. Jacques Seebacher, Introduction to Victor Hugo, *Notre Dame de Paris*, ed. Seebacher (Paris, 1975), 1047–78.

72. Seebacher, Introduction to Hugo, *Notre Dame*, 1063.

73. Peter Lombard, *The Sentences* (Nuremberg, 1474).

74. Hugo, *Notre Dame*, ed. Seebacher, 259.

75. Umberto Eco, Afterword to *The Future of the Book*, ed. Geoffrey Nunberg (Berkeley, 1996), 10.

76. Frances A. Yates, *The Art of Memory* (Chicago, 1966), 131; Eisenstein, *Press as Agent*, 66.

77. Matthew Taunton, review of Jeff Gomez, *Print Is Dead*, *Times Literary Supplement*, 7 March 2008, 32.

78. Patricia Ward, *The Medievalism of Victor Hugo* (University Park, 1975), 11.

79. "Volney" was the pen name of a member of the Angevin gentry actually named Chasseboeuf. His variegated career as a voyager to Syria and Egypt, journalist who sparked one of the first uprisings of the French Revolution, deputy to the Constituent Assembly, Corsican administrator, and author of the international best-seller *Les ruines* deserves to be better known.

80. Lyons, 131.

81. Hugo, *Notre Dame*, ed. Seebacher, 177.

82. Ibid., 182.

83. On Marx's romantic view of "Printing House Square," see below.

84. Alphonse de Lamartine, *Gutenberg: inventeur de l'imprimerie*, 3rd ed. (Paris, 1867), (extracted from *Civilisateur*), 1–2.

85. Thomas Carlyle, "The Hero as Man of Letters" (1840), Lecture V, *On Heroes, Hero Worship and the Heroic in History* (Philadelphia, 1894), 220.

86. Hugo, *Notre Dame*, ed. Seebacher, 187.

87. Ibid., 188.

88. The opening night of *Hernani* (produced in 1830, a year after *Cromwell*) created a battle in the theater that had been planned and stage managed by the author and his friends. Artz, *France Under the Bourbon Restoration*, 324–26.

89. Hugo, *Notre Dame*, ed. Seebacher, 180.

90. Preface to *Cromwell* in *Paths to the Present*, ed. Weber, 44–45.

91. Hugo, *Notre Dame*, ed. Seebacher, Book 3, Chap. 1, 159.

92. Jacques Droz, *Europe Between Revolutions 1815–1848*, trans. Robert Baldick (New York, 1967), 107.

93. Ward, 21.

94. Henri-Jean Martin, "Comment," 20. On Nodier as leader of the first French Romantic school, see also Artz, *Bourbon Restoration*, 321–22.

95. This view, that printing retarded advances made by humanists by replicating earlier scholastic works, is reasserted most vigorously by Lynn Thorndike, *A History of Magic and Experimental Science*, vol. 5, 6 in 1, *The Sixteenth Century* (New York, 1941), passim, and also put forth by Lucien Febvre and Henri-Jean Martin, *L'apparition du livre* (Paris, 1958), 420–21.

96. Cited in Martin, "Comment," 21. See Charles Nodier, "De la perfectibilité . . . et de l'influence de l'imprimerie sur la civilisation," *Rêveries*, in *Oeuvres complètes* (Geneva, 1968 [1832–37]), vol. 5.

97. See Chapter 7, below, on Uzanne.

98. Martin, "Comment," 21.

99. Hugo, preface to *Cromwell*, in *Paths to the Present*, ed. Weber, 53.

100. Bertier de Sauvigny, *The Bourbon Restoration*, trans. Lynn M. Case (Philadelphia, 1966), 378–79.

101. Ibid., 381.

102. Rader, *Journalists*, 17.

103. Alexis Carrel, editor of the liberal newspaper *National* (along with Thiers and Mignet) and a prominent figure in the Revolution of 1830, wrote a book in 1827 about the Glorious Revolution: *Histoire de la contre-révolution en Angleterre* (translated into English by Hazlitt in 1846); see Rader, *Journalists*, 113. For a full account, see Geoffrey Cubitt, "The Political Uses of Seventeenth-Century English History in Bourbon Restoration France," *Historical Journal* 50, 1 (2007): 73–95.

104. *Mémoires de Louis-Philippe, duc d'Orléans, écrits par lui-même*, 2 vols. (Paris, 1973), 1: 4.

105. Oliver Larkin, *Daumier* (Boston, 1966), 14.

106. William Langer, *Political and Social Upheaval, 1832–1852* (New York, 1969), 81.

107. For full account, including German verses, see John Flood, "On Gutenberg's 600th Anniversary," *Journal of the Printing Historical Society* n.s. 1 (2000): 19–20.

108. Freidrich Engels, "On the Invention of Printing: A Poem," in *Gutenbergs-Album*, ed. Heinrich Meyer (Braunschweig, 1840).. http://www.marxists.org/archive/marx/works/1840/04/printing.htm, accessed June 16, 2009.

109. Cited in Flood, "On Gutenberg's 600th Anniversary," 19.

110. There is a reference in Prosper Marchand, *Histoire . . . de l'imprimerie* (The Hague, 1740) to Greek towns fighting over Homer's birthplace.

111. Ironically, in 1640 the German citizens of Strasbourg had anticipated the later French claims of the 1840s. They had celebrated the bicentennial by stressing German exceptionalism: they hailed the "marvelous art which neither the Chinese, nor the Italians, *nor the French*, nor even the Dutch . . . had been able to discover," (my emphasis). They were acclaiming Mentelin, rather than Gutenberg, as the inventor. Glomski, 334.

112. Henri Jouin, *David d'Angers* (Paris, 1878), 2 vols., passim.

113. Martin, "Comment," 23–24.

114. Robert Ranc, "Strasbourg—1840 quatrième centenaire de Gutenberg," *Gutenberg Jahrbuch* (1973): 148.

115. Cited in Ranc, 146, my translation.

116. Martin, "Comment," 24.

117. Anonymous. "Black and White," Review of Gerhard Beier, *Schwarze Kunst und Klassenkampf* (*Black Art and Class War*), *Times Literary Supplement*, July 13, 1967, 612.

118. Alphonse de Lamartine, *Histoire des girondins* (Paris, 1848).

119. Lamartine, *Gutenberg*.

120. See Chapter 6, below.

121. See Frank O'Gorman, "The Paine Burnings of 1792–1793," *Past and Present* 193 (2006): 111–55 for full account of these rituals.

122. Altick, *Common Reader*, 72–3.

123. J. C. D. Clark, *English Society 1688–1832* (Cambridge, 1985), 246.

124. Ibid.

125. Brantlinger, 6.

126. Ibid., 57.

127. Altick, 104.

128. G. H. Spinney, cited in ibid., 75.

129. Ibid., 104–5.

130. Patricia Hollis, *Class and Class Conflict in Nineteenth Century England, 1815–1850* (London, 1973), 144. On Knight, see also below.

131. Elie Halévy, *England in 1815* (London, 1924), 393.

132. William H. Wickwar, *The Struggle for the Freedom of the Press 1819–1832* (London, 1928), describes the two new press laws contained in the Six Acts of 1819.

133. See Rose, 22–29.

134. Joel H. Wiener, *The War of the Unstamped* (Ithaca, 1969), 2.

135. E. P. Thompson, *The Making of the English Working Class* (New York, 1966), 107–8. In an appendix on Paine's works, St. Clair questions "exaggerated" estimates while acknowledging that the circulation was "unusually wide." William St. Clair, *The Reading Nation in the Romantic Period* (Cambridge, 2004), App. 9, 623–24. The first parts of the *Age of Reason* (Paine's polemic against Christianity) were also printed in the 1790s and cost its printer, Daniel Eaton, jail time. See Chapter 4, above.

136. Clark, *English Society*, 381.

137. Altick, 327.

138. Carlile in *The Republican*, v. 279 (1 March 1822), cited in Wickwar, 214–15.

139. Carlile in *The Republican* vii. 683, cited in Wickwar, 75.

140. St. Clair, 27.

141. Olivia Smith, *The Politics of Language, 1791–1819* (Oxford, 1984), 196–200.

142. E. P. Thompson, 767. For a different view of Carlile as a piratical publisher who cut a "foppish" figure in the streets of London and took elaborate precautions against government spies, while spending nineteen years in prison, see St. Clair, 312–13.

143. Wickwar, 95–96.

144. Ibid., 87.

145. Hollis, 209.

146. *Poor Man's Guardian*, 16 July 1831, cited in Geoffrey A. Cranfield, *Press and Society* (London, 1978), 128.

147. Cited in Secord, "Progress in Print," 371–72.

148. Gabriel Rummonds, *Nineteenth Century Printing Practices and the Iron Hand Press*, 2 vols. (Oak Knoll, 2004); Rummonds, *Printing on the Iron Hand Press* (Oak Knoll, 1998); James Moran, *Printing Presses* (Berkeley, 1973), 39ff.

149. Celina Fox, "Political Caricature and the Freedom of the Press in Early Nineteenth Century England," in *Newspaper History from the Seventeenth Century to the Present Day*, ed. George Boyce et al. (London, 1978), 232–35.

150. BM no. 15776 (30 May 1829), reproduced by Celina Fox in Boyce et al., eds., 232, and Secord, "Progress in Print," fig 20.1, 371.

151. On the industrialization of papermaking and printing in France, see Fréderic Barbier, "L'industrialization des techniques," in *Histoire de l'édition*, ed. Henri-Jean Martin and Roger Chartier, 3: 56–68.

152. Secord, "Progress in Print," 370. See also James A. Secord, *Victorian Sensation* (Chicago, 2000) for a detailed account of the printing, publishing, and reception of an early nineteenth-century bestseller.

153. See, e.g., Charles Knight, *William Caxton, The First English Printer*, Facsimile (London, 1976 [1844]).

154. Charles Knight, *The Old Printer and the Modern Press* (London, 1854), 335; see also chap. 21, 323–44 on the invention of printing.

155. Chambers, *Edinburgh Journal* (June 6, 1835), cited in Secord, "Progress in Print," 374.

156. Altick, 130.

157. Louis Dudek, *Literature and the Press* (Toronto, 1960), 161.

158. Altick, 310.

159. Brantlinger, 19.

160. Lamartine, *Gutenberg*, n.p.

161. Altick, 129–30.

162. Simon Maccoby, *English Radicalism, 1786–1832* (London, 1955), 462 cites the issue of June 3, 1827.

163. *Sartor Resartus, Carlyle's Complete Works* (Boston, 1884), 1; Chap. V, lines 26–30 (first serialized in *Frazer's Magazine*, 1833–34).

164. Cited in Dudek, 175.

165. Altick, 131.

166. Thomas Love Peacock, *Crotchet Castle* (London, 1831; rev. 1837).

167. Wiener, *War of the Unstamped*, 229–31.

168. Wickwar, 247, citing from James Mill's article on "Liberty of the Press" for the *Encyclopedia Britannica*, 5th ed. (London, 1821).

169. John Stuart Mill, *Autobiography* (London, 1874), 96.

170. Altick, 131; see also Wiener, 33–35.

171. Cranfield, 194.

172. Wiener, 276.

173. Altick, 341.

174. Secord, *Victorian Sensation*, 173.

175. Isaac d'Israeli, *Isaac d'Israeli on Books*, ed. Martin Spevack (New Castle, 2004), 120.

176. Knight, *William Caxton*, Postscript, 235.

177. Henry Hetherington, cited in Valerie Gray, *Charles Knight* (Aldershot, 2006), 58.

178. Hollis, 20–21.

179. Altick, 133. Samuel Johnson shared Bentham's distaste for poetry and fiction; see Robert DeMaria, Jr. *Johnson's Dictionary* (Chapel Hill, 1986), 288–89.

180. Carlyle, "The Hero as Man of Letters," 235–60.

181. Mill, *Autobiography*, 118.

182. Ibid., 125.

183. Ibid., 125–26.

184. Ibid., 136–37.

185. Ibid., 138.

186. Williams, 100.

187. Ibid., 101–2.

188. Altick, 150.

189. Lewis Mumford, *Technics and Civilization* (New York, 1963 [1934]), 136–37.

190. Charles Knight, *Knowledge Is Power* (London, 1855), 317–18.

191. Knight, *The Old Printer and the Modern Press* (dedication, 14 April 1854).

192. Carlyle, "Hero as Man of Letters," 207.

193. Laurel Brake, *Print in Transition, 1850–1910* (Basingstoke, 2001), 53.

194. Karl Marx, *Preface to the Critique of Political Economy* (1859), in *Selected Works*, 2 vols. (London, 1942), 1:502–6.

195. Knight, *Old Printer Modern Press*, 287.

196. Secord, "Progress in Print," 375.

197. St. Clair, *Reading Nation*, 332.

198. David Perkins, *English Romantic Writers* (New York, 1967), 171.

199. St. Clair, *Reading Nation*, 332.

200. Paul Bénichou, *Le sacre de l'écrivain* (Paris, 1973).

201. Jaucourt's *Encyclopédie* story about Robert Estienne's "perfect" proofread editions was accepted at face value by Isaac d'Israeli, *Books*, 52; see Chapter 4, above.

202. Brantlinger, 198.

203. Walker was a printer and typographer who gave a talk to the arts and crafts exhibit at the New Gallery on Regent Street on 15 November 1888.

204. Brantlinger, 198.

205. William Peterson, Introduction to William Morris, *The Ideal Book*, (Berkeley, 1982), xvi.

206. Altick, 139–40.

207. See Chapter 4 on labeling incunables.

208. George Gissing, *New Grub Street: A Novel*, 3 vols. (London, 1891), 2: 70.

209. Bill Bell, "Fiction in the Market Place," in *Serials and Their Readers*, ed. Robin Myers and Michael Harris (New Castle, 1993), 128.

210. Sainte-Beuve, "De la littérature industrielle," *Revue des Deux Mondes* 4th ser. 19 (Paris): 675–91.

211. See Dudek, 139, and Alvin Kernan, *Printing, Technology, Letters, and Samuel Johnson* (Princeton, 1987), 303–10.

212. César Grana, *Bohemian Versus Bourgeois* (New York, 1964), 56.

213. Halévy, *England in 1815*, 450 describes Balzac as "Scott's successor and disciple."

214. According to Christine Haynes, "An 'Evil' Genius," *French Historical Studies* 30, 4 (Fall 2007): 559–97, portrayals of publishers in early nineteenth-century France were more nuanced than the Balzacian stereotype suggests.

215. Robert Darnton, *The Business of Enlightenment* (Cambridge, 1979), 393.

216. The exception is Charles-Joseph Pancoucke (1736–98), a press baron *avant la lettre* who owned seventeen different journals at the time of the '89 revolution. See Suzanne Tucoo-Chala, *Charles-Joseph Pancoucke et la librairie française* (Paris, 1977).

CHAPTER 6. THE NEWSPAPER PRESS: THE END OF BOOKS

Epigraph: Walter Lippmann, *Liberty and the News* (New York, 1920), 47.

1. Thomas Carlyle, "The Hero as Man of Letters," Lecture V, in *On Heroes, Hero Worship and the Heroic in History* (Philadelphia, 1894), 219.

2. Cited in William St. Clair, *The Reading Nation* (Cambridge, 2004), 309.

3. See Eisenstein, *Grub Street Abroad*, 8–13.

4. Laurel Brake, "The Trepidation of the Spheres: Serial and Book in the Nineteenth Century," in *Serials and Their Readers, 1620–1914*, ed. Robin Myers and Michael Harris (New Castle, 1993), 83–101.

5. Jeremy Popkin citing and translating Pierre-Louis Roederer, *Revolutionary News* (Durham, 1990), 3.

6. Pierre Rétat, "Forme et discours d'un journal révolutionnaire: les révolutions de Paris en 1789," in *L'instrument périodique*, ed. Claude Labrosse, Pierre Rétat, and Henri Duranton (Lyon, 1985), 139–78.

7. Cited in Jeremy Popkin, "The Newspaper Press in French Political Thought," in *Studies in Eighteenth Century Culture*, vol. 10, ed. Harry Payne (Madison, 1981), 127.

8. Jack R. Censer, *Prelude to Power* (Baltimore, 1976), 9; see Table 1.

9. Cited in Eugene Hatin, *Histoire politique et littéraire de la presse en France*, 8 vols. (Paris, 1859–60), 4: 16.

10. Jeremy Popkin, *News and Politics in the Age of Revolution* (Ithaca, 1989).

11. Some 27 journals were being published in Paris in the 1780s, with fourteen foreign papers also in circulation; Hugh Gough, *The Newspaper Press in the French Revolution* (Chicago, 1988), 5. The smaller population of London was being served by at least 85 newspapers in 1760; Robert R. Rea, *The English Press in Politics 1760–1774* (Lincoln, 1963), 7.

12. Rea, 5.

13. Thomas B. Macaulay, *History of England from the Accession of James II*, 2 vols. (1848), 2: chap. 21, cited in James Raven, *The Business of Books* (New Haven, 2007), 86.

14. Ibid.

15. Thomas Babington Macaulay, *History of England from the Accession of James the Second*, 5 vols. (New York, 1849–61), 5: 12–13. This five-volume edition differs from the two-volume one cited in Raven in that it refers to a "licensing act," not act(s).

16. Cited in Raven, 208.

17. Jacob Burckhardt, *The Civilization of the Renaissance in Italy*, trans. S. G. C. Middlemore, 2 vols. (New York, 1958) 1: 170–71.

18. "Aretino's Postures" is the English title assigned to his "Sonnetti Lussuriosi"—

sonnets that accompanied the drawings of sixteen positions (*i modi*) assumed by a heterosexual couple engaged in intercourse. The drawings by Giuliano Romano were engraved by Marcantonio Raimondi for the first edition of 1524 and recopied endlessly thereafter.

19. See Chapter 4, above, regarding Burrows.

20. Paul Grendler, *Critics of the Italian World* (Madison, 1969).

21. See Eisenstein, *Press as Agent*, 394–99.

22. A. G. Dickens, *Reformation and Society in Sixteenth-Century Europe* (New York, 1966), 28.

23. See John J. McCusker, "European Bills of Entry . . . the Origins of the Business Press," *Harvard Library Bulletin* 33 (Summer 1983): 209–56; "The Demise of Distance: The Business Press and the Origins of the Information Revolution," *American Historical Review* 110, 2 (April 2005): 295–320.

24. Joseph Klaits, *Printed Propaganda Under Louis XIV* (Princeton, 1976), 6–7.

25. See essays in Nicolas Russell and Hélène Visentin, eds., *French Ceremonial Entries in the Sixteenth Century* (Toronto, 2007).

26. Folke Dahl, *Dutch Corantos: 1618–1650* (The Hague, 1946). On precursors in Elizabethan London, see Paul J. Voss, *Elizabethan News Pamphlets* (Pittsburgh, 2001).

27. Many other relevant satires are illustrated and described in two Folger Library exhibition catalogues: Elizabeth Walsh, Lu Ellen De Haven and Theresa Helein, eds., *Yesterday's News* (Washington, 1996); and Chris Kyle and Jason Peacey, *Breaking News* (Washington, 2008).

28. D. F. McKenzie, "*The Staple of News* and the Late Plays," in McKenzie, *Making Meaning*, ed. Peter D. McDonald and Michael F. Suarez (Boston, 2002), chap. 7, 197. See also Roger Chartier, *Inscription and Erasure* (Philadelphia, 2006), chap. 4.

29. Julie Stone Peters, *Congreve, the Drama, and the Printed Word* (Stanford, 1990), 10–11. On larger questions pertaining to playwriting, performance, and print see her prize-winning later work: *Theatre of the Book 1480–1880* (Oxford, 2000).

30. James Sutherland, *The Restoration Newspaper and Its Development* (Cambridge, 1986), 97.

31. Christopher Small, *The Printed Word* (Aberdeen, 1982), 73.

32. Theodore Zeldin, *France 1848–1945*, 2 vols. (Oxford, 1977), 2: 439–40; Zeldin is translating from Claude Bellanger et al., *Histoire générale de la presse française*, 4 vols. (Paris, 1969–76), 1: 159, 439.

33. Eisenstein, *Grub Street Abroad*, 139–44.

34. On the changed meaning of this term in eighteenth-century France, see Keith Baker, "French Political Thought at the Accession of Louis XVI," *Journal of Modern History* 50 (June 1978): 290.

35. Camille Desmoulins (1789), trans. from *Révolutions de France et de Brabant* (1789), no. 2; Gough, *Newspaper Press*, 36.

36. Zeldin, 494. Relevant nineteenth-century German and Russian (as well as French) developments are covered by James Billington, *Fire in the Minds of Men* (New York, 1980); see especially chap. 11, "Journalism: The Magic Medium," 306–24.

37. Billington, 314.

38. Bellanger et al., 2: 114, 141.

39. Ibid., 141.

40. *J'accuse* was published on the front-page cover of *L'Aurore* (13 January 1898).

41. Tom Morley, "'The Times' and the Concept of the Fourth Estate," *Journal of Newspaper and Periodical History* 1, 3 (1985): 16.

42. Charles Knight, *The Old Printer and the Modern Press* (London, 1854), pt. 2, chap. viii, 290.

43. Thomas Carlyle, *The French Revolution* (1837) in *The Complete Works*, 3, 2 vols. chap. 4, 304.

44. Carlyle, "Hero as a Man of Letters," 219.

45. According to John Clive, *Not by Fact Alone* (New York, 1989), 46, Macaulay was the first to apply the term to the press, in his essay of 1828 on Hallam's *Constitutional History*.

46. Oscar Wilde, *The Soul of Man Under Socialism* (1908 [1895]), in *The Complete Works of Oscar Wilde*, ed. Josephine M. Guy et al. (Oxford, 2007), 255.

47. Douglas Cater, *The Fourth Branch of Government* (Boston, 1959).

48. Carlyle, *The French Revolution*, 305.

49. Louis Blanc, *Histoire de la révolution française*, 2nd ed. (Paris, 1864), 3: chap. 6, 115–16, 122–23; my translation.

50. John Stuart Mill, *On Liberty* (1859), ed. Albury Castell (New York, 1947), 66.

51. Oswald Spengler, *The Decline of the West*, trans. C. F. Atkinson, 2 vols. (New York, 1928 [1918]), 2: 463.

52. Cited in George Boyce, "The Fourth Estate: Reappraisal," in *Newspaper History*, ed. Boyce et al. (London, 1978), 19.

53. From *New York Herald*, 31 August 1835, cited in Frank Luther Mott, *American Journalism* (New York, 1941), 232–23.

54. *New York Herald*, 28 February 1837; cited in ibid., 229.

55. Cited in ibid., 308.

56. Cited in ibid., 310–11.

57. William Makepeace Thackeray, *The History of Pendennis*, in *The Works of William Makepeace Thackeray*, 13 vols. (London, 1898), 2: chap. 30, 301–2.

58. Cited in John Gross, *The Rise and Fall of the Man of Letters* (New York, 1969), 22–23.

59. Before completing his major two-volume antisemitic work *La France juive* (1886), Edward Drumont had published an article that accused the Jews of "destroying honest journalism and impoverishing native French journalists." Robert F. Byrnes, *Antisemitism in Modern France* (New Brunswick, 1950), 1: 147.

60. See Norman Cohn, *Warrant for Genocide* (New York, 1966), app. II, 277, for texts run in parallel columns from the twelfth dialogue of Joly and the twelfth Protocol.

61. Maurice Joly, *Dialogue aux Enfers entre Machiavel et Montesquieu*, 1st ed. (Brussels, 1864); *The Dialogue in Hell Between Machiavelli and Montesquieu*, trans. and ed. John S. Waggoner (Lanham, 2003), 70–71.

62. The emperor's repressive press policies are summarized in Bellanger et al., 2: 249–83; Zeldin, 2: 547.

63. Joly, *The Dialogue in Hell,* 70–71.

64. Boyce, 19.

65. Trollope, *The Warden* (London and New York, 1902), chap. 14, 227ff. See also chap. 7, "*The Jupiter.*" Cited in Boyce, 19.

66. Gough, 219–20.

67. Cited in David C. Somervell, *English Thought in the Nineteenth Century* (New York, 1940), 56.

68. Cited in Anthony Smith, *The Newspaper* (London, 1979), 102.

69. Karl Bücher, "Die Deutsche Tagespresse Presse und die Kritik," in *Gesammelte Aufsätze zur Zeitungskunde* (1926 [1917]), 377, cited in K. T. Winkler, "The Forces of the Market and the London Newspaper in the First Half of the Eighteenth Century," *Journal of Newspaper and Periodical History* 4, 2 (Spring 1988): 28.

70. See references to Chomsky et al. in Mark Hampton, *Visions of the Press in Britain, 1850–1950* (Urbana, 2004), 3.

71. Theophile Gautier, preface to *Mademoiselle de Maupin (texte complet)* (Paris, 1966 [1834]), 1–39.

72. Ibid.

73. Wordsworth, Preface to *Lyrical Ballads* (1802), in *Paths to the Present,* ed. Eugen Weber (New York: 1960), 21.

74. Louis Dudek, *Literature and the Press* (Toronto, 1960), 47 n.26.

75. Here, as elsewhere, there were eighteenth-century precursors. Swiss physician Samuel-August Tissot linked excessive reading to solitary pleasures and to mental instability caused by masturbation. Chartier, *Inscription,* chap. 7, 113. See also Thomas Laqueur on reading and masturbation, *Solitary Sex* (New York, 2003).

76. Isaac Ray, *Mental Hygiene* (Boston, 1863), 233, 237.

77. Brantlinger, 2.

78. See, e.g., KIPP (Knowledge Is Power Program) schools in Washington, D.C.

CHAPTER 7. TOWARD THE SENSE OF AN ENDING (FIN DE SIÈCLE TO THE PRESENT)

Epigraph: John Gross, *The Rise and Fall of the Man of Letters* (New York, 1969), 232.

1. Carlton J. H. Hayes, *A Generation of Materialism* (New York, 1941), 171–80.

2. Anthony Smith, *The Newspaper* (London, 1979), 143.

3. Ibid. That the modern newspaper had "reduced the dimensions of an entire country to those of an ancient agora" was also asserted by Elie Halévy, *England in 1815* (London, 1924), 149.

4. Patrick Brantlinger, *The Reading Lesson* (Bloomington, 1998), 23.

5. Richard Altick, *The English Common Reader* (Columbus, 1998), 368.

6. See Chapter 6, above.

7. George Boyce, "The Fourth Estate: Reappraisal," in *Newspaper History*, ed. Boyce et al. (London, 1978), 36.

8. John Theobald, *The Media and the Making of History* (Aldershot, 2004), chap. 1.

9. G. M. Young, *Victorian England: Portrait of an Age* (New York, 1954 [1936]), 187.

10. Michel de Montaigne, *The Complete Essays of Montaigne*, trans. and ed. Donald M. Frame (Stanford, 1958), 106.

11. Edward Gibbon, *The Decline and Fall of the Roman Empire*, 3 vols. (1776–89); New York, 1932), 2: chap. 39, 440–42. See also Chapter 3, above (on Wotton).

12. See Chapter 1.

13. Constantine Cavafy, "Waiting for the Barbarians," trans. Edmund Keeley (1904), in *Collected Poems*, trans. Keeley and Philip Sherrard, ed. Georgios P. Savvides (Princeton, 1992), 18–19.

14. George Mosse, *The Crisis of German Ideology* (New York, 1971 [1964]), chaps. 4, 9.

15. Sigfrid Steinberg, *Five Hundred Years of Printing*, 3rd ed. (Harmondsworth, 1974), 306.

16. See Flood, "On Gutenberg's 600th Anniversary."

17. Thomas Laqueur, *Solitary Sex: A Cultural History of Masturbation* (New York, 2003). See also Chapter 6, above (on Tissot).

18. Alfred Austin in the 1880s, cited in Brantlinger, 23.

19. George Gissing, *New Grub Street*, cited in Brantlinger, 194.

20. Brantlinger, 193.

21. Gerhard Masur, *Prophets of Yesterday* (New York, 1961), 15.

22. Cited in Brantlinger, 205.

23. Hayes, *Generation of Materialism* is in the Harvard series, The Rise of Modern Europe, ed. W. Langer. See esp. chap. 7, "Seed-Time of Totalitarian Nationalism," 242–84.

24. Brantlinger, 23.

25. Marshall McLuhan, *The Mechanical Bride* (New York, 1951), 7.

26. Lewis B. Namier, *1848: The Revolution of the Intellectuals* (London, 1964), 110 invokes Benda's "La trahison des clercs" to describe German opposition to Czechs and Poles at the Frankfurt Assembly.

27. See John Morley, *The Life of Richard Cobden* (Boston, 1881); G. M. Trevelyan, *The Life of John Bright* (Boston, 1913).

28. Julien Benda, *The Treason of the Intellectuals* (*La trahison des clercs*) (Paris, 1927), trans. Richard Aldington (New York, 1928), 182.

29. Leo Tolstoy, "That most powerful of ignorance's weapons—the dissemination of printed matter," in *War and Peace*, trans. Ann Dunnigan (New York, 1968), 1440–41.

30. Steinberg, 174.

31. Eisenstein, *Press as Agent*, 362–67.

32. Steinberg, 174.

33. See Chapter 6, above, regarding Carlyle and Louis Blanc.

34. Oswald Spengler, *The Decline of the West*, trans. C. F. Atkinson, 2 vols. (New York, 1928 [1st German ed. 1918]), 2: 461.

35. Octave Uzanne, "The End of Books," illustrated by A. Robida, *Scribner's Magazine Illustrated* (Jul.–Dec. 1894): 221–31.

36. Willa Z. Silverman, "Books Worthy of Our Era? Octave Uzanne, Technology, and the Luxury Book in *Fin de siècle* Paris," *Book History* 7 (2004): 239–84. Among other works, Uzanne authored *The Book Hunter in France: Studies Among the Bookstalls and the Quays*, English trans., Preface Augustine Birrell (London, 1895). I owe thanks to William Barker, Department of English, Memorial University of Newfoundland, for introducing me to Uzanne.

37. On Nodier, see Chapter 5, above, regarding Hugo's companion at the coronation of Charles X.

38. See Chapter 5, above, regarding Morris.

39. According to William S. Peterson, Morris was not a complete purist in his efforts to revive fifteenth-century printing craft, for he also made use of the new technology of photography as an instrument of design. "Tradition and Innovation in Fine Printing," paper presented at a Forum at the Bard Graduate Center, New York, 26 March, 2007.

40. Silverman, 279 notes that Uzanne helped Eduard Drumont find a printer for his virulent, antisemitic *La France juive*. Unlike Maurras, who was a Voltairean skeptic, Uzanne was a devout Catholic (279n.). On the other hand, in his book on transportation, *La locomotion à travers l'histoire et les moeurs* (Paris, 1900), 268–72, he envisioned a utopian future in the twentieth century when trains, bicycles, and family cars would have replaced horse-driven carriages; peaceful commerce between nations would prevail; and prejudice, patriotism, and militarism would have been relegated to the past.

41. By introducing the title of Walter Benjamin's often cited essay I wanted to hint at an affinity between the fin-de-siècle French bibliophile and the mid-twentieth-century German-Jewish connoisseur. At least some of Uzanne's works, such as *The Book Hunter*, seem likely to have been read by Benjamin.

42. Uzanne, "End of Books," 223.

43. Ibid.

44. Marjorie Hope Nicolson, *Voyages to the Moon* (New York, 1960 [1948]), 265 notes that Godwin's book was translated into four languages; 25 editions were issued between 1638 and 1768.

45. Roger Chartier, *Inscription and Erasure* (Philadelphia, 2006), chap. 5, 94.

46. Ibid., 94.

47. Ibid., 63–64.

48. No. 83 (October 1894): 351.

49. Ibid.

50. Geoffrey Nunberg, introduction to *The Future of the Book*, ed. Nunberg (Berkeley, 1996), 10. See also, in the same collection, Paul Duguid, "Material Matters: The Past and Futurology of the Book," esp. "Part 2: The Supersession of the Book," 66ff.

51. In many libraries, hand-copying of sections of printed books by note-takers persisted even after the advent of the photocopier.

52. Curt Bühler, *The Fifteenth-Century Book* (Philadelphia, 1960), 26.

53. See Chapter 6, above.

54. See Chapter 5, above.

55. The completion of the tower of Strasbourg Cathedral was celebrated in 1839–40, together with the unveiling of the statue of Gutenberg; Robert Ranc, "Strasbourg—1840 quatrième centenaire de Gutenberg," *Gutenberg Jahrbuch* (1973): 144.

56. See the idiosyncratic interpretation of *Ivanhoe* noted in chapter 5, above, discussed by Jonathan Rose.

57. James A. Cochrane, *Dr. Johnson's Printer* (Cambridge, 1964), 19n.

58. Ted Striphas, *The Late Age of Print* (New York, 2009), 181–82.

59. Uzanne, "End of Books," 230–31.

60. Filippo Tommaso Marinetti, "Futuristic Manifesto," in *Paths to the Present*, ed. Eugen Weber (New York, 1960), 244–45.

61. Steinberg, 190.

62. See Stephen Bury, ed., *Breaking the Rules: The Printed Face of the European Avant-Garde, 1900–1937* (London, 2007).

63. Brantlinger, 207.

64. Brantlinger, 207–9. The essay of 1917 entitled "Mr. Bennett and Mrs. Brown" first appeared in *The Criterion* and was published by the Woolfs on their Hogarth Press in 1924.

65. *New Age*, December 1910. See Margaret Drabble, "A Lost Art: The Modernist in Arnold Bennett," *Times Literary Supplement*, 21/28 August 2009, 18–19.

66. Drabble, 18–19.

67. Cited in Brantlinger, 208–9.

68. Promotion and marketing of Woolf's books were handled by a long line of competent professional women hired by the Hogarth Press. See Alice Staveley, "Marketing Virginia Woolf," *Book History* 12 (2009): 295–340.

69. Peter Keating, cited in Brantlinger, 207.

70. Gross, *Rise and Fall*, 212.

71. Ibid.

72. Eric Bulson, Review of Suzanne W. Churchill and Adam McKible, eds., *Little Magazines and Modernism* (Aldershot, 2007), *Times Literary Supplement*, 13 February 2009, 32.

73. Janice Radway, *A Feeling for Books* (Chapel Hill, 1991), 70.

74. Richard Terdiman, *Discourse/Counter-Discourse* (Ithaca, 1985), 122, cited in Geoffrey Nunberg, "The Places of Books in the Age of Electronic Reproduction," *Representations* 42 (Spring 1993): 36 n.20.

75. Mike Esbester, "Nineteenth-Century Timetables and the History of Reading," *Book History* 12 (2009): 156–85.

76. McLuhan, *Understanding Media* (New York, 1964), 219.

77. Walter Ong, *The Presence of the Word* (New Haven, 1967), chap. 4, 191.

78. On Blake's affiliation with the pro-Jacobin circle around Joseph Johnson, see

Gerald P. Tyson, "Joseph Johnson, an Eighteenth Century Bookseller," *Studies in Bibliography* 28 (1975): 12–15.

79. Brantlinger, 209–10.

80. Roy Rosenzweig, "Scarcity or Abundance? Preserving the Past in a Digital Era," *American Historical Review* 108 (June 2003): 757.

81. Kathryn Harrison, Review of Lisa Appignanesi, *Mad, Bad and Sad Women and the Mind Doctors, New York Times Sunday Book Review*, 27 April 2008, 13.

82. John Schwartz, "Thinking May Not Be All It's Thought to Be," *New York Times*, 16 January 2005, 12.

83. Ian Donaldson, "The Destruction of the Book," in *Book History*, vol. 1, ed. Ezra Greenspan (University Park, 1998), 8. This estimate probably concerns all printed copies rather than all published titles. With regard to the latter, Robert Darnton, *The Case for Books: Past Present, and Future* (New York, 2009), xiv, cites Bowker's *Global Books in Print* that 700,000 new titles appeared worldwide in 1998 and 976,000 in 2007. He says, "soon a million new books will be published every year." UNESCO's "Worldometer Counter" gives a total of 1,004,725 as of November 2009. Whatever calculation is used, the figures do not suggest declining output.

84. Ibid.

85. Ibid., 7.

86. Henry Fielding in 1752, with reference to Ovid, cited in ibid., 6.

87. As these numerous citations show, I am indebted to Donaldson's article even while noting a need to distinguish more clearly between fear of neglect, recycling, and total destruction.

88. Donaldson, "Destruction," 4.

89. See Chapter 5, above.

90. Donaldson, "Destruction," 7.

91. Blair, *Too Much to Know*, 3.

92. John Brewer, *The Pleasures of the Imagination* (New York, 1997), 190. Brewer is referring to the "Multitude of Books" section in Chambers's *Cyclopaedia* of 1738.

93. Daniel Rosenberg, "Early Modern Information Overload," *Journal of the History of Ideas* 64, 1 (2003): 9.

94. James Raven, *The Business of Books* (New Haven, 2007), 46.

95. Elizabeth L. Eisenstein, "Clio and Chronos," *History and Theory Beiheft: History and the Concept of Time* 6 (1966): 62.

96. Spenser, *Faerie Queene*, Book I, Canto I, 20–22.

97. Ashley Surdin, "In Some Classrooms, Books Are a Thing of the Past," *Washington Post*, 19 October 2009, 3A.

98. Ben Kafka, "Paperwork: The State of the Discipline." *Book History* 12 (2009): 351.

99. Sven Birkerts, *The Gutenberg Elegies* (New York, 1994), 192.

100. Alfred de Musset, *The Confession of a Child of the Century* (New York, 1836); trans. (New York: Bigelow and Smith, 1905), excerpts in *Romantic Reader*, ed. Howard Hugo (New York, 1960), 95.

101. Benedict Anderson, *Imagined Communities* (New York, 1999), 34–35.

102. On the threat posed to newspapers by radio newscasts see Gwenyth L. Jackaway, *Media at War: Radio's Challenge to the Newspapers 1924–1939* (Westport, 1995).

103. Nicholson Baker, *Double Fold* (New York, 2001).

104. Brad Stone, "Amazon Erases Orwell Books from Kindle," *New York Times*, 18 July 2009. I owe thanks to Matthew Pagett for alerting me to this Kindle episode.

105. Monica Hesse, "Notoriety's Missing Links: Online Files Scrubbed After Museum Shooting" *Washington Post*, Friday, 12 June 2009, C5.

106. Paul Duguid, "Saving Paper," Review of Gary Hall, *Digitize This Book*, *Times Literary Supplement*, 31 July 2009, 5.

107. Cory Doctorow cited in Matthew Taunton, "Immortal Pages," review of Jeff Gomez, *Print Is Dead*, *Times Literary Supplement*, 7 March 2008.

108. For present-day provisional guidance, see Darnton, *The Case for Books*.

109. Radway, *Feeling for Books*, 47–48.

110. On the terms "literary" and "literature," see David Scott Kastan, "Humphrey Moseley and the Invention of English Literature" in *Agent of Change* ed. Sabrina A. Baron et al. (Amherst, 2007), 105–12.

111. Chris Snyder, "Google Settles Book-Scan Lawsuit, Everybody Wins," *Wired.com*, 28 October 2008; see also Nicholas Carr, "Is Google Making Us Stupid?" *Atlantic Monthly* (July/August 2008), www.theatlantic.com/doc/200807/google.

112. Emily Walshe, "Kindle e-Reader: A Trojan Horse for Free Thought," *Christian Science Monitor*, 18 March 2009, http://www.csmonitor.com/2009/0318/p09s01-coop.html

Bibliography

Achinstein, Sharon. *Literature and Dissent in Milton's England.* Cambridge: Cambridge University Press, 2003.

AHR Forum: "How Revolutionary Was the Print Revolution?" *American Historical Review* 107, 1 (February 2002): 84–128.

Alexander, Michael. *Medievalism: The Middle Ages in Modern England.* New Haven, Conn.: Yale University Press, 2007.

Allen, James Smith. *In the Public Eye: A History of Reading in Modern France 1800–1940.* Princeton, N.J.: Princeton University Press, 1991.

Allen, P. S. *The Age of Erasmus.* Oxford: Oxford at the Clarendon Press, 1914.

Altick, Richard. *The English Common Reader: A Social History of the Mass Reading Public, 1800–1900.* Columbus: Ohio State University Press, 1998.

Amerbach, Johannes. *The Correspondence of Johann Amerbach.* Selected, trans., and ed. with commentary by Barbara C. Halporn. Ann Arbor: University of Michigan Press, 2000.

Anderson, Benedict. *Imagined Communities: Reflections on the Origin and Spread of Nationalism.* New York: Verso, 1999.

Andrews, William Eusebius. *A Critical and Historical Review of Fox's* [sic] *Book of Martyrs.* 2 vols. London: M. Andrews, 1853.

Anonymous. "Black and White." Review of Gerhard Beier, *Schwarze Kunst und Klassenkampf* (*Black Art and Class War*). *Times Literary Supplement,* July 13, 1967, 612.

Arblaster, Paul. Review of Joad Raymond, ed., *News, Newspapers and Society in Early Modern Britain* (London: Cass, 1999). *Sharp News* 110, 3 (Summer 2001): 6.

Arbuthnot, John, Alexander Pope, Jonathan Swift, John Gay, Thomas Parnell, and Robert Harley (Earl of Oxford). *Memoirs of the Extraordinary Life, Works, and Discoveries of Martinus Scriblerus, written in Collaboration by the Members of the Scribbler's Club.* Ed. Charles Kerby-Miller. New Haven, Conn.: Yale University Press, 1950.

Armstrong, Adrian. *Technique and Technology: Script, Print and Poetics in France 1470–1550.* Oxford: Oxford University Press, 2000.

Armstrong, Elizabeth. *Before Copyright: The French Book-Privilege System, 1498–1526.* Cambridge: Cambridge University Press, 1990.

Arnold, Klaus. *Johannes Trithemius*: Quellen und Forschungen zur Geschichte des Bistums und Hochstifts Würzburg 23. Ed. Theodor Kramer. Würzberg: F. Schöningh, 1971.

Artz, Frederick. *France Under the Bourbon Restoration, 1814–1830*. Cambridge, Mass.: Harvard University Press, 1931.

———. *Reaction and Revolution, 1814–1832*. New York: Harper, 1953.

Aspinall, Arthur. *Politics and the Press c. 1780–1850*. London: Home and Van Thal, 1949.

Aston, Margaret. "John Wycliffe's Reformation Reputation." *Past and Present* (1965): 23–51. Reprinted in Margaret Aston, *Lollards and Reformers: Images and Literacy in Late Medieval Religion*. London: Hambledon Press, 1984.

———. "Lollardry and the Reformation: Survival and Revival." *History* (1964): 149–70. Reprinted in Margaret Aston, *Lollards and Reformers: Images and Literacy in Late Medieval Religion*. London: Hambledon Press, 1984.

Atkins, Stuart. "Motif in Literature: The Faust Theme." In *Dictionary of the History of Ideas*, ed. Philip Wiener et al. New York: Scribner, 1973.

Atkinson, Geoffroy. *Les nouveaux horizons de la renaissance française*. Paris: Droz, 1935.

Atkyns, Richard. *Original* [sic] *and Growth of Printing*. Whitehall: Printed by John Streater, April the 25th, 1664.

Aubrey, John. *Three Prose Works*. Ed. John Buchanan Brown. Sussex: Centaur Press, 1972.

Avrin, Leila. *Scribes, Script, and Books: The Book Arts from Antiquity to the Renaissance*. Chicago: American Library Association, 1991.

Bacon, Francis. *The Advancement of Learning* (1605). In *Advancement of Learning and Novum Organum*, trans. and ed. J. E. Creighton. New York: Willey, 1944.

———. *Francis Bacon: A Selection of His Works*. Ed. Sidney Warhaft. New York: Odyssey Press, 1965.

———. *The Letters and the Life of Francis Bacon Including All His Occasional Works*. Ed. James Spedding. London: Longman, Green, Longman and Roberts, 1861.

———. *The New Organon*. Ed. Lisa Jardine and Michael Silverthorne. Cambridge: Cambridge University Press, 2000.

Bagchi, David V. N. *Luther's Earliest Opponents: Catholic Controversialists, 1518–1525*. Minneapolis: Fortress Press, 1991.

Baines, Paul and Pat Rogers. *Edmund Curll, Bookseller*. Oxford: Oxford University Press, 2007.

Baker, Keith M. *Condorcet: From Natural Philosophy to Social Mathematics*. Chicago: University of Chicago Press, 1975.

———. "French Political Thought at the Accession of Louis XVI." *Journal of Modern History* 50 (June 1978): 279–303.

———. *Inventing the French Revolution*. Cambridge: Cambridge University Press, 1990.

Baker, Nicholson. *Double Fold: Libraries and the Assault on Paper*. New York: Random House, 2001.

Balsamo, Luigi. *Bibliography: History of a Tradition*. Trans. W. A. Pettas. Berkeley, Calif.: Bernard M. Rosenthal, 1990.

———. "Technologia e capitali." In *Studi offerti a Roberto Ridolfi direttore de la bibliofilia*. Biblioteca di Bibliografia Italiana 71. Florence: Olshki, 1973.

Baratin, Marc and Christian Jacob, eds. *Le pouvoir des bibliothèques: la mémoire des livres dans l'Occident*. Paris: A. Michel, 1996.

Barber, Giles. *Book Making in Diderot's "Encyclopédie": A Facsimile Reproduction of Articles and Plates*. Farnborough: Gregg Division McGraw-Hill, 1973.

Barbier, Frédéric. "L'industrialization des techniques." In *Histoire de l'édition française*, ed. Henri-Jean Martin and Roger Chartier, vol. 3, *Du romantisme à la Belle Époque*, 56–68. Paris: Promodis, 1982.

Barker, Nicholas. "A Contemporary Panegyrist of the Invention of Printing." In *Incunabula: Studies in Fifteenth-Century Printed Books Presented to Lotte Hellinga*, ed. Martin Davies. London: British Library, 1999.

Baron, Sabrina A. "Licensing Readers, Licensing Authorities." In *Books and Readers in Early Modern England*, ed. Jennifer Andersen and Elizabeth Sauer. Philadelphia: University of Pennsylvania Press, 2002.

Baron, Sabrina A., Eric N. Lindquist, and Eleanor F. Shevlin, eds. *Agent of Change: Print Culture Studies After Elizabeth L. Eisenstein*. Amherst: University of Massachusetts Press, 2007.

Basnage de Beauval, Henri. *Histoire des ouvrages des savans de la Grande-Bretagne*. 24 vols. 1678–1709. Geneva: Slatkine, 1969.

Beal, Peter. *In Praise of Scribes: Manuscripts and Their Makers in Seventeenth-Century England*. Oxford: Clarendon Press, 1998.

Beard, Mary. "Scrolling Down the Ages." *New York Times Book Review*, Sunday, 16 April 2009, 27.

Belin, Jean Paul. *Le commerce des livres prohibés à Paris de 1750 à 1789*. Paris: Belin Frères, 1913.

Bell, Bill. "Fiction in the Market Place." In *Serials and Their Readers, 1620–1914*, ed. Robin Myers and Michael Harris. New Castle, Del.: Oak Knoll Press, 1993.

Bellanger, Claude, Jacques Godechot, Pierre Guiral, and Fernand Terrou, eds. *Histoire générale de la presse française*. 4 vols. Paris: Presses Universitaires de France, 1969.

Benda, Julien. *The Treason of the Intellectuals (La trahison des clercs)*. Trans. Richard Aldington. New York: Norton, 1928. [Paris: Grasset, 1927]

Bénétruy, Jean. *L'atelier de Mirabeau*. Geneva: A. et J. Picard, 1962.

Bénichou, Paul. *Le sacre de l'écrivain*. Paris: Corti, 1973.

Bennett, H. S. *English Books and Readers, 1475 to 1557; 1558 to 1603; 1603 to 1640*. 3 vols. Cambridge: Cambridge University Press, 1969; 1965; 1970.

Berry, Mary Elizabeth. *Japan in Print: Information and Nation in the Early Modern Period*. Berkeley: University of California Press, 2007.

Bertier de Sauvigny, Guillaume de. *The Bourbon Restoration*. Trans. Lynn Case. Philadelphia: University of Pennsylvania Press, 1966.

———. *La restauration*. Paris: Flammarion, 1955.

Betteridge, Tom. "From Prophetic to Apocalyptic: John Foxe and the Writing of History." In *John Foxe and the English Reformation*, ed. David Loades. Aldershot: Ashgate, 1997.

Bigmore, E. C. and C. W. H. Wyman. *A Bibliography of Printing, with Notes and Illustrations*. 2 vols. London: B. Quaritch, 1881.

Billington, James. *Fire in the Minds of Men.* New York: Basic Books, 1980.

Birkerts, Sven. *The Gutenberg Elegies.* New York: Faber and Faber, 1994.

Black, Joseph, ed. *The Martin Marprelate Tracts: A Modernized and Annotated Edition.* Cambridge: Cambridge University Press, 2008.

———. "The Rhetoric of Reaction: The Martin Marprelate Tracts (1588–89), Anti-Martinism and the Uses of Print in Early Modern England." *Sixteenth Century Journal* 28 (Fall 1997): 707–25.

Black, Scott. "Social and Literary Form in the *Spectator*." *Eighteenth Century Studies* 33, 1 (1999): 21–42.

Blair, Ann. "Annotating and Indexing Natural Philosophy." In *Books and the Sciences in History*, ed. Marina Frasca-Spada and Nicholas Jardine. Cambridge: Cambridge University Press, 2000.

———. "Reading Strategies for Coping with Information Overload, ca. 1550–1700." *Journal of the History of Ideas* 64, 1 (2003): 11–28.

———. *Too Much to Know: Managing Scholarly Information Before the Modern Age.* New Haven, Conn.: Yale University Press, 2010.

Blakey, Dorothy. *The Minerva Press, 1790–1820.* London: Printed for the Bibliographical Society at the University Press, Oxford, 1939.

Blanc, Louis. *Histoire de la révolution française*, 12 vols. Paris: Furne et Cie., 1847–62.

Bloch, R. Howard. *God's Plagiarist.* Chicago: University of Chicago Press, 1994.

Bloom, Edward A. "Johnson on a Free Press: A Study in Liberty and Subordination." *English Literary History* 16, 4 (1949): 251–57.

Blount, Charles and John Milton. *A Just Vindication of Learning: Or, An Humble Address to the High Court of Parliament in Behalf of the Liberty of the Press*, by "Philopatris" (London: [s.n.], 1679). In *The Harleian Miscellany*, ed. William Oldys. London: Printed for Robert Dutton, 1810.

Bodin, Jean. *Method for the Easy Comprehension of History.* Trans. Beatrice Reynolds. New York: Columbia University Press, 1966 [1945].

Bond, Donald F., ed. *The Spectator.* 5 vols. Oxford: Clarendon Press, 1965.

Bond, William. *Thomas Hollis of Lincoln's Inn: A Whig and His Books.* Cambridge: Cambridge University Press, 1990.

Booty, John E., ed. *The Book of Common Prayer, 1559: The Elizabethan Prayer Book.* Charlottesville: Published for the Folger Shakespeare Library by the University Press of Virginia, 1976.

Bossy, John. *Christianity in the West, 1400–1700.* Oxford: Oxford University Press, 1985.

Botein, Stephen. "'Meer Mechanics' and an Open Press." *Perspectives in American History* 9 (1975): 127–275.

Bots, Hans and Lenie van Lieshout, *Contribution à la connaissance des réseaux d'information au début du XVIIIe siècle.* Amsterdam: APA, 1984.

Bottigheimer, Ruth. "Bible Reading, 'Bibles', and the Bible for Children in Early Modern Germany." *Past and Present* 139 (1993): 66–80.

Bourgain, Pascale. "L'édition des manuscrits." In *Histoire de l'édition française*, ed. Henri-Jean Martin and Roger Chartier, vol. 1, *Le livre conquérant*. Paris: Promodis, 1982.

Bouwsma, William. *Concordia Mundi: The Career and Thought of Guillaume Postel (1510–1581)*. Cambridge, Mass.: Harvard University Press, 1957.

Boyce, George, James Curran, and Pauline Wingate, eds. *Newspaper History from the Seventeenth Century to the Present Day*. London: Constable, 1978.

Bracciolini, Poggio and Nicolaus de Niccolis. *Two Renaissance Book Hunters: The Letters of Poggius Bracciolini to Nicolaus de Niccolis*. Trans. and ed. Phyllis Walter Goodhart Gordan. New York: Columbia University Press, 1974.

Brack, O. M., Jr., and Mary Early. "Samuel Johnson's Proposals for the *Harleian Miscellany*." *Studies in Bibliography* 45 (1992): 127–30.

Brake, Laurel. *Print in Transition, 1850–1910*. Basingstoke: Palgrave, 2001.

———."The Trepidation of the Spheres: Serial and Book in the Nineteenth Century." In *Serials and Their Readers, 1620–1914*, ed. Robin Myers and Michael Harris. New Castle, Del.: Oak Knoll Press, 1992. 83–101.

Brann, Noel. *The Abbott Trithemius 1462–1516: The Renaissance of Monastic Humanism*. Leiden: Brill, 1981.

Brant, Sebastian. *The Ship of Fools (Narrenschiff)*. Trans. and ed. Edwin H. Zeydel. New York: Dover, 1962 [New York: Columbia University Press, 1944].

Brantlinger, Patrick. *The Reading Lesson: The Threat of Mass Literacy in Nineteenth-Century British Fiction*. Bloomington: Indiana University Press, 1998.

Braudy, Leo. *The Frenzy of Renown: Fame and Its History*. Oxford: Oxford University Press, 1986.

Bredvold, Louis. "The Gloom of the Tory Satirists." In *Pope and His Contemporaries: Essays Presented to George Sherburn*, ed. James L. Clifford and Louis A. Landa, 1–19. Oxford: Oxford University Press, 1949.

———. *The Intellectual Milieu of John Dryden*. 1934. Ann Arbor: University of Michigan Press, 1966.

Brewer, John. *Party Ideology and Popular Politics at the Accession of George III*. Cambridge: Cambridge University Press, 1976.

———. *The Pleasures of the Imagination: English Culture in the Eighteenth Century*. New York: HarperCollins, 1997.

Bricker, Charles, Gerald R. Crone, and R. V. Tooley, eds. *Landmarks of Mapmaking: An Illustrated Survey of Maps and Mapmakers*. Amsterdam: Elsevier, 1968.

Briggs, Asa. *The Age of Improvement, 1783–1867*. London: Longman, 1959.

Briggs, Asa and Peter Burke. *A Social History of the Media: From Gutenberg to the Internet*. Cambridge: Polity Press, 2002.

Brissot de Warville, Jacques-Pierre. *Mémoires, 1754–1793*. Ed. C. L. Perroud. Paris: [s.i.].

Brokaw, Cynthia. "Book History in Premodern China: The State of the Discipline I." *Book History* 10 (2007): 253–90.

Brooks, Douglas. *From Playhouse to Printing House: Drama and Authorship in Early Modern England*. Cambridge: Cambridge University Press, 2000.

Brooks-Davies, Douglas. *Pope's Dunciad and the Queen of the Night: A Study in Emotional Jacobitism*. Manchester: Manchester University Press, 1985.

Brown, Cynthia. *Poets, Patrons, and Printers: Crisis of Authority in Late Medieval France.* Ithaca, N.Y.: Cornell University Press, 1995.

Brown, Laura. *Alexander Pope.* Rereading Literature. Oxford: Blackwell, 1985.

Browne, Thomas. "To the Reader," *Religio Medici* (1643). In *Prose of Sir Thomas Browne,* ed. Norman Endicott. Garden City, N.Y.: Anchor, 1967.

Bücher, Karl. "Die Deutsche Tagespresse und die Kritik." In *Gesammelte Aufsätze zur Zeitungskunde,* 307–390. 1917. Tübingen: Laup, 1926.

Bühler, Curt. *The Fifteenth-Century Book: The Scribes, the Printers, the Decorators.* Philadelphia: University of Pennsylvania Press, 1960.

Bulson, Eric. Review of Suzanne W. Churchill and Adam McKible, eds., *Little Magazines and Modernism* (Aldershot: Ashgate, 2008). *Times Literary Supplement* (13 February 2009): 32.

Burckhardt, Jacob. *The Civilization of the Renaissance in Italy.* 2 vols. Trans. S. G. C. Middlemore. New York: Harper and Row, 1958.

Burke, Edmund. *Reflections on the Revolution in France.* Dublin: Printed for W. Watson, [etc.], 1790.

———. "Remarks on the Policy of the Allies with Respect to France" (1793). In *The Works of Edmund Burke,* 20 vols. Vol. 3, *Political Miscellanies.* London: George Bell, 1896.

Burke, Peter. *A Social History of Knowledge: From Gutenberg to Diderot.* Oxford: Blackwell, 2000.

Burnett, A. D. "The Engraved Title Page of Bacon's *Instauratio Magna*: An Icon and Paradigm of Science and Its Wider Implication." Thomas Harriot Seminar Occasional Paper 27. Durham: Historical Education Project, 1998.

Burrows, Simon. *Blackmail, Scandal and Revolution: London's French Libellistes 1758–1792.* Manchester: Manchester University Press, 2006.

Bury, J. B. *The Idea of Progress: An Inquiry into Its Origin and Growth.* London: Macmillan, 1920.

Bury, Stephen, ed. *Breaking the Rules: The Printed Face of the European Avant-Garde, 1900–1937.* London: British Library, 2007.

Butler, A. J. "Dante." *Encyclopædia Britannica,* vol. 7. 11th ed. New York: Cambridge University Press, 1910.

Butler, E. M. *The Fortunes of Faust.* Cambridge: Cambridge University Press, 1979.

Butler, Pierce. *The Origin of Printing in Europe.* Chicago: University of Chicago Press, 1940.

Byrnes, Robert F. *Antisemitism in Modern France.* New Brunswick, N.J.: Rutgers University Press, 1950.

Camille, Michael. "Seeing and Reading: Some Visual Implications of Medieval Literacy and Illiteracy." *Art History* 8, 1 (March, 1985): 26–49.

Campbell, James. "Coeur de Midlothian." Review of Murray Pittock, ed., *The Reception of Sir Walter Scott in Europe* (London: Continuum, 2007). *Times Literary Supplement,* 10 August 2007, 32.

Carayol, Elisabeth. *Thémiseul de Saint Hyacinthe 1684–1746.* Studies on Voltaire and the Eighteenth Century 221. Oxford: Voltaire Foundation, 1984.

Carlile, Richard. *Jail Journal: Prison Thoughts and Other Writings*. Ed. and comp. Guy A. Aldred. Glasgow: Strickland Press, 1942.

Carlyle, Thomas. *Carlyle's Complete Works*. 20 vols. Boston: Dana Estes and Charles E. Lauriat, 1884.

———. *The French Revolution: A History*. 2 vols., (1837) in *Complete Works*.

———. "The Hero as Man of Letters" (1840), Lecture V. In *On Heroes, Hero-Worship, and the Heroic in History*. Philadelphia: Henry Altemus, 1894.

Carpo, Mario. *Architecture in the Age of Printing: Orality, Writing, Typography, and Printed Images in the History of Architectural Theory*. Trans. Sarah Benson. Cambridge, Mass.: MIT Press, 2001.

Carr, Nicholas. "Is Google Making Us Stupid?" *Atlantic Monthly* (July/August 2008): 56–63.

Cater, Douglass S.. *The Fourth Branch of Government*. Boston: Houghton Mifflin, 1959.

Cavafy, Constantine. *Collected Poems*. Trans. Edmund Keeley and Philip Sherrard, ed. Georgios P. Savvides. Princeton, N.J.: Princeton University Press, 1992.

Cavallo, Guglielmo and Roger Chartier, eds. *A History of Reading in the West*. Trans. Lydia G. Cochrane. Amherst: University of Massachusetts Press, 1999.

Censer, Jack R. *Prelude to Power: The Parisian Radical Press, 1789–1791*. Baltimore: Johns Hopkins University Press, 1976.

Chakravorty, Swapan and Abhijit Gupta, eds. *Print Areas: Book History in India*. Delhi: Permanent Black, 2004.

Chartier, Roger. "Before and After Gutenberg: A Conversation with Roger Chartier." In *The Book and the Computer: Book Culture at the Crossroads*, Online Symposium, 30 April 2002. http://www.honco.net/os/chartier.html, accessed 25 May 2002.

———. *Culture écrite et société*. Paris: Albin Michel, 1996.

———. "Écriture, publication et lecture dans l'Encyclopédie." In *L'Encyclopédie: du réseau au livre et du livre au réseau*, ed. Robert Morrissey and Philippe Roger. Paris: Champion, 2001.

———. *Inscription and Erasure: Literature and Written Culture from the Eleventh to the Eighteenth Century*. Trans. Arthur Goldhammer. Philadelphia: University of Pennsylvania Press, 2006.

———. *L'ordre des livres*. Paris: Alinéa, 1992.

Clark, J. C. D. *English Society 1688–1832*. Cambridge: Cambridge University Press, 1985.

Clark, William. "On the Bureaucratic Plots of the Research Library." In *Books and the Sciences in History*, ed. Marina Frasca-Spada and Nicholas Jardine. Cambridge: Cambridge University Press, 2000.

Clarke, Arthur C. *Profiles of the Future: An Inquiry into the Limits of the Possible*. New York: Popular Library, 1962.

Claudin, Anatole. *The First Paris Press, an account of the books printed for G. Fichet and J. Heynlin in the Sorbonne, 1470–1472*. London: Printed for the Bibliographical Society at the Chiswick Press, 1898.

Clegg, Cyndia S. *Press Censorship in Elizabethan England*. Cambridge: Cambridge University Press, 1997.

Clive, John. *Not by Fact Alone: Essays on the Writing and Reading of History.* New York: Knopf, 1989.

Cloots, Anacharsis. "Discours prononcé à la barre de l'Assemblée Nationale au nom des imprimeurs par Anacharsis Cloots, orateur du genre humain, le 9 Septembre, 1792, l'an IV de la liberté et le 1er de l'égalité." In *Anacharsis Cloots: écrits révolutionnaires 1790–1794*, ed. Michéle Duval. Paris: Champ Libre, 1979.

Cochrane, James A. *Dr. Johnson's Printer: The Life of William Strahan.* Cambridge, Mass.: Harvard University Press, 1964.

Cohn, Norman. *Warrant for Genocide: The Myth of the Jewish World Conspiracy and the Protocols of the Elders of Zion.* New York: Harper and Row, 1966.

Colclough, David. *Freedom of Speech in Early Stuart England.* Cambridge: Cambridge University Press, 2005.

Cole, Juan R. I. "Printing and Urban Islam in the Mediterranean World, 1890–1920." In *Modernity and Culture from the Mediterranean to the Indian Ocean*, ed. Leila Tarazi Fawaz, C. A. Bayly, and Robert Ilbert, 344–64. New York: Columbia University Press, 2001.

Colley, Linda. *Britons: Forging the Nation 1707–1837.* New Haven, Conn.: Yale University Press, 1992.

Collins, Irene. *The Government and the Newspaper Press in France, 1814–1881.* London: Oxford University Press, 1959.

Collinson, Patrick. "John Foxe and National Consciousness." In *John Foxe and His World*, ed. Christopher Highley and John N. King, 10–36. Aldershot: Ashgate, 2002.

Como, David R. "Secret Printing, the Crisis of 1640, and the Origins of Civil War Radicalism." *Past and Present* 196 (2007): 37–82.

Condorcet, Jean-Antoine-Nicolas de Caritat. *Esquisse d'un tableau historique des progrès de l'esprit humain.* 1793. Ed. Monique Hincker and François Hincker. Paris: Éditions Sociales, 1966.

Contat, Nicolas. *Anecdotes typographiques: où l'on voit la description des coutumes, moeurs et usages singuliers des compagnons imprimeurs* (1762). Ed. Giles Barber. Oxford: Oxford Bibliographical Society, 1980.

Coser, Lewis. *Men of Ideas.* New York: Free Press, 1965.

Cowan, Brian. "Mr. Spectator and the Coffeehouse Public Sphere." *Eighteenth Century Studies* 37 (2004): 345–66.

Crain, Caleb. "Twilight of the Books." *New Yorker* 83, 31 (24 December 2007): 134–39.

Crane, Verner. *Benjamin Franklin's Letters to the Press, 1758–1775.* Chapel Hill: University of North Carolina Press, 1950.

Cranfield, Geoffrey A. *Press and Society: From Caxton to Northcliffe.* London: Longman, 1978.

Cressy, David. *England on Edge: Crisis and Revolution 1640–1642.* Oxford: Oxford University Press, 2006.

Cru, R. Loyalty. *Diderot as a Disciple of English Thought.* New York: Columbia University Press, 1913.

Cubitt, Geoffrey. "The Political Uses of Seventeenth-Century English History in Bourbon Restoration France." *Historical Journal* 50, 1 (2007): 73–95.

Curtius, Ernst. *European Literature and the Latin Middle Ages.* Trans. Willard R. Trask. New York: Harper & Row, 1953.

Dahl, Folke. *Dutch Corantos, 1618–1650: A Bibliography.* The Hague: Koninklijke, 1946.

D'Alembert, Jean Le Rond. *Preliminary Discourse to the Encyclopedia of Diderot.* Trans. Richard N. Schwab. Indianapolis: Bobbs-Merrill, 1963.

Darnton, Robert. *The Business of Enlightenment: A Publishing History of the Encyclopédie, 1775–1800.* Cambridge, Mass.: Harvard University Press, 1979.

———. *The Case for Books: Past, Present, and Future.* New York: PublicAffairs, 2009.

———. *The Devil in the Holy Water, Or the Art of Slander from Louis XIV to Napoleon.* Philadelphia: University of Pennsylvania Press, 2009.

———. "The Heresies of Bibliography." Review article. *New York Review of Books*, 29 May 2003.

———. *The Literary Underground of the Old Regime.* Cambridge, Mass.: Harvard University Press, 1982.

Davidson, Philip. *Propaganda and the American Revolution 1763–1783.* Chapel Hill: University of North Carolina Press, 1941.

Davies, David W. *The World of the Elseviers, 1580–1712.* The Hague: Nijhoff, 1954.

Davies, Martin, "Juan de Carvajal and Early Printing." *The Library* 6th ser. 18 (1996): 193–215.

———. "Making Sense of Pliny in the Quattrocento." *Renaissance Studies* 9 (1995): 240–57.

Davis, Hugh H. Review of Silvia Rizzo, *Il lessico filologico degli umanisti. Renaissance Quarterly* 28 (Autumn 1975): 353.

Davis, Natalie Z. *Society and Culture in Early Modern France: Eight Essays.* Stanford, Calif.: Stanford University Press, 1975.

Deane, Seamus. "Burke and the French Philosophes." *Studies in Burke and His Time* 10, 2 (Winter 1968–69): 113–37.

De Bury, Richard. *Philobiblon.* Ed. Michael Maclagan, trans. E. C. Thomas. Oxford: Blackwell, 1959.

Defoe, Daniel. *History of the Devil.* London: For T. Warner, 1727.

De Frede, Carlo. "Entusiasmi umanistici e allarmi ecclesiastico-politici per l'invenzione della stampa." In *Ricerche per la storia della stampa e la diffusione delle idee riformate nell'Italia del Cinquecento.* Naples: De Simone, 1985.

De Grazia, Margareta. "Imprints: Shakespeare, Gutenberg, Descartes." In *Alternative Shakespeares*, vol. 2, ed. Terence Hawkes, 63–94. New York: CRC Press, 1996.

De Maistre, Joseph. *Considerations on France.* Trans. Richard Lebrun. Cambridge: Cambridge University Press, 1994.

DeMaria, Robert, Jr. *Johnson's Dictionary and the Language of Learning.* Chapel Hill: University of North Carolina Press, 1986.

———. *The Life of Samuel Johnson.* Cambridge, Mass.: Blackwell, 1993.

De Renzi, Silvia, ed. *Instruments in Print: Books from the Whipple Collection*. Cambridge: Whipple Museum of the History of Science, 2000.

Derrida, Jacques. *Of Grammatology*, trans. Gayatri Spivak. Baltimore: Johns Hopkins University Press, 1977.

Descartes, René. *A Discourse on Method*. Trans. John Veitch, intro. A. N. Lindsay. London: J.M. Dent, 1946.

Destutt de Tracy, Antoine Claude. *A Commentary and Review of Montesquieu's "Spirit of the Laws."* Trans. Thomas Jefferson. Philadelphia: William Duane, 1811. New York: Burt Franklin, 1969.

De Vinne, Theodore L. *The Invention of Printing: A Collection of Facts and Opinions*. New York: F. Hart, 1878.

Dickens, A. G. *Reformation and Society in Sixteenth Century Europe*. New York: Harcourt Brace, 1966.

Diderot, Denis. *Encyclopedia Selections*. Trans. and ed. Nelly S. Hoyt and Thomas Cassirer. New York: Macmillan, 1965.

Diderot, Denis and Jean Le Rond d'Alembert, eds. *Encyclopédie ou dictionnaire raisonné des sciences, des arts et des métiers*. 14 vols. Paris: Briasson, 1751–1772.

D'Israeli, Isaac. *Isaac d'Israeli on Books: Pre-Victorian Essays on the History of Literature*. Ed. Martin Spevack. New Castle, Del.: Oak Knoll Press, 2004.

Di Strata, Filippo. *Polemic Against Printing*. Ed. and Intro. Martin Lowry, trans. Shelagh Grier. Birmingham: Hayloft Press, 1986.

Diu, Isabelle. "Medium typographicum et respublica literaria: le rôle de Josse Bade dans le monde de l'édition humaniste." In *Le livre et l'historien: études offertes en l'honneur de professeur Henri-Jean Martin*, ed. Frédéric Barbier et al. Geneva: Droz, 1997: 111–25.

Donaldson, Ian. "The Destruction of the Book." *Book History* 1, 1 (1998): 1–10.

———. *Jonson's Magic Houses: Essays in Interpretation*. Oxford: Oxford University Press, 1997.

Downie, James A. *Robert Harley and the Press: Propaganda and Public Opinion in the Age of Swift and Defoe*. Cambridge: Cambridge University Press, 1979.

Drabble, Margaret. "A Lost Art—The Modernist in Arnold Bennett." *Times Literary Supplement*, 21/28 August 2009, 18–19.

Drogin, Marc. *Anathema! Medieval Scribes and the History of Book Curses*. Totowa, N.J.: Allanheld, Osmun, 1983.

Droz, Jacques. *Europe Between Revolutions 1815–1848*. Trans. R. Baldick. London: Harper and Row, 1967.

Dudek, Louis. *Literature and the Press*. Toronto: Contact Press, 1960.

Duguid, Paul. "Material Matters: The Past and Futurology of the Book." In *The Future of the Book*, ed. Geoffrey Nunberg. Berkeley: University of California Press, 1996.

———. "Saving Paper." Review of Gary Hall, *Digitize This Book*. *Times Literary Supplement*, 31 July 2009, 5.

Dukes, Paul and John Dunkley, eds. *Culture and Revolution*. London: Pinter, 1990.

Dunn, R. D., ed. "Fragment of an Unpublished Essay on Printing by William Camden." *British Library Journal* 12 (1986): 145–49.

Dureau, Jeanne Marie. "Les premiers ateliers français." In *Histoire de l'édition française*, ed. Henri-Jean Martin and Roger Chartier, vol. 1, *Le livre conquérant*. Paris: Promodis, 1983.

Eaton, Daniel. *The Pernicious Effects of the Art of Printing Upon Society Exposed.* London: Printed for Daniel Isaac Eaton, 1794.

Ebel, J. G. "Translation and Cultural Nationalism in the Reign of Elizabeth." *Journal of the History of Ideas* 30, 4 (1969): 593–602.

Echeverria, Durand. *The Maupéou Revolution.* Baton Rouge: Louisiana State University Press, 1985.

———. *Mirage in the West: A History of the French Image of American Society to 1815.* Princeton, N.J.: Princeton University Press, 1957.

Edmunds, Sheila. "From Schoeffer to Vérard: Concerning the Scribes Who Became Printers." In *Printing the Written Word: The Social History of Books, Circa 1450–1520*, ed. Sandra Hindman. Ithaca, N.Y.: Cornell University Press, 1991.

Edwards, Mark. *Printing, Propaganda, and Martin Luther.* Berkeley: University of California Press, 1994.

Eisenstein, Elizabeth L. "Clio and Chronos: An Essay on the Making and Breaking of History-Book Time." *History and Theory* Beiheft 6: *History and the Concept of Time* (1966): 36–64.

———. "The Early Printer as a 'Renaissance Man.'" *Printing History* 3, 1 (1981): 6–17.

———. "The End of the Book? Some Perspectives on Media Change." *American Scholar* 64, 4 (1995): 541–55.

———. "From the Printed Word to the Moving Image." *Social Research* 64, 3 (1997): 1049–66.

———. "Gods, Devils, and Gutenberg: The Eighteenth Century Confronts the Printing Press." In *Studies in Eighteenth Century Culture* 27, ed. Julie C. Hayes and Timothy Erwin, 1–25. Baltimore: Johns Hopkins University Press, 1998.

———. *Grub Street Abroad: Aspects of the French Cosmopolitan Press from the Age of Louis XIV to the French Revolution.* Oxford: Clarendon Press, 1992.

———. "The Libraire-Philosophe: Four Sketches for a Group Portrait." In *Le livre et l'historien: études offertes en l'honneur du professeur Henri-Jean Martin*, ed. Frederic Barbier et al., 539–50. Geneva: Droz, 1997.

———. *The Printing Press as an Agent of Change: Communications and Cultural Transformations in Early Modern Europe.* 2 vols. Cambridge: Cambridge University Press, 1979.

———. *The Printing Revolution in Early Modern Europe.* Cambridge: Cambridge University Press, 1983.

———. "Le publiciste comme démagogue: la *Sentinelle du peuple* de Volney." In *La révolution du journal, 1788–1794*, ed. Pierre Rétat, 181–97. Paris: CNRS, 1989.

———. "The Tribune of the People: A New Species of Demagogue." In *The Press in the*

French Revolution: Papers given at Conference held at University of Haifa, 1988, ed. Harvey Chisick, Ilana Zinger, and Ouzi Elyada, 141–55. Oxford: Voltaire Foundation, 1991.

Ellery, Eloise. *Brissot de Warville: A Study in the History of the French Revolution.* New York: B. Franklin, 1970 [1915].

Elliott, John H. *Europe Divided 1559–1598.* London: Collins, 1968.

Elsky, Martin. *Authorizing Words: Speech, Writing and Print in the Elizabethan Renaissance.* Ithaca, N.Y.: Cornell University Press, 1989.

Emison, Patricia. *Creating the "Divine" Artist: From Dante to Michelangelo.* Leiden: Koninklijke Brill NV, 2004.

Engels, Friedrich. "On the Invention of Printing: A Poem." In *Gutenbergs-Album,* ed. Heinrich Meyer. Braunschweig: J.H. Meyer, 1840. http://www.marxists.org/archive/marx/works/1840/04/printing.htm, accessed 16 June 2009.

Erasmus, Desiderius. *The Adages of Erasmus: A Study with Translations.* Ed. Margaret Mann Phillips. Cambridge: Cambridge University Press, 1964.

———. *The Colloquies of Erasmus.* Trans. and ed. Craig Thompson. Chicago: University of Chicago Press, 1965.

———. *Erasmus on His Times.* Ed. Margaret Mann Phillips. Cambridge: Cambridge University Press, 1967.

Esbester, Mike. "Nineteenth-Century Timetables and the History of Reading." *Book History* 12 (2009): 156–85.

Estienne, Henri. *The Frankfort Book Fair: The Frankofordiense Emporium of Henri Estienne.* Ed. James Westfall Thompson. Chicago: Caxton Club, 1911.

Eusebius. *Chronicon.* Venice: Erhard Ratdolt, 1483.

Evenden, Elizabeth. *Patents, Pictures, Patronage: John Day and the Tudor Book Trade.* Aldershot: Ashgate, 2008.

Evenden, Elizabeth and Thomas Freeman. "John Foxe, John Day and the Printing of the *Book of Martyrs.*" In *Lives in Print: Biography and the Book Trade,* ed. Robin Myers, Michael Harris, and Giles Mandelbrote. London: British Library; New Castle, Del.: Oak Knoll Press, 2002.

———. "Print, Profit and Propaganda: The Elizabethan Privy Council and the 1570 Edition of Foxe's 'Book of Martyrs.'" *English Historical Review* 119 (November 2004): 1288–1307.

Evennett, H. Outram. *The Spirit of the Counter-Reformation.* The Birkbeck Lectures in Ecclesiastical History, 1951. Ed. John Bossy. Cambridge: Cambridge University Press, 1968.

Fairfield, Leslie. *John Bale: Mythmaker for the English Reformation.* West Lafayette, Ind.: Purdue University Press, 1976.

Febvre, Lucien and Henri-Jean Martin. *L'apparition du livre.* Paris: Éditions Albin Michel, 1958.

Felch, Susan. "Shaping the Reader." In *John Foxe and the English Reformation,* ed. David Loades, 52–65. Aldershot: Ashgate, 1997.

Feld, M. D. "Sweynheim and Pannartz, Cardinal Bessarion, Neoplatonism, Renaissance, Humanism and Two Early Printers' Choice of Texts." *Harvard Library Bulletin* 30 (1982): 282–335.

Firth, Katharine R. *The Apocalyptic Tradition in Reformation Britain, 1530–1645.* Oxford: Oxford University Press, 1979.

Fixler, Michael. *Milton and the Kingdoms of God.* Evanston, Ill.: Northwestern University Press, 1964.

Fliegelman, Jay. *Declaring Independence: Jefferson, Natural Language, and the Culture of Performance.* Stanford, Calif.: Stanford University Press, 1993.

———. *Prodigals and Pilgrims: The American Revolution Against Patriarchal Authority 1750–1800.* Cambridge: Cambridge University Press, 1982.

Flood, John L. "Nationalistic Currents in Early German Typography." *The Library* 6th ser. 15 (1993): 125–41.

———. "On Gutenberg's 600th Anniversary: Towards a History of Jubilees of Printing." *Journal of the Printing Historical Society* n.s. 1 (2000): 5–36.

Fox, Adam. *Oral and Literate Culture in England, 1500–1700.* Oxford: Oxford University Press, 2000.

Fox, Celina. "Political Caricature and the Freedom of the Press in Early Nineteenth Century England." In *Newspaper History from the Seventeenth Century to the Present Day,* ed. George Boyce, James Curran, and Pauline Wingate. London: Constable, 1978.

Foxe, John. *Actes and Monuments . . .* London: By John Daye, 1583.

———. *The Actes and Monuments of John Foxe.* Rev. Josiah Pratt, intro. John Stoughton. 8 vols. London: Religious Tract. Society, 1877.

———. "Preface to the Christian Reader." In *The Whole Works of W. Tyndall, John Frith and Doct. Barnes, three worthy Martyrs, and principall Teachers of the Church of England.* London: By John Daye, 1573.

Foxon, David. *Pope and the Early Eighteenth Century Book Trade.* The Lyell Lectures, Oxford 1975–1976. Ed. James McLaverty. Oxford: Clarendon Press, 1991.

Franklin, Benjamin. *Benjamin Franklin: The Autobiography and Other Writings.* Ed. L. Jesse Lemisch. New York: Signet Classic New American Library, 1961.

Frasca-Spada, Marina. "Compendious Footnotes." In *Books and the Sciences in History,* ed. Marina Frasca-Spada and Nicholas Jardine, 171–89. Cambridge: Cambridge University Press, 2000.

Fraser, Robert and Mary Hammond, eds. *Books Without Borders.* 2 vols. Basingstoke: Palgrave Macmillan, 2008.

Freeman, Thomas. "Texts, Lies, and Microfilm: Reading and Misreading Foxe's 'Book of Martyrs.'" *Sixteenth Century Journal* 30 (1999): 23–47.

Fumaroli, Marc. "Rhetoric, Politics, and Society." Trans. Ruth B. York. In *Renaissance Eloquence: Studies in the Theory and Pratcice of Renaissance Rhetoric,* ed. James J. Murphy. Berkeley: University of California Press, 1983.

Fussner, F. Smith. *Tudor History and the Historians.* New York: Basic Books, 1970.

Gaisser, Julia H. *Catullus and His Renaissance Readers*. Oxford: Clarendon Press, 1993.

Garat, Dominique-Joseph (Comte). *Mémoires historiques sur la vie de M. Suard, sur ses écrits, et sur le XVIIIe siècle*. Paris: A. Belin, 1820.

Garin, Eugenio. *Italian Humanism: Philosophy and Civic Life in the Renaissance*. Trans. Peter Munz. Oxford: Blackwell, 1965.

Gautier, Théophile. *Mademoiselle de Maupin (texte complet)*. 1836. Paris: Garnier, 1966.

George, M. Dorothy. *English Political Caricature: A Study in Opinion and Propaganda*. 2 vols. Oxford: Clarendon Press, 1959.

Ghosh, Anindita. Review of Rochelle Pinto, *Between Empires: Print and Politics in Goa* (Oxford: Oxford University Press, 2007). *American Historical Review* 114 (June 2009): 744–45.

Gibbon, Edward. *The Decline and Fall of the Roman Empire*. 3 vols. New York: Random House, 1932.

Gilmartin, Kevin. *Writing Against Revolution: Literary Conservatism in Britain, 1790–1832*. Cambridge: Cambridge University Press, 2007.

Gilmont, Jean François, ed. *La Reforme et le livre: l'Europe de l'imprimé (1517–1570)*. Paris: Cerf, 1990.

Gilmore, Myron P. *The World of Humanism 1453–1517*. New York: Harper and Brothers, 1952.

Gissing, George. *New Grub Street: A Novel*. 3 vols. London: Smith, Elder, 1891.

Glomski, Jacqueline. "Incunabula Typographiae: Seventeenth Century Views on Early Printing." *The Library* 7th ser. 2, 4 (Dec. 2001): 334–48.

Goldgar, Anne. *Impolite Learning: Conduct and Community in the Republic of Letters, 1680–1750*. New Haven, Conn.: Yale University Press, 1995.

Goodwin, Albert. *The Friends of Liberty: The English Democratic Movement in the Age of the French Revolution*. London: Hutchinson, 1979.

Gordon, Daniel. "Philosophy, Sociology and Gender in the Enlightenment Conception of Public Opinion." *French Historical Studies* 17, 4 (1992): 882–911.

Gough, Hugh. *The Newspaper Press in the French Revolution*. Chicago: Dorsey, 1988.

Grafton, Anthony. *Bring Out Your Dead: The Past as Revelation*. Cambridge, Mass.: Harvard University Press, 2001.

———. "The Importance of Being Printed." *Journal of Interdisciplinary History* 11 (1980): 265–286.

———. *New Worlds, Ancient Texts: The Power of Tradition and the Shock of Discovery*. Cambridge, Mass.: Harvard University Press, 1995.

Grana, César. *Bohemian Versus Bourgeois: French Society and the French Man of Letters in the Nineteenth Century*. New York: Basic Books, 1964.

Granger, Bruce I. "Franklin as Press Agent in England." In *The Oldest Revolutionary: Essays on Benjamin Franklin*, ed. Joseph A. Leo LeMay, 21–32. Philadelphia: University of Pennsylvania Press, 1976. 21–32

Gray, Valerie. *Charles Knight: Educator, Publisher, Writer*. Aldershot: Ashgate, 2006.

Green, James N. and Peter Stallybrass. *Benjamin Franklin: Writer and Printer*. New Castle, Del.: Oak Knoll Press, 2006.

Greengrass, Mark, Michael Leslie, and Timothy Raylor, eds. *Samuel Hartlib and Universal Reformation: Studies in Intellectual Communication.* Cambridge: Cambridge University Press, 1994.

Greenslade, Stanley L. *The Cambridge History of the Bible.* Cambridge: Cambridge University Press, 1963.

Gregg, Pauline. *Free-Born John: A Biography of John Lilburne.* London: Harrap, 1961.

Gregory the Great. *Moralia, sive Expositio in Job* (Rome, 1475); item 135 in *Le livre,* ed. Marie-Rose Seguy and Michel Brunet. Catalogue of the Bibliothèque Nationale Exhibition Held in 1972. Paris: Bibliothèque Nationale, 1972.

Grendler, Paul. *Critics of the Italian World, 1530–1560: Anton Francesco Doni, Nicolò Franco, and Ortensio Lando.* Madison: University of Wisconsin Press, 1969.

Grierson, Constantia. "The Art of Printing. A Poem." 1764. Epigraph to *London Chronicle* (28–30 June 1785).

Griffin, Dustin. "Critical Opinion: Fictions of Eighteenth Century Authorship." *Essays in Criticism* 43 (1993): 181–94.

———. *Literary Patronage in England, 1650–1800.* Cambridge: Cambridge University Press, 1996.

Griffith, Reginald H. *Alexander Pope: A Bibliography.* Austin: University of Texas, 1927 [1922].

Gross, John. *The Rise and Fall of the Man of Letters: A Study of the Idiosyncratic and the Humane in Modern Literature.* New York: Macmillan, 1969.

Gunn, J. A. W. *Queen of the World: Opinion in the Public Life of France from the Renaissance to the Revolution.* Studies on Voltaire and the Eighteenth Century 328. Oxford: Voltaire Foundation, 1995.

Gustafson, Sandra. *Eloquence Is Power: Oratory and Performance in Early America.* Chapel Hill: University of North Carolina Press, 2000.

Halasz, Alexandra. *The Marketplace of Print: Pamphlets and the Public Sphere in Early Modern England.* Cambridge Studies in Renaissance Literature and Culture 17. Cambridge: Cambridge University Press, 1997.

Hale, J. R. "Gunpowder and the Renaissance." In *From the Renaissance to the Counter Reformation: Essays in Honor of Garrett Mattingly,* ed. Charles Howard Carter. New York: Random House, 1965.

Halévy, Elie. *England in 1815.* Vol. 1 of *A History of the English People in the Nineteenth Century.* Trans. E. I. Watkin and D. A. Barker. London: T. F. Unwin, 1924.

Hall, David. *Cultures of Print: Essays in the History of the Book.* Amherst: University of Massachusetts Press, 1966.

Haller, William. *The Elect Nation: The Meaning and Relevance of Foxe's "Book of Martyrs".* New York: Harper and Row, 1963.

———. *The Rise of Puritanism: Or, The Way to the New Jerusalem as Set Forth in Pulpit and Press from Thomas Cartwright to John Lilburne and John Milton, 1570–1643.* New York: Harper, 1957.

———, ed. *Tracts on Liberty in the Puritan Revolution, 1638–1647.* 3 vols. New York: Columbia University Press, 1934.

Hallman, Barbara M. "Italian 'Natural Superiority' and the Lutheran Question, 1517–1546." *Archiv für Reformationsgeschichte* 71 (1980): 134–48.

Halporn, Barbara. "Libraries and Printers in the Fifteenth Century." *Journal of Library History* 16 (1981): 134–42.

———. "Sebastian Brant's Editions of Classical Authors." *Publishing History* 16 (1984): 33–41.

Hammond, Breen S. *Professional Imaginative Writing in England 1670–1740: "Hackney for Bread."* Oxford: Clarendon Press, 1997.

Hamowy, Ronald. "Cato's Letters, John Locke, and the Republican Paradigm." *History of Political Thought* 11 (Summer 1990): 273–94.

Hampton, Mark. *Visions of the Press in Britain 1850–1950.* Urbana: University of Illinois Press, 2004.

Hanson, Laurence. *Government and the Press 1695–1763.* Oxford: Clarendon Press, 1936.

Haraszti, Zoltán. *John Adams and the Prophets of Progress.* 1952. New York: Grosset and Dunlap, 1964.

Harleian Miscellany: A Collection of Scarce, Curious, and Entertaining Pamphlets and Tracts, as Well in Manuscript as in Print. 8 vols. Ed. William Oldys 1744–46. Reprinted in 10 vols. and edited by Thomas Park (1808–13). London: Printed for Robert Dutton, 1810.

Harris, John. *Lexicon Technicum, or, An universal English dictionary of arts and sciences.* London: Printed for Dan Brown et al., 1704–1710.

Harrison, Kathryn. Review of Lisa Appignanesi, *Mad, Bad and Sad: Women and the Mind Doctors* (New York: Norton, 2007). *New York Times Sunday Book Review*, 27 April 2008.

Harvey, Gabriel. *The Works of Gabriel Harvey.* Ed. Alexander B. Grosart. 3 vols. New York: AMS Press, 1966.

Hatin, Eugene. *Histoire politique et littéraire de la presse en France.* 8 vols. Paris: Poulet-Malassis et de Broise, 1859–60.

Hauser, Henri. *La naissance du protestantisme.* Paris: Presses Universitaires de France, 1962 [1940].

Hay, Denys. *Polydore Vergil, Renaissance Historian and Man of Letters.* Oxford: Clarendon Press, 1952.

Haydn, Hiram. *The Counter-Renaissance.* New York: Scribner, 1950.

Hayes, Carlton J. H. *A Generation of Materialism, 1871–1900: The Rise of Modern Europe.* Ed. William Langer. New York: Harper and Brothers, 1941.

Haynes, Christine. "An 'Evil' Genius." *French Historical Studies* 30, 4 (Fall 2007): 559–97.

Hayum, Andrée. "Dürer's Portrait of Erasmus and the *Ars Typographorum.*" *Renaissance Quarterly* 38 (1985): 650–87.

Hazlitt, William. "Lectures on the English Poets." In *The Romantic Reader*, ed. Howard Hugo. New York: Viking, 1960.

———. *The Life of Napoleon Buonaparte.* Philadelphia: J.B. Lippincott, 1878.

Headley, John. *Tommaso Campanella and the Transformation of the World.* Princeton, N.J.: Princeton University Press, 1997.

Hellinga, Lotte. "Analytical Bibliography and the Study of Early Printed Books with a Case Study of the Mainz *Catholicon*." *Gutenberg Jahrbuch* 64 (1989): 47–96.

Herman, Peter C. "Authorship and the Royal 'I': James VI/I and the Politics of Monarchic Verse." *Renaissance Quarterly* 54, 4, part 2 (2001): 1495–1530.

Hesse, Carla. *Publishing and Cultural Politics in Revolutionary Paris*. Berkeley: University of California Press, 1991.

Hesse, Monica. "Notoriety's Missing Links: Online Files Scrubbed After Museum Shooting." *Washington Post*, Friday, 12 June 2009, C5.

Higman, Francis M. *Censorship and the Sorbonne: A Bibliographical Study of Books in French Censured by the Faculty of Theology of the University of Paris, 1520–1551*. Geneva: Droz, 1979.

———. *Lire et découvrir: la circulation des idées au temps de la Réforme*. Geneva: Droz, 1998.

Hill, Christopher. *The Century of Revolution, 1603–1714*. New York: Norton, 1982.

Hillhouse, James Theodore. *The Grub Street Journal*. Durham, N.C.: Duke University Press, 1928.

Hirsch, Rudolph. "Bulla super Impressione Librorum, 1515." *Gutenberg Jahrbuch* 48 (1973): 248–51.

———. *Printing, Selling, and Reading, 1450–1550*. Wiesbaden: Harrassowitz, 1967.

Hoffman, George. *Montaigne's Career*. Oxford: Clarendon Press, 1998.

———. "Writing Without Leisure: Proofreading as Work in the Renaissance." *Journal of Medieval and Renaissance Studies* 25 (1995): 17–31.

Holborn, Hajo. *Ulrich von Hutten and the German Reformation*. Trans. Roland H. Bainton. Yale Historical Publications 11. New Haven, Conn.: Yale University Press, 1937.

Hollis, Patricia. *Class and Class Conflict in Nineteenth Century England, 1815–1850*. London: Routledge and Kegan Paul, 1973.

Holmes, Richard. *The Age of Wonder*. New York: Pantheon, 2008.

Holt, Mack P. *The French Wars of Religion, 1562–1629*. Cambridge: Cambridge University Press, 1995.

Holtman, Robert B. *Napoleonic Propaganda*. Baton Rouge: Louisiana State University Press, 1950.

Hughes, Ann. "Approaches to Presbyterian Print Culture: Thomas Edwards's *Gangraena* as Source and Text." In *Books and Readers in Early Modern England*, ed. Jennifer Andersen and Elizabeth Sauer. Philadelphia: University of Pennsylvania Press, 2002.

———. *Gangraena and the Struggle for English Revolution*. Oxford: Oxford University Press, 2004.

Hugo, Howard, ed. *The Romantic Reader*. New York: Viking, 1960.

Hugo, Victor. *Notre Dame de Paris*. Ed., anno., and intro. Jacques Seebacher. Paris: Gallimard, 1975.

———. "'*Quentin Durward*' ou l'Écossais à la coeur de Louis XI, par Sir Walter Scott." *La Muse Française* (July 1823). In *Oeuvres complètes*, ed. Jean Massin. 18 vols. Paris: Club Français du Livre, 1967.

Hume, David, *Enquiry Concerning the Principles of Morals: A Critical Edition*. Ed. Tom L. Beauchamp. Oxford: Clarendon Press, 2006.

Hunter, J. Paul. *Before Novels: The Cultural Contexts of Eighteenth-Century English Fiction*. New York: Norton, 1990.

İnalcık, Halil. *The Ottoman Empire: The Classical Age 1300–1600*. Trans. Norman Itzkowitz and Colin Imber. London: Praeger, 1973.

Ingrassia, Catherine and Claudia N. Thomas, eds. *"More Solid Learning": New Perspectives on Alexander Pope's Dunciad*. Lewisburg, Pa.: Bucknell University Press, 2000.

Israel, Jonathan. "Enlightenment! Which Enlightenment?" *Journal of the History of Ideas* 67, 3 (2006): 523–45.

Jacob, Margaret. *The Radical Enlightenment: Pantheists, Freemasons, and Republicans*. London: Allen and Unwin, 1981.

Jackaway, Gwenyth L. *Media at War: Radio's Challenge to the Newspapers 1924–1939*. Westport, Conn.: Praeger, 1995.

Jardine, Lisa. *Worldly Goods: A New History of the Renaissance*. New York: Norton, 1996.

Jarrett, Derek. *The Begetters of Revolution: England's Involvement with France, 1759–1789*. Totowa, N.J.: Rowman and Littlefield, 1973.

Johns, Adrian. *The Nature of the Book: Print and Knowledge in the Making*. Chicago: University of Chicago Press, 1998.

Johnson, Odai. *Rehearsing the Revolution: Radical Performance, Radical Politics in the English Revolution*. Newark, Del.: University of Delaware Press, 2000.

Joly, Maurice. *Dialogue aux enfers entre Machiavel et Montesquieu; ou, La politique de Machiavel au XIXe siècle*. Paris, Calmann-Lévy, 1948.

———. *The Dialogue in Hell Between Machiavelli and Montesquieu: Humanitarian Despotism and the Conditions of Modern Tyranny*. Trans. and ed. John S. Waggoner. Lanham, Md.: Lexington Books, 2003.

Jones, Richard F. *Ancients and Moderns: A Study of the Rise of the Scientific Movement in Seventeenth-Century England*. Berkeley: University of California Press, 1965 [St. Louis: Washington University, 1961].

Jones, Stephen. *A New Biographical Dictionary: Containing a Brief Account of the Lives and Writings of the Most Eminent Persons and Remarkable Characters in Every Age and Nation*. London: Printed for Longman, Hurst [etc.], 1811.

Jouin, Henri. *David d'Angers, sa vie, son oeuvre, ses écrits et ses contemporains*. 2 vols. Paris: Plon, 1878.

Judex, Matthäus. *De Typographiae Inventione, et De Praelorum Legitima Inspectione, Libellus Brevis et Utilis*. Copenhagen: Johannes Zimmermann, 1566.

Kafka, Ben. "Paperwork: The State of the Discipline." *Book History* 12 (2009): 340–53.

Kafker, Frank A., James M. Laux, and Darlene Gay Levy. *The French Revolution: Conflicting Interpretations*. 3rd ed. Malabar, Fla.: Krieger, 1983.

Kahn, Didier. "The Rosicrucian Hoax in France (1623–24)." In *Secrets of Nature: Astrology and Alchemy in Early Modern Europe*, ed. Anthony Grafton and William R. Newman. Cambridge, Mass.: MIT Press, 2001.

Kaplan, Justin. *Mr. Clemens and Mark Twain: A Biography.* New York: Simon and Schuster, 1991 [1966].

Kapr, Albert. *Johann Gutenberg: The Man and His Invention.* Trans. Douglas Martin. Aldershot: Ashgate, 1996.

Kastan, David Scott. "Humphrey Moseley and the Invention of English Literature." In *Agent of Change: Print Culture Studies After Elizabeth L. Eisenstein,* ed. Sabrina A. Baron, Eric N. Lindquist, and Eleanor F. Shevlin. Amherst: University of Massachusetts Press, 2007.

———."Little Foxes." In *John Foxe and His World,* ed. Christopher Highley and John N. King, 117–320. Aldershot: Ashgate, 2002.

Kates, Gary. *The "Cercle Social," the Girondins and the French Revolution.* Princeton, N.J.: Princeton University Press, 1985.

Keller, Alex. "A Renaissance Humanist Looks at 'New' Inventions: The Article on 'Horologium' in Giovanni Tortelli's *De Orthographia.*" *Technology and Culture* 11 (1970): 345–65.

Kelley, Donald. *The Beginning of Ideology: Consciousness and Society in the French Reformation.* Cambridge: Cambridge University Press, 1981.

———. "Johann Sleidan and the Origin of History as a Profession." *Journal of Modern History* 52 (1980): 573–98.

Kelly, Ann Cline. *Jonathan Swift and Popular Culture: Myth, Media, and the Man.* New York: Palgrave, 2002.

———. "Swift's Battle of the Books: Fame in the Modern Age." In *Reading Swift: Papers from the Third Münster Symposium on Jonathan Swift,* ed. Hermann Josef Real and Helgard Stöver-Leidig, 91–101. Munich: Wilhelm Fink, 1998.

Kernan, Alvin. *Printing Technology, Letters, and Samuel Johnson.* Princeton, N.J.: Princeton University Press, 1987.

Keymer, Thomas and Peter Saybor. *Pamela in the Market Place: Literary Controversy and Print Culture in Eighteenth Century Britain and Ireland.* Cambridge: Cambridge University Press, 2005.

King, John N. "The Light of Printing: William Tyndale, Foxe, Day and Early Modern Print Culture." *Renaissance Quarterly* 54 (Spring 2001): 52–85.

Kingdon, Robert McCune. *Geneva and the Coming of the Wars of Religion in France, 1555–1563.* Geneva: Droz, 1956.

Klaasen, Walter. *Living at the End of the Ages: Apocalyptic Expectation in the Radical Reformation.* New York: University Press of America, 1992.

Klaits, Joseph. *Printed Propaganda Under Louis XIV: Absolute Monarchy and Public Opinion.* Princeton, N.J.: Princeton University Press, 1976.

Kline, Michael. *Rabelais and the Age of Printing.* Études Rabelaisiennes 4, Travaux d'Humanisme et Renaissance 60. Geneva: Droz, 1963. 1–59.

Knachel, Philip. *England and the Fronde: The Impact of the English Civil War and Revolution on France.* Ithaca, N.Y.: Published for the Folger Shakespeare Library by Cornell University Press, 1967.

Knight, Charles. *Knowledge Is Power: A View of the Productive Forces of Modern Society, and the Results of Labour, Capital, and Skill.* London: John Murray, 1855.

———. *The Old Printer and the Modern Press.* London: John Murray, 1854.

———. *William Caxton, The First English Printer: A Biography.* London: Facsimile Printed for the Wynken de Worde Society, 1976 [London: Charles Knight and Co., 1844].

Knights, Mark. *Representation and Misrepresentation in Later Stuart Britain: Partisanship and Political Culture.* Oxford: Oxford University Press, 2005.

Kolb, Robert. "The Book Trade as Christian Calling." In *Books Have Their Own Destiny*, ed. Robin B. Barnes et al., 61–72. Sixteenth Century Essays and Studies 50. Kirksville, Mo.: Thomas Jefferson University Press, 1998.

König, Eberhard. "New Perspectives on the History of Mainz Printing." In *Printing the Written Word: The Social History of Books, Circa 1450–1520*, ed. Sandra Hindman. Ithaca, N.Y.: Cornell University Press, 1991.

Kornicki, Peter. *The Book in Japan: A Cultural History from the Beginnings to the Nineteenth Century, Part 5.* Vol. 7 of *Handbuch der Orientalistik. Funfte Abteilung, Japan.* Leiden: Koninklijke Brill, 1998.

Krevans, Nita. "Print and the Tudor Poets." In *Reconsidering the Renaissance: Papers from the Twenty-First Annual Conference*, ed. Mario. A. DiCesare. Center for Medieval and Early Renaissance Studies 21. Binghamton, N.Y.: Medieval and Renaissance Texts and Studies, 1992.

Kyle, Chris and Jason Peacey, eds. *Breaking News: Renaissance Journalism and the Birth of the Newspaper.* Exhibition at Folger Shakespeare Library, Washington, D.C., 25 September 2008–31 January 2009. Seattle: University of Washington Press, 2009.

Lamartine, Alphonse de. *Gutenberg: inventeur de l'imprimerie.* Paris: Hachette, 1867.

———. *Histoire des girondins.* Paris: Furne et Cie, W. Coquebert, 1848.

Lamont, William. *Godly Rule: Politics and Religion 1603–1660.* London: Macmillan, 1969.

Lander, Jesse. "Foxe's Books of Martyrs: Printing and Popularizing the *Acts and Monuments*." In *Religion and Culture in Renaissance England*, ed. Claire E. McEachern and Deborah K. Shuger, 69–92. Cambridge: Cambridge University Press, 1997.

———. *Inventing Polemic: Religion, Print, and Literary Culture in Early Modern England.* Cambridge: Cambridge University Press, 2006.

Langer, Ullrich. *Invention, Death, and Self-Definitions in the Poetry of Pierre Ronsard.* Stanford French and Italian Studies 45. Saratoga, Calif.: Anman Libre, 1986.

Langer, William. *Political and Social Upheaval, 1832–1852.* New York: Harper and Row, 1969.

Lankhorst, Otto S. "Le rôle des libraire-imprimeurs néerlandais dans l'édition des journaux littéraires de langue française (1684–1750)." In *La diffusion et la lecture des journaux de langue française sous l'Ancien Régime*, ed. Hans Bots, 1–11. Amsterdam: APA Holland University Press, 1988.

Laqueur, Thomas. *Solitary Sex: A Cultural History of Masturbation.* New York: Zone Books, 2003.

Larkin, Oliver. *Daumier: Man of His Time*. Boston: McGraw-Hill, 1966.

Latreille, André and René Remond. *Histoire du catholicisme en France*. 3 vols. Paris: Éditions Spes, 1962.

Lee, Felicia R. "In Brief." *New York Times*, June 19, 2004, A9.

Legouis, Pierre. *Andrew Marvell: Poet, Puritan, Patriot*. Oxford: Clarendon Press, 1968.

Lehmann-Haupt, Hellmut. *Peter Schoeffer of Gernsheim and Mainz: With a List of His Surviving Books and Broadsides*. Rochester, N.Y.: Leo Hart, 1950.

LeMay, Joseph A. Leo, ed. *The Oldest Revolutionary: Essays on Benjamin Franklin*. Philadelphia: University of Pennsylvania Press, 1976.

LeRoy, Louis. *De la vicissitude ou variété des choses en l'univers*. 1575. Ed. B. W. Bates. Princeton, N.J.: Princeton University Press, 1944. Trans. James B. Ross in *The Renaissance Reader*, ed. Ross and Mary M. McLaughlin, 91–108. New York: Viking, 1972.

Lilti, Antoine. "The Writing of Paranoia: Jean Jacques Rousseau and the Paradoxes of Celebrity." *Representations* (Summer 2008): 53–83.

Lippmann, Walter. *Liberty and the News*. New York: Harcourt Brace, 1920.

Loewenstein, Joseph. *The Author's Due: Printing and the Prehistory of Copyright*. Chicago: University of Chicago Press, 2002.

———. *Ben Jonson and Possessive Authorship*. Cambridge: Cambridge University Press, 2003.

———. "The Script in the Marketplace." *Representations* 12 (1985): 101–14.

Lombard, Peter. *The Sentences*. Nuremberg: A. Koberger, 1474.

Louis-Philippe, King of the French. *Mémoires de Louis-Philippe, duc d'Orléans, écrits par lui-même*. 2 vols. Paris: Plon, 1973.

Lowry, Martin. *Nicholas Jenson and the Rise of Venetian Publishing in Renaissance Europe*. Oxford: Blackwell, 1991.

———. *The World of Aldus Manutius: Business and Scholarship in Renaissance Venice*. Ithaca, N.Y.: Cornell University Press, 1979.

Lüsebrink, Hans-Jürgen. "'Hommage à l'écriture' et 'éloge à l'imprimerie.'" In *Livre et révolution*, ed. Daniel Roche and Roger Chartier, 133–44. Mélanges de la Bibliothèque de la Sorbonne 9. Paris: Amateurs du Livre, 1989.

Luther, Martin. *Luther's Works*. Ed. Jaroslav Pelikan and H. T. Lehmann. 55 vols. St. Louis and Philadelphia: Concordia and Fortress/Muhlenberg, 1955–86.

Lutz, Cora. "Manuscripts Copied from Printed Books." In Lutz, *Essays on Manuscripts and Rare Books*, 129–65. Hamden, Conn.: Archon Books, 1975.

Lyon, Gregory. "Baudouin, Flacius and the Plan for the *Magdeburg Centuries*." *Journal of the History of Ideas* 64 (2003): 253–72.

Lyons, Martyn. *Le triomphe du livre: une histoire sociologique de la lecture dans la France du XIXe siècle*. Paris: Promodis, 1987.

Macaulay, Thomas Babington. *History of England from the Accession of James the Second*. 5 vols. New York: Harpers, 1879–.

———. *Miscellaneous Works of Lord Macaulay*. 5 vols. Ed. Lady Trevelyan. 1824. New York: Harper, 1880-.

Maccoby, Simon. *English Radicalism, 1786–1832: From Paine to Cobbett.* London: Allen and Unwin, 1955.

Madan, Falconer. "Early Representations of the Printing Press," In *Bibliographica.* 3 vols. London: K. Paul, Trench, Trübner, 1895. 1:223–48, 499–502.

Maguire, Laurie. "The Craft of Printing (1600)." In *A Companion to Shakespeare*, ed. David Scott Kastan, 434–49. Oxford: Blackwell, 1999.

Malesherbes, Guillaume-Chrétien de Lamoignon (de). "Discours de réception à l'Académie Française (1775)." In *Malesherbes: le pouvoir et les lumières (textes réunies par Marek Wyrwa).* Paris: France-Empire, 1989.

Mallinckrodt, Bernard von. *De ortu et progressu artis typographicae (On the Origin and Progress of Printing).* Cologne: Apud Ioannem Kinchium, 1639.

Manuel, Frank E. *The Prophets of Paris.* Cambridge, Mass.: Harvard University Press, 1962.

Marchand, Prosper. *Dictionnaire historique, ou mémoires critiques et littéraires, concernant la vie et les ouvrages de diverses personnes distinguées dans la république des lettres.* Ed. J. N. S. Allemand. 2 tomes in 1 folio vol. The Hague: Pierre de Hondt, 1758.

———. *Histoire de l'origine et des premiers progrès de l'imprimerie.* The Hague: Paupie, 1740.

Mardersteig, Giovanni. *The Remarkable Story of a Book Made in Padua in 1477.* Trans. Hans Schmoller. London: Nattali & Marrice, 1967.

Marinetti, Filippo Tommaso. "Futuristic Manifesto." In *Paths to the Present: Aspects of European Thought from Romanticism to Existentialism*, ed. Eugen Weber, 242–46. New York: Dodd, Mead, 1960.

Marker, Gary. *Publishing, Printing, and the Origins of Intellectual Life in Russia, 1700–1800.* Princeton, N.J.: Princeton University Press, 1985.

Marotti, Arthur. "Malleable and Fixed Texts: Manuscript and Printed Miscellanies and the Transmission of Lyric Poetry in the English Renaissance." In *New Ways of Looking at Old Texts: Papers of the Renaissance English Text Society, 1985–1991*, ed. W. Speed Hill. Binghamton, N.Y.: Medieval and Renaissance Texts and Studies, 1993.

———. *Manuscript, Print, and the English Renaissance Lyric.* Ithaca, N.Y.: Cornell University Press, 1995.

Martin, Henri-Jean. "Comment on écrivit l'histoire du livre." In *Le livre français sous l'Ancien Régime*, ed. Martin. Paris: Promodis, 1987.

Martin, Henri-Jean and Roger Chartier, eds. *Histoire de l'édition française.* 4 vols. Paris: Promodis, 1982

Marvell, Andrew. *The Rehearsal Transpros'd.* London: Printed by J. D. for the Assigns of John Calvin and Theodore Beza [etc.], 1672.

Marx, Karl. *Introduction to the Critique of Political Economy* (1859). In *Selected Works*, ed. V. Adoratsky and C.P. Dutt, 1: 502–6. London: Lawrence and Wishart, 1942.

Mason, Haydn T., ed. *The Darnton Debate: Books and Revolution in the Eighteenth Century.* Studies on Voltaire and the Eighteenth Century 359. Oxford: Voltaire Foundation, 1998.

Masur, Gerhard. *Prophets of Yesterday: Studies in European Culture, 1890–1914.* New York: Macmillan, 1961.

May, Steven. "Tudor Aristocrats and the 'Stigma of Print'." *Renaissance Papers* 10 (1980): 11–18.

McCusker, John J. "The Demise of Distance: The Business Press and the Origins of the Information Revolution in the Early Modern Atlantic World." *American Historical Review* 110, 2 (April 2005): 295–320.

———. "European Bills of Entry and Marine Lists: Early Commercial Publications and the Origins of the Business Press." *Harvard Library Bulletin* 33 (Summer 1983): 209–56.

McDayter, Mark. "The Haunting of St. James's Library: Librarians, Literature, and the Battle of the Books." *Huntington Library Quarterly* 66 (2003): 1–27.

McGinty, Alice B. "Stradanus (Jan Van der Straet): His Role in the Visual Communication of Renaissance Discoveries, Technologies, and Values." Ph.D. dissertation, Tufts University, 1974.

McKenzie, Alan T. "Giuseppe Baretti and the 'Republic of Letters' in the Eighteenth Century." *Studies on Voltaire and the Eighteenth Century* 193 (1980): 1813–22.

———. "The Solemn Owl and the Laden Ass: The Iconography of the Frontispieces to The Dunciad." *Harvard Library Bulletin* 24 (1976): 25–39.

McKenzie, Donald F. *"Making Meaning: "Printers of the Mind" and Other Essays,* ed. Peter D. McDonald and Michael F. Suarez. Amherst, Mass.: University of Massachusetts Press, 2002.

McKitterick, David. *Print, Manuscript and the Search for Order.* Cambridge: Cambridge University Press, 2003.

McLaverty, James. *Pope, Print and Meaning.* Oxford: Oxford University Press, 2001.

McLuhan, Marshall. *The Gutenberg Galaxy: The Making of Typographic Man.* Toronto: University of Toronto Press, 1962.

———. *The Mechanical Bride: Folklore of Industrial Man.* New York: Vanguard, 1951.

———. *Understanding Media: The Extensions of Man.* New York: McGraw-Hill, 1964.

McMahon, Darrin. *Enemies of the Enlightenment: The French Counter-Enlightenment and the Making of Modernity.* Oxford: Oxford University Press, 2001.

McManners, John. *The French Revolution and the Church.* New York: Harper, 1970.

Mehl, James V. "Printing the Metaphor of Light and Dark." In *Books Have Their Own Destiny,* ed. Robin B. Barnes et al., 83–92. Sixteenth Century Essays and Studies 50. Kirksville, Mo.: Thomas Jefferson University Press, 1998.

Mendle, Michael. "Preserving the Ephemeral." In *Books and Readers in Early Modern England,* ed. Jennifer Andersen and Elizabeth Sauer, 201–16. Philadelphia: University of Pennsylvania Press, 2002.

Mengel, Elias. "The Dunciad Illustrations." *Eighteenth Century Studies* 7 (Winter 1973–74): 161–78.

Mill, John Stuart. *Autobiography.* London: Longmans, Green, Reader and Dyer, 1874.

———. *On Liberty.* Ed. Albury Castell. New York, Appleton-Century-Crofts, 1947. [London: J.W. Parker and Son, 1859].

Miller, Peter N. *Peiresc's Europe: Learning and Virtue in the Seventeenth Century*. New Haven, Conn.: Yale University Press, 2000.

Milton, John. *Complete Prose Works of John Milton*. Ed. Don M. Wolfe. 8 vols. New Haven, Conn.: Yale University Press, 1953–58.

———. *John Milton: Selected Prose*. Ed. Constantinos A. Patrides. Columbia: University of Missouri Press 1985.

Monfasani, John. "The First Call for Press Censorship: Niccolò Perotti, Giovanni Andrea Bussi, Antonio Moreto, and the Editing of Pliny's *Natural History*." *Renaissance Quarterly* 41, 1 (1988): 1–31.

Montaigne, Michel de. *The Complete Essays of Montaigne*. Trans. and ed. Donald M. Frame. Stanford, Calif.: Stanford University Press, 1958.

Montesquieu, Charles de Secondat (Baron de). *The Spirit of the Laws: A Compendium of the First English Edition*. Ed. David W. Carrithers. Berkeley: University of California Press, 1977.

Moran, James. *Printing Presses: History and Development from the Fifteenth Century to Modern Times*. Berkeley: University of California Press, 1973.

Morison, Samuel Eliot. *Admiral of the Ocean Sea: A Life of Christopher Columbus*. Boston: Little, Brown, 1942.

Morley, John. *The Life of Richard Cobden*. Boston: Roberts Brothers, 1881.

Morley, Tom. "'The Times' and the Concept of the Fourth Estate: Theory and Practice in Mid-Nineteenth Century Britain." *Journal of Newspaper and Periodical History* 1, 3 (1985): 11–23.

Morris, William. *The Ideal Book: Essays and Lectures on the Arts of the Book*. Edited by William Peterson. Berkeley: University of California Press, 1982.

Mosse, George. *The Crisis of German Ideology: Intellectual Origins of the Third Reich*. New York: Grosset and Dunlap, 1971 [1964].

Mott, Frank Luther. *American Journalism: A History of Newspapers in the United States Through 250 Years*. New York: Macmillan, 1940.

Moxon, Joseph. Preface to *Mechanick Exercises on the Whole Art of Printing*. London: Printed for Joseph Moxon on the Westside of Fleet-ditch, at the sign of the Atlas, 1683. Facsimile ed. ed. Herbert Davis and Harry Carter. New York: Dover, 1978.

Mozley, John. *John Foxe and His Books*. London: Society for Promoting Christian Knowledge, 1940.

Mumford, Lewis. *Technics and Civilization*. New York: Harcourt Brace, 1963 [1934].

Myers, Robin and Michael Harris, eds. *Serials and Their Readers, 1620–1914*. New Castle, Del.: Oak Knoll Press, 1993.

Namier, Lewis B. *1848: The Revolution of the Intellectuals*. London: Oxford University Press, 1964.

Napoleon I, Emperor of the French. *Napoleon Self-Revealed: In Three Hundred Selected Letters*. Trans. and ed. James M. Thompson. Boston: Houghton Mifflin, 1934.

National Endowment for the Arts. *Reading at Risk: A Survey of Literary Reading in America*. Research Division Report 46. Washington, D.C.: National Endowment for the Arts, 8 June 2004.

Naudé, Gabriel. *Advice on Establishing a Library.* [Avis pour dresser une Bibliothèque, 1627] Intro. and trans. Archer Taylor. Berkeley: University of California Press, 1950.

Nauert, Charles G., Jr. "Humanists, Scientists, and Pliny: Changing Approaches to a Classical Author." *American Historical Review* 84 (February 1979): 72–85.

Needham, Paul. "*Haec sancta ars*: Gutenberg's Invention as a Divine Gift." *Gazette of the Grolier Club* 42 (1990): 101–20.

Nelson, Eric. "True Liberty: Isocrates and Milton's *Areopagitica*." In *Milton Studies 40*, ed. Albert C. Labriola. Pittsburgh: University of Pittsburgh Press, 2002.

Nicholson, Eirwen. "Eighteenth Century Foxe." In *John Foxe and the English Reformation*, ed. David Loades. Aldershot: Ashgate, 1997. 143–77

Nicolson, Marjorie H. *Newton Demands the Muse: Newton's Opticks and the Eighteenth Century Poets.* Princeton, N.J.: Princeton University Press, 1966 [1946].

———. *Science and Imagination.* Ithaca, N.Y.: Cornell University Press, 1956.

———. *Voyages to the Moon.* New York: Macmillan, 1960 [1948].

Nodier, Charles. "De la perfectiblité . . . et de l'influence de l'imprimerie sur la civilisation." *Rêveries*, 1832, vol. 5. In *Oeuvres complètes.* Geneva: Slatkine, 1968 [Paris: Renduel, 1832–37].

Norbrook, David. "*Areopagitica*, Censorship and the Early Modern Public Sphere." in *The Administration of Aesthetics: Censorship, Political Criticism, and the Public Sphere*, ed. Richard Burt, 3–33. Minneapolis: University of Minnesota Press, 1994.

Nunberg, Geoffrey. "The Places of Books in the Age of Electronic Reproduction." *Representations* 42 (Spring 1993): 13–37.

———, ed. and intro. *The Future of the Book.* Afterword Umberto Eco. Berkeley: University of California Press, 2006.

Nussbaum, Damian. "Appropriating Martyrdom: Fears of Renewed Persecution and the 1632 Edition of *Acts and Monuments*." In *John Foxe and the English Reformation*, ed. David Loades. Aldershot: Ashgate, 1997.

Oastler, Christopher L. *John Day, the Elizabethan Printer.* Oxford: Oxford Bibliographical Society, 1975.

O'Connell, Sheila. *The Popular Print in England, 1550–1850.* London: British Museum Press, 1999.

O'Gorman, Frank. "The Paine Burnings of 1792–1793." *Past and Present* 193 (2006): 111–55.

Olsen, V. Norskov. *John Foxe and the Elizabethan Church.* Berkeley: University of California Press, 1973.

Ong, Walter. *The Presence of the Word: Some Prolegomena for Cultural and Religious History.* New Haven, Conn.: Yale University Press, 1967.

Paine, Thomas. *Rights of Man.* Ed. Philip Foner. New York: Citadel, 1974.

Palmer, Paul A. "The Concept of Public Opinion in Political Theory." In *Essays on History and Political Theory in Honor of Charles H. McIlwain*, ed. Carl F. Wittke, 230–57. Cambridge, Mass.: Harvard University Press, 1936.

Palmer, Robert R. *The Age of the Democratic Revolution.* 2 vols. Princeton, N.J.: Princeton University Press, 1959.

———. *Catholics and Unbelievers in Eighteenth-Century France.* Princeton, N.J.: Princeton University Press, 1939.

Palmer, Samuel. *A General History of Printing from the First Invention of it in the City of Mentz to its Propagation and Origins through most of the kingdoms of Europe, particularly the Introduction and Success of it here in England.* London: Printed for A. Bettesworth, C. Hitch, and C. Davis, 1733.

Parkes, Malcolm B. *Scribes, Scripts and Readers: Studies in the Communication, Presentation and Dissemination of Medieval Texts.* London: Hambledon, 1991.

Parks, Stephen. *John Dunton and the English Book Trade: A Study of His Career with a Checklist of His Publications.* New York: Garland, 1976.

Patterson, Annabel. *Censorship and Interpretation: The Conditions of Writing and Reading in Early Modern England.* Madison: University of Wisconsin Press, 1984.

———. *Marvell and the Civic Crown.* Princeton, N.J.: Princeton University Press, 1978.

P. D. "Epigram on the Frontispiece to 'The Dunciad.'" *Notes and Queries* 2nd ser. 36 (September 6, 1856): 182.

Peacey, Jason. *Politicians and Pamphleteers: Propaganda During the English Civil Wars and Interregnum.* Aldershot: Ashgate, 2004.

Peacock, Thomas Love. *Crotchet Castle.* London: Wildside Press, 1831; revised 1837.

Penny, Andrew. "John Foxe, the *Acts and Monuments* and the Development of the Prophetic Interpretation." In *John Foxe and the English Reformation*, ed. David Loades, 252–77. Aldershot: Ashgate, 1997.

Perkins, David. *English Romantic Writers.* New York: Harcourt, Brace, and World, 1967.

Peters, Julie Stone. *Congreve, the Drama, and the Printed Word.* Stanford, Calif.: Stanford University Press, 1990.

———. *Theatre of the Book 1480–1880: Print, Text and Performance in Europe.* Oxford: Oxford University Press, 2000.

Peters, Kate. *Print Culture and the Early Quakers.* Cambridge: Cambridge University Press, 2005.

Peterson, William S. "Tradition and Innovation in Fine Printing." Paper presented at a Forum at the Bard Graduate Center, New York, March 26, 2007.

Petrucci, Armando. *Writers and Readers in Medieval Italy.* Trans. and ed. Charles M. Radding. New Haven, Conn.: Yale University Press, 1995.

Pettegree, Andrew. "Illustrating the Book: A Protestant Dilemma." In *John Foxe and His World*, ed. Christopher Highley and John N. King, 133–44. Aldershot: Ashgate, 2002.

Pitcher, John. "Editing Daniel." In *New Ways of Looking at Old Texts*, ed. W. Speed Hill, 57–73. Binghamton, N.Y.: Medieval and Renaissance Texts and Studies, 1993.

Plant, Marjorie. *The English Book Trade: An Economic History of the Making and Sale of Books.* 2nd rev. ed. London: Allen and Unwin, 1965.

Plantin, Christopher. *An Account of Printing and Calligraphy in the Sixteenth Century* (1567). Trans. and ed. Ray Nash. Cambridge, Mass.: Department of Printing and Graphic Arts, Harvard College Library, 1940.

Pollard, Alfred. *An Essay on Colophons with Specimens and Translations.* Intro. Richard Garnett. Chicago: Caxton Club, 1905.

Poole, Kristen. *Radical Religion from Shakespeare to Milton: Figures of Nonconformity in Early Modern England.* Cambridge: Cambridge University Press, 2000.

Pope, Alexander. *The Dunciad Variorum with the Prolegoma of Scriblerus.* Facsimile of 1729 ed. Ed. James Sutherland. London: Methuen, 1943.

Popkin, Jeremy. "The Business of Political Enlightenment in France, 177–1800." Paper presented at French Historical Studies Meeting, University of Kentucky; Lexington, 15 December 1990.

———. *News and Politics in the Age of Revolution.* Ithaca, N.Y.: Cornell University Press, 1989.

———. "The Newspaper Press in French Political Thought 1789–99." In *Studies in Eighteenth Century Culture*, vol. 10, ed. Harry Payne, 113–33. Madison: University of Wisconsin Press, 1981.

———. *Revolutionary News: The Press in France, 1789–1799.* Durham, N.C.: Duke University Press, 1990.

Porter, Roy. *The Enlightenment: Britain and the Creation of the Modern World.* London: Allen Lane, 2000.

Postman, Neil. *Amusing Ourselves to Death.* New York: Penguin, 1985.

Preus, Robert. *The Inspiration of Scripture: A Study of the Theology of the Seventeenth Century Lutheran Dogmaticians.* Edinburgh: Oliver and Boyd, 1957.

Proust, Jacques. *Diderot et l'Encyclopédie.* Paris: A. Colin, 1982 [1962].

Rabelais, François. *Gargantua and Pantagruel.* Trans. Thomas Urquhart 1653. London: David Nutt at the Sign of the Phoenix, Long Acre, 1900.

Racaut, Luc. *Hatred in Print: Catholic Propaganda and Protestant Identity During the French Wars of Religion.* Aldershot: Ashgate, 2002.

Rader, Daniel L. *The Journalists and the July Revolution in France: The Role of the Political Press in the Overthrow of the Bourbon Restoration 1827 1830.* The Hague: Nijhoff, 1973.

Radway, Janice. *A Feeling for Books: The Book-of-the-Month Club, Literary Taste, and Middle-Class Desire.* Chapel Hill: University of North Carolina Press, 1997.

———. *Reading the Romance: Women, Patriarchy, and Popular Literature.* Chapel Hill: University of North Carolina Press, 1991.

Ranc, Robert. "Strasbourg—1840 quatrième centenaire de Gutenberg." *Gutenberg Jahrbuch* 48 (1973): 144–48.

Raven, James. *The Business of Books: Booksellers and the English Book Trade, 1450–1850.* New Haven, Conn.: Yale University Press, 2007.

Ray, Isaac. *Mental Hygiene.* Boston: Ticknor and Fields, 1863.

Raymond, Joad. *Invention of the Newspaper: English Newsbooks, 1641–1649.* Oxford: Oxford University Press, 1996.

———. *Pamphlets and Pamphleteering in Early Modern Britain.* Cambridge: Cambridge University Press, 2003.

Rea, Robert R. *The English Press in Politics 1760–1774.* Lincoln: University of Nebraska Press, 1963.

Redgrave, Gilbert. *Erhard Ratdolt and His Work at Venice: A Paper Read Before the Bibliographical Society November 20, 1893.* London: Printed for the Bibliographical Society, 1899.

Reed, Christopher A. "Gutenberg and Modern Chinese Print Culture: The State of the Discipline II." *Book History* 10 (2007): 291–315.

Reed, Walter. *An Exemplary History of the Novel: The Quixotic Versus the Picaresque.* Chicago: University of Chicago Press, 1981.

Rétat, Pierre. "Forme et discours d'un journal révolutionnaire: les révolutions de Paris en 1789." In *L'instrument périodique: la fonction de la presse au XVIIIe siècle,* ed. Claude Labrosse, Pierre Rétat, and Henri Duranton, 139–78. Lyon: Presses Universitaires de Lyon, 1985.

Richardson, Brian. "The Debates on Printing in Renaissance Italy," *Bibliofilia* 100 (1998): 134–55.

———. *Printing, Writers and Readers in Renaissance Italy.* Cambridge: Cambridge University Press, 1999.

Rizzo, Silvia. *Il lessico filologica degli umanisti.* Sussidi Eruditi 26. Rome: Edizioni di Storia e letteratura, 1973.

Robbins, Caroline. "The Strenuous Whig: Thomas Hollis of Lincoln's Inn." *William and Mary Quarterly* 3rd ser. 7 (1950): 406–53.

Robinson, Francis. "Technology and Religious Change: Islam and the Impact of Print." *Modern Asian Studies* 27, 1 (1993): 229–51.

Robinson, Marsha S. *Writing the Reformation: Actes and Monuments and the Jacobean History Play.* Aldershot: Ashgate, 2002.

Roelker, Nancy L. *One King, One Faith: The Parlement of Paris and the Religious Reformations of the Sixteenth Century.* Berkeley: University of California Press, 1996.

Rogers, Pat. *Hacks and Dunces: Pope, Swift and Grub Street.* London: Methuen, 1980. Abridged from *Grub Street: Studies in a Subculture.* London: Methuen, 1972.

———. "Nameless Names: Pope, Curll and the Uses of Anonymity." *New Literary History* 33 (2002): 233–45.

Rose, Jonathan. *Intellectual Life of the British Working Classes.* New Haven, Conn.: Yale University Press, 2001.

Rosen, Edward. "In Defense of Kepler." In *Aspects of the Renaissance: A Symposium,* ed. Archibald R. Lewis. Austin: University of Texas Press, 1967.

———. "The Invention of Eyeglasses." *Journal of the History of Medicine* 11 (1956): 13–46, 183–218.

Rosenberg, Daniel. "Early Modern Information Overload." *Journal of the History of Ideas* 64, 1 (2003): 1–9.

Rosenzweig, Roy. "Scarcity or Abundance? Preserving the Past in a Digital Era." *American Historical Review* 108 (June 2003): 735–62.

Rossi, Paolo. *Philosophy, Technology, and the Arts in the Early Modern Era.* Trans. Salvator Attanasio, ed. Benjamin Nelson. New York: Harper and Row, 1970.

Rouse, Mary A. and Richard H. Rouse. *Cartolai, Illuminators, and Printers in Fifteenth-*

Century Italy. UCLA Occasional Papers 1. Los Angeles: Department of Special Collections, University Research Library, University of California, 1988.

———. "Nicolaus Gupalatinus and the Arrival of Print in Italy." *La Bibliofilia* 88 (1986): 221–53.

Rousseau, Jean Jacques. "Discourse . . . on the question 'Has the Restoration of the sciences and arts tended to purify morals?'" (1750). In *The First and Second Discourses*, trans. and ed. Roger D. Masters. New York: St. Martin's, 1964.

Rowland, Ingrid. "Revenge of the Regensburg Humanists, 1493." *Sixteenth Century Journal* 25, 2 (1994): 307–22.

Rudé, George. *Wilkes and Liberty: A Social Study of 1763 to 1774*. London: Oxford University Press, 1962.

Ruhlière, Claude Carloman de. *Oeuvres de Rulhière*. 2 vols. Paris: Ménard et Desenne Fils, 1819.

Rummonds, Gabriel. *Nineteenth-Century Printing Practices and the Iron Hand Press*. 2 vols. New Castle, Del.: Oak Knoll Press, 2004.

———. *Printing on the Iron Hand Press*. New Castle, Del.: Oak Knoll Press, 1998.

Russell, Nicolas and Hélène Visentin, eds. *French Ceremonial Entries in the Sixteenth Century: Event, Image, Text*. Toronto: Centre for Reformation and Renaissance Studies, 2007.

Ryan, Michael. Review of Marc Baratin and Christian Jacob, eds., *Pouvoir des bibliothèques: la mémoire des livres dans l'Occident*. *Bryn Mawr Classical Review* (23 September 1997).

Saint-Hyacinthe, Thémiseul de. *Le chef d'oeuvre d'un inconnu: poème heureusement découvert et mise au jour avec des remarques savantes et recherchées par M. le docteur Chrysostome Mathanasius*. The Hague: La Compagnie [Pierre Gosse], 1714.

Sainte-Beuve, Charles Augustin. "De la littérature industrielle." *Revue des Deux Mondes* 19, 4 (1839): 675–91.

Saisselin, Rémy G. *The Literary Enterprise in Eighteenth-Century France*. Detroit: Wayne State University Press, 1979.

Salmon, John H., ed. *The French Wars of Religion*. Boston: Heath, 1967.

———. *Renaissance and Revolt: Essays in the Intellectual and Social History of Early Modern France*. Cambridge: Cambridge University Press, 1987.

Sarton, George. *Six Wings: Men of Science in the Renaissance*. Bloomington: Indiana University Press, 1957.

Saunders, David and Ian Hunter. "Lessons from 'the Literatory.'" *Critical Inquiry* 17 (1991): 479–509.

Saunders, J. W. "The Stigma of Print: A Note on the Social Bases of Tudor Poetry." *Essays in Criticism* 1 (1951): 137–64.

Sawyer, Jeffrey. *Printed Poison: Pamphlet-Propaganda, Faction, Politics, and the Public Sphere in Early Seventeenth-Century France*. Berkeley: University of California Press, 1990.

Saxl, Fritz. "Veritas Filia Temporis." In *Philosophy and History: Essays Presented to Ernst*

Cassirer, ed. Raymond Klibansky and H. J. Paton, 196–221. New York: Harper and Row, 1963 [London: Clarendon Press, 1936].

Schiffman, Robyn L. "A Concert of Werthers." *Eighteenth Century Studies* 43, 2 (Winter 2010): 207–22.

Schlegel, Dorothy. "Freemasonry and the Encyclopédie Reconsidered." *Studies on Voltaire and the Eighteenth Century* 90, 1433–60. Oxford: Voltaire Foundation, 1972.

Schlup, Michel. "Diffusion et lecture du *Journal Helvétique*, au temps de la Société Typographique de Neuchâtel." In *La diffusion et la lecture des journaux de langue française sous l'Ancien Régime*, ed. Hans Bots, 59–71. Amsterdam: APA Holland University Press, 1988.

———. "La lecture et ses institutions dans la Principauté de Neuchâtel au tournant des Lumières." *Revue Française d'Histoire du Livre* 55/56 (1987): 463–500.

Schölderer, Victor. "Printers and Readers in Italy in the Fifteenth Century." Annual Italian Lecture of the British Academy Brochure. *Proceedings of the British Academy* 35 (1949): 25–47.

Schwartz, John. "Thinking May Not Be All It's Thought to Be." *New York Times*, Sunday, 16 January 2005.

Schwoerer, Lois. *The Ingenious Mr. Henry Care, Restoration Publicist*. Baltimore: Johns Hopkins University Press, 2001.

———. "Liberty of the Press and Public Opinion, 1660–1695." In *Liberty Secured? Britain Before and After 1688*, ed. James R. Jones. Stanford, Calif.: Stanford University Press, 1992.

Scott, Walter. *Waverley: Or, 'Tis Sixty Years Since*. 3 vols. in 2. Philadelphia: E.T. Scott, 1821.

Scott-Warren, Jason. *Early Modern English Literature*. Cambridge: Polity Press, 2005.

Scribner, Robert. *For the Sake of Simple Folk: Popular Propaganda for the German Reformation*. Oxford: Oxford University Press, 1994.

Secord, James A. *Victorian Sensation: The Extraordinary Publication, Reception, and Secret Authorship of Vestiges of the Natural History of Creation*. Chicago: University of Chicago Press, 2000.

———. "Progress in Print." In *Books and the Sciences in History*, ed. Marina Frasca-Spada and Nicholas Jardine, 369–93. Cambridge: Cambridge University Press, 2000.

Shaw, David. "*Ars formularia*: Neo-Latin Synonyms for Printing." *The Library* 6th ser. 11, 3 (1989): 220–30.

Shell, Alison. *Catholicism, Controversy and the English Literary Imagination, 1558–1660*. Cambridge: Cambridge University Press, 1999.

Sheppard, Leslie Alfred. "A Fifteenth-Century Humanist: F. Filelfo." *The Library* 4th ser. 16 (1936): 1–27.

Sher, Richard B. "1688 and 1788: William Robertson on Revolution in Britain and France." In *Culture and Revolution*, ed. Paul Dukes and John Dunkley, 98–109. London: Pinter, 1990.

Sherburn, George. *The Early Career of Alexander Pope*. Oxford: Clarendon Press, 1934.

Siebert, Fred Seaton. *Freedom of the Press in England, 1476–1776: The Rise and Decline of Government Control.* Urbana: University of Illinois Press, 1952.

Silverman, Willa Z. "Books Worthy of Our Era? Octave Uzanne, Technology and the Luxury Book in *Fin de siècle* France." *Book History* 7 (2004): 239–84.

Small, Christopher. *The Printed Word: An Instrument of Popularity.* Aberdeen: Aberdeen University Press, 1982.

Smith, Anthony. *The Newspaper: An International History.* London: Thames and Hudson, 1979.

Smith, Olivia. *The Politics of Language: 1791–1819.* Oxford: Clarendon Press 1984.

Smith, Preserved. *A History of Modern Culture, 1687–1776.* Vol. 2, *The Enlightenment.* New York: H. Holt, 1934.

Snyder, Chris. "Google Settles Book-Scan Lawsuit, Everybody Wins." *Wired.com*, 28 October 2008. http://www.wired.com.

Solomon, Howard. *Public Welfare, Science, and Propaganda in Seventeenth-Century France: The Innovations of Théophraste Renaudot.* Princeton, N.J.: Princeton University Press, 1972.

Somervell, David C. *English Thought in the Nineteenth Century.* New York: Longmans, Green, 1940.

Spengler, Oswald. *The Decline of the West.* Trans. C. F. Atkinson. 2 vols. New York: Knopf, 1928 [first German ed. 1918].

Spitz, Lewis W. *The Religious Renaissance of the German Humanists.* Cambridge, Mass.: Harvard University Press, 1963.

Sprat, Thomas (Bishop). *History of the Royal Society for the Improving of Natural Knowledge.* 2nd ed. London: Printed for Robert Scot, Richard Chiswell and Thomas Chapman, 1702 [London: Printed by J. R. for T. Martyn, 1667].

St. Clair, William. *The Reading Nation in the Romantic Period.* Cambridge: Cambridge University Press, 2004.

Stallybrass, Peter and Allon White. *The Politics and Poetics of Transgression.* Ithaca, N.Y.: Cornell University Press, 1986.

Starobinski, Jean. "Eloquence Antique, Eloquence Future." In *The French Revolution and the Creation of Modern Political Culture*, vol. 1, *The Political Culture of the Old Regime*, ed. Keith M. Baker et al., 311–39. Oxford: Pergamon Press, 1987.

Staveley, Alice. "Marketing Virginia Woolf." *Book History* 12 (2009): 295–340.

Steinberg, Sigfrid Henry. *Five Hundred Years of Printing.* 3rd ed. Harmondsworth: Penguin, 1974.

Stone, Brad. "Amazon Erases Orwell Books from Kindle." *New York Times*, 18 July 2009.

Straus, Ralph. *The Unspeakable Curll; being some account of Edmund Curll, bookseller, to which is added a full list of his books.* New York: Chapman and Hall, 1927.

Strauss, Gerald. *Luther's House of Learning: Indoctrination of the Young in the German Reformation.* Baltimore: Johns Hopkins University Press, 1978.

———. "The Course of German History." In *Renaissance: Studies in Honor of Hans Baron*, ed. Anthony Molho and John A. Tedeschi. DeKalb: Northern Illinois University Press, 1971.

Striphas, Ted. *The Late Age of Print: Everyday Book Culture from Consumerism to Control.* New York: Columbia University Press, 2009.

Surdin, Ashley. "In Some Classrooms, Books Are a Thing of the Past." *Washington Post,* October 19, 2009, 3A.

Sutherland, James R. *The Restoration Newspaper and Its Development.* Cambridge: Cambridge University Press, 1986.

Swift, Jonathan. *A Tale of a Tub, to which is added the Battle of the Books and the Mechanical Operation of the Spirit.* Ed. Adolph C. Guthkelch and David Nichol Smith. Oxford: Clarendon Press, 1958.

———. *A Tale of a Tub. Written for the Universal Improvement of Mankind . . . To which is added an Account of a Battel between the Antient and Modern Books in St. James Library. With the Author's Apology and Explanatory Notes.* Ed. W. W-tt-n, B. D., and others. London: Printed for J. Nutt, 1710 [1704].

Taunton, Matthew. Review of Jeff Gomez, *Print Is Dead: Books in Our Digital Age. Times Literary Supplement,* March 7, 2008.

Terdiman, Richard. *Discourse/Counter-Discourse: The Theory and Practice of Symbolic Resistance in Nineteenth-Century France.* Ithaca, N.Y.: Cornell University Press, 1985.

Thackeray, William Makepeace. *The History of Pendennis: His Fortunes and Misfortunes, His Friends, and His Greatest Enemy.* In *The Works of William Makepeace Thackeray,* ed. Anne Thackeray Ritchie. 13 vols. London: Harper and Brothers, 1898.

Theobald, John. *The Media and the Making of History.* Aldershot: Ashgate, 2004.

Thiem, Jon. "The Great Library of Alexandria Burnt: Towards the History of a Symbol." *Journal of the History of Ideas* 40 (December 1979): 507–26.

Thomas, Isaiah. *History of Printing in America.* 2 vols. 2nd ed. Albany, N.Y.: Isaiah Thomas, 1874 [Worcester, Mass.: Isaiah Thomas, jun. Isaac Sturtevant, printer, 1810].

Thompson, Edward Palmer. *The Making of the English Working Class.* New York: Vintage, 1966.

Thompson, James M. *Napoleon Bonaparte: His Rise and Fall.* Oxford: Blackwell, 1952.

Thomson, Ian. "The Scholar as Hero in Ianus Pannonius' Panegyric." *Renaissance Quarterly* 44, 2 (1991): 197–213.

Thorndike, Lynn. *A History of Magic and Experimental Science.* Volumes 5 and 6 in one vol., *The Sixteenth Century.* New York: Columbia University Press, 1941.

Thurston, Benjamin. "Joseph de Maistre." *2000: The European Journal* 2 (2002): 2.

Tolstoy, Leo. *War and Peace.* Trans. Ann Dunnigan. New York: Signet, 1968.

Tottel, Richard. *Tottel's Miscellany (1557–1587).* Ed. Hyder Edward Rollins. Cambridge, Mass.: Harvard University Press, 1928–9.

Tournoy, Gilbert. "Juan Luis Vives and the World of Printing." *Gutenberg Jahrbuch* 69 (1994): 128–48.

Tracy, Clarence. "Johnson and the Common Reader." Roy M. Wiles Memorial Lecture, 17 March 1976. Hamilton, Ont.: McMaster University Publication, 1976.

Trevelyan, G. M. *The Life of John Bright.* Boston: Houghton Mifflin, 1913.

Trevor-Roper, Hugh R. *The Crisis of the Seventeenth Century: Religion, the Reformation and Social Change.* New York: Harper and Row, 1968.

Tribble, Evelyn B. *Margins and Marginality: The Printed Page in Early Modern England.* Charlottesville: University Press of Virginia, 1993.

―――. "Godly Reading: John Foxe's *Actes and Monuments* (1583)." In *The Reader Revealed: Catalogue of Folger Library Exhibition (2001–2).* Comp. and ed. Sabrina Alcorn Baron et al. Washington, D.C.: Folger Shakespeare Library, 2001.

Trithemius, Johannes . *Annales Hirsaugienses.* 2 vols. St. Gall: Joannes Georgius Schlegel, 1690.

―――. *In Praise of Scribes* (*De Laude Scriptorum*). Trans. and ed. Klaus Arnold. Lawrence, Kan.: Coronado Press, 1974.

Trollope, Anthony. *The Warden.* London and New York: John Lane, 1902.

Tucoo-Chala, Suzanne. *Charles-Joseph Panckoucke et la librairie française de 1736–1798.* Paris: Touzot, 1977.

Turgot, Anne Robert Jacques. "A Philosophical Review of the Successive Advances of the Human Mind" (December 11, 1750). In *Turgot on Progress, Sociology, Economics*, ed. and trans. Ronald L. Meek. Cambridge: Cambridge University Press, 1973.

Tuveson, Ernst R. *Millennium and Utopia: A Study in the Background of the Idea of Progress.* New York: Harper and Row, 1964 [1949].

Twain, Mark. *Life on the Mississippi.* New York: Harper, 1901 [1883].

Tyson, Gerald P. *Joseph Johnson: A Liberal Publisher.* Iowa City: University of Iowa Press, 1979.

―――. "Joseph Johnson, an Eighteenth Century Bookseller." *Studies in Bibliography* 28 (1975): 1–16.

Uzanne, Octave. *The Book Hunter in Paris: Studies Among the Bookstalls and the Quays.* Pref. to English ed. Augustine Birrell. London: Eliot Stock, 1895.

―――. *The End of Books.* Illustrations by A. Robida. *Scribner's Magazine Illustrated* (Jul.-Dec., 1894): 221–31.

―――. *La locomotion à travers l'histoire et les mœurs.* Paris: Ollendorff, 1900.

Vann, Richard T., ed. *Century of Genius: European Thought 1600–1700.* Englewood Cliffs, N.J.: Prentice-Hall, 1967.

Venturi, Franco. *Utopia and Reform in the Enlightenment.* Cambridge: Cambridge University Press, 1971.

Vergil, Polydore. *De Inventoribus Rerum.* 1499; expanded 1521. Trans., ed., and intro. Beno Weiss and Louis C. Pérez. Nieuwkoop: De Graaf, 1997.

―――. *On Discovery.* Trans. and ed. Brian P. Copenhaver. Cambridge, Mass.: Harvard University Press, 2002.

Voltaire. "Liberty of the Press." *Philosophical Dictionary.* In *The Portable Age of Reason Reader.* Ed. Crane Brinton. New York: Viking, 1956.

―――. *Philosophical Letters.* Trans. and ed. Ernest Dilworth. Indianapolis: Bobbs-Merrill, 1961.

Voss, Paul J. *Elizabethan News Pamphlets.* Pittsburgh: Duquesne University Press, 2001.

Waddington, Raymond B. "*Meretrix est stampificata*: Gendering the Printing Press." In *Books Have Their Own Destiny*, ed. Robert Barnes et al., 131–43. Sixteenth Century Essays and Studies 50. Kirksville, Mo.: Thomas Jefferson University Press, 1998.

Walker, Mack, ed. *Metternich's Europe*. New York: Harper and Row, 1968.

Wall, John. "The Reformation in England and the Typographical Revolution." In *Print and Culture in the Renaissance: Essays on the Advent of Printing in Europe*, ed. Gerald P. Tyson and Sylvia S. Wagonheim, 208–21. Wilmington: University of Delaware Press, 1986.

Wall, Wendy. *The Imprint of Gender: Authorship and Publication in the English Renaissance*. Ithaca, N.Y.: Cornell University Press, 1993.

Wallas, Graham. *The Life of Francis Place, 1771–1854*. London: Longmans, Green and Co., 1898.

Walsh, Elizabeth, Lu Ellen De Haven, and Theresa Helein, eds. *Yesterday's News: Seventeenth-Century English Broadsides and Newsbooks*. Washington, D.C.: Folger Library, 1996.

Walsh, Marcus. "The Superfoetation of Literature: Attitudes to the Printed Book in the Eighteenth Century." *British Journal for Eighteenth Century Studies* 15 (1992): 151–61.

———. "Text, 'Text' and Swift's *Tale of the Tub*." *Modern Language Review* 85, 2 (April, 1990): 290–303.

Walsham, Alexandra. "'Domme Preachers'? Post-Reformation English Catholicism and the Culture of Print." *Past and Present* 168 (August 2000): 72–122.

———. *Providence in Early Modern England*. Oxford: Oxford University Press, 1999.

———. "Unclasping the Book? Post-Reformation English Catholicism and the Vernacular Bible." *Journal of British Studies* 1 (2003): 141–66.

Walshe, Emily. "Kindle e-Reader: A Trojan Horse for Free Thought." *Christian Science Monitor*, 18 March 2009. http://www.csmonitor.com/2009/0318/p09s01-coop.html.

Walter, Gérard. *Marat*. Geneva: Famot, 1977.

Waquet, Françoise. "Qu'est-ce que la république des lettres?" *Bibliothèque de l'École des Chartes* 147 (1989): 473–502.

Ward, Patricia. *The Medievalism of Victor Hugo*. University Park: Pennsylvania State University Press, 1975.

Warner, Michael. *The Letters of the Republic: Publication and the Public Sphere in Eighteenth Century America*. Cambridge, Mass.: Harvard University Press, 1990.

Warren, Jason Scott. *Early Modern English Literature*. Cambridge: Polity Press, 2005.

Watt, Ian. *The Rise of the Novel: Studies in Defoe, Richardson, and Fielding*. Berkeley: University of California Press, 1957.

Weber, Eugen, ed. *Paths to the Present: Aspects of European Thought from Romanticism to Existentialism*. New York: Dodd, Mead., 1960.

Weber, Harold. "The 'Garbage Heap' of Memory: At Play in Pope's Archives of Dulness." *Eighteenth Century Studies* 33 (1999): 1–20.

———. *Paper Bullets: Print and Kingship Under Charles II*. Lexington: University Press of Kentucky, 1996.

Webster, Charles. *The Great Instauration: Science, Medicine and Reform, 1626–1660*. London: Duckworth, 1975.

Wedgwood, C. V. "Good King Charles's Golden Days." In *The Restoration of the Stuarts, Blessing or Disaster?* 4–29. Washington, D.C.: Folger Shakespeare Library. 1960.

Weinstein, Mark A. *The Prefaces to the Waverley Novels.* Lincoln: University of Nebraska Press, 1978.

Wells-Cole, Anthony. *Art and Decoration in Elizabethan and Jacobean England: The Influence of Continental Prints, 1558–1625.* New Haven, Conn.: Yale University Press, 1997.

Whelan, Timothy. "William Fox, Martha Gurney and Radical Discourse of the 1790s." *Eighteenth Century Studies* 42, 3 (2009): 397–411.

White, Lynn. *Medieval Technology and Social Change.* Oxford: Clarendon Press, 1962.

Wickwar, William H. *The Struggle for the Freedom of the Press 1819–1832.* London, 1928.

Wiener, Joel H. *The War of the Unstamped: The Movement to Repeal the British Newspaper Tax, 1830–1836.* Ithaca, N.Y.: Cornell University Press, 1969.

Wieruszowski, Helene. "Burckhardt and Vespasiano." In *Philosophy and Humanism: Essays in Honor of P. O. Kristeller,* ed. Edward P. Mahoney. New York: Columbia University Press, 1976.

Wilde, Oscar. *The Complete Works of Oscar Wilde.* Vol. 4, *Criticism: Historical Criticism, Intentions, The Soul of Man.* Ed. Josephine M. Guy. Oxford: Oxford University Press, 2007.

Williams, Raymond. *Culture and Society, 1780–1950.* New York: Columbia University Press, 1983.

Wilson, Adrian. *The Making of the Nuremberg Chronicle.* Amsterdam: Nico Israel, 1976.

Wilson, Arthur. *Diderot, the Testing Years: 1713–1759.* New York: Oxford University Press, 1957.

Winkler, K. T. "The Forces of the Market and the London Newspaper in the First Half of the Eighteenth Century." *Journal of Newspaper and Periodical History* 4, 2 (Spring 1988): 22–35.

Winn, James. "On Pope, Printers, and Publishers." *Eighteenth Century Life* 6 (January-May 1981): 93–102.

Winn, Mary Beth. *Anthoine Vérard, Parisian Publisher 1485–1512.* Geneva: Droz, 1997.

Woloch, Isser. *Jacobin Legacy: The Democratic Movement Under the Directory.* Princeton, N.J.: Princeton University Press, 1970.

Wolper, Roy S. "The Rhetoric of Gunpowder and the Idea of Progress." *Journal of the History of Ideas* 31 (1970): 589–98.

Wood, Christopher S. *Forgery, Replica, Fiction: Temporalities of German Renaissance Art.* Chicago: University of Chicago Press, 2008.

Wooding, Lucy E. C. *Rethinking Catholicism in Reformation England.* Oxford: Oxford University Press, 2000.

Worden, Blair. "Puritan Propaganda." *Times Literary Supplement,* 21 February 1997, 26.

Wordsworth, William. "The Tables Turned." In *Lyrical Ballads, with a few other poems.* London: Printed by Biggs and Cottle, for T.N. Longman, 1798.

Wotton, William. *Reflections upon Ancient and Modern Learning.* London: Printed by J. Leake, for Peter Buck, 1694.

Woudhuysen, H. R. *Sir Philip Sidney and the Circulation of Manuscripts, 1558–1640.* Oxford: Oxford University Press, 1996.

Yates, Frances A. *The Art of Memory*. Chicago: University of Chicago Press, 1966.

Yeo, Richard. *Encyclopaedic Visions: Scientific Dictionaries and Enlightenment Culture*. Cambridge: Cambridge University Press, 2001.

———. "Encyclopedic Knowledge." In *Books and the Sciences in History*, ed. Marina Frasca-Spada and Nicholas Jardine, 207–25. Cambridge: Cambridge University Press, 2000.

———. "A Solution to the Multitude of Books." *Journal of the History of Ideas* 64, 1 (2003): 64–65.

Young, G. M. *Victorian England: Portrait of an Age*. New York: Doubleday 1954 [Oxford: Oxford University Press, 1936].

Zaret, David. *Origins of Democratic Culture: Printing, Petitions, and the Public Sphere in Early-Modern England*. Princeton, N.J.: Princeton University Press, 2000.

Zeldin, Theodore. *France 1848–1945*. 2 vols. Oxford: Clarendon Press, 1977.

Ziff, Larzer. *Writing in the New Nation: Prose, Print, and Politics in the Early United States*. New Haven, Conn.: Yale University Press, 1991.

Index

We of this age have discovered a shorter and more prudent way to become scholars and wits, without the fatigue of reading or thinking. The most accomplished way of using books at present is two fold: either first to . . . learn their titles exactly and then brag of their acquaintance; or secondly . . . to get a thorough insight into the index by which the whole book is governed . . . the arts are all in a flying march and therefore more easily subdued by attacking them in the rear. . . . Thus men catch knowledge by throwing their wit upon the posteriors of a book. (Jonathan Swift, *The Tale of a Tub*, Section VII, "A Digression in Praise of Digressions") [94–95, 280n139]

Page references in italics refer to illustrations

Acknowledgments

I owe special thanks to Maura Elford, who provided indispensable editorial assistance and computer expertise during the many months when my work was underway and took charge of getting my final version to the press.

Thanks are also due to the participants in the Folger Institute Seminar, Fall Term, 1999, with whom I discussed several of the topics that are covered in this book. One of them, Sabrina Alcorn Baron, later helped with revising and illustrating an early draft. While I was engaged in research, Betsy Walsh, Owen Williams, Georgianna Ziegler, and many other members of the staff of the Folger Shakespeare Library came to my aid repeatedly.

I am also grateful to Margaret Aston, Ann Blair, Carol Armbruster, Jack R. Censer, Roger Chartier, Robert DeMaria, Thomas Freeman, Barbara Halporn, Ann Cline Kelly, Robert Kingdon, Alberto Manguel, Jason Rosenblatt, Lois Schwoerer, Richard Sher, William Sherman, Eleanor Shevlin, and Peter Stallybrass, who made suggestions, read selected chapters, and offered informed criticism. Others who performed similar services, will, I hope, forgive me for being inadvertently omitted from this list. It would be incomplete without a word of thanks to my son Ted Eisenstein, who proofread my next-to-last draft.

A final acknowledgment is due to the editors and publishers who have allowed me to rework material first published in the following books and journals:

"Clio and Chronos: An Essay on the Making and. Breaking of History-Book Time," *History and Theory Beiheft* 6: *History and the Concept of Time* (1966): 36–64.

"Gods, Devils and Gutenberg: The Eighteenth Century Confronts the Printing Press," in *Studies in Eighteenth Century Culture* 27, ed. Julie C Hayes and Timothy Erwin (Baltimore: Johns Hopkins University Press, 1998).

"Le publiciste comme démagogue: La *Sentinelle du Peuple* de Volney," in *La Révolution du Journal, 1788–1794*, ed. Pierre Rétat (Paris: CNRS, 1989).

"Printing as Divine Art: Celebrating Western Technology in the Age of the Hand Press," Harold Jantz Memorial Lecture, Oberlin College, 4 November 1995 (Oberlin, Ohio, 1996).

"The Libraire-Philosophe: Four Sketches for a Group Portrait," in *Le livre et l'historien: études offertes en l'honneur du professeur Henri-Jean Martin*, ed. Frederic Barbier et al. (Geneva: Droz, 1997).

The Printing Revolution in Early Modern Europe (Cambridge: Cambridge University Press, 1983).

The Printing Press as an Agent of Change: Communications and Cultural Transformations in Early Modern Europe, 2 vols. (Cambridge: Cambridge University Press, 1979).

"The Tribune of the People: A New Species of Demagogue," in *The Press in the French Revolution*, ed. Harvey Chisick, Ilana Zinger, and Ouzi Elyada (Oxford: Voltaire Foundation, 1991).

Grub Street Abroad: Aspects of the French Cosmopolitan Press from the Age of Louis XIV to the French Revolution (Oxford: Clarendon Press, 1992).

"The Early Printer as a 'Renaissance Man,'" *Printing History* 3, 1 (1981): 6–17.

"The End of the Book? Some Perspectives on Media Change," *American Scholar* 64, 4 (1995): 541–55.

"From the Printed Word to the Moving Image." *Social Research* 64, 3 (1997): 1049–66.

Thanks are also due to the following institutions for permission to reproduce the illustrations:

Bridgeman Art Library
City Museum of Paris, Musée Carnavalet
Folger Shakespeare Library
Musée National de l'Éducation,_ I.N.R.P., Rouen, France.
Smithsonian Institution Libraries
University of Maryland, Baltimore County
Yale University Library